DATE			
APR 17 79			
FEB 23 81			
OCT 21 1987			
AUG 25 1990			
SEP 20 1994			
AUG 14 2000			

A Tool of Power

*To form a broad conception of the true
implications of what is going on day by
day in one's own time is a difficult but
most interesting task, to which intelligent
observation will always be attracted.*

GUSTAV CASSEL
The Downfall of the Gold Standard (1936)

A TOOL OF POWER

The Political History of Money

WILLIAM WISELEY

A WILEY-INTERSCIENCE PUBLICATION

JOHN WILEY AND SONS, New York · London · Sydney · Toronto

Library of Congress Cataloging in Publication Data

Wiseley, William, 1928–
    A tool of power.

    "A Wiley-Interscience publication."
    Bibliography: p.
    Includes index.
        1. Money—History. 2. International finance—
History. I. Title.
HG231.W57   332.4'9   76-57701
ISBN 0-471-02235-7

Printed in the United States of America

10 9 8 7 6 5 4 3 2 1

For

F.M.W. and M.C.W.

Preface

The beginning of spring is always a hopeful time of year. In 1972 the wide-spread optimism seemed warranted, even though a few careful readers of the London *Times* noted uncertain auguries. On Monday, March 21, naturalists were delighted to see that a company oddly named Rio Tinto-Zinc had abandoned its schemes to dredge for alluvial gold in the rivers of Wales. Readers also witnessed the Editor's solemn assurance that "Political and economic judgment alike require the Chancellor of the Exchequer to go all out for full employment." In his Spring Budget, presented in the House of Commons that day, he did indeed announce both tax cuts and pension increases. The Leader of the Labour Opposition praised him as "a repenting sinner," but others found it politic to carp. A trade union leader denounced the new Budget as "a good thing for the Stock Exchange but not so hot for the Labour Exchange . . . the Chancellor has not seized a golden opportunity to strike a blow at the hard core of poverty in Britain." The human species are insatiable. That Budget was the largest and most inflationary attempt to stimulate domestic demand Great Britain's economy has ever experienced. The immediate reactions of the London markets were mixed. Bank shares welcomed the news and promptly rose. The exchange rate of the British pound declined 10 points, to $2.6180. Gold fell 5 cents to $48.40 per ounce, but tin abruptly soared to its highest price since the preceding April.

Unnoted by both the press and the public, a monetary landmark had passed. After weighing the political considerations at home and abroad, the British Prime Minister had quietly decided that he was no longer willing to defend that fixed exchange rate for the pound. In Boston, on March 25, an angry American Secretary of the Treasury therefore warned Republicans gathered at the 107-year-old Middlesex Club that other nations would have to "change the rules of the game" to enable the United States to earn a balance-of-payments surplus. He declared that the first requirement in any negotiated reform of the international monetary system. If others would not permit the United States to earn payments surpluses, he cautioned "We've got to be prepared to look after our own interests." The same day in Vienna, another disgruntled spokesman was heard. The Organization of Petroleum Exporting Countries (OPEC) announced that it would take collective action against any oil companies unwilling to accept "participation"—transfer of the ownership of oil production facilities to the member governments of OPEC. And on Sunday, March 26, another intriguing coincidence appeared. The Deputy Prime Minister of Egypt arrived in London to open an exhibition at the British Museum of the 3300-year-old relics excavated from the tomb of the Pharaoh Tutankhamun. He also began discreet talks with the British Foreign Secretary on the situation in the Middle East. Even in the most modern of cities, many ancient methods and interests remain. That day in Bonn, a massive barter deal was completed between West Germany and the Soviet Union to trade steel pipe for gas valued at more than $340 million.

Human progress has always been cautious and halting. In Washington, on March 27, emphasizing the commitment of the United States to diminish the monetary role of gold, reports circulated that the Treasury had begun studies on the possibility of selling part of its gold reserves on the world's free markets. The Secretary was said to be "attracted by the idea." Though later repudiated, those rumors had the effects intended. The next morning, on European free markets, gold fell 25 cents to $48.15 per ounce. And in Paris a senior American Treasury official informed his European colleagues that

> The basic constitutional issue facing the leading economic powers was who would play the role of the United States in the 1970s now that there were multiple centers of economic power rather than a single dominating country to provide the matching deficits for other countries' surpluses and to sustain the International Monetary Fund.

On March 20 the London *Times* informed its readers

> The Queen spent forty minutes looking at the treasures of Tutankhamun yesterday afternoon after officially opening the exhibition at the British Museum. . . . The Queen showed particular interest in the great golden funerary mask, the three gilded figures of Tutankhamun . . . and the little golden shrine which had never before been allowed to leave Egypt.

The following week, another *Times* reporter recorded the interests of less exalted visitors.

> Nearly 3000 schoolchildren and teachers from many parts of Britain visited the Tutankhamun exhibition at the British Museum yesterday. It was the first of the regular Monday . . . viewings set aside for school parties. Unquestionably the star attraction was the golden funerary mask, which seemed particularly to grip the imagination of the boys. I asked a group of fifty boys waiting on the staircase

. . . which exhibit they had liked best. "The mask," they chorused. Why was that, I asked a freckled 12-year-old. "Because it's solid gold," he answered. His friends, each clutching a souvenir, nodded in agreement.

Gold's fascination will persist, long after it has ceased to serve as money.

* * *

At the end of a road, it is always a pleasure to record thanks to those who have helped along the way. First place should go to Professor William N. Locke of the Massachusetts Institute of Technology. I shall also remain grateful to the late Professor Karl Loewenstein of Amherst College, for a quarter-century of encouragement.

The search began in London. Professor Sir Roy Harrod advised me to meet Professor Friedrich Lutz, who kindly opened the libraries of the University of Zürich. Dr. Max Iklé provided further guidance. The late Mr. Ernst Bigler and Dr. Hans Mast were consistently helpful, even though they must have found me an unprofitable client. Dr. John Lademann generously provided the private library of the Swiss National Bank, at a time when its relations with the United States were most sensitive. And in Basle, the candor of Mr. Michael Dealtry was an encouraging contrast to the reticence I had been led to expect at the Bank for International Settlements.

In London, I am indebted for many favors to Miss Violet Conolly. Mr. Willis Coburn Armstrong steered my hazardous course through the many Washington offices in which decisions are made and unmade, and introduced me to Dr. Miroslav Kriz in New York. Dr. Mast, Mr. Dealtry, Dr. Hans-Eckart Scharrer and Dr. Klaus Boeck of Hamburg have read the preliminary draft. I regret that in Paris I have not been able to consult M Baquiast before completing the final draft, but I trust that I have amply considered French views. Someone has said that to write on money without mentioning France would resemble staging *The Merchant of Venice* without the Jew.

Let me end this journey by thanking those who have helped in many other ways to uncover the facts, fables and foibles of man's experience with money. They will hasten to remind readers that I alone am responsible for all errors, and for the opinions expressed.

WILLIAM WISELEY

Zürich–Oxford
May 1970–August 1976

Contents

A Tool of Power

1 = Gold and Its Competitors to 1815

The most ancient forms of money can still be found in the more primitive societies of our own times.

In the Paleolithic Age, the oldest recorded period of human existence, man had slight influence on the natural forces surrounding him. The most ancient remains of human culture date from approximately 300,000 B.C., and the earliest type of social organization was the tribe. Its behavior was strongly affected by nature, against which it had few defenses. Ancient peoples made no conscious, deliberate efforts to change their social structure, and the species were so small in number that they could not affect their environment. Nevertheless, they had an extraordinary instinct for survival. By the Young Paleolithic Age (30,000 B.C. to 10,000 B.C.) human life had become comparatively sophisticated. Plants were cultivated, and by 7500 B.C. animals had been domesticated. The economic structures of agriculture had appeared that have remained the foundations of all later civilizations. Tribes tended to hold inflexibly to orderly, religious and traditional ways of life, with unwritten rules. Though one tribe's religion might be another's heresy, it was an apparent defense against nature and the night. The needs of the tribe were supreme, each individual's worth being determined by his or her comparative utility. Primitive crafts had begun to appear, and many new tools—axes, knives, lances, bows and arrows. Hunting and food gathering had become more skillful, and the natural division of labor began.

Necessity required early tribes to be nomadic, and whenever one encoun-

1

tered another, opportunities appeared to exchange not only tools and crafts but also the jewelry so important in their religious rites. Shells, strings of stones, rock crystal, the teeth of fish and animals, coral, ivory, amber, jet—all were valued. North European amber has been found as far south as the Pyrenees, and Red Sea shells have been excavated from sites in Switzerland. Those earliest exchanges were by chance, rather than organized. The production of goods was still intended to satisfy the immediate needs of the tribe, and only occasional, accidental surpluses were available for barter.

ANCIENT MONEYS

The earliest capital formation began after 10,000 B.C. Man began to preserve surplus products and to hire servants paid in them or in goods obtained by barter. Violence was a frequent, and often the preferred, way to gain slaves, animals and land. Pure barter was difficult, because lengthy search was so often needed to find goods a trading partner could use. Consequently, perhaps as early as the Paleolithic Age, societies began to give preference to wares everyone considered desirable for economic or religious reasons. Those were the beginnings of money, defined as the means of valuation and exchange widely recognized and used as standards in certain fields of economic activity. Cattle and slaves are examples. At the same time, materials valued as jewelry tended to be used as money. Other forms were used in many parts of the world. "Cloths money" (textiles, furs and leather of a definite quantity and quality) was always known in town civilizations as unrelated as Egypt, Mesopotamia and China. Shell and bead money were characteristic in the Americas, and "tool money" was common throughout Europe. The quantity and quality of the materials used in that "tool money" appear to have been unimportant. Value derived from the traditional shape, an innovation from which later coin forms would evolve. However, those earliest forms of money could not be lent out for interest. The most ancient moneylending began with "food money" and "animal money," which added a third purpose to the original characteristics of money—as a medium of exchange and as a standard of value.

With the passage of time, man would perceive further refinements. Certain forms of money could be considered stores of value and liquid reserves. Means and standards of deferred payments appeared. And by 7500 B.C. man had begun to think in the abstract. Money as a medium of exchange is a material commodity. As a standard of value it is an abstraction as intangible as any religious deity. Today no one should be surprised that there has always been a popular tendency to mistake one for the other by attributing supernatural qualities to material and often prosaic objects.

In the Mesolithic and Neolithic Ages, seeking to improve the quality of life, mankind began to mine for materials of value. As early as 5000 B.C. they were able to dig shafts to a depth of 20 meters and more, to use piles to support those shafts, and to construct horizontal galleries. Picks were often made of antlers, and trees were used as ladders. Flint seems to have been the material first and most frequently sought, but there were cultures that had begun to use copper, tin, gold, silver and meteoric iron for their jewelry and ornaments. That occurred quite early, especially in countries where minerals were easily found, such as Hungary, parts of Egypt and certain districts of India. In the course of the Neolithic Age, man learned to work these materials, their scarcity determining their use for luxury purposes. The earliest Sumerians and Egyptians knew gold and silver well, even though their everyday life remained as primitive as it had been in the Stone Age. Sometime after 4000 B.C. tin began to be used in Asia Minor, Syria, Iran, Egypt, India and Malaya. Between 2500 B.C. and 2000 B.C. it was alloyed with copper to form bronze. And after 3000 B.C. the first earthly iron was obtained as a by-product of refining of gold. Both bronze- and iron-smelting techniques had their origins in cultures begun near deposits of gold, silver, copper and tin for the specific purpose of extracting them.

In the Neolithic Age gold, silver, their alloys and other metals were fashioned into the jewelry, religious objects and magical implements man has always craved. The unusual properties of gold had been recognized by its earliest discoverers. It was attractive to the eye and malleable by the most primitive craftsmen. Yet it could not be tarnished or corroded by nature, and therefore seemed to possess a permanence that man himself so conspicuously lacked. That was a winning combination of attributes, and from the beginning gold's rarity reserved it for uncommon uses. Early tribal leaders often united in themselves both political and religious functions. Gold adorned them, to distinguish their rank. It also served as gifts or tribute whenever one leader met another. When tribes were in conflict, it was the obvious plunder that enabled all observers to see which tribe was the victor and which the vanquished. Thus gold has always been a symbol of power, both temporal and spiritual.

Modern archeologists have assembled a clear and reasonably accurate picture of those earliest civilizations. Recent radiocarbon research has made it possible to assign dates to them. We now know that the results of human thought and the traditions of many cultures were first written and recorded in the Middle East. Many of those civilizations had slight effect on others, then disappeared for millennia, and are now known only to specialists. Egypt was the exception. At the height of its powers ancient Egypt had profound influence on its neighbors, and its heritage has affected human development ever since.

The origins of Egyptian civilization are to be found in the centuries just before and after 4000 B.C. Primitive towns of predynastic Egypt appeared after 3500 B.C., and the era known as the "Old Kingdom" began around 3000 B.C. Those oldest city cultures created the foundations of every planned state society and organization that has succeeded them. Ruling classes of conquerors appeared, and the evidence available indicates that the material welfare of dependent classes actually improved. Regardless of wars and destruction, archeological excavations reveal continuing improvements in economic conditions. Except for a few everyday tools, metals continued to be used primarily for luxury purposes. But usury was far more important in those town civilizations than it had been in nomadic tribes, and the earliest use of bar gold as money dates from approximately 3000 B.C.

Among those ancient Middle Eastern peoples—Sumerian, Accadian, Hittite and Egyptian—first appeared the concept of a universal monarchy responsible for central planning that has been so significant in the political and economic development of imperial powers ever since. Ancient Egypt has always provided the prototype of the living king and divine representative endowed with the power and the right to rule the world. With planning centralized in a small ruling class, capital development in ancient Egypt was rapid and revolutionized civilization.

In that Third Millennium B.C. the money of the Middle East consisted of materials considered exchangeable because they could be weighed or measured out. The forms in which metals were used as money varied widely from one region to another and from one period to the next—rough flat cakes, rings, spirals, wire, grains, bars, lumps of gold and silver, copper or lead, and rough shapes such as animals' heads and tongues. Metal rings were a preferred form, and rings of gold, silver and copper have been found in European sites of the Bronze Age as well as in Egypt, Crete, the Near and Far East, and Central Asia.

Where every kind of exchangeable material could be used as money, there were ample opportunities for misunderstandings, real and fancied. Therefore, in many epochs, efforts were made to stabilize exchange rates by publishing lists of rates authorized and strictly controlled by the state. Many of those lists have been found, and they resemble the tables of currency exchange rates printed daily in modern newspapers. Their purpose was to prevent political difficulties and social unrest by stabilizing prices, wages and the cost of living for all classes. Those official, compulsory valuations of the many different types of money apparently achieved considerable success, and they demonstrate that rulers' economic power was indeed real. Nevertheless that monetary system was clumsy and complicated. It also tended to favor the rich against the poor, a relationship always fraught with social and political hazards.

After 3000 B.C. the growth in foreign trade transformed the Middle East, from Africa and Crete to Iran and India, into an integrated bloc for the exchange of certain goods, especially luxuries. Encouraged by increasing purchasing power and by the invention of better means of transport, man began to enjoy the products of foreign labor. Gold from Egypt and Nubia, from Iran and Asia Minor, and later from Hungary, played an important part in that traffic. And in those advancing circumstances, money almost entirely replaced barter. Well-organized merchant associations developed from 3000 B.C. onward, but trading capital was usually owned by the state—either by the king's treasury or by temples under state supervision. Legal sciences and systems of weights and measures were by-products of that increasing international trade. And mining, as a branch of primary production, rose to full importance for the first time. The exploitation of mineral deposits was carried out by gangs of serfs or by dependent peasants, supervised and financed by the holders of capital. Most of those early capitalists were kings and temples, but there were also a few private individuals rich enough to buy mines or to lend capital to entrepreneurs.

Though mining techniques had improved considerably when cheap iron had become available and iron tools were therefore introduced, the Iron Age witnessed enormous fluctuations in the prices of metals as their production fitfully responded to increasing demand. For example, gold was valued against silver at 8–1 in Babylonia somewhat before 2000 B.C. Then it rose to 10–1 around 2000 B.C. but quickly fell to 7–1. By the time of Hammurapi (circa 1728–1686 B.C.) gold compared with silver had fallen to a ratio of 6–1, and even to 3–1, because of increased imports from Egypt, which was rich in gold deposits. The mines that established and supported the political power and widespread influence of the Egyptian rulers were at Coptos and Edfu, and in Nubia. Nubia alone produced annually between 300 and 400 kilograms of gold under Thutmoses III (circa 1515–1436 B.C.). In the Old Kingdom of Egypt, silver had been so much scarcer than gold that it had been the more highly valued of the two. Between 1500 B.C. and 1200 B.C. Egypt and Mesopotamia simultaneously reached 10–1 valuations for gold and silver. Then a breakdown in foreign trade almost entirely separated Egypt from its sources of imported silver, and the rate of exchange between gold and silver fell to 1.87–1. After that exorbitant increase in the price of silver, mining throughout the known world increased substantially. During the 22nd Dynasty of Egypt, approximately 900 B.C., silver fell to less than one-fortieth of the price of gold. Those violent changes in the exchange rates between gold and silver are the first recorded difficulties man has experienced with metallic moneys whose supply was entirely unpredictable. It would be entertaining to know how Egyptian treasury officials explained to their pharaohs the consistent failure of their budget forecasts. Unhappily no record of those reports has been found.

The splendor of an empire such as ancient Egypt has always provoked not only envy and attack but also imitation and emulation. By the 8th and 7th centuries B.C. Egyptian influences had become pronounced in the cultural life, art, religion and economic affairs of Asia Minor, Greece and regions as far West as Etruria. In Egypt itself transactions were still conducted in metals, grain and many other materials that were weighed and measured out. But metal bars had become more carefully cut and standardized, because the invention of hardened iron tools had made the punching of metal inexpensive.

According to Homer metal bars were also known as money in Greece. Similarly the Phoenicians, Italians, Spaniards, Syrians and Arabs followed Egyptian example by weighing out bits of metals as money. The Phoenicians invented another form—leather bags of silver stamped with the seal of a Phoenician town, and money of that kind was circulated by Carthage as late as the 4th century B.C. There were also other forms of money in use on the northern shores of the Mediterranean that were unrelated to Egyptian and other Middle Eastern traditions, the most important being the "tool money" that had survived from the European village cultures of earlier millennia. Copper, iron, lead, gold and silver were used in those European metal pieces, their weight being unimportant. They were acceptable if, and only if, they were in the shape of traditional tools. In archaic Greece the most common forms were basins, tripods and other genuine utensils. Homer also recorded that ax money was common. But the circulation of each variety of tool money was restricted to the territory of a few tribes. Between that form and the Egyptian method of carefully weighing out money materials a combination or compromise appeared in the Greek city-states of Asia Minor during the 8th and 7th centuries B.C. Evolving from the bars that had become an internationally acceptable form, the coin developed.

Most historians have attributed invention of the first of those coins to Gyges, King of Lydia (687–652 B.C.), around the year 670 B.C. Yet there has always been a tendency for similar ideas to occur to many people at approximately the same time and in comparable circumstances. It is certain that Miletus, Ephesus, Samos, Phocaea and Lydia were the first of the Greek city-states and kingdoms in Asia Minor to adopt coin money. Smyrna, Chios, Cyzicus and Lampsakos soon followed. The metal first used was exclusively electrum, the natural alloy of gold and silver found in Asia Minor. Each piece of metal to be used as money received the stamp of a private person or a royal estate, a city-state or a sovereign king, to guarantee its exact weight and the purity of its metallic content. Those earliest coins were large and valuable pieces, intended only for exchange into objects of considerable value and for payment of large sums. They were probably used to pay the mercenary troops hired by Gyges and the Greek city-states. If so, the invention of coinage was only another example of a monetary innovation devised to meet military or wartime needs.[1] The coin form was accepted by the island of Aigina around 630 B.C. By 610 B.C. the city of Corinth had begun to follow the trend. Finally Athens began to try coins in the second or first decade of the 6th century B.C. The metal used by the Athenians was silver, small denominations being introduced because they were convenient in everyday trade. An Athenian tyrant, Peisistratos, devised the unified city mint and the coins bearing the Attic owl that became famous throughout the known world in the following centuries. Coinage quickly spread throughout Greece and extensively stimulated commerce. A similar development was taking place in China at approximately the same time. Around 700 B.C. Greek script was also created and Greek overseas colonization began. It was an era fertile in new ideas and in rapid development of older traditions.

During earlier centuries of the First Millennium B.C. the Phoenicians had been the leaders in the foreign trade of the Mediterranean, and primarily they had sought metals. Phoenicians had exploited mines as distant as Spain and had worked them with native labor or with slaves captured in war and piratical ventures. Phoenician trading posts had often been located near those mines to control and protect them. Tyre and Israel had undertaken joint ventures across the Red Sea during the reign of Solomon and every 3 years the legendary voyage to Ophir had returned with gold and silver, ivory, apes and peacocks, ebony and precious stones. Phoenician rulers had been both owners of ships and moneylenders in that foreign trade. Less often temples and prominent nobles had undertaken such voyages. As yet there had not been everyday traffic by merchants.

The Greek colonizing ventures of the 8th and 7th centuries B.C. were of a different character. They began with agrarian settlements, fishing stations and the construction of castles by political overlords, though several Greek settlements were pirate strongholds or mining outposts. The valuable gifts they sent annually to the principal temple of the mother city usually took the form of bars of precious metals, which became the war reserves of that city-state. No coin hoards have been found that date before 560 B.C., indicating that Greek trading in the Mediterranean became frequent only after that time.

The 6th century B.C. also witnessed the founding of the first banks outside Babylonia. Sale of specie and money exchange began with coin money and among goldsmiths and silversmiths rather than among rich capitalists.

Piracy, robbery and war continued to play an important part in the circulation of goods and were often more effective than peaceful methods of trade. As late as the 4th century B.C. Aristotle considered robbery by land and sea to

---

[1] Heichelheim, *An Ancient Economic History*, vol. 1, p. 216.

be quite lawful, and Thucydides declared that piracy was the oldest method of Greek acquisition throughout the Mediterranean. Though Greeks were less active in mining than the Phoenicians, traces of Greek operations during the 7th and 6th centuries B.C. have been found in Macedonia, Thrace, Lydia, Egypt, Cyprus, Italy and Sicily.

Several modern scholars believe that the new coin economy hastened the transition from aristocratic to democratic government in the Greek city-states by enabling small landowners to sell their surplus produce for money they could save and thereby establish their independence. Public expenses, particularly the cost of wars, were met by irregular contributions from the people, by the payments of allies and by use of earlier booty the state had carefully preserved. Increasingly state reserves took the form of precious metals, both in bars and in coin.

By 560 B.C. the economies of those Greek city-states had become quite sophisticated. Bimetallism had been introduced into Lydia by Croesus, and his small silver coins became commonplace in marketplaces throughout Asia Minor. Cyrus the Great, the Persian ruler who subdued Lydia, spread that usage throughout his empire. Persian *darics* in gold and silver were introduced after 514 B.C. and gradually replaced more ancient forms of money in Syria, Egypt and Mesopotamia. By the time of the Persian Wars coins had become the most common form of money as far west as Spain, and north beyond the Black Sea. Several coin standards gained widespread acceptance. During the 5th century B.C. the Attic silver currency became the principal system of valuation used by trading states, occasionally supplemented by Persian gold, Corinthian silver and Cyzicene electrum. During the 4th century B.C. Corinthian silver money was as widely accepted as that of Athens. And in the last quarter of the 5th century B.C. bronze coins had been introduced. They have been preferred ever since for local trade and for small denominations.

The rates of exchange among the four standard coinage metals—gold, silver, electrum and bronze—fluctuated considerably because of frequent changes in production and demand. Each of those changes affected the weights in which coins were issued and varied the exchange rates in the money markets. Therefore mint unions were tried. Various mints sought in vain to achieve permanent agreement between the commercial and the metallic values of their coins. In principle all four metals were equally legal tender—declared officially acceptable by local authorities everywhere. None of the four achieved definite superiority, so far as acceptance was involved. Often fluctuations in their relative values had political origins. Just before the Peloponnesian War many of Athens' tributary towns seceded, and it was denied a large part of the gold production from the Balkan peninsula. The price of gold rose, and Athens was compelled to use the gold reserves in its treasury. The price promptly fell.

After the beginning of the 4th century B.C. the value of gold continued to decline as the Persian kings used their massive reserves to pay mercenary armies. In the "Holy War" the metallic reserves of Delphi were minted and put into circulation. Then Philip II of Macedon began to use the enormous production of his Thracian and Macedonian mines for his political ventures into the Greek world. When the price of gold fell remarkably, Philip tried to stabilize his Macedonian currency system at a ratio of 10–1 for gold and silver. His new bimetallic gold and silver coinage became dominant in the money markets of Greece, as he prepared the political groundwork for his victories at Chaeronea and Granicus. Ten to one became the normal rate of exchange between gold and silver for many years thereafter.

During the 3rd century B.C., the heyday of the Greek city-states, increasing demand for gold and silver began to exhaust their domestic mines at Siphnos, Thasos and Laurion. During the 2nd century B.C. those deposits were worked out and abandoned. But to the north the vast Macedonian mines continued to provide the financial foundations for the policies of imperial expansion pursued by Philip, his son Alexander and later Macedonian kings. Ever since their example has spurred ambitious rulers to seek control over ample sources for the production of money.

Alexander himself utterly transformed the known world. Among other achievements he simplified and standardized its monetary systems thoroughly and remarkably. Because Philip had adopted the Attic standard for his gold coinage, Alexander accepted it for silver, then released upon a startled world vast reserves of captured Persian metals. All of their successors except the Ptolemeans of Egypt followed that tradition. The standard of Alexander the Great dominated in most of the states from the Indus River to Naples and Syracuse. Both in Southern Arabia and in Northern Europe the coins of Philip and Alexander were so popular that they would be copied and counterfeited for centuries. Thus they provided a striking example of the widespread popular acceptance a ruler's political achievements could confer upon his currency. The influence of the Ptolemean kings of Egypt, who adopted the standard of the Phoenician coinage, was restricted to the territories under their immediate control. By the end of the 3rd century B.C. those two coinage standards had divided between them the known world.

Recently attempts have been made to relate modern monetary theory to the experience of ancient civilizations.[2] The results have been questionable because of the dearth of reliable statistical evidence. Yet sufficient research has been done to demonstrate that the monetary disorders of the 20th century have been minor by comparison with those endured by ancient peoples.

Several aspects of primitive moneys should be remembered. The multiplic-

[2] Notably by Paul Einzig, in his *Primitive Money*.

ity of forms vastly increased the possibilities of error and the need for caution in every transaction. Moreover most early forms of money served both monetary and nonmonetary purposes. Therefore nonmonetary demand often became the determining factor in the value of money, and that has remained true wherever gold and silver have been used. In ancient times price levels were often simply unknowable from one day to the next, because the frequent, unpredictable fluctuations in the supply and demand for metals were so severe. The limited scope of ancient forms of money, both in geographic acceptance and in commercial utility, further restricted the development of trade. Thus the most lasting benefit conferred by Alexander the Great may have been his establishment of a simple and uniform monetary standard for so much of the world known in his day. The stimulus to trade, and therefore to human welfare, was extraordinary.

OLD ROME AND NEW ROME

Whenever republican Rome was compared with the flourishing economies of the Hellenistic world, whose trade in luxuries was lavishly financed by gold and silver, it appeared not only rude and primitive but quite barbaric. Nevertheless those early Romans demonstrated the remarkable expansion that could be achieved by a warlike tribe, even though it lacked the metallic moneys considered essential by its more sophisticated neighbors. The original Rome would never overcome the difficulties caused by its shortages of gold and silver bullion.

The first metallic money of the Romans was the *as*, a copper rod 1 Roman foot long and ½ inch in diameter. By immemorial custom, one hundred of those copper rods were valued at one cow. The first Roman silver *denarius* was modeled on the *drachma*, the Hellenic unit of account, and minted in 269 B.C. That exclusively silver coinage accompanied the Roman legions as they completed their conquest of the Italian peninsula and Sicily, then invaded Gaul and Spain. By the latter part of the 1st century B.C. the Roman *denarius* had become the dominant monetary standard of Western Europe. The Romans also proved to be more ruthless conquerors than the Greeks and the Macedonians. Whereas Alexander and his successors had tolerated the continuing existence of many local coinages, because all were based on the Attic standard, the Romans suppressed them, melted down those symbols of competing power and minted their metals into Roman coins. In the 2nd and 1st centuries B.C. local minting of *denarii* began to appear from Gaul to Rumania as tangible evidence of expanding Roman political power. In republican Rome there were no permanent state treasuries that handled foreign-exchange operations comparable to the treasuries of the Greek city-states. There were only the private professions of *nummularii* and *spectatores*, ill esteemed by a people who valued most highly the military virtues. Rome had no deposit banks, though interest was paid on capital sums advanced by private banks or private individuals. Because the banking of Ptolemaic Egypt was far more sophisticated, it served as an example for Romans interested in the economic development of their own state. During the 3rd century B.C. the state banking system of Egypt had reached its most advanced era and had enabled the Ptolemaic kings to become the largest moneylenders in the Mediterranean.

Though the output of the Macedonian gold and silver mines had surpassed those available to Rome in the 3rd century B.C., in the 2nd century B.C. they suffered setbacks from which they never recovered. For political reasons all independent states began to develop whatever resources of gold and silver could be found within their own borders, to supply as best they could their own needs for money. In troubled times a policy of self-sufficiency has always had obvious merits. The quantities of precious metals obtained from Carthaginian lands in Africa had equaled those available to Alexander's heirs in Asia, and they excited the competitive spirit of the Romans. In the 3rd century B.C. they had begun to exploit the silver mines of Sardinia and the deposits of gold found in the Po River valley and in the Carinthian Alps. In the 2nd century B.C. Rome gradually occupied the Spanish gold and silver mines that had been extensively worked by the Carthaginians. Gold and tin mines were also opened in Dalmatia and in Gaul. The Romans of the republican period did not make any innovations in mining techniques, but they took full advantage of the methods developed by the Greeks and Carthaginians. And they apparently decided quite consciously that it was easier to obtain precious metals by plunder and as tribute, rather than to find new deposits.

In its valuation of silver and gold republican Rome had remained independent of the Hellenic East, probably because of the high freight rates in the Mediterranean. In the 3rd century B.C. the Roman ratio of silver to gold was 1–15. That fell to 1–10 in the 2nd century B.C., when new gold mines were discovered, then rose to 1–12 in the reign of Augustus.

For the first time accurate data have been preserved that permit the study of currency crises. A series of severe inflationary periods began during the Second Punic War, when Rome was threatened by Hannibal. Then Carthage suffered from that scourge after its defeat. Next inflation troubled Macedonia and Syria, Rhodes and Egypt, even Parthia and Bactria, wherever Roman armies marched. Price stability was not restored until the time of Augustus, concurrent with the establishment of political security for the entire world known at that time.

Though the average Roman of the republican period seems to have been more prosperous than a citizen of the Hellenic states, the few rich Romans were not as conspicuous as Eastern princes. In the 2nd century B.C. the Elder Scipio amassed some 200 talents. In the 1st century B.C. the enterprising

Pompey bequeathed 11,000 talents and was said to have been the richest Roman of his day. Crassus held some 7000 to 8000 talents, and Lucullus approximately 4200. That did not compare with the wealth of Eastern rulers, and almost all the remaining Roman fortunes of the 1st century B.C. were less than 1000 talents each. The habits of the Roman ruling classes tended to be spendthrift and often caused catastrophic debts, one of the reasons for their downfall.

Minting of the *aureus*, the gold coin that provided the second monetary standard for the later Roman Empire, began with Julius Caesar. Apparently he had grasped that a gold coinage was one of the symbolic ways in which Rome could emulate earlier world conquerors. It now had ample gold reserves for that purpose, and the weight of the new *aureus* was established at 40 to the pound. Though his plans were soon terminated by assassination and can never be fully known, it is indicative that minting of the *aureus* was undertaken by his personal decree, without the authorization of the Senate.

The coinage reforms begun by Julius Caesar were completed by his adopted son Augustus. Though less universal in his ambitions, Augustus had greater opportunities and used them so fruitfully that his age is still recalled with nostalgia. The *aureus* became popular as far away as India, and was supported everywhere by the prestige of Roman armies. Augustus took minting of the silver *denarius* from the Senate and stabilized its exchange rate with the *aureus* at 25 to 1, so that the ratio between silver and gold remained at approximately 1–12 for a long period. Nevertheless neither Augustus nor his successor Tiberius could meet the demand for gold and silver from the borderlands of the Roman Empire, from Britain to Central Asia. Their inability to provide adequate quantities of acceptable money hampered the development of trade and may have had harmful effects on the political unity of their empire. Deflationary troubles began, accompanied by urban unemployment and social disorders, which have always characterized the stagnation or contraction of international trade.

Deterioration of the Roman coinage began in the time of Nero. At the heart of the Roman Empire copper and silver had remained the coins used in everyday transactions. Under Nero the silver *denarius* suffered a slow but increasing addition of copper. There were many and varied causes: the export of coinage in the course of trade; the exhaustion of old mines and the failure to find new ones; and the lavish expenditures of several emperors, for whom the regular revenues of the state did not suffice. Limited debasement of the coinage would have been accepted if the credit of Rome had remained high and commerce had flourished. But the difficult wars of Marcus Aurelius and the civil wars of Septimus Severus caused economic instability. New and productive enterprises became too hazardous. Gold and silver coins were hoarded, their disappearance from circulation increasing commercial difficulties. Because existing mines could not remedy those deficiencies, the state began to require the payment of taxes in kind. In turn that stimulated increases in the prices of commodities. Debasement of the coinage had further adverse effects abroad. In outlying areas such as India the *denarius* ceased to circulate, only the golden *aureus* continuing to be acceptable. Beyond the immediate reach of its armies the influence of Rome began to decline. Trajan's conquest of Dacia brought rich plunder and the gold and silver mines of Hungary. But a modern critic has observed that "no war booty, however large, lasts long, and no amount of silver and gold can ultimately give vigor to a weakened economic structure." [3]

In the 3rd century A.D., under the Emperor Commodus, the Augustan system of coinage collapsed. To revive it, varied experiments were tried. But the diverse restrictions imposed served only to bewilder the citizenry and to disrupt trade further. There was no longer any way to disguise the financial embarrassment of the Roman Empire. The *aureus* became a much lighter piece of gold, and the *denarius* fell to half of its earlier value. By the 4th century A.D. copper's ratio to silver was 1–125. Silver's ratio to gold was 1–14 and sometimes as high as 1–18. It has been estimated that, if the demand for precious metals had remained constant in the internal economy of the Empire from the time of Augustus to the 4th century A.D., more than half of the silver and two-thirds of the gold stock must have disappeared in the course of three centuries.

All confidence was lost in the coin money developed by Hellenic cultures, then unified by Caesar and Augustus. The accompaniment was severe trade recessions, urban unrest and still heavier restrictions on the circulation of money. A new era in monetary history began, a reversion to the primitive weighing out of metals of a millennium before. When its coin money systems collapsed, the Roman Empire had no alternative except to resort to a system of state barter exchange. And diminishing state revenues in metallic moneys added to the difficulties of later emperors, because their troops demanded payment in coin.

We now take for granted that a prosperous economy is a principal purpose of any government, with peace and political stability as essential preconditions. But the early Romans had scorned peace and never achieved a type of government that could provide stability for more than a few years. Their Republic had succumbed to the first ruthless Caesar, and his family's efforts to establish the dynastic principle had ended ingloriously in Nero. By the reign of Commodus the civil wars of competing generals had so thoroughly ravaged the Empire that they have become cautionary examples cited by all modern scholars.

[3] Rostovtzeff, *Social and Economic History of the Roman Empire,* vol. 2, p. 694, n. 1.

Rather than revert to the republican modesty that had served early Rome so well, later Roman emperors, beginning with Diocletian, audaciously assumed divine status, hoping that theatrics would quell internal disorders and forestall external threats. He was neither the first nor the last political leader who has vainly tried monetary magic in an effort to rebuild quickly the shattered foundations of production and commerce that provided his revenues. Diocletian's reform of the Roman coinage began in 295 A.D. and was continued after his abdication in 305 by his principal successor, Constantine I. Though a conservative effort to restore confidence in the golden *aureus* by recalling the earlier grandeur of Rome, Diocletian's experiments with its weight were not the way to achieve that purpose. First he tried a weight of 70 to the pound, then of 60 to the pound, which weighed about 327 grams in his time. Benefiting from that experience, Constantine I later fixed the weight at 72 to the pound and established such firm quality controls for his new coinage that it became known as the *solidus,* or *obryziacus.* Diocletian had also founded a network of sixteen mints throughout the Empire to provide payment for his armies. The coins they issued were subjected for the first time to regulations intended to ensure uniformity of quality and weight for gold coinage issued throughout the Empire. The coin took the form of a small gold bar stamped by the state mint as a guarantee of weight and gold content. Struck primarily for private circulation, the *solidus* provided a standard that was steadily maintained for the next 700 years, a unique achievement in the history of money. No debasement of that coinage began until after 1042.

Yet gold had never been commonly used in everyday commerce. Both Diocletian and his successors failed to find a remedy for the far more difficult problem of the debased and discredited *denarius* by providing a new and more acceptable silver coinage. A new silver coin called the *argenteus* (or *denarius siliqua*) of 3.41 grams was indeed introduced, its weight fixed at that of the Neronic *denarius.* Once again, however, insufficient bullion was available. Diocletian could not mint enough of the *argentii* to meet the demand for them and never tried to standardize their weight and quality. Constantine I was compelled to authorize continuing use of those *denarii* that had maintained their credit in circulation. Their value tended to fluctuate considerably, influenced by the quantity in circulation, their purity, the successive reform efforts, public confidence and political unrest.

The catastrophic inflationary difficulties of that period have been recorded, and one example should suffice to indicate their disruptive effects. In 301 Diocletian tried to stabilize the debased *denarius* by fixing its value at 50,000 to the gold pound. By 305, however, the exchange rate had fallen to 100,000 to the gold pound. Having failed to obtain rapid economic recovery by his experiments with the coinage, in 301 Diocletian had also tried futile price controls. He began the persistent, arbitrary intervention in the economy that had previously been attempted only in crises. Later emperors would continue that practice and repeatedly ban the export of gold, an expedient used ever since by rulers burdened with excessive expenditures and inadequate revenues.

The hazardous political and military instincts of the Roman emperors had led to overextension. Early conquests had only stimulated their appetite for more. In the 3rd century the city of Rome itself was abandoned by those emperors, because they disliked the continuing pretensions of its senators and citizens. Nor had Diocletian enhanced his popularity there by imposing taxes, from which they had previously been exempt. Rome's supreme rulers became vagabonds, roaming the Empire to suppress internal disorders and to protect frontiers. In 322–323, during a campaign against the rebel Licinius, Constantine I noted the strategic advantages of the ancient city of Byzantium. Though its climate was unpleasant, its importance as a fortress had been known since the Peloponnesian War. It controlled the traffic by water between the Mediterranean and the Black Sea and trade by land between Europe and Asia. Moreover it was near the increasingly important Danubian and Armeno–Syrian frontiers. Construction of fortifications began in November 324. And on May 11, 330, Constantine the Great formally entered his new capital, the city of New Rome. Most men called it Constantinople in his honor.

Few cities have ever enjoyed the commercial advantages Constantinople later derived from its geographic position and its standing as the capital of the predominant state between West and East. Though the West could produce its own necessities, it craved luxuries only the East could provide. Spices, herbs and sandalwood from the Indies; the silks of China; jewels from Ceylon; Baltic amber; Russian furs and slaves; and the metals of Central Europe all found their way to the warehouses and marketplaces of Constantinople. Throughout the 5th and 6th centuries the diplomacy of the Empire was intended to secure free trade routes, especially through the Central Asian steppes and across the Red Sea. Though sometimes disrupted by the incursions of Tatars, Arabs or Bulgars, the trade of Constantinople continued to prosper through the 9th and 10th centuries.[4]

The money preferred by Eastern merchants of all races was the imperial coinage of Byzantium. And in the legal code prepared under Theodosius (379–395) the doctrine was first proclaimed that money is minted in the service of the public and is not in any way a commodity but rather an official instrument of exchange. So firmly did that concept take root that, even after the fall of the Western Empire, the emperors of Byzantium continued to claim the right to monopolize the minting of gold coinage throughout the length and breadth of the former Roman Empire. From Constantine I to Constantine IX Monomachus (1042–1055) the unimpaired and monometal-

[4] Runciman, *Byzantine Civilization*, p. 163 et seq.

lic gold coinage of the Byzantine Empire provided an indispensable instrument that attracted to Constantinople its virtual monopoly of international trade. Though the *solidus* became known as the *nomisma* or *bezant*, its purity and weight remained constant, at 72 to the pound. It was divided into twelve *miliaressia*, each of which could be further subdivided. But maintenance of the purity and weight of the *nomisma* or *bezant* for seven centuries did not in itself secure stability of domestic prices throughout that period. In Constantinople price stability was maintained only by rigorously policed state controls and by the peace and political security conferred upon its citizens by strong walls and armies. Beyond those walls, on the borders of the Empire, the citizens of New Rome continued to suffer from inflationary and deflationary disorders caused by natural disasters and political unrest.[5]

The resplendent, hierarchic Byzantine court and bureaucracy were the wonder of the Middle Ages and a phenomenon from which the world has never recovered. Though the crown was elective, laws codified by Justinian after 527 provided political stability and continuity. Byzantine budgets were calculated annually, and the principal revenues of the emperors were drawn from customs duties and land taxes. Lesser amounts were obtained from patents and monopolies, mines and arsenals, and the produce of extensive crown lands. Constantine I had placed the financial affairs of the Empire in the hands of two ministers and the Praetorian Prefects, but eventually their responsibilities were divided among eight quite independent ministries. A General Logothete collected taxes and received the bullion from state mines, while a Military Logothete administered the treasury that paid troops and other military expenses. The Special Treasury controlled public factories, and the Chartulary of the Wardrobe was also master of the mint. The imperial estates were administered by two central offices, and there were separate offices for the herds of military horses in Asia and the stables in Constantinople itself. The central treasurer of the state, the Sakellarios, bore the responsibility of general comptroller. To his misfortune, however, the eight finance ministries were not subordinate to him. Their waste and corruption became legendary and could be supported only in times of prosperity. Public expenditures tended to be inconstant. Under an ambitious emperor military campaigns and public buildings absorbed state revenues. Empresses were prone to spend their incomes on the church and charities. Wastrels dissipated the resources of the Empire on entertainments and favorites.

There is little reliable evidence on the actual revenues of the Byzantine Empire during that millennium. Costly, lavish display had become habitual, to impress the crowds at home and to sustain Byzantine prestige abroad. But emperors and their treasurers were secretive about their incomes. Well aware of the influence of their gold, they frequently brandished it with considerable

[5] Baynes and Moss, *Byzantium*, pp. 64 et seq.

effect. Where its real quantity was unknown, it could be and presumably was exaggerated. We do know, however, that the Emperor Anastasius bequeathed 340,000 pounds of gold, Theophilus and Theodora 135,000 pounds, and Basil I 235,000 pounds. Those sums seem large, but Byzantium had no credit system of any kind. An emperor's gold reserves therefore represented the total disposable wealth of the state, and historians have marveled how rarely they were bankrupt.

In the Byzantine economy, whenever a sum was owed, actual transport of the gold was required. In 809 a Bulgarian king captured 11,000 pounds of gold a Byzantine army had been carrying in its baggage train for the payment of troops. In 949 the Emperor Constantine VII recorded that an expedition of 14,459 men sent to Crete had cost him 3706 pounds of gold. Construction of the Church of St. Sophia cost 300,000 gold pounds. And in the 12th century the island of Corcyra yielded an annual revenue of 1500 gold pounds. Though fragmentary those sums indicate the magnitudes of the revenues available to Byzantine rulers long after internal decay had begun. During the 11th century the civil bureaucracy so detested the military aristocracy that they systematically reduced the numbers and the quality of Byzantine armies and thereby exposed Constantinople to repeated attacks. As the borders of the Empire contracted, income from land taxes diminished and crown lands were lost. As foreign trade declined, customs duties decreased. Deterioration in revenues was not accompanied by retrenchment in state expenditures until much too late, for fear of losing prestige. Then desperate, futile expedients were tried. Constantine IX Monomachus quietly began debasement of the gold coinage, and it became a public scandal during the reign of Nicephorus III Botaneiates.

During the crusades of the 11th century Byzantium enjoyed renewed prominence, and Alexius I Comnenus tried to restore the ancient coinage. By the end of his reign, however, he was forced to pay expenses in a new coin he had invented, a *nomisma* of brass that was legally fixed at two-thirds the value of the gold *nomisma*. It simply was not acceptable, regardless of his decrees. After 1204, during the rule of the Paleologi, the gold *nomisma* rapidly fell to one-sixth of its former weight and ceased to circulate outside the Empire. Though the city of Constantinople did not fall to the Turks until 1453, its last emperors had become so impoverished that they could no longer struggle against the social and financial chaos that had accompanied the collapse of their coinage.

MEDIEVAL EUROPE

Regardless of economic distress and political disorder the Roman Empire of the West might have survived much longer if it had not been besieged by the incessant attacks of barbarian tribes. Rome's profitable conquests had ended in the reign of Trajan. From the time of Marcus Aurelius onward Rome was compelled to maintain exhausting defenses on all frontiers. In the 5th century the successors of Theodosius were minors and weaklings who permitted barbarian settlements within the Empire. Roman troops were withdrawn from Britain in 411. The Vandals began their conquest of Africa in 429, and in 455 they pillaged Italy as far as the gates of Rome. By 456 the Goths had conquered the greater part of Spain, and by 470 the Burgundians had absorbed most of Gaul. By 476 the Empire had lost most of the West, and in Italy itself the authority of the emperors existed largely in theory. Gothic kings had become the real rulers. The 6th century "reconquest" by the Emperor Justinian, begun in 526, was a brief revival of imperial ambition that ruined and depopulated every African and European province in which his wars were waged. Though successful in their campaigns to defend Eastern frontiers, Byzantine emperors were forced to recognize new rulers in the West.

Of the many Romano–Germanic states born amid that chaos in the West, only the kingdom of the Franks was sufficiently stable to endure for more than a few decades. Recognizing the prestige and moral authority of Rome, the Franks found a way to live with it by accepting the legal fiction that they were *federates,* in Roman service. First prominent under Childeric (464–476), the Frankish tribes remained disunited until the accession of his son Clovis in 481. The ambitions of that 15-year-old King of Touraine were boundless. Skillful and audacious, he quickly defeated the last remnants of the Roman armies and authority in Gaul. Sometime between 486 and 499 Clovis had himself baptized at Rheims and thus became the only Christian head of state in the West. Though the Burgundians and the Goths remained rivals, the Roman Church therefore became his ally. Helped by its funds and many friends, by 509 Clovis had defeated all of his opponents between the Pyrenees and the Rhine. Then he installed himself in Paris, where he died in 511, at the age of 45.

Like other barbarian leaders, the Frankish kings who succeeded Clovis chose to imitate the Roman monetary system Constantine I had restored. But the Gallic gold coinage had a lighter weight of 84 *solidi* or *sous* to the Roman gold pound of 327 grams, whereas in Italy the weight remained 72 to the pound. In practice the Franks preferred half *sous* or thirds of a *sou*, and most gold coins were issued in those denominations. The silver coinage of the Franks retained the old Roman name of *denarius*, a coin equal in value to the Romano–Byzantine half *siliqua*, which usually weighed 1.30 grams. However, neither Clovis nor his successors made any effort to maintain those coins as standards. Their weight and the quality of their metallic content were irregular. The common commercial practice was to weigh them in every transaction and to melt down coins into bullion whenever large sums were needed.

Several historians have expressed surprise that the minting of gold continued in the West long after its trade had collapsed and its economy had been
exhausted by war. Yet considerable amounts of gold had remained, not in
circulation but in private hoards. During the 4th century a new class of great
landowners and officials had appeared, and they survived all the efforts of
Christian emperors and barbarian kings to tax them. Aside from vast landed
estates they held large fortunes in gold and silver bars and in specie. Those
hoards were secretly passed from one generation to the next. Heirs of the
latifundia, those large landowners survived the barbarian invasions to emerge
as the senatorial nobility under the Merovingian kings. They also established
the propensity to hoard gold that has persisted to our own day among the
French *haute bourgeoisie*, for similar reasons. The rich, whenever they distrust
their own governments, will always find ways to evade taxation. At the opposite end of the social scale common folk used a small copper coin called the
denarius communis, whose weight and purchasing power were inconstant.
French historians have described it as "the currency of inflation."[6]

In the 7th century the right of coining, a right royal prerogative, passed to
episcopal and monastic churches and even to private individuals, though the
treasuries of many petty European princes continued to share the profits.
Mints multiplied in towns, and the Franks alone are said to have had more
than 700 of them. Towns, castles and even villas issued coins, because the
demand for them was considerable, no matter how debased they became.
That proliferation of mints symbolized the disintegration of royal power and
the division of the West into hundreds of petty principalities.

In the 8th century the minting of gold coins almost ceased. Only the provinces of Southern Italy and Sicily under Byzantine control continued to issue
them regularly. Isolated by the expansion of Norman and Mohammedan
power, Europe's foreign trade almost vanished. It became an agricultural
economy that could support only local trade. Even silver tended to disappear
from circulation, and payments were commonly made in cattle, horses, grain
and other commodities, though prices were still expressed in the old coinage.
For more than 500 years the West would buy from the East when and as it
could, but it rarely sold anything there. Regular gold coinage would not
reappear in France until the reign of Louis IX, in the 13th century.

Regardless of that disappearance of gold, an economic revival had begun
in late 8th century Gaul that would demonstrate the dispensability of any
single form of money. Whenever one form becomes too scarce, another will be
substituted. First begun by Pepin the Short (751–768), then continued by his
son Charlemagne (768–814), an entirely new monetary system was established. It was a logical, almost essential corollary of their political efforts to

[6] Latouche, *The Birth of Western Economy*, p.16.

reunify the West. The system was monometallic, and the Frankish silver *denier* (*denarius*) became the universal coinage throughout their Carolingian Empire. Legally the basis of that coinage was a silver pound that weighed 491 grams, much heavier than the earlier Roman pound of 327 grams. The pound of Charlemagne was divided into 240 *deniers* or *pence* of pure silver, each of which weighed approximately 2 grams. Those silver *deniers* or *pence*, and the *half-pence*, were the only tangible coins. However, there were also abstract units of account, mere numerical expressions, that were used for accounting purposes. Each corresponded to a fixed number of *pence*. The *sou* or *shilling* (*solidus*) was the equivalent of 12 *pence*, and 20 *sous* or *shillings* equaled 1 *pound*. Though ill suited for large-scale commerce, that coinage was well adapted to the needs of an age in which the vast majority of transactions were petty retail payments.

Pepin and Charlemagne were quite conscious of their Roman imperial heritage and apparently were not aware that they were doing anything new and revolutionary. In their eyes they were only reforming abuses that had become troublesome. A systematic series of Capitularies was issued to enforce conformance. The state reserved to itself the right of coining and concentrated it in a few mints under royal supervision. Rigorous punishment was prescribed for anyone so rash as to counterfeit or refuse the royal *deniers*. The silver bullion available to the Carolingians consisted of stocks of old coins and new production from the few Frankish mines, principally those of Melle in Aquitaine, supplemented by several in the Harz Mountains and in Bohemia. After a half-century of strict controls Charlemagne's heirs became too weak to continue them. Counts who had been responsible for the mints as royal officials began to appropriate their income, with or without royal permission. Nevertheless the Carolingian monetary system remained in use in all the European states born from the division of his empire. All retained the silver *denier* as their tangible money, with the *sou* and the *livre* as units of account. Regardless of differences in language, a *pfennig* or a *penny*, a *sou* or a *shilling*, a *livre*, *pound* or *pfund*, the reality was the same. In Britain that Carolingian monetary system was retained until the introduction of decimal coinage in 1971.

Commerce with the East began to revive in the 9th and 10th centuries, led by the nascent capitalists of Venice, Pisa and Genoa. In Alexandria they sold slaves, wood and weapons from the West and returned with spices, textiles and some gold. Often, however, that gold was spent in Constantinople to buy silks, dyes and other luxuries. Though dissolution of the Carolingian Empire in the latter half of the 9th century caused a reversion to monetary chaos, and there were soon as many debased types of *deniers* in circulation as there were feudal European princes, most men were content with coins that were acceptable only within quite limited territories. Beginning in the 11th century,

Charlemagne's silver *livre* of 491 grams was replaced in the Germanies by a new monetary unit, the silver *mark* of 218 grams, which was probably of Scandinavian origin.

North of the Alps, trade revived in the 12th century, fed by new supplies of silver obtained from mines discovered near Freiburg. But the bullion available remained insufficient until the 15th century, when entrepreneurs such as the Fuggers began thoroughly to exploit the deposits of Saxony, Bohemia, the Tyrol, Salzburg and Hungary. Where every petty prince had the right to coin, it was invariably used to secure maximum profit for the prince. From the 13th century onward coins were continually recalled, recast and reissued in more debased condition than before. By contrast, in England the right to coin became a jealously guarded royal prerogative. The quality of English coins was therefore maintained more consistently than on the Continent, and they tended to fetch a premium in transactions.

Both in England and in France those royal efforts to recover and preserve regalia, the royal rights and privileges that included coining, were a conscious part of the medieval struggle for supremacy between kings and their great vassals. A mint was a valuable source of revenue, and money in coin enabled a strong monarch to buy the troops and political support needed to sustain his rule. Where money was lacking, kings weakened and dynasties fell. In France, by the end of the 14th century, the number of vassals who still retained the right to coin had been reduced to thirty. Nevertheless the coins issued by the royal mints were as debased as those of competing nobles. Coining techniques had remained so rudimentary that it was too difficult to guarantee uniformity in weight and quality of content.

Badly needed reforms began, not in the royal mints of Europe, but in Venice—the greatest commercial center of 12th century Europe. In a carefully calculated effort to compete with Constantinople, whose Eastern trade the Venetians had begun to invade, in 1192 the Doge Henry Dandolo struck an entirely new kind of silver coin called the *gros*, *groat* or *matapan*. Weighing a little more than 2 grams, it had a value equivalent to the Carolingian *sou*, or 12 of the old *deniers*. Rapidly the *groat* became the money of commerce, debased *deniers* being reduced to small change throughout Northern Italy. Imitating that Italian example, in 1266 Louis IX of France created the *gros tournois* and the heavier *gros parisis*. Those coins spread throughout Europe, and from 1276 onward they began to appear in the Germanies as *groschen*. In England the *sterling* coin, an improved *denier*, appeared at the end of the 12th century. It was also accepted throughout Continental trade. Those new coins were not a break with the Carolingian system but rather efforts to improve it, to provide commerce with instruments of exchange adequate to the expanding needs for them.

In 1231 the extravagant Emperor Frederick II of Hohenstauffen, King of

Sicily and Jerusalem, popularly hailed as *Stupor Mundi*, struck a new gold coin called the *Augustale*. He did so to remind the world that he alone, not the Pope, had inherited the ancient Roman Empire. Though limited in circulation, that coin also provided an outstanding example of the fine craftsmanship that could now be achieved in minting by any prince willing to spend money for that purpose. Italian trading cities, intent upon profiting from the opportunities provided by reopening Mediterranean commerce, quickly followed his example. In 1252 Florence coined the first golden *florins*, so called because they were stamped with a lily, the *fiorino* that served as the city's emblem. Genoa issued a similar coin in the same year, and in 1284 Venice produced the *ducat* or *zecchino*. Adequate supplies of bullion had become available to those Italian city-states. After the capture of Constantinople by the Franks in 1203 Venice had gained not only large quantities of Byzantine treasure but also three-eighths of its lands, including the gold mines of the Crimea. Both the *florin* and the *ducat* weighed 3½ grams of gold, which at that time had a value of 1 silver *pound gros*. Thus the *pound*, like the *shilling*, was transformed from a unit of account into a real coin.

North of the Alps, adequate supplies of gold bullion were not available. But when the Italian city-states began the fashion for gold coinage, others felt obliged to follow, in the competitive quest for both commercial advantage and political prestige. The first golden French *denier* was probably struck by Louis IX in 1266. In Spain regular gold coinage began to appear in the reign of Alfonso XI of Castille (1312–1350). Bohemia was the first of the Germanic states to issue gold coins, in 1325. Since the time of the Saxons the coinage of England had been exclusively silver. Yet Henry III had issued a few gold *pennies* in 1257, and Edward III struck a gold *florin* in 1344. Gold coinage had also appeared in the Low Countries, in the 1330s and 1340s.

Revived awareness of gold stimulated renewed search for it—first in Europe, then along the coasts of Africa, and finally across unknown seas to legendary continents. Folk tales of Marco Polo's travels and visionary accounts of a distant *El Dorado* spread widely throughout Europe. Yet the Renaissance return to gold coinage was subject to all of the old abuses. Kings and princes once again debased their coins and fixed official valuations that traders would not accept.

A 14th century French churchman and writer named Nicholas Oresme is said to have been the first in a long succession of modern scholars who have pleaded with governments to adopt sound monetary policies. In France the extortionate practices of Philip IV, so oddly nicknamed "the Fair," had been symptomatic of the monetary difficulties experienced throughout Europe. His first act in that field had been to suspend the feudal right to coin gold and silver. Next he had demonetized the old coinage and had then issued a new and lighter one. Philip encouraged the import of bullion and forbade its export. Industrial use of gold was restricted by sumptuary laws. Efforts were made to prevent the market price from rising above the mint price, and private holdings of both gold and silver were sometimes seized and coined by force. Philip himself profited hugely from those manipulations of money and had massive debts as an excuse for them. But his debasement of the coinage had unhappy effects on his subjects. Between 1277 and 1309 Parisian prices and rents rose sharply, owing largely to the decline in the purchasing power of money. Popular unrest increased proportionately.

Between 1337 and 1350 the exigencies of war caused no less than twenty-four changes in the French coinage, and public distress was loudly voiced. Acting on the advice of Nicholas Oresme, Charles V created a new coinage in 1360, seeking to restore stability by issuing coins of unalloyed gold and silver whose values represented the ratio then prevailing between those two metals. In his famous *Traité de la première invention des monnaies* Oresme proclaimed that it was "unjust and tyrannous" for a prince to change "the natural ratio" between gold and silver. Alas, conflicting concepts of morality have always plagued money, and *raisons d'état* have invariably prevailed. Oresme also pointed out what would later become known as "Gresham's Law"—that if a prince issued bad money, it would drive good money out of circulation and was therefore a cause of hoarding. Oresme held that "strong money" would preserve "the just balance" between gold and silver and thus prevent hoarding. Unfortunately he had not allowed for the effects of fluctuations in new supplies of gold and silver bullion. Though Charles V was converted to Oresme's concepts and suppressed the debased coinage of his predecessors, his new "strong money" did not outlast his own reign. Mankind have learned little from history.

Partly because of the persistent shortages of bullion, throughout the 15th century there was a universal tendency toward debasement of coinage. Confidence in the German and Austrian *pfennigs* completely disappeared, and for a time the Hungarian golden *gulden* served as the standard of value in Central Europe. Wherever possible, merchants paid in debased coin but demanded gold in payment for the goods they sold. "Buy cheap and sell dear" has always been an unwritten precept in unregulated market economies, and it is unlikely ever to change. During the Hundred Years War between England and France the latter was flooded with debased coins of every description and degree of fineness, including many counterfeits—some of which had been issued by the rival kings. Even in the lawful coins of France forty-one changes were made between 1422 and 1428. Much of the gold and silver in the form of jewelry and plate was consumed in those wars. Quantities of sound coins disappeared into hoards. The old mines of Europe appeared to be nearing exhaustion. When Charles VII began in 1438 to reconstruct France, he was compelled by circumstance to issue monetary decrees as pitiless as those of

Philip IV. England and the Low Countries had been more fortunate, but everywhere the shortages of gold and silver bullion had induced those straitened conditions in which new forms of money could and did appear.

The origins of credit money are still obscure and are hotly debated by many scholars. It seems probable that they are to be found in the 11th and 12th centuries, when the recovery of trade and the stimulus of the crusades revived ancient business methods and encouraged innovations.[7] The perennial problem of transporting gold and silver was partly solved by the Knights Templar. Among their many commanderies throughout Europe and the Middle East and aboard their own ships they carried money whenever and wherever it was needed, for their own purposes and those of others. It was a natural though revolutionary step to substitute a letter of credit or a bill of exchange, rather than to transport the specie. Various types of documents appeared in the 12th century—the promissory note and bills payable in different forms and places at varying times.

Scholars are not agreed on the origin of the bill of exchange, which may have been Arabic. The earliest of record (though doubtless not the earliest) is one dated August 25, 1199, in which King John of England promised to pay the sum of 2125 marks to several merchants of Piacenza. And when Louis IX of France went to Egypt on his crusade, he was able to use the letter patent for his borrowing. In northern Europe a similar device appeared early in the 13th century—the *lettres de foire*, which were promissory notes or drafts drawn by merchants who frequented the trade fairs that provided regular times and places for the settlement of debts. The promissory notes of national governments are, of course, the form of money that has since become dominant in every trading economy. But paper money has met many obstacles over the the past eight centuries.

An early opponent of credit money was the Christian Church. During the first millennium of its existence it had become the indispensable moneylender. In times of war or famine the treasuries of the Church had yielded gold and silver, not always willingly, against the borrowers' pledges to repay. Usually those pledges had taken the form of land. The Biblical prohibition against usury did not apply, because the money lent did not in itself produce any interest. However, the revival of commerce, by rediscovering the productivity of liquid capital, caused endless arguments over the rights and wrongs of usury. In the 14th and 15th centuries, after long conflict with temporal princes, the Roman Church lost its claim to rule this world and was forced to content itself with the hereafter.

Private owners of capital took heart and began the development of commerce on a large scale. As early as the 10th century Venetians had begun to

---

[7] Thompson, *Economic and Social History of Europe in the Later Middle Ages,* pp. 432–440.

invest money in shipbuilding ventures. Soon Genoese and Pisan nobles and burgesses began to risk their capital in trading ventures by sea. The sums were small, investors hedging the risks by taking "parts" of several ships at a time. Lenders advanced money to borrowers for shares in anticipated profits, and the documents recording those agreements could be transferred. Medieval bankers were both merchants and moneylenders and could evade charges of usury by claiming that interest was in fact a sum of money that had been earned by the owner of the capital employed. Yet commercial credit used only part of the liquid capital available. The greater part was used for loans to public authorities or to individuals. Often merchants were unable to refuse powerful borrowers. Though risks were often high, prospective profits must have been more attractive.

By 1160 an Englishman named William Cade had begun to supply large sums for the kings and court of England. In the Low Countries many towns became banking centers. Arras was famous for its moneylenders, and the Louchard and Crespin families were legendary symbols of cupidity. Towns and monasteries also had recourse to the merchants' moneybags. However, in documents intended for the public eye, the reality of usury was concealed. Usually the borrower agreed to repay, at a certain time, a sum larger than he received. The difference was the interest paid: Italians rapidly became the most sophisticated of those financiers, aided by the favorable laws of their towns. The part played by Jews appears to have been exaggerated. Everywhere they were the outsiders who served as scapegoats for the popular dislike of usurers. In 1261 a dying Duke of Brabant ordered all usurers expelled from his lands, a pious decree that was promptly rescinded by his widow. Edward I of England and Philip IV of France adopted similar measures in 1290 and 1306. By 1393, however, another generation of usurers had become so prominent that the French crown again tried banishment as a sop to popular discontent. Exchangers participated both in the trade in money and in the handling of credit. Usually moneychangers enjoyed a semiofficial position, because the right to exercise their trade was granted by princes in exchange for rents. The commerce in gold and silver was entrusted to them, and it became customary to deposit sums with them for safekeeping. They also received funds under arrest and frequently served as agents of payment. By the end of the 13th century the Christian Church had ceased to serve as a moneylender and was often obliged to borrow from those financiers whose practices it had so vehemently condemned.

THE EXPANSION OF EUROPE

European rulers of the 14th and 15th centuries had limited understanding of the needs of international trade and of the benefits they might have derived from it. Each had but one constant thought—to maintain or increase the treasure of his own realm, primarily for military purposes. Each fought to secure his own head and land and often found ready weapons against his neighbors in the monetary turmoil of those years. Where so many coinages circulated, any variation in the price of gold or silver served as a lever with which one metal could be used to force out the other. Every commodity has always tended to flow towards the highest bidder, without regard for his political beliefs or ethical standards.

The behavior of bimetallic systems was therefore inimical to the development of international trade. Rulers threatened with exports of gold found they could stop them, and sometimes turn them to profit at an enemy's expense, by increasing gold's price in terms of silver. But any excessive change in the ratio, whether in favor of gold or silver, caused the disappearance from circulation of the metal that had become undervalued. Monetary use of either metal alone would have been feasible if adequate supplies of bullion had been available, so that its price would have remained stable and coins could have been fixed at constant values for long periods. But where both metals were used as money, each served as a weapon against the other, to the ultimate undoing of both. In less than 30 years after Edward III's introduction of a fine gold *florin* England was stripped of both gold and silver coinage in the normal course of trade with France and the Low Countries, where ratios were often changed with an eye to their political effects. English domestic trade slowed for lack of acceptable money, its rulers being confronted with the most daunting of all monetary situations, a trade recession accompanied by price inflation, with no new supplies of bullion at hand. Only one group of men grasped the facts, without necessarily understanding why they had occurred. In all ages and lands, whenever presented with opportunities for profit by arbitrage, merchant moneychangers have taken full advantage of them. Neither the English nor the French kings were able to stop that profiteering by beheading a few moneychangers as cautionary examples for others.

The many Christian kingdoms of the Iberian peninsula, so often at war with one another or with the Moors, devised a different remedy for their shortages of specie and bullion. Rather than continue to plunder their neighbors or impose still heavier taxes upon their groaning subjects, they sought new sources of gold and silver beyond the seas in ventures that were as highly speculative as they were ultimately profitable. First the Portuguese kings sent exploratory expeditions along the western coast of Africa, where they were later joined by the Dutch. Guinea began to supply gold for Europe. Then the rulers of Aragon and Castille financed those voyages to the Indies that opened an entirely new age in world history. The search for money has often had unforeseen consequences.

The grandson of Ferdinand and Isabella, Charles I of Spain, was elected

Holy Roman Emperor in 1519, when the riches of Mexico and Peru were first becoming fully known. His accession as Charles V to that imperial throne of his Habsburg ancestors was widely heralded as a restoration of the glories of ancient Rome. The conquests of his Spanish subjects in the Americas not only justified that historic claim but also provided the funds for further expansion. The year 1519 was the same in which Cortés began his march to Mexico City. And in 1534 Pizarro returned to Spain with the first booty from Peru. Early supplies of gold ornaments stripped from Aztec and Incan princes were soon supplemented by new bullion from mines. In 1545 the rich silver deposits at Potosì in Peru, and in 1555 those of Guadalcanal in Mexico, began to supply far larger quantities of silver than of gold. Throughout the 16th century 181,235 kilograms of gold and 16,632,648 kilograms of silver reached Spain, to mention only shipments officially recorded. Additional amounts were smuggled or were lost to pirates.

As a young man Charles I and V had been fully conscious of the antique concept of world monarchy, and Rome provided a model that ill served Spain. Martial virtues were extolled and commerce was despised. The 15th century wars against the Moors, and depressed agricultural prices, had stimulated the growth of large estates. Unemployed or dispossessed *hidalgos* were encouraged to become adventurers abroad, seeking military glory in Europe or material wealth in the New World. Not only the trade with the Indies but also the industrial and financial inadequacies of Spain itself attracted large numbers of German and Genoese merchants. They gained a virtual monopoly in finance. As early as 1515 the Spanish governmental units called the *Cortes* tried to restrict the activities of those foreign moneymen. But the total revenues of Spain, added to those from his other European territories and to the bullion supplied by the New World, were not enough to pay for the wars Charles conducted throughout Europe. Funds were also needed for widespread distribution of political bribes and subsidies. Charles became increasingly dependent on foreign moneylenders such as the Fuggers, the Haros and the Grimaldi, to whom the gold and silver remittances from the Americas were mortgaged. By 1598, at the death of his son Philip II, the national debt of Spain exceeded 100 million ducats—a sum without precedent. The Roman example of profligacy in blood and treasure had encouraged similar overextension of Spanish power.

Increasing production of gold and silver in the New World also became an important cause of price inflation. It was first experienced in Spain, then spread northward as far as Scandinavia, and troubled England into the 17th century. In Spain itself prices and rents more than quadrupled during the 16th century. Spanish governments assumed their supplies of bullion were inexhaustible, and therefore the only function of government should be maintenance of a sound coinage. They were so successful that their *coronas*, *escudos* and *reals* were exported as rapidly as they could be minted. Italian, French, Flemish and English merchants were eager to pay a premium for coins of such high quality. In 1523 the *Cortes* of Valladolid petitioned Charles to lower the gold and silver content "so that in weight and value they may pass equal with the crowns of the sun that are made in France, so that by these means they will no longer draw our gold from the kingdom." But Charles did not accept that measure until 1537. The only other monetary restriction recorded in his reign occurred in 1552, when Spanish coins of billon (the alloys of gold and silver with base metals) were lightened. Charles dryly noted on the margin of his decree that the unending export of Spanish coin seemed in some way to be related to the fact that they contained more precious metals than could be found in the coins of other countries.[8] But the Spanish balance of trade was always in deficit, and by the end of the 16th century the predicaments of the Spanish treasury had become severe. Manufactures of all kinds, and even grain, were imported from France, England and the Netherlands because higher prices were paid in Spain. Its domestic farmers and craftsmen could not compete.

The legend lingers that Spain was finally defeated in 1588 by Sir Francis Drake and his doughty English sailors, who destroyed the mighty Armada. In reality, however, the ambitions of Charles V and Philip II had been curbed much earlier, during their long, exhausting wars with France. In the last half of the 16th century France was also drastically weakened by religious and civil wars subsidized by Spanish gold. In 1577 a serious reform of the French coinage was attempted. The old reckoning by *livres* was abolished, and that of *écus* or *crowns* was substituted. Circulation of all foreign coins was prohibited, with the exception of those prized Spanish and Portuguese *ducats*. It was a major advance in monetary thinking. Since the evil was a badly regulated bimetallic system, subject to frequent fluctuations and therefore constantly disturbed by the arbitrage operations of moneychangers, the remedy was correctly seen to be establishment of a monometallic system using the gold *écu* as its standard. But money alone has never determined the prosperity of a state. The last kings of the ancient House of Valois had become so weak and discredited that they could not secure public acceptance for reforms of any kind. They were regarded as failures because price inflation continued, regardless of their coinage changes and monetary decrees.

French royal power was not only restored but enhanced by the first Bourbon, Henry IV of France and Navarre, who inherited the throne in 1589. His finance minister and master of artillery, who united those two key offices in one pair of trusted hands, was an able Huguenot named Maximilien de Bé-

---

[8] Shaw, *The History of Currency, 1252 to 1894*, pp. 109–110. See also Haring, *Trade and Navigation Between Spain and the Indies*, pp. 153 et seq.; Morrell, *The Gold Rushes*, pp. 17–41.

thune, who became Duke of Sully. In 1602 bimetallism was reestablished. And in the next 7 years of peace, the purchasing power of the *écu* continued to depreciate as rapidly as it had throughout the preceding quarter-century of war and civil disorder.

The effects of increasing bullion imports on prices were still not understood. In 1615 the ratio of gold to silver was fixed at 13.9–1. It remained almost unchanged until 1640, when a coin called the *louis d'or* was issued to establish a new monetary standard comparable to that of Spain. Gold's ratio to silver was fixed at 13½–1, then changed in 1656 to 14 ⁵⁄₇–1. The quality of that standard was declared to be 22 carats fine, and it would remain in effect until 1709. Europe's kings had at last obtained sufficient specie to suppress their vassals at home and to wage war more freely against their neighbors. However, the inflation fueled by bullion from the New World had caused novel problems. The wars of the Reformation in 16th century France and in 17th century Germany had been economic and social as well as religious, and had become vehicles for the expression of widespread discontent. Not all emigrants to the Americas were religious dissenters. Many sought opportunities there to escape from the social and economic distress prevalent in Europe.

During the 17th and 18th centuries a school of economic thought developed in France that has profoundly influenced money and trade ever since. For 18 years, from 1624 to 1642, the country was in fact governed by Louis XIII's first minister, the Cardinal de Richelieu. He believed the importance of money was so self-evident that kings should never be permitted to ignore it. In his *Testament politique*, he wrote: "People have always said that financial resources are the sinews of a state, and it is true that they are the fulcrum of Archimedes, which being firmly established gives the means of moving the the whole world." According to Richelieu: "A needy Prince can undertake no glorious action . . . Gold and silver are the tyrants of the world." He held that there were four bases for the power of a prince: an army, reputation, the loyalty of his subjects, and "a notable sum of money in his coffers." His rules for the successful conduct of war included "an abundance of money," because "he gains more in it who spends more on it." Money was "not only the sinew of war but also the grease of peace."

Like many of his contemporaries, Richelieu believed that the greatness of Spain "proceeds only from the money which comes to them from the Indies." He became absorbed in the problems of taxation and in eliminating extravagance from government. "France wastes more," he complained, "than other nations spend." Commerce also interested him, because he considered it the normal source of a nation's wealth. "It is a saying, common but true, that while states often increase their territory by war, they ordinarily increase their wealth by commerce, in times of peace." Noting the potential self-sufficiency of France, Richelieu added: "It would be easy for us to deprive

ourselves of the commerce that could only serve to foster our idleness and
nourish our luxury, and to attach ourselves solidly to that which can increase
our wealth." Therefore he urged that the fiscal and commercial policies of
France be designed to amass large amounts of gold and silver for needs of
state. He and the "bullionists" who followed him argued that it was eminently desirable for a nation to attract and to retain within its own borders as
much gold and silver as possible.

Richelieu's policies were not continued by Cardinal Mazarin (1642–1661).
But the philosophy of the bullionists and mercantilists became dominant,
because the resources of France were so blatantly dissipated by Mazarin on
foreign wars and domestic strife. Mazarin himself was interested in economic
matters only if they promised to increase his personal fortune. The real heir
of Richelieu was Jean-Baptiste Colbert, who became Intendant of Finances
in 1661 and later the most important of Louis XIV's ministers. To that
master, Colbert once wrote: "I declare to Your Majesty that as for me, a
useless banquet costing a thousand écus gives me incredible anguish; yet
when it is a question of millions of gold for Poland, I would sell out all my
property, I would hire out my wife and children, and I would go afoot all my
life to supply the necessary money." He concluded that letter with these
significant words: "It is a beautiful maxim that it is necessary to save five sous
on unessential things, and to pour out millions when it is a question of your
glory."

The intellectual heirs of Sully, Richelieu and Colbert have continued ever
since to control the finances of France. Secure behind watery moats, English
and American scholars have been quick to criticize those rival policies and
practices of the vulnerable French. But their beliefs were suited to the real
needs of France in the economic conditions of the 16th and 17th centuries. It
was a considerable advance to be able to collect taxes in gold and silver coin,
rather than in kind. Yet France lacked adequate supplies of bullion, either
from domestic mines or from colonies abroad. Wars were still financed on a
current basis by prompt payments of coin, and France's Spanish enemies had
it in large quantity. So long as troops were paid, diplomats were bribed and
allies were subsidized in coin, obviously it was wise to hold a substantial stock
of it. Finally, where so much domestic commerce was transacted in coin, the
amounts available had significant effects on the general prosperity of the
country, as well as on price levels. If coin and bullion could be obtained only
from foreign trade, it was logical that French kings should seek to import as
much as possible and to deter export.[9]

Credit money, the antithesis to that bullionist philosophy, provided an
alternative remedy for shortages of metallic coin and bullion. But credit mon-

[9] Cole, *Colbert and a Century of French Mercantilism*, passim.

ey systems had developed successfully only where private banking and commerce were strong, and were virtually independent of any royal authority, as in 16th century Genoa and 17th century Antwerp. Public opinion held that merchants might be trusted with money, whereas kings must not be. Too often kings had debased the coinages or had seized the treasure of their subjects. The first European experiment with paper bank notes served as a warning. It occurred in a Sweden exhausted by war. From 1661 to 1664 the Bank of Sweden issued notes based on a copper standard. But when that copper was exported, those notes had to be discontinued. The origins of English bank notes have been traced to the years of the Civil War and Commonwealth, when many landowners and merchants transferred liquid cash from the care of stewards and scriveners to the custody of goldsmiths in London. Those goldsmiths were prepared not only to offer safety but also to pay interest on money deposited with them. By 1688 their handwritten deposit receipts had become negotiable. Soon those receipts were described as cash "notes" or "bills," and the practice began of making them payable to a named payee "or bearer." By 1729, when Child's Bank first used printed notes, bearer notes had become common.[10]

The first issue of English fiduciary currency[11] had occurred in the reign of Charles II, in the form of tallies that were claims upon future tax revenues owing to the Exchequer. Wooden tallies, familiar since Norman times, were replaced in 1667 by paper orders or assignments of revenue issued to anyone who advanced money or supplied goods to the king. However, when war against Holland was declared in 1672, royal expenditures had already so exceeded anticipated revenues that further payments were stopped for 12 months. The paper orders of Charles immediately fell to a heavy discount, wherever people could be presuaded to accept them. A serious crisis developed in the City of London, where many bankers stopped their own payments. Those who held considerable quantities of the royal paper never fully recovered from that blow to their credit, and it caused widespread ruin among depositors. Nothing was done for them until 1674, and as late as 1705 many would continue to clamor unsuccessfully for satisfaction of their claims. The stoppage of 1672 had been confined to the paper tallies and had confirmed public belief in "the unsafe condition of a bank under a monarchy," as Samuel Pepys wryly described that situation. A central bank would appear soon after, with the grant of a charter to the Bank of England in May 1694, but it would be securely placed in private hands.

When war with France broke out in 1689, William III would have been in

[10] Feaveryear, *The Pound Sterling*, pp. 105–118.
[11] So called because it rested entirely on trust and confidence, and did not represent a deposit of specie.

dire financial difficulties even if the British coinage had been in sound condition. Though Parliament had increased the royal revenue to more than £2 million per annum, by 1694 he was spending £2.5 million each year on the army alone. By 1697 he had incurred debts that exceeded £20 million. The Bank of England was founded to help fund those royal debts. From the beginning it was essentially a bank of issue rather than of deposit. Its purpose was to create a credit currency. Of the initial issue of capital, which totaled £1.2 million, 60 percent was paid to the government in cash and £480,000 in notes under the seal of the Bank. The government of the day immediately paid out those notes for army supplies, and soon they were accepted at par in payments throughout the country. Though the public continued to distrust the paper of the king, they would and did accept the handsomely engraved "bills" of the private Bank of England, which accepted the onerous task of collecting from the royal revenues—plus interest for its pains. That was a strikingly successful way to bypass public distrust of kingly ways with money, and the Bank of England's stock of gold and silver coin and bullion became the final national reserve against all credit issues.

Throughout the 17th century persistent fluctuations in the relative values of English gold and silver coins had continued, and there had been no shortage of proposals for reforming the coinage. There never is. By 1695 the depreciation of coin money had become such a widespread concern that a parliamentary committee was appointed to inquire into it. For the first time since 1299 a recoinage was effected that restored entirely the standard that had existed before the debasement. And for the first time in English history a large part of the cost was borne by the Exchequer. The English philosopher John Locke played a part, by establishing certain concepts that have been strongly upheld by others ever since. Where a new era of parliamentary government had begun, Locke argued in *Further Considerations Concerning Raising the Value of Money* that the public faith was pledged and that no government should alter the standard of the mint on any pretext whatever. The mint weights of coins were to be regarded as immutable. After 1696, largely as the result of Locke's influence, £3.17s.10½d. per ounce was considered the fixed and unchangeable price for gold, a price from which Great Britain should never stray. During most of the next two and a half centuries, when gold served as the effective monetary standard, its real value gradually declined. The burden of debt was lightened, and producers were encouraged, largely at the expense of long-term creditors. However, the decline in gold's value was so gradual that it did not awaken any sense of grievance. The public continued to believe that their currency was far more stable than it could have been if it had been subject to frequent manipulation by royal authority.

Once firmly established in England, credit money supported remarkable expansion of trade overseas, which the bullionists of France could only observe with increasing envy and dismay. By the end of the 17th century, imports of gold and silver from the Americas were becoming inadequate for the expanding needs of government and commerce. A taste for the luxuries of the Far East had spread among the rich of Europe, and there was nothing that Oriental traders would accept so readily as silver. There was still no single international monetary standard nor a generally accepted ratio for the precious metals. In 17th century Spain the ratio of gold to silver was usually around 16–1, depending on fluctuations in the receipt of new supplies from the Americas. In the Orient, however, the ratio was only 9 or 10–1. The East India companies of the English, French and Dutch played the leading part in an inevitable, profitable movement eastward of European silver. In Europe that served to maintain an approximately constant ratio between gold and silver throughout the 18th century. In England its primary effect was the natural establishment and gradual public acceptance of a monometallic gold standard.

Only much later, after considerable controversy and deliberate legislation, did the gold standard become acceptable on the Continent of Europe. Continental experiments with credit money were also slower, and one sorry experience has been cited ever since by French advocates of gold. After the conclusion of peace with England in 1714 the enormous debts of Louis XIV were inherited by a reckless Regent who authorized the Scottish adventurer John Law to form the Banque Royale as a bank of issue in May 1716. Law had persuaded the Regent and his spendthrift court that royal debts could be funded and excessive state expenditures paid by unregulated printing of paper currency without reserves of specie. In January 1720 he was therefore named Controller–General of Finances, and the speculative boom began that became known as the "Mississippi Bubble." It ended abruptly in October 1720, when further circulation of Law's notes was suspended. The failure of that Banque Royale dominated 18th century French thinking on credit, convincing many of the French that British thinking on money was essentially unsound.

In Great Britain gold never became the coin used in everyday transactions or to pay wages. However, supplies were sufficient, and strict mint regulations assured full-weight coins for the uses of the rich. Remedies were never found for the consistent shortage of sound silver coins. During most of the 18th century the English mint was virtually closed to the coinage of silver, and by 1773 the silver coins still in circulation were considerably lighter than standard weight. Domestic mining of copper and tin encouraged experiments with token coinage, but it proved impossible to regulate their issue and prevent counterfeiting. Consequent loss of value and public objections to the mint's profits from token coinage caused frequent unrest.

Meanwhile the varied types of credit currency were also competing among themselves for dominance. To foil forgers, engraved and watermarked bank notes were developed, and an Act of 1704 had given the holder the same legal protection accorded bills of exchange. The notes of private bankers were supplemented by drafts or checks, by Bank of England bills and notes, by Exchequer bills, malt tickets and lottery tickets. Through most of the 18th century credit currency was used only in large transactions. Few notes were issued in small denominations. In 1765, when the first measures were taken to restrict credit currency, their purpose was not to control value but to protect the public from the worst excesses of the power to issue notes. English private bankers have always insisted that they be permitted to do as they please, and in 1776 their *laissez-faire* creed was stamped with intellectual respectability by Adam Smith's *The Wealth of Nations*. In the last quarter of the 18th century the shortage of silver coin began to cause the appearance of paper bills in small denominations, issued by country banks, which totaled almost 400 by the year 1793. Their reserves were kept on deposit with London bankers, not in Bank of England notes. The ease with which they forgot the prudence expected of them was demonstrated in the crises of 1783 and 1793, caused largely by their overexpansion of credit.

During the American Revolutionary War the export of gold for payment of military expenses had caused the Bank of England's reserves to fall from £4.2 million in August 1780 to £2 million in August 1782. If the American colonies had not been allowed to go their own way, the Bank of England would soon have been bankrupt. British bankers never entirely forgot that political lesson. The American rebels had had no reserves of gold and silver. Specie had always been scarce in those colonies, and barter had therefore been prevalent in their commerce. The coin most widely known throughout the Americas had not been British but rather the Spanish silver *dollar*. To finance a long war, the Americans had been compelled to resort to issues of fiduciary currency that had rapidly depreciated in value. Many American troops were paid off in land grants at the end of that war, and the American people would never forget the early political difficulties caused by their lack of acceptable cash. As soon as circumstances permitted, the financial affairs of the new Republic were therefore placed in the hands of conservatives intent on forming a national reserve of gold and silver. Though the American Constitution forbade the separate states to issue their own currencies, and its original intent was to restrict the Federal government to specie, the latter provision was impracticable. When the First United States Bank was chartered in 1791, to supply credit money, its reserves of specie totaled $2 million. That was estimated to be a third, and perhaps even half, of the entire stock of gold and silver coin in the country.

Both Great Britain and the United States benefited from the trade boom that had accompanied restoration of peace in January 1783, but it was soon disturbed by outbreak of revolution in France. English country banks had not rebuilt sufficient reserves, and their credit collapsed completely in February 1793, when France suddenly declared war against Great Britain. The Bank of England had replenished its own stock of bullion and coin, to more than £8 million. But that fell to £4 million during the crisis of 1793. The only expedient available to finance British military and naval expenditures was short-term government bills discounted by the Bank of England. By the end of 1795 they totaled nearly £13 million.

The French revolutionary government had also been experimenting with paper money—the *assignats*, supposedly secured by lands confiscated from the French crown and the church. But they soon failed as conspicuously as the unsupported American currencies had. In 1795 the French revolutionary assembly therefore began to debate a return to metallic coinage. In itself that sufficed to reverse the flight of French specie to Great Britain, and by February 1796 the reserves of the Bank of England had fallen to £2.5 million. On February 26 George III signed an Order in Council that stopped further payment of gold and silver by the Bank of England, and every means was used to persuade the British people to accept its notes instead of demanding gold.

Until the end of the Napoleonic Wars the British used an unregulated paper pound whose value was not tied in any way to gold or silver. The purchasing power of that pound declined slowly in 1797 and 1798, when domestic harvests were good. But the harvest of 1799 was a failure, and wheat doubled in price. The need for imports turned the exchanges against the pound. Speculation began in commodities, financed by large quantities of paper money. That speculative bubble burst in Hamburg, spreading panic, business failures and deflation over large parts of Europe. Further strains were imposed by Brisish military expenditures abroad, which rose from £400,000 in 1797–1798 to £2.4 million in 1799–1800. Gold was collected for export, its price accordingly rising to £4.6s. per ounce in 1800. Nevertheless within 2 years the effects of those varied crises had passed. Gold fell to £4.1s. per ounce, the paper pound returned to near par on the exchanges, and commodity prices declined. To the anger of the French the Bank of England's emergency note issues had not failed. Monetary conditions in Great Britain remained quiet, and the commercial community refrained from excessive speculation. Inflation remained within tolerable limits. British paper currency thus sustained its first severe test by war, because commerce flourished and the British people were confident of the outcome. War was still considered a normal occupation of mankind and was subject to civilized constraints.

French experience during those war years had been quite different and had equally marked effects on the subsequent evolution of money. By Law of

7-17 Germinal an XI (March 28, 1803) a new and metallic French monetary system had been established. The gold *livres tournois* of the former Bourbon regime had been officially replaced by coins of 20 and 40 gold *francs,* and the decimal system had been introduced. For both gold and silver, the standard had been fixed at .900 purity. Though the silver *franc* had been declared the basic monetary unit, and the ratio of gold and silver was 15½–1, in practice the system became bimetallic and the two metals often fluctuated in price. Napoleonic conquests throughout Europe had supplied France with large quantities of gold and silver, to which the astute Napoleon had given ample publicity. However, his regime had lacked sufficient specie to provide for all the needs of government and commerce throughout his newly formed Continental System. A central Bank of France had therefore been created in 1808 and had been granted the exclusive right to issue notes. It had also been required to discount even the smallest bills, whenever they might benefit French trade. The administration of that new central bank had been so conservative and its currency issues so limited that it did not have to suspend specie payments even in the most difficult days of 1814 and 1815. In practice the imperial coinage of the first Napoleon would be supplemented by continuing use of the old gold coins of 12, 24 and 48 *livres* until 1829, the old billon coins until 1845, and inferior coins of earlier Bourbon issues until 1852–1856. Less trustful of their rulers than the British, the French people continued to prefer specie to paper. Perforce French governments remained bullionists at heart, because all political leaders are restrained by the prejudices of the peoples they claim to rule.[12]

(12) See also Heckscher, *The Continental System.*

2 = Gold and Empire
1815–1914

In recent centuries, only colonial empires with ample supplies of bullion from their own mines have been able to maintain gold standards for long periods of time. Their purpose in creating gold coinages has been twofold—to gain political prestige and to provide the specie needed for their worldwide trade. Those empires have sold their manufactures to, and have bought raw materials from, protected and primitive areas of the world where gold and silver have continued to be valued and paper money has been suspect. In times of war those empires have also found gold useful in obtaining scarce commodities, even from enemy traders.

For almost three centuries, since the discovery of precious metals in the Americas, Europe had been largely dependent on Spanish mines in Mexico and Peru for new supplies of bullion. Their annual production had reached an average value of £10 million during the first decade of the 19th century, but Napoleon's invasion of Spain had abruptly curtailed those supplies. In 1808 revolutionary disorders had begun in the Spanish colonies. Mines were abandoned, capital was withdrawn, and the entire colonial system of bullion production and transport began to disintegrate. During the second decade annual supplies fell to an average value of £6 million. Encouraged by British and American merchants eager to break Spain's monopoly on trade within its empire, Mexico declared itself independent in 1822, and the last Spanish royalist strongholds in Peru surrendered in 1824. Though the British doctrine of free trade was becoming profitable for some, France was no longer in a position to gain from the decay of the Spanish Empire. The French fleet had been destroyed. By the Treaty of Paris, signed May 30, 1815, France had also been limited to its old borders of 1791 and had lost many of its own colonies to Great Britain. Moreover, the Allies had imposed a punitive though not crippling indemnity of 700 million francs and had stationed troops in France to ensure payment. Austria had been sadly weakened by a quarter-century of war, and neither Prussia nor Russia had any grand dreams of world conquest at that time. Only Great Britain was in a position to expand its trading and colonial possessions, and was impelled to do so by peculiar domestic circumstances.

EUROPE DEFLATED

Whereas the Napoleonic Wars had brought prosperity to Great Britain, the return of peace threatened to bring ruin and anarchy. By the end of 1813 it had become obvious that Napoleon's glittering career could not continue much longer. Within Great Britain the circulation of paper money had reached its highest level, commodity prices were near their peak, and the price of gold was £5.10s. per ounce. By October 1814 it had fallen to £4.5s. per ounce. During the "Hundred Days" of Napoleon's brief return to power it rose to £5.7s. per ounce, then began to decline in the period of uncertainty that followed the battle of Waterloo. In the autumn of 1815 there was a serious crash. Agriculture and industry had received stimuli in war for which there was no counterpart in peace. Government orders for military supplies were canceled, leaving merchants with goods for which they had no markets. As their credit began to diminish, they were compelled to dump goods in seaports at home and abroad, for any price they could get. That brought ruin to foreign industries and no benefit to British traders. European harvests had been abundant in 1813 and 1814 but were no longer bought by governments to feed troops. The hundreds of thousands of demobilized soldiers disrupted established relationships between labor and industry, until the unemployed in Great Britain alone were estimated at a half-million. Hundreds of country banks closed, and high interest rates held only because money was simply not loaned. Wartime prosperity had concealed social inequities laid bare by peace, and the Parliament of Great Britain began to fear revolt and civil disorder at home.[1]

Because of the importance of gold in foreign trade, Parliament had begun to urge the Bank of England to resume specie payments as soon as peace could be foreseen. An Act of 1814 had stated that resumption was "highly desirable as soon as possible," but the government of the day had preferred to

[1] Jenks, *The Migration of British Capital to 1875*, pp. 25 et seq.

reform the currency before allowing gold to circulate freely. Eventually, on June 22, 1816, the Act (56 Geo.III, c. 68) was passed on which the British currency system would rest for the next century. Experts had recommended immediate coinage of both gold and silver but had emphasized that gold alone should be declared the standard measure of value and legal tender for payment without any limitations on amount. Silver was to be token coinage, legal tender only for payments not exceeding 40 shillings. A gold coin in a new denomination was authorized, the *sovereign* of 20 shillings, which was to weigh "five pennyweights, three grains $2740/10,000$ troy weight of standard gold." By that time the market price of gold had fallen almost to the mint price. When the old gold *guineas* of the 18th century began to be dishoarded, many were found to be deficient in weight. Later that year half-sovereigns were also declared current coins. The exchanging of old silver for new was carried out in February 1817, and the minting of gold began, £4.275 million worth of sovereigns and half-sovereigns being coined in 1817, and £2.862 million in 1818.

Because no one could estimate how much would be needed under a system of free circulation, British officials proceeded by trial and error. That has always been the only certain test of monetary proposals. Partial resumption of specie payments had begun in November 1816, in exchange for small notes. The new sovereigns were ready in July 1817, but officials were disconcerted to find that the British people were simply not interested in them. They had become accustomed to paper notes and preferred them. By comparison gold coins were too inconvenient to handle and too expensive to transport. Most of the first issue of new sovereigns, which the British themselves would not use, were therefore shipped to France, melted down and promptly turned into French coins at the Paris mint. All Europe was trying to resume specie payments at the same time and had been joined by the United States. Thus bullion from all sources was in great demand, with scant prospect of any growth in new supplies from the Americas.

The consequent rise in the price of gold, and the drain of gold from Great Britain, continued to frustrate British efforts to resume specie payments. Moreover merchants and manufacturers throughout the country were petitioning against resumption. The economist David Ricardo argued in his *Plan for the Establishment of a National Bank* (1819) that the increased demand for gold required by coinage would only seriously worsen deflation. Instead he proposed that the notes of the Bank of England be convertible into bullion only, that gold coins not be put into circulation, and that small notes be made legal tender as substitutes. However, in the considerations of the Parliamentary leaders who prevailed, the needs of foreign trade were dominant. In the absence of internationally accepted credit systems and organizations, there was simply no substitute for specie. With Russia and the Orient continuing to drain gold and silver from Europe, the stock of metallic moneys available to the commercial countries actually began to decline—from an estimated £380 million in 1808, to £313 million in 1829, and £270 million in 1838. That tended to deflate commodity prices throughout the Western world.

The postwar depression in Great Britain was only the first of a series that dominated business cycles until the middle of the 19th century. The price indices of British domestic and imported commodities, as calculated by Gayer, Rostow and Schwartz, steadily sank from a high of 168.9 in 1813, to 118.6 in 1816, to 113 in 1825, to 84.5 in 1835, to 83.3 in 1845, and to 73.5 in 1850. That was the low point of the century. Definite reversal of the deflationary trend in prices awaited either discovery of new bullion supplies or the development of stable credit mechanisms for the conduct of international trade.

During those decades of depressed world trading conditions richer classes of British consumers benefited from increasingly cheap imports. Everywhere the rich enjoyed those years. But successive British governments were hard pressed to find a balance between the conflicting needs of domestic producers, who sought higher prices and expanding markets for their manufactures, and the insistence of exporters that specie was essential for their complex financial transactions on all seas and continents. The Bank of England therefore bought gold at a loss until its reserves reached £11.9 million in 1821, the highest level in its history. Long postponed, specie payments were then resumed. As Ricardo had foreseen, that did tend to deflate domestic prices further. However, a revival in industrial activity was noticeable in 1822 and 1823, especially in manufactures for export. It was accompanied by considerable speculation in commodities and shares, and a crash followed in 1825. The price of gold fell to mint price and below. Runs on the Bank of England depleted its reserves of gold and silver to £1 million by the end of 1825. A mere decade after Waterloo, France provided the Bank of England with gold in exchange for silver. The Duke of Wellington commented that "had it not been for the most extraordinary exertions—above all on the part of old Rothschild—the Bank must have stopped payment in 1826"[2]

Distress at home and disorder abroad had not deterred British bankers from foreign ventures. The City of London had begun to consider investment abroad potentially more profitable than the possibilities at home. Much of the speculation in shares that swept Great Britain in 1824 and 1825 had been kindled by the promoters of joint-stock companies, who persuaded investors that money could be made in a wide range of new ventures—not only railroads in England, coal in Wales and iron in Staffordshire, but also wool in Australia, a canal in Suez and real estate in Canada.

The companies that most stirred the London markets were those encour-

[2] Clapham, *The Bank of England*, vol. 2, pp. 50–185.

aged by the Canning Government to send British machines and steam engines in search of South American gold. The products of the Industrial Revolution, harnessed by British bankers, were to remedy the shortages of bullion by reopening abandoned mines in the newly independent republics of South America. British investors were urged to "patronize infant liberty and liberal principles," and those new countries welcomed investment. Their agents in London offered mining concessions in return for loans. British adventurers in South America were freely granted leases by local authorities, and companies multiplied to exploit them. So certain was London of favorable results that their boards of directors included every well-known firm in the City, with the exception of Baring and Rothschild. The Lord Chancellor himself speculated in those mines. Collapse of the South American gold ventures was therefore the most striking of the reverses suffered in the crash of 1825, but it did not end the search for new sources of gold.

Recovery from the depression of 1826 was slow. By 1830, however, industry had begun to revive. Once again it was stimulated by rising exports and by large loans to the United States. In that year the British also experienced political troubles at home and revolutions abroad, which inevitably caused tumult in the bullion markets. Though the Directors of the Bank of England had become skilled in bullion and foreign exchange operations, the net result of their trading during the Parisian revolt against the last of the Bourbon kings was a loss of £3 million. For neither the first nor the last time, they had gambled on a loser.

The French had wearied of kings and would tolerate only the compliant Louis-Philippe of Orléans. The Industrial Revolution had only begun to affect France, which would remain primarily an agricultural society. In the 1820s landed property represented two-thirds of the national wealth of France, and two-thirds of the French lived in country districts. Throughout all vicissitudes they had remained profoundly conservative. The richness of French farmland became an actual hindrance to industrial and commercial growth. In sharp contrast with the British, French peasants were prosperous and contented and had no desire to exchange their country life for the misery in workshops and towns. Nor were they disposed to emigrate. All French governments since 1789 had shown a preference for the middle classes and had believed in the sacredness of private property. Yet none had accepted the laissez-faire philosophy of the British. By regulations and subsidies they had tried to encourage commercial enterprises of all kinds. Unfortunately the losses in manpower, the depreciation and then the fluctuations in money, and the exhaustion induced by a quarter-century of civil and foreign wars had caused torpor. Industries were short of capital, raw materials and skilled labor. The paralysis of commerce and industry had begun soon after 1810 and had aroused more opposition to Napoleon than his defeats abroad had.

His downfall in 1815 had therefore been accepted calmly by French commercial classes, even though it had meant national humiliation.

Nevertheless since 1815 France had remained the predominant commercial country on the Continent, and its financial recovery had been rapid. Napoleon's policy of making his wars pay for themselves by confiscating foreign treasure and other resources had enabled France to emerge from those wars with less public debt than Great Britain. By 1827 that debt had been fully retired, and there was a surplus in the French Treasury. The restored Bourbons had accepted all the financial obligations of Napoleon's Empire and had thereby established confidence in their financial soundness, both at home and abroad. By 1828 France had more specie in circulation than any other European power. Bimetallic systems prevailed throughout Western Europe, except in Great Britain. The Bank of France usually cashed notes in silver, and both silver and gold circulated freely. Prices had not declined substantially, partly because the increasing use of credit money tended to offset the increasing supply of goods. Deposits in the Bank of France had risen from 46 million francs in 1814 to 145 million in 1830. During that period its gold reserves also grew—from 93 million francs to 172 million. Several financial panics were skillfully handled. Nations were beginning to be so closely interrelated by commerce that disorders in any major center were felt in all others. Under the last Bourbon kings the closely regulated Bank of France cooperated fully with the far more independent Bank of England. French colonial trade had fallen from 165 million francs in 1789 to a mere 37 million in 1818, but the restored Bourbons had had no interest either in rebuilding their navy or in ventures abroad. Their concerns had been overwhelmingly domestic, and the French people had become indifferent to the worldwide expansion of British finance and trade. Though bankers and industrial capitalists had begun to play a larger role in French affairs than ever before, from 1818 to 1825 French exports had grown only slightly, from 502 million francs to 544 million. Imports consisted almost entirely of raw materials. Essentially self-sufficient, France had no compelling reasons to challenge the expanding world power of Great Britain. [3]

AMERICAN DEBTORS

For both Great Britain and France the United States had become an important customer. To their increasing anxiety it was also becoming a major debtor. During the 20 years of its operations, from 1791 to 1811, the First Bank of the United States had prudently guided the financial affairs of that new Republic. It had assumed all the wartime debts of the states, and Euro-

[3] Artz, *France Under the Bourbon Restoration*, pp. 172–233.

pean hopes had been high that Americans would become staunch defenders of monetary and financial orthodoxy. Alas, such hopes have always been futile. From its beginnings the Federal government of the United States had been plagued by monetary difficulties and controversies. The first currency act passed by Congress in 1792 had valued the new American dollar at 24.75 grains of gold (the weight of the Spanish milled dollar) and had established the decimal system. The ratio of gold to silver had been fixed at 15–1, both had been made full legal tender, and free, unlimited coinage had been authorized. Nevertheless, little bullion had been brought to the new Federal mint for coining, partly because silver had been slightly overvalued at that ratio. It had become increasingly overvalued as new discoveries of Mexican silver had depreciated its market price. Any gold coined at the Philadelphia mint had been quickly shipped out of the country, primarily to settle commercial debts in London. The United States had soon been reduced in practice to a silver standard. Even then Yankee traders had found that their silver dollars could be exchanged in the West Indies for the slightly heavier Spanish dollars, which could be profitably reconverted into American coin by presenting them as bullion at the Philadelphia mint. President Jefferson, a fastidious Virginian, had learned of that sly trade in 1806. He had promptly ended the coinage of American silver dollars, and it was not resumed for 30 years.

Until changed in 1834, the currency of the United States consisted of paper money, token coins of small denominations, and foreign coins. When the charter of the specie-issuing First Bank of the United States had expired in 1811, numerous state banks had been founded, their number increasing from 88 to 246 in 5 years. The quantity of money in circulation rose from $45 million to $100 million. The various notes of the state banks circulated at a discount, sometimes as much as 50 percent. Monetary confusion had been compounded by the War of 1812, financed by public loans and Treasury notes. Congress lacked the courage to increase domestic taxation, and that timidity toward taxpayers would continue to characterize American fiscal practices in times of war. Unwilling to pay for those wars by taxation, Americans would subsequently pay in inflation.

When the Second Bank of the United States was chartered in 1816, its conservative supporters expected its paper notes, redeemable in specie on demand, to restore order by forcing the state banks to resume specie payments or see their own notes driven out of circulation. Instead the renewed controversy between advocates of cheap and dear money became a continuing bone of contention between political parties and a central issue in the presidential election of 1832. The victory of the Democratic Party, led by Andrew Jackson, doomed the Second Bank. Its directors tried to frighten the public into supporting them by producing the credit squeeze known as

"Biddle's Panic." They merely convinced Congress and the public that bankers had become too powerful. Though President Jackson had to remove two Secretaries of the Treasury before he could find one willing to carry out his orders, eventually he succeeded, and the Second Bank of the United States lost its Federal charter in 1836.[4]

That is the extent to which the story of Jackson's encounter with the Second Bank is usually retold in American histories, but there had been international ramifications that were more intriguing. Persistent shortages of bullion and specie had continued to hinder the development of American trade abroad, and the seemingly endless Congressional arguments about the forms of money to be used in the United States had alarmed its creditors in London.

British bankers were sympathetic toward the aspirations of their American cousins. Regardless of political differences and tariff barriers the United States had remained the principal customer of Great Britain. During the 1820s, 36 percent of American exports had gone to Great Britain, and the latter had shipped 16 percent of its own exports to American seaports. As early as 1791 London had also begun to own the major share of American securities held abroad. By 1805 British investments in American securities had totaled £5.747 million, including at least $7 million in the shares of the First Bank of the United States. In 1817 and 1818 temporary loans of bullion had been made to the Second Bank and had become the basis of a permanent investment in the shares of that institution. By 1820 the British stake in the central bank of the United States had reached $3 million. Another million dollars was added in 1828, and that British investment rose to $8 million in 1831. Of the 300,000 shares held in private hands approximately one-quarter was owned by British investors. And of the $19 million in American public indebtedness held by Europeans in 1828, $14 million was owned by the British. After the London crash of 1825 they had lost all interest in supporting political causes abroad with further loans. Instead they had become quite anxious about the safety of their existing investments in the United States. Discreet pressures had begun.

However, General Jackson had met the British before. Once again he outmaneuvered them. Between 1830 and 1836 the volume of Anglo–American trade had doubled and by 1836 the United States was incurring a trade deficit of some $60 million per year. Decades of British capital imports had created a relationship that could be sustained only by still larger loans. Though the exports of the United States were expected to increase, its needs for investment capital were far larger. Perhaps only a President with the radical reputation of Andrew Jackson could have obtained passage by Congress of the conservative American Banking Act of 1834. With one hand

[4] Faulkner, *American Economic History*, pp. 152–168.

Jackson suppressed his conservative opponents, led by the Second Bank of the United States and its not-so-silent British partners. With the other he regained foreign confidence by a series of measures they could only applaud. Though never suspected by his followers of being an expert on finance, Jackson had been known to the public as a canny "hard-money man" who distrusted paper currencies. Still stronger had been his dislike of the political power paper money conferred on those empowered to issue it. Therefore his policy was to substitute a gold currency for the silver and paper currencies to which Americans had become addicted. The Banking Act of 1834 fixed a ratio of approximately 16–1 for gold and silver, which slightly overvalued gold and thus encouraged both gold imports and dishoarding. At the same time Jackson insisted that France and Naples should pay in gold the indemnities they owed to the United States. Consequently, from 1833 to 1836, the United States imported an annual surplus of $10 million in gold. During those years the Federal government was also paying off the public debt. Regardless of the panic of 1837 the total quantity of British capital invested in the United States continued to equal the debts incurred by the separate states. And in 1840 Jackson's chosen successor founded the Federal Treasury's practice of encouraging the use of specie by collecting Federal taxes in coin and by making Federal payments in coin. The credit of the United States was preserved, and the concept of a privately owned central bank authorized to issue notes and to control the national currency was buried forever.

Unhappily no way had been found to limit the banking powers of the separate states. And in 1840 the United States Senate disclaimed any Federal responsibility for their debts. In 1841 and 1842 nine states refused to pay the interest owing on their bonds, which had been issued in quantities far beyond their means. Debtor classes had begun to gain political power. At the same time slackening British demand for cotton brought disaster to those American bankers who had long speculated in it, led by the Second Bank of the United States. In 1841 that bank suspended payments for the last time and went into receivership. A wave of bankruptcies swept across the United States, and shocked British bankers found they held more than $100 million in doubtful American state securities, plus additional losses on their American banking, canal and mercantile investments. Those securities had been purchased, often at a premium, by large numbers of the governing classes of Great Britain. They began to express the keenest resentment against anything and everything American. The United States was held collectively responsible for the shortcomings of each and every American citizen. Yet Congress steadfastly refused to assume those state debts. British bankers who had encouraged excessive indebtedness were told that defaults should have been foreseen. The arguments were heated and lasting. Anglo–American trade dwindled by half, and fully a generation passed before British investors began once again to venture with confidence into American securities. Nevertheless the United States continued to believe firmly in credit money, because without credit it could not have become the United States. At the same time, in deference to the prejudices of Europeans, the Federal Treasury continued the expedient practice of maintaining a large national reserve of specie and bullion.

THE HEYDAY OF THE BRITISH EMPIRE

The American crisis of 1837 had not affected the domestic economy of Great Britain. The British people were enjoying improved living conditions and were better able to consume their own manufactures and imports from their colonies. Industrial activity was at a high level. The price of grain had been increased by a series of bad harvests, but other prices had not risen substantially. There was no inflation of country-bank credit, no speculative boom on the exchanges, and no unusual increase in imports, except for grain. In 1838, however, banking failures in France and Belgium seriously drained the reserves of the Bank of England. They fell from £9.5 million in January to £2.5 million in August and were maintained at that level only by special measures that included use of credits in Hamburg and Paris. That crisis exposed the Bank of England to severe criticism; public debate began on the adequacy of its policies and practices. A parliamentary committee of inquiry was appointed in 1839, but little was known of its deliberations until the Bank Charter Act of 1844 was introduced in the House of Commons.

Passed after brief debate and against slight opposition, the Bank Charter Act of 1844 required the Bank of England's paper notes to be mere bullion certificates fully backed by gold and silver. Because strict observance would have compelled the Bank to double its stock of bullion, it was allowed a fiduciary issue of £14 million that could be reduced but not increased. Beyond that amount all notes were to be fully covered by gold coin or gold or silver bullion. Silver was not to exceed one-fifth of the total metallic cover, and the Bank was required to issue notes in exchange for all bullion offered to it, at the official price of £3.17s.9d. per ounce of standard gold. The Act of 1844 then dealt with the notes issued by country banks. Only bankers who had been permitted to issue such notes before May 6, 1844, were allowed to continue, and provision was made for the gradual extinction of their rights to do so. The Peel Government was determined to prevent excessive issues of paper money, such as those in the United States. The Act of 1844, extended to Scotland in 1845, removed any danger that banks of issue might be unable to redeem their notes with gold and silver. It substituted, however, another risk—that they might be unable to meet the claims of their depositors with notes. The gold reserves of the Bank of England could be exhausted only if its note issue fell to £14 million, a contingency considered highly improbable. By freezing part of the Bank's stock of gold, Parliament sought to render it invulnerable and to guarantee its reputation. Unlike the Second Bank of the United States, the Bank of England would not be permitted to fail.

Severely criticized as restrictionist, that Act of 1844 reflected the overriding concerns of the British governing classes—to safeguard their deposits, to preserve the purchasing power of their money, and to strengthen the political stability of their institutions, in a period of bullion shortages, deflation and domestic unrest. Throughout the 19th century, only the phlegmatic British and the superstitious Russians were able to preserve their ancient forms of government, while rulers elsewhere in Europe were being swept aside. The Act of 1844 so firmly established the prestige of the Bank of England that it continued to operate under the same rules for the next 70 years.

The crisis of 1847 arose from reckless speculation in railroads, both at home and abroad, and from bad harvests in England and in Ireland. The Act of 1844 was immediately suspended, but unnecessarily. Throughout 1847 the bullion reserves of the Bank of England never dropped below £8 million, a comfortable figure at that time. And through the worst of that crisis there was no greatly increased demand for the Bank's notes. The needs of the London money market were for credit at the Bank of England, against which checks might be drawn. That could be obtained by Bank advances against securities. Credit money reached maturity, as the use of checks became widespread. The commerce of Great Britain rapidly recovered from that crisis, exports more than doubling between 1847 and 1857. During that decade the joint-stock banks of London increased their deposits from £8.850 million to £43 million. The Bank of England found itself the central support for a far larger volume of credit money than ever before, regardless of the restrictions within which it labored. By 1852 its Directors were delighted to announce that their bullion reserves exceeded £22 million, mostly in gold.

Vital changes had begun. In February of 1848 the French had dethroned the thrifty Louis-Philippe of Orléans. After more than a generation of deflationary conditions debtor classes throughout Europe had become desperate. As political disorders had spread across the continent, capital had fled to the safety of London. And in far-off California an unemployed Swiss Guardsman who had been carried westward by the great wave of emigration to the United States had found gold in his mill sluice. As the largest creditor of the United States, London had obtained the first of that newly discovered Californian gold. British chroniclers happily recorded that by Christmas of 1849 some £600,000 of it had been shipped to London in bars via Panama. That accidental finding of gold in the United States had stimulated deliberate search elsewhere. In 1851 the Bendigo and Ballarat mines had been discovered in the Australian province of Victoria. Monetary conditions in Great

Britain became easy. The persistent shortages of gold that had troubled Europe for a half-century disappeared entirely, and after 1848 the Bank of England would buy little silver. Because gold better served its purposes, after 1861 the Bank of England ceased holding silver bullion. There was so much new gold pouring into Europe that it began to affect prices generally. From the low point of the century in 1850 a gradual rise began that continued intermittently until 1873. Yet the Bank of England continued to offer the old, constant price of £3.17s.9d. per ounce, and the general public did not perceive that it was becoming cheaper. The provisions of the Bank Charter Act of 1844 had become the object of almost religious veneration by the British people.

There are conflicting estimates of the quantities of new gold produced in those years. Total world production of both gold and silver had approximated $1 billion[5] between 1811 and 1840, and all had been drained from circulation by the Orient. Russian discoveries in the Ural Mountains increased annual supplies by 4 or 5 percent between 1837 and 1848, but the Russian tsars had no need to export that gold for the uses of Western Europe. They continued to enjoy large annual payments surpluses, because they were major exporters of naval stores and grain. The average annual production of gold during the 1840s was approximately $36.4 million. Then from 1850 to 1855 it soared to $132.5 million per annum. In the years 1850 to 1870, aided by improved mining techniques, larger quantities of new gold reached European markets than the mines of Spanish America had produced since the days of Cortés and Pizarro.

For the economic history of those years that rapidly growing world stock of gold provided the keystone upon which a vast increase in world trade would be built. The growing hoard in the vaults of the Bank of England helped keep interest rates low, and in turn that encouraged all kinds of new ventures and increasing foreign use of the London money market. The export of British capital reached new heights during the first quarter-century after Sutter's discovery of gold in California. Though British harvests were frequently bad and grain imports often large, free trade had become an economic doctrine that enabled Great Britain to compensate for its own deficiencies in raw materials and foodstuffs and to encourage foreign demand for its manufactures by deployment of London's financial services. Other nations, in different circumstances, continued to cling stubbornly to protectionism—to the frequent indignation of British exporters.

In 1852 Napoleon III became Emperor of the French and renewed the

---

[5] Jenks, op. cit., p. 161. The American term *billion* will be used rather than the older English *thousand millions* or the French *milliard*, because it is the usage of the International Monetary Fund.

rivalry with Great Britain that had lapsed for more than a generation. In that year he also formed the Crédit Mobilier to attract the savings of the French public and use them for the finance of French industry and railroads. Appalled, conservative French financiers predicted disaster. They were wrong. The discoveries of gold were exciting successful speculation and industrial development in many parts of the world. Moreover the growing wealth and self-confidence of Europe's commercial, industrial and financial middle classes gained them political power. Allied with the bankers of London and Paris, the *bourgeoisie* gradually replaced feudal governments throughout Europe.

France and Belgium had been the first to welcome British entrepreneurs, who then began to venture into Piedmont, Switzerland and Spain. Having suppressed a Hungarian revolt by abolishing feudal privileges, the Habsburg emperors found it expedient to invite British bankers into their realms. The kings of Prussia soon followed that trend. After the Crimean War both Russia and Turkey offered concessions for the bids of foreign capitalists. By the end of the 1850s the epidemic of railroad building had spread to Asia Minor, Algiers, Portugal and Brazil, and Americans were planning the first transcontinental railroad to link their capital to California. Political and national objectives were served by that economic growth and were stimulated by British capital. In most of the countries that emulated the Second Empire of Napoleon III it was as inconvenient to borrow money at home as it was to levy taxes. Even France—during the Crimean War and again in 1870–1871—relied on London for large loans. Austria–Hungary and Russia habitually met fiscal emergencies by issuing inconvertible paper money. In 1848 and 1854, respectively, they permanently suspended payments in specie. Neither empire subsequently struck a gold coinage until the 1890s, when they found that by nominally joining Great Britain's gold standard they could enhance their attractiveness to British and French investors.

Recent advocates of gold as money have often regarded those years of prosperity, the heyday of British financial supremacy, as proof that price stability can be obtained by central banking policies that require full gold backing for all paper money issued. However, there is no evidence to support their arguments. Nostalgia has always been a bad guide. In 1850 Great Britain occupied a unique position, unlike that of any other power before or since. The Bank Charter Act of 1844 was preserved intact for so many years only because ample gold imports had become available. British consumers of all classes enjoyed low prices because imported raw materials and foodstuffs were cheap and could be paid for with manufactures Great Britain alone could supply. British payments accounts were therefore consistently in surplus. The British Isles were overpopulated, wages remained low and the rich retained political control. To the extent that large imports of gold affected domestic prices, those effects were inflationary. Yet the annual rate of that inflation was so small that it disturbed no one.

Those were also years in which British fleets sailed unchallenged on every sea. British traders therefore dominated the economies of Africa and Asia as never before or since. In 1873 Sir Charles Trevelyan bluntly observed: "India is at our mercy; we can charge her what we wish." And foreigners did not question the wisdom of the Bank of England, whose favors they so frequently needed. Between 1854 and 1869 London invested some £150 million in India, and that subcontinent imported another £200 million in precious metals. Its appetite for gold and silver has always been voracious. Between 1860 and 1876 London also loaned £50 million to the governments of Australasia and another £25 million to Canada and smaller colonies. Those loans having fostered the possessive attitudes of London's bankers, the foreign policies they supported became self-consciously imperial. It was an extraordinary era, in which the defenses of old England were believed to depend on holding the Northwest Frontier passes of India, to prevent Russian invasions. And the glamor of the Orient had captured Queen Victoria. On January 1, 1878, she had herself proclaimed Empress of India at Delhi. A skeptical courtier commented:

> That night at Windsor she came to dinner a mass of Oriental jewellery . . . though effective as a blaze of colour, they did not suit her Majesty, as they required a large and a dark woman to carry them effectively.

Under the Disraeli Government the movement had begun to identify the symbolism of monarchy with the symbolism of empire. And in British schools the dominant study was Rome. Yet those halcyon years would not last much longer. When Victoria assumed an imperial crown, the power of Great Britain had already passed its zenith.

THE FRENCH AND GERMAN EMPIRES

Queen Victoria disliked all republicans, profoundly distrusting the French in particular. The alliance between the Bank of England and the Bank of France became one of convenience. They were no longer bound by natural sympathies and the dependence of the French. Napoleon III had begun to rebuild a competitive French navy and had restored the gold reserves of France. Throughout the 18th century and under the last kings of the houses of Bourbon and Orléans the coinage of France had been principally and sometimes exclusively silver. In 1851 the reserves of the Bank of France totaled 478 million francs in silver and a mere 83 million in gold. By 1869 they contained 798 million francs in silver and 461 million in gold. The first Napoleon had flourished gold, and his nephew was determined to restore the glories of France. During his reign it became a substantial net importer of gold in every year except 1861. Silver, becoming undervalued, tended to disappear from circulation.

In 1861 Napoleon III therefore named a commission to study the problems of bimetallic systems. That led to formation in 1865 of the Latin Union, the first international effort to regulate the exchange rates of currencies. Belgium had adopted the French monetary system in 1832 and later had been joined by Switzerland and Italy. In 1865 they agreed that

> This convention places in the front rank gold money, and reduces the pieces of silver of 2 francs and less to the role of token money. It therefore definitely establishes the ascendancy of the gold francs and solves practical difficulties arising from the double standard.

Throughout history many monetary experts have had a similar weakness for propounding "final solutions." France was moving toward a monometallic gold standard similar to that of Great Britain, even though Napoleon was well aware that France lacked secure supplies of bullion. During the years 1861–1863 all Europe had experienced temporary shortages of gold and silver caused by the American Civil War. Nevertheless the convention establishing the Latin Union became effective in August 1869 and lasted for 15 years. Four sovereign powers had agreed on a common monetary system, and the French gold *Napoleons* of 1850 were accepted throughout the Latin Union, together with its 5-franc silver coin of 1865. Needless to add, the French began to be ardent advocates of fixed exchange rates.[6]

The Latin Union formed in 1869 was widely interpreted as a revival of French imperial pretensions, its competitive monetary system being regarded with suspicion by the City of London. Nor had the British been reassured during the joint intervention of the French, British and Spanish governments in Mexico in 1861. As early as 1837 Napoleon III had been interested in the riches of Mexico. Shorn of Texas and California, and torn by revolutionary governments, Mexico had remained the largest country in Central America and the richest in natural resources. Its silver mines were still the most important in the Americas. Quarrels had arisen between the French and British leaders of the expeditionary force, and rebel Mexican leaders had disclosed that their predecessors had formed privy agreements with European bankers close to the French government. A Mexican loan floated in London and Paris completely failed to interest British investors and succeeded in France only because Napoleon coerced the Crédit Mobilier into taking a large part of the issue. He persistently refused to withdraw French troops from Mexico unless he could do so "with honor," and the British and Americans were not alone in their desire that he should lose it.

Tension had also been growing between France and Prussia, where Count

(6) Shaw, op. cit., pp. 166–197.

Bismarck had become Prime Minister in 1862. When the Prussians began to consider unbearable the growing French influence in the Rhineland and in Poland, Bismarck countered by proposing a Hohenzollern candidate for the vacant throne of Spain. Enticed into war with Prussia, Napoleon III was decisively defeated at Sédan in 1870. Queen Victoria was pleased. One competitive empire had vanished, though another even stronger had begun to appear.

On January 18, 1871, the many German princes and the heads of the German corps of generals assembled in the Hall of Mirrors at the French palace of Versailles to proclaim William of Prussia the German Emperor. Martial memories of the old Holy Roman Empire were deliberately revived, to symbolize the restored power and glory of the German people, who had been divided for so many centuries into hundreds of petty principalities. It was the glittering climax in a decade of sustained effort. In 1861 a Handelstag assembled in Heidelberg had recommended a common currency system for all the Germanic states. In 1865 the third Handelstag at Frankfurt had proposed minting a gold piece identical with the French 20-franc gold Napoleon, and in 1868 the fourth Handelstag in Berlin had advised adoption of a gold standard. Though debased silver thalers had served for centuries, they would not suffice for the purposes of the new and unified Germany. In June 1870 the Bundesrat of the recently formed North German Union had approved reform and unification of the German paper moneys, and the plan eventually approved by the new Reichstag in December 1871 also called for a gold coinage. The ratio of gold to silver was fixed at 15½–1, identical to the ratio prevailing in the neighboring Latin Union. The basic unit of the German system was the gold *mark*, coined into pieces of 10 and 20 marks and divisible on a decimal basis. New silver marks were also authorized and (with the Austrian silver thalers) were declared legal tender for payments of no more than 20 marks. From 1872 until 1878 a total of 1,205,786 pounds of gold were minted into those new German coins, and approximately one-third of that gold had been obtained by melting down French Napoleons. In the tradition of the first French Emperor an indemnity of 5 billion francs had been imposed upon France after its defeat at Sédan. Allowing for the value of French railroads in the annexed provinces of Alsace and Lorraine, Bismarck gradually obtained gold for the balance. It was used not only to create the new German imperial coinage but also to replenish the Prussian war chest kept in the Julius Tower at Spandau. Accomplished primarily through the London money market, that transfer of funds was not completed until 1873.[7]

For the next four decades Germany became consistently the largest net importer of gold on the Continent of Europe. Built upon the Prussian Bank

[7] Morgan, *Central Banking 1797–1913*, pp. 181–184.

founded in 1847, the Reichsbank was chartered in March 1875. By the late 1870s its reserves of specie totaled the equivalent of £30 million, and by the late 1880s they rose to £45 million. The Reichsbank was not, however, the only bank of issue in the German Empire. For political reasons many of the Germanic states had been allowed to keep the power to create money. Gradually those independent banks were reduced in number, by being forbidden to undertake more profitable types of banking. Eventually only Bavaria, Saxony, Wurtemberg and Baden retained one bank each that was permitted to issue small quantities of paper money.

REVIVAL OF THE BIMETALLIC CONTROVERSY

Though the years 1870 to 1875 were a high point in British investment abroad, especially to governments, the industrial and financial strength of Great Britain ceased to be unique. During the 1860s and 1870s rapid industrialization soon made the United States and Germany self-sufficient. Deprived of those principal markets, Great Britain was becoming increasingly dependent on its colonies. Other nations were also intensively developing their own banking systems, to contest the leadership of London and Paris. Adoption of a gold standard by the new German Reich was quickly imitated in 1872 by the Scandinavian kingdoms. In 1871 the Emperor of Japan had made an unsuccessful attempt to create a gold standard, as one feature in the opening of his country to foreign trade. Then in 1874 the United States, which had suspended specie payments during its Civil War, announced that it too would return to a gold standard on January 1, 1879. But American mining of new gold had begun to decline, and in 1873 a worldwide crash caused a fall in commodity prices that continued almost without interruption until it reached bottom in 1896.

During those years the annual production of new gold was a steadily dwindling percentage of the total world output of precious metals. New sources of silver had been found, of which the largest were in Nevada. People began to ask whether the abandonment of silver coinage and the increasingly exclusive use of gold as the only standard coin might be largely responsible for the prolonged fall in prices and the stubborn economic depression that was most keenly felt by agricultural producers everywhere. The old bimetallic controversies were resumed and became heated. In retrospect the arguments themselves are tedious to read. Yet they sharply displayed the fierce antagonisms of the conflicting interest groups.

By 1876 the fall in the price of silver had become severe. Commissions were appointed in both London and Washington to investigate the problem. The British commission merely discussed the causes without recommending any remedies. Its members feared disturbing the monetary assumptions upon which the Bank of England was so firmly seated. But the American commission ardently recommended remonetization of silver. Fully supported by American mining interests, in 1878 it presented their case to an international conference in Paris. There it met the combined opposition of Great Britain, Switzerland and Norway. The British representative declared that his government could not consent to any serious modifications in its monometallic gold system. Germany was not represented, and France remained silent. Then in 1879 the agricultural interests of Germany persuaded Bismarck to reopen the discussions, and in 1881 another conference was held in Paris. As president the French representative promptly declared for bimetallism. He was joined by the United States, Italy, Austria–Hungary, the Netherlands and British India. Great Britain and Germany temporized, refusing to alter their own monometallic gold standards and conceding only that increased monetary use might be found for silver—if full agreement could be obtained from all the major powers. Then Belgium, Switzerland, Greece and the Scandinavian countries spoke against silver. The outcome had been well arranged.

Austria–Hungary joined the gold standard in 1891, Russia and Japan in 1897, and by 1900 even Italy was struggling to maintain its currency at a gold parity. All had become chronic debtors and therefore tended to follow the guidance of London and Paris. But the bimetallic controversy continued to embitter relations between Great Britain and the United States until the American presidential election of 1896. The Democratic candidate was William Jennings Bryan, a Midwestern populist who campaigned on the platform that mankind should not be "crucified on a cross of gold." Though his defeat was warmly applauded by the Bank of England, silver advocates were still so strong in the United States Senate that the gold standard was not officially adopted by Americans until 4 years later. Having found new supplies of gold in Colorado and Alaska, the United States briefly caught the imperial fever. In a spirit of "Manifest Destiny" President Theodore Roosevelt secured passage of the Currency Act of 1900. It declared the gold dollar of "25.8 grains nine-tenths fine" the American unit of value. All other forms of money used in the United States were to be maintained at par with that gold dollar. The American Treasury was required to hold a gold reserve of $150 million, equal to the gold reserve of the Bank of England. Nevertheless gold was never recognized as money throughout the United States. West of the Allegheny Mountains, advocates of cheap money remained active and often dominant. Gold continued to be identified with the Republican Party and its banking supporters along the Atlantic coast.

The animosities aroused continued to fret diplomatic relations between the United States and Great Britain. In the years 1913–1915, when the British needed American support to cope with a powerful and increasingly arrogant

German Empire, William Jennings Bryan was the American Secretary of State, widely regarded by the American people as the "Grand Old Man" of the ruling Democratic Party.

IMPERIAL RIVALRIES

Germany had been a latecomer in the quest for colonies. There had been some interest among merchants of the Hanseatic seaports as early as the middle of the 19th century. Factories and trading stations had been founded on the east, west and southwest coasts of Africa, and in 1868 an association had been formed in Berlin to promote German interests abroad. All kinds of schemes had been proposed by men eager for action, and most of them had promised to find another *El Dorado*. Many did find financial backers in that era of renewed Germanic pride and expansion. However, during the Franco–Prussian War of 1870, Bismarck had ignored the clamor for seizure of the French colonies abroad. He had been intent first upon consolidating Germany's gains in Europe, and he therefore chose to overlook opportunities to obstruct consolidation of British influence in the southern half of Africa.

A trader of Bremen forced Bismarck's hand by informing Berlin in 1882 that he intended to acquire land and found trading stations in South Africa. He asked for German Imperial protection. Bismarck invited the British government to declare whether it claimed jurisdiction there, and in turn the British Foreign Office asked the government of the Cape Colony to express its opinion. That colony immediately urged annexation of the southwest coast of Africa before it could fall into German possession. But messages were delayed, and British Foreign Office officials were not interested. After waiting 6 months for a reply from London, Bismarck granted the Bremen trader the Imperial protection he had requested. That finally aroused the British government to protest, but Bismarck replied in 1884 that he could not accept their views. He was somewhat bemused by the British argument that territory Great Britain had never claimed could not be claimed by any other power. He refused to agree that Great Britain could apply a kind of "Monroe Doctrine" to Africa. Germany began its annexation of Southwest African territories and soon found extensive mineral deposits there, including gold, silver and diamonds.

The influence of the German colonial movement in Berlin reached its height in 1887–1888, when the British announced discovery of the Witwatersrand gold deposits in the Transvaal. The German Emperor was moved to declare that it was a solemn duty for Germany "to win the Dark Continent for Christian civilization." But the search for gold soon became a greedy scramble between rival German and British adventurers, and the protection of its new colonies required Germany to reconsider its needs for a navy.

British anger increased during the Boer War, in which Germany unofficially but warmly supported the Afrikaners. British Army officers began to talk openly of "the inevitable conflict with Germany." Though Sir Cecil Rhodes was described in Germany as the foulest of villains, he became a hero in London and in Oxford. As soon as Queen Victoria was securely buried, her successor began secret naval and military discussions with the French.[8]

By the end of the 19th century nations that lacked ready access to sources of new gold had learned how to live without them. Specie was no longer needed in any of the advanced societies of Europe or the Americas, and it had ceased to have a dominating effect on their price and wage levels. Central bankers had also learned how to cope with fluctuations in supplies of new gold.[9] Credit money had gained sufficient acceptance in world trade, and gold might have been replaced by silver and paper if it had continued to disappear from circulation—either into hoards or in settlement of accounts with the Orient. Yet powerful interest groups had developed who considered it their patriotic and profitable duty to defend gold as the paramount form of money. It is an irony of history that the largest and most influential group of gold supporters appeared in London, where development of credit money had been most pronounced since the 17th century. Those British partisans of gold drew sustenance primarily from the huge deposits found in the African Transvaal. New supplies of gold had fallen to a low of some £20 million in 1882. By 1894, when West Australian fields also began to deliver, the world's total annual production rose to £37 million. In 1899, after the discoveries in Alaska, total world supplies reached £63.026 million. By 1908 annual world production soared to £98.225 million—one-third from the Transvaal. Production during the period 1906–1911 alone was almost as large as the total stock of gold in both Europe and the Americas at the end of the year 1848.

Most of those new supplies of gold continued to find their way to the London bullion market. During the years 1903–1906 the treasure of the Bank of England's Issue Department averaged only £33 million, but it could obtain large quantities whenever they were needed. During the American banking crisis of 1907 some £17 million in gold left London within 60 days. The consequent anxieties of London's banking leaders were loudly voiced, with true British overstatement. By raising bank rate to 7 percent, a level then considered preposterous, the Bank of England was able to draw £7 million in gold from Germany and £3.5 million from France. Mining colonies provided an additional £6.5 million and India £2.5 million. The relationships among central banks were informal yet adequate for the most severe strains that could be imposed upon them by banking disorders. Then in 1911 France,

---

[8] Dawson, *The Evolution of Modern Germany*, pp. 344–378.

[9] Among others, see Hobson, *Gold, Prices and Wages*.

Germany and Russia began to compete for the gold supplies without which everyone assumed that no nation could hope to wage war successfully.[10]

By 1914 Germany had become one of the three great industrial nations of the world. France had fallen hopelessly behind, and Germany had begun to surpass Great Britain in the race for European economic leadership. Germany had achieved double or more than double the British output in iron and steel, machinery, electrotechnical products and chemicals. It lagged behind only in coal and textiles. The German merchant fleet was exceeded in tonnage only by the British, and German investments had become worldwide. Only the United States surpassed Germany in industrial output. If peace had continued, American supremacy might soon have been challenged.

World trade had been growing at an annual rate of approximately 3 percent, doubling every 25 years. The increase in gold supplies was sufficient to support that rate of growth, but many experts had begun to foresee that the necessary growth in gold reserves might not be adequate much longer. Among central banks a scramble had begun to increase their gold reserves, partly because public opinion held that they gave a nation's currency a value unrelated to the latter's own scarcity. Thus there was constant public and parliamentary discussion on the "gold cover" of each national currency, and it fostered the popular belief that the national welfare depended upon the extent to which the currency was "covered" by gold. Large parts of national reserves were therefore effectively frozen, and only "excessive reserves" were available for the purposes for which national reserves have always been held. One consequence was a general tendency toward deflation and protectionism. Where gold was taken in payment for goods exported, people tended to look upon exports as desirable in themselves and were unwilling to accept foreign goods and services in payment.

That trait was particularly noticeable in the countries that had belonged to the Latin Union, where policies continued to adhere to the old tenets of bullionism and mercantilism. British and American advocates of free trade argued vainly that the obsession with accumulating gold reserves hindered world economic growth, which depended on the willingness of creditor nations to invest their surpluses abroad. For political purposes, sometimes the French did invest heavily abroad—as in their carefully calculated financial support for their Russian ally.[11] But the French public believed that the principal merit of the gold standard lay in providing the private holder of paper currency with something tangible and of intrinsic value into which he might freely convert that paper. Without comment on the "intrinsic" value of

[10] For statistical details on the gold reserves held by the major powers in 1913, see the Appendix.

[11] Feis, *Europe: The World's Banker, 1870–1914*, passim.

a metal for which the demand was primarily monetary rather than industrial, readers should note that before 1914 only the convertibility or "redeemability" of the British currency was beyond doubt. In other countries, where central banks were more intent on protecting their gold reserves, small sums of gold coin could be obtained for domestic circulation, but large sums of gold for export were often refused.

When 1914 began, Egypt was the only country in which gold coins were still commonly used in everyday commerce. Its merchants and *fellahin* recognized only British gold sovereigns as real money. Elsewhere paper and token coins of silver and bronze had become the predominant forms in general usage. Widespread use of checks in Great Britain had been imitated throughout the English-speaking world. The leading British historians of those years have commented:

> The English monetary system in the generation before the first World War has sometimes been represented as unchanging, largely automatic, and as near perfection as can be expected of any human institution; . . . it was none of these things. The international gold standard, with London as its center, gave stability in exchange rates and provided a means by which very large international payments, both on current and capital account, could be financed smoothly and with great economy of gold. At home the system gave a stable banking structure, immune from the purely financial crises that had occurred early in the century. It did not prevent cyclical fluctuations in trade, and it did not avoid considerable fluctuations in the value of money.[12]

Wholesale prices in Great Britain had risen approximately 35 percent between 1850 and 1873, during the influx of new gold from California and Australia. They had fallen 40 percent from the middle of the 1870s to the middle of the 1890s. Then they had risen again, some 25 percent between 1895 and 1914, with the imports of gold bullion from South Africa, Colorado and Alaska. In the 33 years after 1880 trade union unemployment in Great Britain had averaged 4.7 percent. During 21 of those years it had been less. Though bankers and economists were well aware of flaws in the gold standard, there was no public discussion of them. It had become a symbol of British power and prestige, one of the foundations of Empire the public took for granted.

Not only the smooth functioning of that monetary system but also its very survival depended on London's ability to remain a substantial creditor in the short-term credit markets. In 1914 total British long-term investments abroad totaled £4 billion, the net being approximately £3.5 billion. Because of its acceptance and discount business London was also the short-term creditor of the world for several hundred million pounds. The latter were the credits the

[12] Feaveryear (revised by Morgan), *op. cit.*, pp. 334–336.

Bank of England could manipulate with bank rate, to cope with any run on its gold reserves. By 1914, however, France had also become a major creditor. The possibility existed that the Bank of England and the Bank of France might someday act at cross-purposes. Germany was in a less favorable financial position—a creditor for many of its neighbors but often a debtor in settlements with France, Great Britain and the United States. Next in rank were Russia and Austria–Hungary—rich and powerful, with large reserves of gold, but debtor nations dependent in the short-term capital markets on their neighbors. And those debtor nations, beginning with Austria–Hungary and the United States, had already begun in international conferences to argue the merits of a "gold-exchange system" that would permit maximum economy in the monetary use of gold.[13]

Thus the continuing existence of the international gold standard, as it had been known for several decades in both Europe and the Americas, was entirely dependent on the restraint of Great Britain. If for any reason London had become a debtor, that gold standard would have disappeared forever. And it did.

[13] Keynes, *Indian Currency and Finance*, pp.15–36.

3 = The Test of War
1914–1918

If that international gold standard had had any inherent meaning, behind its façade of constitutional provisions and international agreements, its guiding principle would have been the constant and inalienable right of any individual to convert paper currency into gold for any purpose. At the very outbreak of the First World War that popular notion was permanently destroyed. To safeguard national reserves for other needs, the convertibility of currencies was suspended almost everywhere. Governments demonstrated that in any serious emergency the "national interest" would always take precedence over the rights of individual citizens. Even their private holdings of gold were gradually drawn into central banks by methods that were more or less coercive.

THE ALLIED POWERS

In London the traditional planning of the British War Office had called for denying to any potential enemy the Channel ports of the Low Countries. The Foreign Office had also been dismayed by the growing might of Germany. Both had agreed that the German Empire could not be permitted to establish hegemony on the Continent. The Treasury and the Bank of England had been consulted and had urged caution. Yet they too had assumed that in time of war Great Britain could again rely on its navy and would serve primarily as the paymaster for Continental allies, as it had in the Napoleonic Wars a century before. They were as ignorant of the exigencies of modern mass warfare as the generals, the admirals and the diplomats. The British people were enjoying a fine summer, complacently unaware that their government had abandoned "splendid isolation," the dominant principle of Victorian policies. Relations with Germany had appeared to be reasonably good. On the day following the assassination of the Archduke Franz Ferdinand the British Foreign Secretary asked the House of Commons to approve his settlement of several long-standing difficulties with Germany. The Baghdad railroad was the best known. On June 29, 1914, Sir Edward Grey "prefaced his statement in moving the vote with an expression of sympathy with the Austrian people and their venerable Sovereign at the tragic loss they had suffered. . . . There was not the slightest suspicion that the effects of that murder could not be confined to the Austrian Empire." [1]

The progress of negotiations between Austria–Hungary and Serbia had little effect on the London markets, and even the Austrian ultimatum to Serbia on July 23 did not cause serious uneasiness. Balkan alarms had been frequent for decades. Then on July 25 a panic began on the Vienna Bourse and was immediately transmitted to the London Stock Exchange. Within 24 hours after the Austrian declaration of war on July 28 all major stock exchanges had closed except London and the British provincial exchanges, New York and the official ("parquet") exchange in Paris. Anticipating a run on its gold reserves, the Bank of England raised bank rate to 4 percent on July 30. Except from the United States, foreign remittances of all kinds ceased to reach London. As the world's largest stock exchange, it had many firms that specialized in business on behalf of foreign clients, and it held at least £350 million in outstanding bills of exchange. Most bore the name of a merchant banker or a joint-stock bank, which were entirely dependent on prompt payment by their clients. Though they had resources sufficient to cover an occasional default, they were helpless against a general failure to pay.

In 1914 there were essentially four ways by which those international payments could be made—by sending goods, by shipping gold, by selling securities or by incurring a new loan. Shipment of goods was slow at the best of times, and owners of cargo ships had begun to keep them in port. Submarines and mines had recently become feared weapons of naval warfare, and the German navy was known to have many surface raiders. Where gold was obtainable, both shipping and insurance costs became prohibitive. The closing of so many stock exchanges made the sale of securities impossible, and the issue of new long-term foreign loans ended abruptly. Suddenly cautious, British bankers preferred to call in existing short-term loans rather than issue new ones. The flow of sterling into foreign hands was reduced to a trickle. That

[1] Lawson, *British War Finance 1914–1915,* pp. 2–3.

breakdown in the mechanisms of international payments caused a severe crisis in London, first felt on the Stock Exchange. Both from home and abroad it was subjected to a wave of selling. As one European stock exchange after another closed, the pressure increased on those that remained open.[2]

On July 31 the Paris Stock Exchange announced that it was postponing settlements for a month. That was regarded as the last straw by many London firms that dealt with Paris. Dozens of them threatened to declare bankruptcy the next day. Therefore the London Stock Exchange also closed on July 31 and was immediately followed by New York. Only the "parquet" in Paris continued restricted dealings, until at last it too was forced to close as German armies approached Paris. With the closing of those stock exchanges, securities held by banks became unsaleable. Then the banks found themselves in dangerous straits. Before absolute paralysis began, considerable sums were withdrawn. The exchange rate of the French franc turned heavily against the pound, and the Bank of England exported more than £4 million in gold during the last week before Great Britain's declaration of war. Yet that withdrawal of foreign funds from London was soon offset by recall of British funds from abroad. Almost all exchange rates except that of the French franc turned in favor of the pound. Bills on London became unobtainable, and foreign debtors were unable to meet obligations falling due, no matter how able and eager they were to pay.

More than a decade later a punctilious Japanese Finance Minister would recall:

> I remember only too well how in those days we used to send bills to London by the Trans-Siberian Mail, but all communication with London via Siberia was suspended when the war broke out; we wanted to make payments in London, but we had no money there; we wanted to get bills onto the London discount market, but we could not do it. . . . We felt that if this state of things was going to last any length of time, the country would be defaulting in its interest payments. . . . It was a nerve-wracking experience: we really thought that this country was well down the road to bankruptcy. . . . It was, Gentlemen, one long, evil nightmare, and the memory of it still haunts my dreams.[3]

That critical, confused state of affairs lasted for more than 6 months, further complicated by the proclamation of various kinds of moratoria on debts by most of the principal countries.

In London the burden of those difficulties fell upon accepting houses and then upon discount houses and banks. On July 31 the Bank of England asked the clearing banks to help the market, and a number of the big banks moved to rescue their smaller brethren. They also took large quantities of gold and notes from the Bank of England and then invented obstacles to avoid having

---

[2] Morgan, *Studies in British Financial Policy 1914–1925,* pp. 1 et seq.
[3] Inouye, *Problems of the Japanese Exchange 1914–1926,* pp. 5–6.

to pay out that gold to their depositors. Instead they offered notes. As the keeper of the country's gold reserves and its lender of last resort, the Bank of England was much criticized for that practice. In reality, however, it had only limited control over the great commercial banks. No further demand for the export of gold appeared, because of the hazards of shipping. The real threat was internal demand, which almost exhausted the treasure of the Bank of England. Between July 22 and August 1 its gold reserves fell from £29.3 million to less than £10 million. That reduced its sacrosanct cover on paper notes outstanding from 52 percent to 14. On August 1, when Germany declared war against Russia and France, the Directors of the Bank of England began a series of worried discussions with the Prime Minister and the Chancellor of the Exchequer.

News arrived on August 4 that German troops were invading Belgium, and the British government sent a tardy ultimatum to Germany. There is no evidence that they had weighed economic considerations. Sir Edward Grey had been prepared to resign if his commitments to the French had not been honored by his Cabinet colleagues, many of whom had remained entirely ignorant of their "understandings" with France. The British ultimatum expired at midnight, and David Lloyd George cried "Doom, doom, doom!" as he listened to Big Ben strike that hour. A surprised and oddly jubilant Great Britain awoke on August 5 to find itself at war.

As Chancellor of the Exchequer, Lloyd George hastened to reassure the British public by informing the House of Commons that specie payments would be maintained. He urged loyal subjects not to hoard gold. His next step, on August 6, was to introduce the emergency Currency and Banknotes Act of 1914. It passed through Parliament and received the royal assent within a single day. The Treasury was authorized to issue paper notes in denominations of 1 pound and 10 shillings. In one of the more deceptive measures of an increasingly deceitful war those notes were also declared convertible into gold at the Bank of England. In fact, however, at that point the Bank ceased to pay out gold on demand to individuals. In 1796 it had openly suspended specie payments. By 1914 it had become the central banker of an Empire and was determined to preserve appearances at all costs. British subjects who believed what they read in their newspapers were politely turned away when they quoted the Act of 1914 to tellers at the Bank of England.

The first instinct of many London bankers was to worry more about their American competitors than their German enemies. A chronicler of the London markets wrote:

> If any country stood to gain by the war, and should therefore have been ready to make the most of it, it was the United States. It might have been expected to rush into the foreign markets from which Germany and Austria–Hungary had

been completely cut off. The best of these lay at its own door in South America, and had long been coveted by American manufacturers and exporters. At the same time a splendid opening offered itself to New York financiers for capturing the monetary supremacy which London appeared to be in danger of losing for good and all. A still more fascinating prospect unfolded itself before the American growers of food and raw materials. With record crops of wheat and cotton, fortunes were to be made if only normal prices were to be obtained for them.[4]

However, Americans generally were not aware of those splendid opportunities. Unlike Great Britain the United States had never become dependent on exports. Most Americans therefore remained happily heedless of the intricacies of international finance. Unlike the City of London, New York had never been the political capital of the United States. There had been times when the influence of New York's bankers had not extended beyond the Hudson River. So it was in 1914.

In Washington the new Democratic Administration of the puritanical Woodrow Wilson was watching with growing horror old Europe's stubbornness in error. Wilson's overriding concern was to protect the United States from contamination by European follies. And Secretary of State Bryan was determined to remain strictly neutral by refusing American loans to all belligerents. His ability to do so was limited by the Federal government's slight control over private banking. In 1913, after the United States had existed without any central bank for almost 80 years, one of the first official acts of President Wilson had been to secure passage by Congress of legislation that had virtually ended the Treasury's practice of dealing through "pet banks." Well aware of banking abuses, Wilson had frequently reminded colleagues that Federal control of note issue was a Democratic doctrine in the tradition of Jefferson and Jackson. The Federal Reserve System, and the Federal Reserve Board that would supervise it, had been established to end application of the political "spoils system" in banking. They were intended to be independent, free from interference by political parties, private interests and foreign influences. The Republican bankers of New York had recognized punishment when they saw it and had howled. The Bank of England was therefore concerned to retain the cooperation of those American private bankers, headed by Morgan Brothers, while seeking support from the new President and his fledgling central bankers. As Governor of the Bank of England, Lord Walter Cunliffe found those disparate tasks quite difficult.

On the money exchanges of London the two currencies most in trouble were the dollar and the ruble. The United States was usually in debt to London in late summer, a debt liquidated later in the year from proceeds of the autumn sales of grain and cotton. Thus the crisis of 1914 had caught

---

[4] Lawson, *op. cit.,* p. 159.

American banks with low foreign balances. European sales of securities on American stock exchanges increased the remittances required, and during the week beginning July 20 New York exported large quantities of gold. From July 27 onward it became practically impossible to discount bills in London and prohibitively risky to ship gold. Foreign currencies became unobtainable in New York. Private arrangements were therefore made with France, Italy, Switzerland and Austria to provide credits in New York against payments falling due, at nominal rates of exchange. Foreign creditors could exchange them for credits in their own countries. In London, however, similar private negotiations broke down and the dollar fell to the unprecedented rate of $6.50 on August 1. Americans were quite disturbed. Moreover, cotton exports were becoming unsaleable and an issue of $500 million in New York City notes was due for payment beginning in September. $400 million of that American indebtedness was held by British and French investors. American bankers became highly disturbed. By August 6 they had devised an extraordinary expedient. The American cruiser *Tennessee* sailed for Great Britain carrying $7.5 million in gold—two-thirds from New York's bankers and one-third from the Federal government. London's bankers were temporarily appeased.

To restore peace between the bankers of London and New York, on August 12 the Bank of England announced a simpler way to overcome the difficulties of shipping gold in wartime. It opened an account with the Canadian Ministry of Finance in Ottawa, in which gold could be deposited. Against it, sterling would be provided in London at the rate of $4.90. Though the dollar was still far below that rate, there was no immediate export of gold from New York to Ottawa, because American bankers were refusing to pay in that form. Then on September 1 a conference of New York bankers agreed to form a gold fund of $100 million for the purpose. Three weeks later that scheme was approved by the Federal Reserve Board in Washington as one of its first official decisions. A total of $104 million in American gold was deposited in Ottawa, most of it by mid-October. By the end of that year the improvement in the cotton trade and the beginning of Allied war purchases in the United States had returned the dollar–pound exchange rate to its prewar parity, and for several months thereafter no further official intervention was required to stabilize it. Because London's bankers had so sharply stipulated gold for payments owing to them, American bankers became equally rigorous in demanding Allied payments in gold for the increasing quantities of supplies Great Britain and France began to seek in the United States.

In the case of the ruble large gold purchases just before the outbreak of war had practically exhausted Russia's sterling balances. Purchases abroad of war materiel increased its needs for foreign currencies at a time when it became impossible to export autumn wheat surpluses. The ruble therefore remained weak. In November Russia shipped £8 million in gold to London, in return for a credit of £20 million, the balance of which was raised by discounting Russian Treasury bills. Further credits were raised as the war progressed, but the underlying causes of weakness remained. Russia could not pay with its usual exports, and the costs of shipping gold had become exorbitant. After the defeats of the Russian armies that had invaded East Prussia in August, London's bankers had also become doubtful about the competence of the Tsarist government and its high command. Few in London knew that those rash attacks had been deliberate efforts to distract German attention from Paris and thus to demonstrate Russia's loyalty to its French ally. What London's bankers did recognize quite suddenly was that in wartime even gold could not always liquidate debts. An ally might be rich in gold and yet be a bad credit risk. The situation was replete with ironies, often tragic.

As of July 29, just before the Tsar's declaration of war against Austria–Hungary, the Russian State Bank had held 1.6 billion rubles in gold against outstanding notes of 1.63 billion. That had represented gold cover of 92.2 percent for paper rubles in circulation, and the ruble had therefore been considered one of the world's "strongest" currencies. Then the Law of July 27 (August 9 New Style) had hastily suspended specie payments and had authorized the first issue of credit notes unbacked by gold to a total of 1.5 billion rubles.[5] In France a curiously similar government decree of August 5 had limited savings bank withdrawals, authorized the unrestricted issue of 5- and 20-franc notes and suspended specie payments.[6]

It was becoming clear to a few expert observers that the war plans of all the major powers had called for unlimited issue of paper notes—a ruinously inflationary method of war finance, as had been demonstrated so often before. Yet the peoples of Great Britain, France and Russia remained trusting, quite unconscious of the excesses that had begun.

THE CENTRAL POWERS

Though more thorough, the planning of the Central Powers proved equally inadequate. In every capital, general staffs eager for glory had promised their rulers that quick, decisive victories could and would be achieved. Everywhere the public had believed that no war could be sustained for more than a few months, if only because the costs of modern armaments had become so excessive.

An important change had occurred in the character of the Austro–German

[5] Katzenellenbaum, *Russian Currency and Banking, 1914–1924, pp. 7 et seq.*
[6] Dulles, *The French Franc,* pp. 86 et seq.

alliance since the days of Bismarck and the elder Moltke. Bismarck had always been unwilling to permit combined planning by the two general staffs or any binding military agreements. He had rightly feared that, if Austria–Hungary became too dependent on Germany, the politicians in Vienna would become too adventurous in their Balkan policies and would slacken their own military spending. After his fall from office Berlin had become increasingly openhanded with pledges to Vienna. Kaiser Wilhelm had frequently reassured the Austrian ambassador that "Emperor Franz Josef is a field-marshal of Prussia. Thus he has but to command and the whole Prussian army will follow him." A combined offensive against Russia had been the essence of the elder Moltke's war plan. Not until 1909 were the Austrians fully informed of German thinking, and by then Schlieffen had redrawn German plans to direct the major strike at France while leaving only holding forces on the eastern front to prevent Russia from advancing on Berlin.

From 1909 onward German and Austro–Hungarian finance ministers and central bankers had also begun to coordinate their planning. The relationship between them clearly illustrated the perils in an alliance of unequals. The Austrians were always fearful that the Germans would not keep their commitments and would fail to help Austria–Hungary if war with Serbia should ever begin. Therefore they were willing to make major concessions, such as the transfer of their remaining gold reserves of $206 million to the custody of the Reichsbank soon after the outbreak of war. Yet in 1914 it was the rashness of Austria–Hungary that precipitated hostilities, and Germany then found it a costly, increasingly helpless ally, in need of constant troop, materiel and financial support. Within the first 18 months of war Germany supplied subsidies to Austria-Hungary that exceeded 260 million Reichsmarks.

Both Germany and Austria–Hungary had suspended specie payments on August 4, 1914. Both were unable to obtain from abroad not only further supplies of gold but also many commodities more essential to their war effort. With the imposition of the British naval blockade, and Italy's entry into the war in May 1915, the Central Powers found they could obtain imports only with the greatest difficulty, principally through the neutral Netherlands and Sweden. Exchange crises developed very early.[7] By the end of 1914 the Reichsmark had depreciated 10 percent and the Austrian crown 16 percent on the Geneva exchange, while the French franc and the British pound remained slightly above their prewar gold parities. Partly for reasons of prestige French and British financial officials had already begun to support their currencies on foreign-exchange markets. The Germans and Austrians were slow to do so, because they had not anticipated the need. The Reichsmark

[7] Helfferich, *Der Weltkrieg*, pp. 141–295.

depreciated 20 percent from prewar parity by the end of 1915, 34 percent by the end of 1916 and 50 percent by the middle of 1917. After rallying when Russia collapsed, the Reichsmark depreciated again and stood at a 40 percent loss against its 1914 parity when the war ended in November 1918.

Germany and Austria–Hungary had held much smaller quantities of foreign securities than Great Britain and France, and parted with them more reluctantly to stabilize their exchange rates. The Central Powers also had major difficulties obtaining external credits. Therefore in January 1916 Germany established a Central Foreign Exchange Office in Berlin, and it was granted arbitrary powers. German citizens who held bills on foreign countries were compelled to surrender them; anyone who needed foreign exchange was required to apply there. The Office itself fixed the Reichsmark's rates of exchange with other currencies, its intervention helping to mitigate the Reichsmark's slow depreciation. In the course of the war the Reichsbank also sold some 450 million gold Reichsmarks to support its exchange rate in the Netherlands, Switzerland and Sweden. Nevertheless the supply of means for external payments was simply inadequate to the demands upon it. Berlin's exchange rate for the Reichsmark always tended to be higher than that quoted on exchanges abroad. Foreign debtors therefore preferred to pay German exporters with those cheaper Reichsmarks available abroad, and the rules of the Central Foreign Exchange Office were often confounded. Opportunities had appeared for the most complex, profitable speculation in currencies. Many Germans also began to keep small emergency reserves of foreign currencies, a form of hoarding they would continue to prefer to the traditional French practice of secreting gold.

For the entire period of the war Germany had a foreign-trade deficit of approximately 15 billion gold marks. To settle those accounts, approximately 1 billion Reichsmarks worth of gold actually left the country, shipped mostly by the Reichsbank. In addition an estimated 3 billion Reichsmarks worth of foreign securities and 1 billion in German securities were sold in foreign countries. Of the remaining 10 billion in indebtedness an estimated one-third was temporarily covered by foreign-currency credits, and the remaining two-thirds was financed either by the assumption of new mark indebtedness or by the sale of mark notes and mark balances to foreign speculators. In nearby neutral cities, such as Amsterdam and Zürich, that speculation was keen. Regardless of the increasing depreciation of the Reichsmark, many foreigners were willing to buy and hold, in the belief that after the war the German government would return the Reichsmark to its prewar gold parity.

From the outbreak of war the Reichsbank had made the most strenuous efforts to increase its gold reserves. All public departments that handled cash, especially the posts and railroads, forwarded all gold coin received. Elaborate propaganda urged the surrender of gold by loyal German citizens. They were persuaded by the press, the churches and the schools. A decree of November 23, 1914, authorized punishment by fines and imprisonment for all private dealings in German gold coin. The gold stocks of the Reichsbank, 1.253 billion Reichsmarks on July 31, 1914, rose to 2.092 billion at the end of that year. Most of the increase was gold coin withdrawn from circulation. By June 15, 1917, that central gold reserve had reached a peak of 2.533 billion Reichsmarks. Private gold exports had been prohibited. Industrial users of gold were rigorously restricted, and in mid-1916 the Reichsbank began to buy jewelry and other objects of gold. Patriotic subjects who surrendered prized jewelry were awarded an iron medal inscribed: *Gold gab ich zur Wehr, Eisen nahm ich zur Ehr*. More than a billion Reichsmarks in gold coin alone were withdrawn from circulation during those war years.[8]

The Reichsbank continued to publish its regular reports openly. In the first 18 months of war more than 25 billion Reichsmarks were raised by war loans placed by the Reichsbank and subscribed by the German people. In later years an additional 73 billion in loans were similarly placed. Swiftly generations of investments in commercial and industrial properties accumulated by the German middle classes were converted into securities guaranteed by the Empire. The primary responsibility for the choice of that method of financing rested with the German Finance Ministry, not the Reichsbank. The error was a political, not a banking, miscalculation. Treasury bills and bonds were discounted by the Reichsbank, the floating debt incurred being funded twice each year by the public issue of those long-term loans. The first four War Loans, issued in 1914–1916, were oversubscribed. They exceeded the Treasury's debt to the Reichsbank by 6.6 billion Reichsmarks. However, a weakening in public fervor began to appear in the fifth War Loan. Subscriptions failed to meet expectations, leaving 2.1 billion Reichsmarks of the floating debt unfunded. By the end of the war that unfunded debt had gradually increased to 39 billion Reichsmarks. Not only the German people but also most of their leaders had failed to grasp that severe inflation was an inevitable consequence of exclusive reliance on that method of war finance. The popular belief was that the Allied blockade and the shortages of consumer goods of all kinds were entirely responsible for the rise in prices.

Though the year 1914–1915 had witnessed reduced yield from taxes, customs and public enterprises of more than a billion Reichsmarks and increased expenditure of more than a billion Reichsmarks for interest on the national debt alone, the German government had done nothing to increase the revenue of the "Ordinary Budget." Instead one-half, and later the entire cost, of current army and navy expenditures was thrown onto the "Extraordinary (War Costs) Budget." Until 1916 the procedure followed was quite

---

[8] Schacht, *The Stabilization of the Mark*, pp. 11–34.

similar to that used in France. Not even the peacetime expenditures of the state could have been paid from current revenues. Yet as late as August 20, 1915, Secretary of State Helfferich informed the Reichstag: "We do not mean during the war to increase by taxation the gigantic burden on the shoulders of our people, so long as there is no pressing need for us to do so." Eight days later he rejected the Reichstag's demand for a tax on war profits, saying: "We take the view that such a tax cannot be imposed until the war is over, since it will not be possible until then to survey the financial effects of the war." Tacitly he conceded that German financial leaders did not know how to cope with the prolonged warfare that had developed. In the same sitting of the Reichstag he warned: "If God gives us the victory, those who provoked the war will have to carry for decades to come the dead weight of the billions spent." Both the French and the British overheard that threat.

Not until June 1916, when the deficit in the Ordinary Budget estimates had risen to 500 million Reichsmarks, were a war profits tax and taxes on consumption and business introduced. Taxes on income or on capital gains were never used. That contrasted sharply with the policies followed in Great Britain, which had doubled income tax rates in the autumn of 1914, had increased them another 40 percent in September 1915, and then raised them again in April 1916. In Germany, only 6 percent of total war costs was met by taxation and the remainder from loans, whereas in Great Britain 20 percent was paid by taxation. In France the entire cost of the war was met by loans, 43 percent raised by domestic borrowing, 21 percent by foreign loans and the remaining 36 percent by increasing the floating debt.

The London *Economist* for September 25, 1915, bitterly commented:

> A war on this scale, which is plunging thousands of families into mourning week after week, ought not to be surrounded and accompanied by an atmosphere of general prosperity, of war bonuses for the working classes, or of huge war profits for the contractors and for those who manufacture for the Government.

Yet precisely that heady atmosphere of profits and prosperity prevailed in London, Paris and Berlin. Before the war the French had had no income taxes at all. One was introduced in 1916, and many taxes on consumption were increased. But the revenue from all those sources did not suffice to pay the normal expenses of the French government, those that had existed before the war. And Paris was so near the trenches that in April 1917 the French Army was compelled to suppress mutiny among its own resentful troops. General Pétain, the "Hero of Verdun," resorted to decimation by firing squads. In Berlin many of the profiteers who so scandalized patriots were Jewish refugees from Eastern Europe, living hand to mouth in any way they could.

In peacetime Germany the circulation of notes had fluctuated around 2 billion Reichsmarks. It had remained at approximately 4 billion in November 1914, a billion representing notes that had replaced gold coins withdrawn. In December there was a rapid rise, and at the end of 1914 the total of all means of payment in circulation was 7.2 billion Reichsmarks. By the end of 1915 the total had risen to 9.7 billion, and by the end of 1916 to 12.9 billion. The rate of progression was rising. In 1917 the Hindenburg Program was introduced, to stimulate maximum efforts by industry. Highly profitable contracts for war materiel were offered. By the end of 1917 the total note circulation was 19.5 billion, and by November 1918 it had reached 28.4 billion. 17 billion of that total were Reichsbank notes and 9.6 billion were the so-called *Darlehnskassenscheine* or loan-bank notes. Throughout the war, circulation per capita rose from 110 Reichsmarks to approximately 430. So long as the additional purchasing power represented by that increase of notes in circulation was used to purchase war bonds or the bonds of the floating debt, inflation was held in check. But as the war continued, the German government obtained less and less benefit from the additional purchasing power it was creating. By the end of 1917 not less than half of the 28.5 billion in Treasury bonds issued was still on the hands of the Reichsbank. On November 7, 1918, the total floating debt of the German Empire, in the form of discounted Treasury bonds, was 48.5 billion Reichsmarks. Of that total 19.2 billion was held by the Reichsbank for its own account, and a corresponding quantity of notes had been put into circulation.

The damaging course of inflation could be read in recorded wholesale prices. If the average number for 1913 is taken as 100, the average for 1914 was 105. For the next 4 years the average numbers were 142, 152, 179 and 217. In November 1918 the average was 234. The annual average price for rye rose from 164 Reichsmarks per 1000 kilograms in 1914 to 305 Reichsmarks in 1918. Raw iron increased from 82 Reichsmarks per 1000 kilograms to 223 Reichsmarks. In Berlin an egg cost 9 pfennigs in 1914 and 48 in 1918. If August 1914 is taken as 100, workmen's wages reached 248 in 1918. There was no unemployment, and until quite late German workers continued to believe they were profiting from the war. When that delusion vanished, the "home front" collapsed.

Another source of inflation, which would later assume grotesque proportions, had appeared during the first weeks of war. An acute shortage of small coins and notes had been experienced, primarily for the needs of the Army. An attempt had been made to remedy that situation by a decree of August 31, 1914, that had ordered the issue of *Darlehnskassenscheine* for 1 and 2 marks. Before they could be printed, however, many districts of Germany had already resorted to temporary issues of *Notgeld,* or emergency money. Regardless of a half-century of empire local particularism had remained strong. In small denominations from 5 pfennigs to 3 marks some two hundred municipalities, districts and savings banks, plus more than a hundred industrial companies and other private organizations, issued more than 10 million marks.

By the middle of 1916 the rise in the cost of living and the continuing expansion of the areas of military occupation had led to further shortages of small notes and coins. That was intensified by the withdrawal of metallic coins from circulation. Silver coins were being hoarded, and copper and nickel were needed for war purposes. The silver held by the Reichsbank still totaled 40 million Reichsmarks in 1915, but by the last quarter of 1916 it had dropped to 17 million. Holdings of copper and nickel coins had been reduced from 3.5 million Reichsmarks to 0.750 million. To ease that problem, 5- and 10-pfennig pieces of iron and zinc were minted, and further issues of *Notgeld* were authorized in denominations of 50 pfennigs or less. In all, 2251 public and private institutions were permitted to create money, until long after the end of the war. Their issues were legally covered by a block credit for 300 million marks at the Reichsbank. Interest coupons of the war loan bonds were also declared legal tender.

The disintegration of the German Empire can be traced in that gradual loss of central control over note issue.

THE EFFECTS UPON NEUTRALS

For decades before the war the gold parities of currencies had represented their comparative purchasing power. The peacetime economies of European countries had become closely related, and the gold standard had prevented any artificial undervaluation or overvaluation of their currencies. When the belligerent nations suspended specie payments, their currencies began to drift away from those traditional moorings. The direction was almost always down. Their depreciation on the foreign-exchange markets reflected not only speculation and the belligerents' needs for foreign commodities but also the progress of domestic inflation. Those economic effects of war were concealed from the peoples of the warring powers by rigorous censorship and patriotic propaganda, but no illusions blinded the inhabitants of neutral countries. Their newspapers trumpeted protests, and their governments vainly sought to benefit from the war by increasing exports without importing inflation. All failed. All incurred losses, as well as gains.

One of the early casualties of that war was the old belief that its first phase could and would be financed by accumulated gold reserves. Wherever possible, belligerent governments evaded doing so. They preferred to retain their gold for still graver emergencies. Nevertheless, beginning in 1915, some gold was used—for necessities from abroad and to support loan operations on foreign markets. The latter proved to be the most effective way to procure the largest possible quantities of foreign currencies. Foreign markets were willing to issue larger loans if a gold "sweetener" was offered. France's gold exports to Great Britain and Franco–British gold exports to the United States were soon used for that purpose. In one way or another gold was slowly transferred from all the belligerents to all the neutrals. Quickly it converted the United States and Japan from prewar debtors into substantial creditors.

World gold production actually increased during the first few years of war, rising from $459.9 million in 1913 and $439.1 million in 1914 to a peak of $470.5 million in 1915. Then the inevitable decline began. New production fell to $454.2 million in 1916, to $423.6 million in 1917, to $380.0 million in 1918 and to $365.2 million in 1919. During the years 1913–1919 the proportion that entered the world's national reserves totaled $1.345 billion. In addition approximately $1.9 billion in gold coinage was withdrawn from circulation in the belligerent countries of Europe and was added to their prewar reserves. The amount of gold offered on the world markets became extraordinary, at a time when monetary demand was limited to the minimal quantities the central banks and treasuries of the neutral countries, the United States and Japan were prepared to accept for their own reserves. The market for gold became totally disorganized, its price falling sharply. Measured against the general levels of wholesale commodity prices, between 1913 and 1920 gold fell to an estimated 40 percent of its prewar value. That was a monetary revolution more violent than any previously recorded, and the depreciation in the value of gold was one of the most remarkable phenomena of a war in which so many ancient beliefs were being shattered. The accepted opinion that gold could and would maintain its "intrinsic" value throughout the worst disasters was therefore discarded by monetary experts, though speculators and the public continued to believe in it blindly.

Essentially the problem was that gold could neither be eaten nor fired from cannon. After the first year of war, only essential commodities were in great demand. Both belligerents and neutrals were competing for dwindling supplies of commodities far more useful than gold. The extent of its depreciation in value was largely dependent on the reception central bankers of the gold-standard neutral countries gave to the gold that poured in upon them. If the influx had been comparatively moderate, and if those central banks had admitted gold into their central reserves without increasing their note circulation, then the value of gold might have been maintained at its prewar level. But for neutrals that influx of gold was quite large. Faithful to prewar rules central banks in every neutral country built upon those increasing gold reserves an increasing quantity of means of payment. That increased purchasing power forced up the price levels of other commodities, which was the equivalent of a reduction in the purchasing power of gold. Even where neutral central banks did not increase their note circulation in proportion to the increase in their gold stocks (as in the Netherlands, Switzerland and Spain), they did not impose ceilings on those increases. And wherever the supply of means of payment increased in absolute figures, the artifically expanded purchasing power stimulated a rise in commodity prices. Logically that was not a cause of worry to the belligerents. Their purpose was to obtain for themselves the largest possible supply of essential commodities without paying out any useful commodities in return. If neutrals would accept large quantities of paper securities sweetened with small amounts of gold, rather than iron or coal, in exchange for their wheat and cotton, who benefited? Obviously neutrals were the fools.

In some of the gold-receiving countries the creation of new purchasing power caused by that influx of gold was forced to such extremes that the value of their currencies fell lower than that of gold. Then it became useless for belligerents to export any more gold to them. With each expansion of inflation in the neutrals the market for gold became narrower. At last the United States became the only country that could take more. The American people were pleased to see so much gold returning to the country from which so much of it had been mined. American Treasury and Federal Reserve officials decided that they would have to accept gold, because the Allies no longer exported anything worth taking in payment. And the United States Congress was quite aware that growing gold reserves would enhance American political prestige abroad. But the belligerents continued to ship gold not only to the United States but also to countries where it had little purchasing power, such as Japan, whose consequent inflation became severe. Not until the war ended, and some freedom of trade had been restored, would there be any widespread recognition that many countries had permitted inflation of their currencies to such extremes that they had fallen far below gold in value. That was the case in all the neutral countries of Europe.

Sweden had been the first to grasp that to trade its scarce iron ore, timber and foodstuffs for German government securities and gold was simply not a sound economic transaction. In a special law passed February 8, 1916, and by subsequent royal decrees, Sweden tried to protect itself from the undesirable effects of excessive gold imports by excluding gold from its monetary system. Known as the "gold-exclusion policy," that effort was one of the more interesting experiments in the history of money. Gold imports were not forbidden, but free coinage was suspended and the central bank was freed from its obligation to buy gold at a fixed price. By this severing of its currency from any connection to gold the value of the Swedish paper crown was permitted to rise above its gold parity. The gold reserves of the Riksbank, which had totaled 108.5 million crowns at the end of 1914 and had reached only 124.6 million crowns at the end of 1915, had suddenly risen to 142.3 million on January 31, 1916, and to 160.3 million on February 5. The Riksbank simply could not absorb any more gold. Therefore the right of free coinage was suspended effective April 28, so that agreements could be formed with Norway and Denmark, with which Sweden had been allied in a monetary union. Yet by the end of 1917 the Riksbank's gold reserves had increased another 84.2 million crowns, as other Scandinavian gold coin was imported to settle Norwegian and Danish debts. Their currencies were depreciating, as the Swedish crown appreciated.

That Swedish policy of "gold exclusion" proved to be a valiant miscalculation. Though the paper crown briefly remained above its old gold parity, inflation continued and reached such extremes that the crown's purchasing power against commodities eventually dropped far below that of gold. The central banks in Norway and Denmark had continued to buy gold on a large scale at prices considerably below par. In the Netherlands, where the gold standard was officially retained and gold was accepted at par, the central bank nevertheless had the power to decide how much gold it wanted to buy. After large increases in its gold stocks during the first 2 years of war it reduced its gold buying during the final 2 years.

Thus all neutrals quickly learned the obvious lesson that the real value or purchasing power of a currency was not related in any way to its gold backing or "cover" but rather depended primarily on the quantity in circulation.[9]

AMERICAN ENTRY

By the end of 1916 the First World War had become an endurance test for all the countries engaged. Both industrial and agrarian societies had demonstrated far greater staying power than anyone had believed possible. After the first 30 months of war both the Allied and the Central Powers had not only imposed rigorous controls on their domestic economies but had also begun to develop the weapons of economic warfare. The Allies had not been using their navies for the offensive strikes long anticipated, because both sides feared the possibly decisive effects of surface engagements. Instead the British Home Fleet found itself imposing an increasingly relentless blockade on Germany and Austria–Hungary, to starve them into submission. The German Navy sought to break out and to cut the maritime supply lines on which Great Britain and France were so dependent by deploying ever larger numbers of long-range submarines. Neither side had been able to gain any decisive advantages either at sea or on land. Both Allied and Central Powers had therefore been employing all their wiles, to obtain allies and to suborn enemies. Though the Allies had gained Italy and Japan, Bulgaria and Turkey

(9) Cassel, *Money and Foreign Exchange after 1914,* passim.

had joined the Central Powers. None had tipped the balance to one side or the other on the scales of power.[10]

Like all other neutrals, the United States had been subjected to increasing propaganda and to pressures intended to compel it to take sides. Yet most Americans had considered the war a European affair, caused by Europeans and fought for their advantage. The majority of the American people saw no reason for the United States to become involved. It is doubtful that they would ever have entered if all belligerents had abstained from desperate measures that challenged the freedom of American ships to sail wherever they pleased. In January 1917, however, Germany resorted to unrestricted submarine warfare in the Atlantic. Kaiser Wilhelm mistakenly believed that President Wilson could be frightened into withholding American shipments of war materiel to the Allied Powers. By April the United States was at war with Germany and Austria–Hungary, and had begun to supply its hard-pressed Allies with aid on a scale never before seen. Though American support eventually tilted the balance, many Europeans continued to regret that they had invited the United States to intervene in their affairs. Nor had Americans any reasons to rejoice in doing so. A seasoned observer of Washington's follies sighed:

> The old isolation is finished. We are no longer aloof from Europe, we are no longer aloof from the rest of the world. For weal or woe, whatever happens now concerns us, and from none of it can be withheld the force of our influence.[11]

In 1914 the trade surplus of the United States had been $435.8 million. The New York Federal Reserve Bank had opened for business in mid-November of that year, and the New York exchanges had reopened December 15. Between January 1915 and March 1917, more than $1 billion in gold entered the United States. Most of it found its way into bank vaults, where it augmented reserves and stimulated credit expansion of several billion dollars. Inflation rapidly followed. Wholesale prices rose 75 percent between mid-1914 and April 1917. By January of 1917, the district banks of the Federal Reserve System held more than $400 million in excess of required gold reserves. If their member banks had called upon them to do so, they could have rediscounted to the extent of $1 billion, issuing notes for that amount. But those excessive gold reserves established only the possibility rather than the necessity for credit expansion, and Americans had been learning from European experience. The decision was reached to "freeze" superfluous gold, rather than allow it further to expand note issue. War orders continued to flood

[10] Jack, *Studies in Economic Warfare*, pp. 82–145.
[11] Link, *Wilson*, vol. 5, p. 431.

American industry, creating an overwhelming demand for increased business credits. By 1917 the annual trade surplus of the United States had risen to $3.568 billion. The Allies had liquidated some $2 billion in American securities owned by their own citizens, before they had begun to pay in gold. They were borrowing to the very limits of their credit, until in late 1916 the Federal Reserve Board had to caution American bankers about lending them more. Yet British and French Treasury officials promised such handsome profits that American bankers continued to lend readily. By the end of 1916 the British Treasury alone had to raise £5 million per day to finance British war expenditures. Of that sum, it was seeking to borrow at least £2 million per day in the United States.

Between June 1914 and June 1917 total domestic bank loans in the United States had increased from $15.250 billion to $20.5 billion. That had been over-expansion of credit, far in excess of normal production and consumption requirements. If the increasing demand had been terminated suddenly, readjustment would have been painful. However, when the United States entered the war, the years 1915–1917 proved to have been a fortunate preparation. Industries were already functioning smoothly in large-scale operations and needed only to raise their production goals. As the Allies exhausted their foreign securities and credit abroad, the gold stocks of the United States rose to a peak of $3.22 billion in June 1917. The Federal Reserve system alone held $1.295 billion in gold. Private banks stubbornly clung to some $700 million, and another $200 million was held by the Federal Treasury. The remainder was the gold coin in circulation. Then, by Law of June 21, 1917, the Federal Reserve Board was authorized to exercise direct control over all international gold shipments to and from the United States. Arrangements had also begun to fund Allied purchases in the United States by extending Federal loans to them. By the end of the war the United States would find that it had lent those Allies a gross total of $11.853 billion, a sum beyond the comprehension of most Americans.[12]

In 1914 the Federal Reserve Bank of New York had been designated the official agent of the United States in foreign exchange and gold operations, a role it has played ever since. Its first Governor was Benjamin Strong, who had been a private banker. A forthright New Yorker, he had family connections with Princeton, President Wilson's university. Among his purposes Strong intended to reform the American currency, to amass large gold stocks in the Federal Reserve Banks and to develop a major international money market in New York. That implied keener competition with the older financial centers of Europe, and from the beginning Strong sought closer cooperation with their central bankers. Early in 1916 he sailed for Europe not only to meet

(12) Shultz and Caine, *Financial Development of the United States*, pp. 493–497.

financial leaders in Great Britain and France but also to open negotiations with those central banks. In London he was warmly welcomed and began relations that would become close in the next decade. In Paris, where traditionalists at the Bank of France tended to regard all Americans with suspicion, he achieved no tangible results. In both capitals he explored methods of war finance and studied the effects of war on their finances, central banking policies, money market organization and foreign exchange operations. He found that everyone had underestimated the increases in government expenditures. And on April 5, 1917, when the American Secretary of the Treasury estimated the expenses of the United States from that date to mid-1918, he guessed they would be $8.4 billion. Later they would prove to be $13 billion and would rise beyond $18.5 billion in the following fiscal year. Whenever dealing with generals, one must always at least double the estimates they present.

The legislation President Wilson had signed on June 21, 1917, had been intended primarily to concentrate gold in the Reserve Banks of the United States. Federal Reserve notes were to be issued for gold, and all member banks were required to keep their legal reserves in the form of deposits at the Reserve Banks. Yet Federal Reserve officials had to plead with commercial banks and clearing houses to relinquish their gold and gold certificates. The Reserve Banks assumed all related costs, and severely discouraged payments in gold and gold certificates to the public. Until the end of the war and beyond, the policy of the Federal Reserve Board and of the Treasury would be to conserve gold and to discourage its circulation, on grounds that it no longer served any useful purpose in domestic transactions and should be regarded as the foundation of national reserves, kept for settlement of international transactions. Strong had obtained that bit of monetary philosophy from the Bank of England. Every effort was made to persuade Americans that it was somehow unpatriotic to hold gold coin.

In retrospect those efforts seem extraordinary, at a time when the United States was importing so much gold and was becoming the world's largest creditor. Yet old debtor-nation ways of thought had persisted, and many officials had feared that when the war ended there would be a collapse of credit and a run on national reserves unless measures were taken to forestall it. Strong's efforts were quite successful. At the end of 1916 the gold stocks of the Reserve Banks had been $720 million, a mere 28 percent of the monetary gold in the country. By the end of 1918 they had increased to $2.134 billion, 74 percent of the total national monetary stock. Strong had also urged that war costs be paid from current taxation. In the event, however, tax receipts

(13) Chandler, *Benjamin Strong*, pp. 41–133.

actually covered less than 30 percent. He had proposed methods for selling Federal securities that became the five Liberty Loan and Victory Loan campaigns, to which the American people subscribed $21.465 billion. The national debt grew from less than $1 billion in 1917 to more than $25 billion at the end of 1918, and it was widely spread among all major sectors of the American economy.[13]

While in London Strong had confirmed arrangements with the Bank of England and the Bank of France to peg the exchange rate of the dollar. Early in 1915 it had begun to appreciate against both the pound and the franc. After a committee of London bankers had failed to stabilize the pound's rate against the dollar, in August the Bank of England had been compelled to intervene. Eventually the official exchange rate had been pegged at $4.76. With the Defence of the Realm Act in December 1916, which had prohibited the melting down of British gold coin, and a widening network of controls on all types of foreign transactions, Allied monetary authorities had been able to preserve the legal fiction that the prewar gold standard was still intact. The official dollar exchange rate was crucial to Great Britain and France, because they depended on an adequate supply of dollars at a reasonable price to sustain their vast purchasing program in the United States. The rate of $4.76 was therefore a substantial concession by the United States, because it represented a concealed subsidy. Nonetheless substantial British and French resources were required to support it. Between financial year 1915–1916 and financial year 1918–1919 they spent $2.021 billion for that purpose.

That exchange rate was near the prewar standard parity of the pound. Yet behind that façade of normalcy on the foreign exchange markets, international wage, cost and price levels had begun to diverge sharply under the stress of war. The franc was never pegged as rigidly as the dollar, and fluctuated between 27.15 and 27.55 to the pound, between 93 and 91 percent of its prewar parity. The Italian lira proved to be even weaker than the franc. Opening at 26.35 to the pound at the beginning of 1915, it fell as low as 32.45 to the pound in January 1916. As the end of the war neared, there was a strong rally of sterling on most neutral exchanges, and a rally of the weak Allied currencies against sterling. In October 1918 the pound's supposed value as a percentage of prewar parity was 98 against the American dollar, 100 against the Canadian dollar, 103 against the French franc, 93 against the Dutch guilder, 120 against the Italian lira, 92 against the Spanish peseta, 87 against the Swedish crown, 89 against the Japanese yen and 91 against the Argentine peso. Those rates represented, not the forces of supply and demand, but rather official intervention and some private speculation. Though the war had drastically weakened London's position as an international banker, there was no way to determine what new and realistic exchange rates might be until currencies could be freed from those deceptive wartime controls.[14]

Like the Bank of England and the Reichsbank, the Bank of France had been hoarding gold—calling in gold coinage from circulation, demanding gold in payment from weaker Allies and paying it out to the stronger only when compelled to do so. Like the British and the Germans, the French had also been confidently anticipating that wartime costs could be fully recovered by levying indemnities upon defeated enemies.[15] They had retained vivid memories of the sums extracted from France after its defeats in 1815 and 1870. Therefore the primary method of war finance had been advances by the Bank of France to the Finance Ministry, and that Bank's note circulation had increased accordingly, from 6.638 billion francs in July 1914 to 29.072 billion in November 1918. Though huge, that increase had been kept to a minimum only by raising funds from abroad and from the French people— the *bons de la défense nationale.* Issued in denominations of 100 and 1000 francs through every bank and post office, the total of those national bonds outstanding had risen from 1.619 billion francs at the end of 1914 to 22.235 billion at the end of 1918. Regardless of rudimentary efforts to control wages and prices, inflation had got out of hand. Though the foreign-exchange rate of the franc still appeared to be sound, between July 1914 and the end of 1918 wholesale prices rose from 100 to 300. Good French *bourgeois,* whether suspicious patriots or cynical profiteers, had become furious. In a rising chorus they had begun to ask whether they had been duped by the French governments that had called in their gold and had sold them such vast amounts of paper securities. As peace drew near, Premier Georges Clemenceau sought ways to distract their attention.

Despite the armies of men, money and materiel shipped across the Atlantic to help France in the years 1917–1918, American participation in "Mr. Wilson's War" was never wholehearted. Private talks with the Central Powers had continued. On January 8, 1918, President Wilson had announced to Congress the "Fourteen Points" upon which the United States desired peace to be founded. Point Three called for "The removal, so far as possible, of all economic barriers and the establishment of an equality of trade conditions among all the nations consenting to the peace and associating themselves for its maintenance." Point Five required "A free, open-minded and absolutely impartial adjustment of all colonial claims." Points Six, Seven, Eight and

---

[14] Morgan, *Studies in British Financial Policy, 1914–1925,* pp. 303–361.
[15] British studies on a war indemnity had begun in 1915. The Treasury had estimated that over time Germany would be able to pay between £200 million and £300 million. But a Cabinet committee later appointed insisted on full payment of all Allied war costs. Their preliminary estimate was £24 billion. Keynes, *Collected Writings,* vol. 16, pp. 311–386.

Eleven stipulated evacuation and restoration of all territory invaded by Germany and compensation for all damages done to civilians and their property.

The German government addressed a brief, formal note to President Wilson on October 5, accepting those Fourteen Points and asking for peace negotiations. Wilson's reply of October 8 demanded confirmation that "the terms laid down" had been accepted, and he added that evacuation of all occupied territories would be a precondition for an armistice. On October 12 the German government replied with an unconditional affirmative, and on October 20 it agreed to an absolute cessation of hostilities prior to the continuation of discussions. President Wilson was also informed that Germany now had a constitution and a government responsible to the Reichstag rather than to the Kaiser. The Allies' "desire for his abdication had been noted." After consulting all associated governments, Wilson informed Berlin on November 5 that the French Marshal Foch had been authorized to communicate the terms of an armistice to the German Army. He also told Berlin that the Allies were willing to make peace on the basis of the Fourteen Points, plus two additional qualifications. They reserved to themselves the complete freedom of the seas, and they required full understanding that compensation would be made by Germany for all damages done to the civilian population of the Allies and to their property by the aggression of Germany on land, at sea and from the air.

On November 11 representatives of the German General Staff signed that armistice in a railroad car on a siding in the French forest of Compiègne. A month later, on December 13, President Wilson arrived in the French port of Brest aboard the old troopship *George Washington.* Throughout the world hopes were high. At great cost in blood and treasure it had at last been made "safe for democracy." Surely wise statesmen could and would secure peace and prosperity for all time to come. However, Wilson's own prophetic observation during his crossing had been: "People will endure their tyrants for years, but they tear their deliverers to pieces if a millennium is not created immediately."

4 = Revolution, Recovery, Relapse 1917–1931

Zürich is an ancient town of severe charm, huddled in the valley of the River Limmat, where it leaves Lake Zürich to flow northward toward the Rhine. For several thousand years it has been the center for Switzerland's trade with the Germanies, its largest customers and suppliers. Therefore it became a financial center of importance, and by the 1880s a modest trader and net importer of gold and silver. In 1889 annual Swiss imports of bullion and specie totaled £3.4 million (Sfr. 85.6 million), and its exports some £1.2 million (Sfr. 28.9 million). Because long and sobering experience with religious and civil wars had rendered the Swiss remarkably tolerant, Zürich had also become the principal center for the activities of German Social Democrats no longer welcome in their own homelands. There were a few Russian exiles, though most of that nationality preferred the gentler clime of Geneva. By law the right of asylum should have been revoked for those who advocated regicide or insurrection and organized conspiracies against foreign governments. But when the First World War began, the cantonal police had a small budget and were understrength for the more important task of watching the swarms of foreign speculators who descended on Zürich to trade in gold, currencies, securities, war materiel and contraband of all kinds. Surrounded by four powerful belligerents—Germany, Austria–Hungary, France and Italy—the staid burghers of Zürich were suddenly affronted by a spectacle they had never before witnessed. Every luxury hotel near the Paradeplatz was crowded with frantic speculators, who traded in gold by the kilogram and currencies by the bale, and consumed as by right the very finest foods and wines available.

THE RISE OF BOLSHEVISM

Intently observing them, from the other side of the River Limmat, was one Vladimir Ilyich Ulyanov. In exile he had taken the name *Lenin*. By 1916, at the age of 46, he had decided to settle in Zürich because he needed its fine libraries, for which he had and would retain the highest respect. Though Lenin deeply hated the "intelligentsia" and Europe's middle classes generally, he was a Russian provincial and petty noble who judged a city's cultural achievements by its libraries. With his wife, Nadezhda Krupskaya, he had found an apt address in the old town, at Spiegelgasse 14. It was a few minutes' walk from the University, the Central Library and the cheap bars on the Niederdorf. The recent death of his mother had ended his regular allowance from Russia, and wartime inflation had sharpened the hostilities of a needy writer who had become dependent on his pen. His international research culminated that year in a treatise, *On Imperialism*, derived primarily from a book with the same title first published in 1902 by an English radical, John Hobson. Inspired by the Boer War, the Hobson–Lenin thesis argued that imperialism was the final stage in the development of capitalism, and Lenin was convinced that it had also been the basic cause of the First World War.

A compulsive moralizer, Lenin had long proclaimed through the Russian émigré journal *Iskra* that capitalism could not be reformed. He urged total destruction of the bourgeoisie and their *laissez-faire* apologists, and transfer of power to a dictatorship of industrial workers. Neither a scholar nor an analyst, Lenin's grasp of economics was feeble. Essentially he was an agitator and a pamphleteer who used libraries only to glean those ideas and statistics that served his preconceived conviction that Russian Tsarist autocracy must be overthrown. Yet there was a modicum of truth at the heart of that Hobson–Lenin thesis on imperialism, regardless of the unreal embroideries later built upon it. To this day former colonies have continued to howl for "social justice," repayment in goods and cash for their exploitation by the colonial empires of the 19th century. Because of its simplicity and emotional appeal that anti-imperial doctrine of Hobson and Lenin would become one of the most influential beliefs of modern times. European liberals, hagridden by self-doubt, have scurried to oblige the lazy servants of their ancestors. Which are the greater fools, readers must judge for themselves.[1]

While Lenin in Zürich was growing anxious for money, the German gov-

[1] Ulam, *Lenin and the Bolsheviks*, pp. 269–381.

ernment in Berlin was becoming desperate for ways to end that war. In January 1917, when Kaiser Wilhelm decided on unrestricted submarine warfare in the Atlantic, he also chose to encourage revolution in Russia. German representatives in Switzerland had kept the Foreign Office in Berlin well informed on the activities of the Russian émigrés, and contacts had already been made. Yet everyone was surprised by the February revolt in Petrograd, followed so soon by abdication of the Tsar. Berlin was perturbed, because the Russian threat had revived. The provisional government of Kerensky was promising its Allies that it would continue the war against Germany to the bitter end. By contrast the wing of the Russian Social Democrats who followed Lenin had been crying out for peace at any price. Quiet negotiations began through a Swiss Socialist. On April 9 Lenin, his wife and twenty members of his group left Zürich bound for Petrograd. They traveled via Germany, Sweden and Finland. Anticipating charges that he was a mere hireling of the Germans, Lenin had stipulated that the railroad car carrying him through Germany should enjoy the extraterritorial privileges of a diplomatic mission. All dealings with German authorities were conducted through the neutral Swiss Socialist who had negotiated the agreement. The only formal obligation Lenin incurred was to plead in Petrograd for the release of an equivalent number of German prisoners of war held in Russia. The German Foreign Office was delighted to be able to inject so disruptive an opponent into the midst of its enemies.[2]

In Petrograd Lenin found chaos and a dearth of effective leadership that would soon deliver power into his own hands. Yet he remained sorely in need of money, that indispensable implement of authority. Russian finances had become completely disorganized, and huge wartime budget deficits had caused indirect inflation. For the years 1914–1917 those deficits had totaled 47 billion rubles, 75 percent of total public expenditures for that period. The national debt, 9.3 billion rubles in 1914, had increased to 33.6 billion at the beginning of 1917. Much of that increase represented debts to Allies. Despite the withdrawal of gold coinage from circulation and the continuing production of bullion from mines in the Ural Mountains and Siberia, gold reserves held by the State Bank in Russia itself had fallen from 1.604 billion rubles in 1914 to 1.292 billion in October 1917. The quantity of paper currency in circulation had increased from 1.630 billion rubles in July 1914 to 18.917 billion on October 23, 1917. Inflation had been tolerable during the first 2 years of war. If 1913 is taken as 1, the price index of twenty-six basic commodities sold in Moscow had risen to 1.01 in 1914, 1.30 in 1915 and 2.08 on July 1, 1916. Then both inflation and speculative excesses had begun to get out of control. Tsarist Treasury officials had been notoriously incompetent. As had happened elsewhere, their primitive technique of financing war pri-

(2) Hahlweg, *Lenins Rückkehr nach Russland 1917*, passim.

marily by having Treasury bills discounted by the State Bank had proved
totally inadequate for the needs of prolonged hostilities. As they continued to
pour notes into circulation, the wholesale price index rose to 3.15 on January
1, 1917. By July 1 it had jumped to 7.73. Four months later, at the time of the
October Revolution, it soared to almost 15. Public confidence in paper currency simply disappeared, as the Russian people lost confidence in the ability
of Kerensky's provisional government to control events.

Revolutionary changes in Russia had begun to cast shadows over the rest
of Europe, and Western observers would soon begin to charge Lenin and his
Bolsheviks with deliberate inflation and depreciation of the ruble, as part of
a general policy intended to repudiate Russian debts abroad, to impoverish
the Russian bourgeoisie and thereby to reorganize Russian society.[3] It is
true that many Social Democrats had dreamed of an ideal, moneyless economy. And when Lenin gained power, he permitted many experiments. Yet
foreign critics then and ever since have tended to overestimate the extent of
the control Lenin could and did exercise. They also assumed that Lenin's
government was competent. It was not. Nor was it in Lenin's interest to
inform those foreigners how little real power he had. Throughout history the
inefficiency of Russian governments has surpassed Western belief and accounts for much of the violence and brutality with which Russian leaders
have customarily sought to enforce their will.

For the record and for Russia, Lenin spoke firmly against inflation, though
the jejune remedies he proposed thoroughly terrified bankers at home and
abroad. In a pamphlet on *Financial Collapse and Measures to Combat It*, published
in late October 1917, he wrote.

> Everybody admits that the emission of paper money constitutes the worst form of
> compulsory loan, that it affects most of all the conditions of the workers, the
> poorest section of the population, and that it is the chief evil engendered by
> financial disorder. . . . Immense issues of paper money encourage profiteering,
> enable the capitalists to make millions of rubles, and place tremendous difficul-
> ties in the way of a very necessary expansion of production. . . . The workers
> and peasants, organized in unions, by nationalizing the banks, making the use of
> checks compulsory for all rich persons, abolishing commercial secrecy, imposing
> confiscation of property as a penalty for concealment of incomes, etc., might with
> extreme ease render control both effective and universal. This requires a revolu-
> tionary dictatorship of the democracy, headed by the revolutionary proletariat.

A few days after those provocative words were written, Lenin and his
Bolsheviks suddenly gained the ruling positions needed to test their theses in
practice. On December 14 (27), 1917, he informed the All-Russian Central

[3] Keynes, Jack et al. For a sympathetic, disinterested sketch of conditions in Russia at that
time, see Brown, *The Groping Giant.*

Executive Committee that banks had been nationalized. Confronted with *force majeure,* the resistance of both public and private banking officials quickly collapsed. Admitted to their vaults, Lenin's followers obtained from the State Bank alone the equivalent of £114 million in gold. Both foreigners and Russians themselves were flabbergasted, as they watched men who had survived Tsarist rule by robbing banks become literal autocrats of the ancient treasury of the Romanovs. The foreign-exchange market vanished underground. Absence of banks and markets made the usual operations with gold and foreign exchange impossible. Hoarding of gold became extensive. Russians who owned gold and foreign currencies made every effort to transmit that capital abroad. At the end of 1918 the Soviet government began to require delivery of all gold and foreign exchange to the state, and its demands became intense in 1919–1920. Nevertheless, illegal exchanges continued to exist in every major Russian city, the principal object of speculation being gold specie and bullion, as a means of protecting and preserving capital through the storms of inflation and revolution. Late in 1920 some demand also appeared for gold with which to pay for contraband smuggled from abroad.

The responsibilities of power transformed Lenin's thinking. With only a small group of wayward ideologues to assist him, he had found that he could not simultaneously seek peace with Russia's enemies abroad, subdue domestic rivals and foes, provide for the essential expenditures of state, and curb inflation. Events imposed their own priorities on him. While his emissaries parleyed with Germany, Austria–Hungary, Bulgaria and Turkey, he had no choice but to continue using the mint's printing presses. In the treaty signed at Brest–Litovsk on March 3, 1918, Russia almost lost eighteen ancient provinces and would have lost them if the Allies had not abrogated that treaty in November. At Brest–Litovsk Germany also squeezed £10 million in gold from the shrinking treasury of the Soviet Union. By July 1, 1918, the price index had risen to 123.20 in Moscow and 100 elsewhere in Russia. By January 1, 1919, it stood at 278 for Moscow and 164 for all of Russia. By January 1, 1920, Lenin's government was fully engaged in civil war against the "White" counterrevolution of conservative Russians, aided by the intervention of foreign armies. The price index had taken a huge jump, to 4180 for Moscow and 2420 for the rest of Russia.

No effort was made to conceal the fact that currency inflation was being used as a means to secure purchasing power independently of the normal methods of taxation. The fiscal apparatus of the Russian state had disintegrated. *Nécessité fait loi* had therefore become Lenin's guiding principle. As inflation and depreciation of the ruble became more rapid, that method of financing became less effective. By January 1, 1921, the price index had risen to 24,600 in Moscow and 16,800 elsewhere in Russia. Lenin was compelled to resort to taxation in kind, simply to obtain the grain and fuel needed to maintain life in the cities. Russian peasants were no longer willing to sell their produce for any amounts of paper money. Consequently, in 1921, Lenin relaxed Bolshevik prohibitions against free enterprise by introducing his "New Economic Policy." When trade in agricultural products was declared free, commodities began to reappear in urban shops.

As late as 1921, among leading members of the Communist Party, the opinion prevailed that it would become possible to manage society without money and to carry on trade by "direct barter." Those illusions were abandoned when it became obvious that all efforts to organize trade between towns and the country would fail without the medium of money. Peasants were simply too primitive to grasp and accept the visions of the Party's leading thinkers and were distrustful of all innovations. By the autumn of 1921 the "black" markets were operating openly in Moscow, Petrograd and other towns. In addition to the dishoarded gold coins that had been the principal objects of trade in 1919–1920, gold bullion from the Urals and Siberia began to appear. Output from State enterprises went to the Treasury, but gold found by private miners was sold on the uncontrolled exchanges in 1921 and 1922. Lenin, having shed many of his prejudices, had turned for advice to several old Tsarist monetary experts. In his meetings with foreign traders who visited Russia seeking business opportunities, he had also gained a lively understanding of their interest in Russian gold and its consequent usefulness to him.

In October 1921 a new State Bank had been founded. And in a tract dated November 5, on *The Importance of Gold Now and After the Complete Victory of Socialism,* Lenin informed his followers of the Soviet government's revised policies.

> What grounds are there for assuming that the "great, victorious, world" revolution can and must employ only revolutionary methods? There are none at all. . . . When we are victorious on a world scale I think we shall use gold for the purpose of building public lavatories in the streets of some of the largest cities of the world. This would be the most "just" and most educational way of utilizing gold for the benefit of those generations which have not forgotten how, for the sake of gold, ten million men were killed and thirty million maimed in the "great war for freedom," in the war of 1914–18, in the war that was waged to decide the great question of which peace was the worst, the Brest Peace or the Versailles Peace; and how, for the sake of this gold, they certainly intend to kill twenty million men and to maim sixty million in a war, say, in 1925, or 1928, between, say, Japan and America, or between Britain and America, or something like that. . . . But however "just," useful or humane it would be to utilize gold for that purpose, we nevertheless say: let us work for another decade or two with the same intensity and the same success as in the 1917–1921 period, in order to reach this stage. Meanwhile, we must save the gold in the R.S.F.S.R., sell it at the highest price; buy goods with it at the lowest price. "When you live among wolves, you must howl like a wolf." As for exterminating all the wolves, as should

be done in a rational human society, we shall act up to the wise Russian proverb: "Boast not before but after the battle."[4]

Alas, those golden *pissoirs* have never been built, though both Moscow and Zürich need them so badly. Like all the other wolves, the Bank for Foreign Trade of the USSR has continued to sell its gold to the bankers of Zürich, Paris and London, for the highest prices it can get. Successive Soviet governments have found that, among the primitive peoples of this world, gold can lend prestige even to a dictatorship of the proletariat.

By the end of 1921 Lenin's government considered it necessary not only to reestablish a monetary system but also to relate it in some way to gold—though without putting gold coins into circulation. The Ninth All-Russian Congress of Soviets decided in favor of "a sound monetary system on a gold basis" and delegated the thankless task of accomplishing it to the Commissariat of Finance. On November 18, 1921, an attempt was therefore made to restore the prewar or gold ruble as the unit of account, by declaring 1 prewar ruble equal to 60,000 current rubles—the latter figure being the multiple by which the price index had risen between 1913 and that date. However, there are times and circumstances in which a logical, essential decree simply does not suffice. By March 1922 the ruble had soared to 200,000, in defiance of Lenin and his decrees. That attempt to reestablish the old Russian monetary standard was therefore abandoned. The problem of stabilizing the currency would remain, awaiting invention of a stable unit of account that could command widespread public confidence and acceptance.

By decree of April 4, 1922, ownership of precious metals and foreign currencies was freed from restrictions, and the new State Bank was authorized to trade in them. The number of foreign businessmen visiting the Soviet Union having increased in 1922, they introduced a new supply of foreign currencies in payment of their expenses. By the end of 1922 some foreign commercial deals were being arranged. Other sources of foreign currencies had appeared, among them charities such as the American Relief Administration and remittances from emigrants abroad. That last source had almost vanished during the years 1917–1921. Late in 1922 exports were resumed, proceeds going to the State Bank and other state institutions. Finally, by decree of February 15, 1923, foreign exchanges were permitted to trade in gold and silver bullion, and in foreign currencies. Only Russian gold and silver coins were forbidden, to prevent any revival of their free circulation.

Lenin died on January 21, 1924, after a series of strokes. Yet he had lived long enough to see Russia survive war, revolution and his own preconceptions. Slow recovery had begun.[5]

---

[4] *Pravda* for November 6–7, 1921

[5] Katzenellenbaum, *op. cit.;* and Yurovsky, *Currency Problems and Policy of the Soviet Union;* passim.

THE VERSAILLES DIKTAT

Four mighty empires had disappeared. The Russian Tsar had been merely the first to go. On October 18, 1918, the Grand Vizier of the Ottoman Empire informed the Austrian ambassador in Constantinople that his Sultan would be compelled to ask the Allies for an armistice and peace. Soon thereafter he was deposed. On October 26 the Austrian Emperor Karl telegraphed similar bad news to Berlin. Encouraged by the Allies, nationalist revolts were breaking out in Prague, Budapest, Agram, Fiume and Laibach. Karl relinquished power on November 11 and was forced to seek refuge in neutral Switzerland because he refused to abdicate formally. He left behind in Vienna a treasury stripped of its reserves, and officials helpless to prevent dismemberment of his realm. Europe's frightened *bourgeoisie* were convinced that the revolutions sweeping across their continent were being financed by the Romanov gold that had fallen into Lenin's hands, though there is scant evidence of that. Socialist propaganda was widespread, and Social Democrats had been the only open opponents of the Central European monarchies. Willy-nilly they had therefore become collaborators of the Allies, who had deliberately sought to break up the Central Powers by subsidizing the nationalist, separatist and republican movements in Germany and Austria–Hungary. Wilson's concept of "self-determination for all nations and peoples" was more subversive than Bolshevism.

Yet the German Empire received its *coup de grâce* from that navy for which the Kaiser had sacrificed prewar opportunities to reconcile his disputes with Great Britain. Because the German Navy had seen little action, its disgruntled admirals were plotting to disrupt armistice negotiations by steaming into the North Sea to seek a decisive battle with the British Home Fleet. Though they kept that secret from the German Chancellor, their crews learned what was planned from the nature of their preparations. On October 29 the stokers of the German fleet went on strike. By November 4 the red flag flew from every ship. Revolutionary bands of sailors wandered from the seaports to other cities, spreading terror and rebellion wherever they went. German Social Democrats had been urging peace for several years. On November 7 they threatened to withdraw from the new coalition government if Kaiser Wilhelm would not abdicate. The following day a republic was proclaimed in Munich, and Bavaria's Wittelsbachs were deposed. The German Army was also disintegrating; on November 9 its Supreme Command advised the last of the Hohenzollern emperors to abdicate. Abruptly he did so and sought asylum in the neutral Netherlands.[6]

[6] Eyck, *A History of the Weimar Republic,* vol 1, pp. 1–128.

Suddenly the stunned German people found themselves not only a republic but a Social Democratic republic compelled from the beginning to struggle for maintenance of domestic order and national unity while seeking peace with enemies determined to divide and subdue them permanently. The "Weimar governments" would never be sufficiently strong to carry those burdens In 1918 the fierce French Premier Clemenceau, who had witnessed the defeat and humiliation of Napoleon III in 1870, was convinced that France could not permit any revival of German power. At the moment of victory nothing seemed more reasonable and logical to French voters than Clemenceau's assertions that defeated Germany could and should be made to pay for everything France had lost or suffered. The French were also persuaded that their only security in future lay in a Rhine River border that would strip from Germany its provinces on the western bank.

When the German delegation arrived at the palace of Versailles in January 1919 to plead for generous terms in those same halls where modern Germany had been born in 1871, they found a conference dominated by the bitter, hardened Clemenceau. Cynically he refused to sign any peace treaty that would not fully satisfy French demands for reconstruction and protection. For France the costs of war had been very high—almost 1,400,000 dead and 3,750,000 wounded. Almost half the soldiers under the age of 30 had been killed. More than 4000 villages had been ruined, and 20,000 shops and factories destroyed. Mere money could never repair such damages. The naive President Wilson could not fully comprehend them or fathom the depths of European hatreds. The devious Lloyd George scarcely tried to restrain the victorious demands of France. In his own capital of London he too was besieged by voters' insistence that Germany should pay, and pay and pay. Few thought to ask the obvious questions. After 4 years and 4 months of near total war how could Germany pay? Could lasting peace be secured by crippling rather than reconciling a proud enemy?[7]

On January 12, 1919, the Allied representatives assembled in Paris decided to raise the blockade of Germany partially and to provide food and especially fat supplies on a large scale. That was made conditional upon delivery of the German fleet to the Allies. Hunger and even starvation had become so widespread in Germany that the new republican government in Berlin was not in a position to refuse anything. At the beginning of February it was compelled to reduce the weekly ration of potatoes to 5 pounds per person. Nevertheless many German ship captains attempted to scuttle rather than surrender their commands, and Germany had cause to complain of the food supplies delivered to them. A large part were aged, spoiling and of low quality.

---

[7] Full credit where credit is due. See Keynes, *The Economic Consequences of the Peace*. For an eloquent restatement of the French case, see Mantoux, *The Carthaginian Peace*.

The Allies had long had their eyes on German gold reserves as assets that were readily transferable. The British Treasury had carefully noted that, as of November 30, 1918, the gold reserves of the Reichsbank had totaled the mark equivalent of £115,417,900—much larger than its prewar stock. Germany was required to pay in full, in gold or in foreign securities, for all the food supplied. During the first half of 1919 the Reichsbank therefore paid the Allies more than a billion marks in gold for foodstuffs. Naturally Paris and London were also concerned about the safety of the Reichsbank's note-issuing plant. Sparticist rebels had occupied it for 2 days during their Berlin uprising in November and December 1918. When they had occupied the Imperial Palace, the Social Democratic Chancellor Ebert had been appalled by the parallel with events in Petrograd. German delegates therefore agreed to move their gold stocks and note-issuing presses farther to the West, where Allied precautions could be taken to defend them. Within the first few months of 1919, in fulfilment of the armistice terms, Germany also handed over 5000 locomotives, 150,000 railroad cars, 5000 trucks and all the gold taken from banks in occupied territories. Moreover Germany agreed to pay the maintenance costs of Allied occupation troops. Yet the economic blockade of Germany continued. Six months later the drafting of the Versailles Peace Treaty was at last completed, and was presented to the German delegates for their signatures. After anguished negotiations and futile arguments they signed on June 28, 1919. Then and then only, 2 weeks later, that blockade was raised.

In addition to clauses intended to enforce complete demilitarization of Germany, the Versailles Treaty contained far-reaching territorial and economic provisions. The Allied occupation of the left bank of the Rhine and of bridgeheads across that river was to continue in full strength for 5 years and was not to be entirely terminated until 1935. Alsace and Lorraine, with the coal mines of the Saar, were ceded to France. Three small districts were given to Belgium, and the Duchy of Luxemburg was detached from the German customs union. The upper part of Schleswig was given to Denmark, and large parts of Posen, Silesia and West Prussia to the new Poland. Danzig was declared a free city, and Memel was internationalized. Thus East Prussia, popularly assumed in Allied countries to be the heart of German militarism, was severed from the body of Germany. Poland was given access to the Baltic Sea. Outside Europe the Treaty obliterated the German colonial empire. By the device of "mandatories" those colonies were divided among the Allies. As a mandate from the League of Nations, South Africa obtained the gold-rich Southwest African territories it had coveted since 1882. A young German pilot named Hermann Goering, the son of a former Resident of Southwest Africa, considered himself disinherited and dispossessed by that provision of the Versailles Treaty.

The economic clauses required more. For 10 years Germany was to deliver

38 million tons of coal per annum to France, in compensation for French mines that had been ruined. Large quantities of benzol, coal tar, ammonium sulfate and other chemicals and dyes were to be delivered to the Allies. Literally millions of German livestock were to be requisitioned, and all merchant ships of more than 1600 tons' burden. In addition to paying the costs of all Allied occupation forces and commissions, Germany relinquished all private property in Allied countries, and agreed to grant them most-favored-nation and other commercial concessions in Germany without any *quid pro quo.* Moreover Germany agreed to compensate for all damages done by its armies to the peoples of the Allied powers. The amount of those damages was not specified in the Treaty itself but was to be determined by an Allied commission no later than May 1, 1921. By that date Germany was to pay the sum of 20 billion gold marks and to give bonds or the promise to issue bonds for an additional 80 billion. Those were the so-called reparations clauses that would become the focal point for the disputes and struggles of the next decade and more. By submitting to them, Germany's delegates had signed a huge blank check. If they had not done so, the economic blockade of Germany would not have been lifted.

Thus Germany was compelled to commit itself to pay a vast, unspecified sum, to be determined by its recent, still vengeful enemies. Outraged German critics promptly cried that they were "bleeding Germany white," which did not perturb the French. Even then those arrangements might have become workable if the Allies had held to their original, limited definition of "war damages." They did not. Under the pressure of domestic politics, especially in France, and under the obligation to keep at least some of the rash promises they had made to their voters, Allied politicians later extended the term to include not only physical damages but also all pensions and other allowances to Allied soldiers, sailors and their beneficiaries. The result was that reparations claims more than doubled. On May 1, 1921, the Allied Reparations Commission announced that the sum required from Germany would be 132 billion gold marks, or some $31.5 billion. Even the prosperous, prewar Germany would have found such payments impossible. To the leaders of the prostrate postwar Germany they seemed a cruel joke.[8]

Neutral monetary experts immediately declared unworkable the stipulation that reparations be paid in gold. That precluded any restoration of stability in the world's monetary system, enhanced the value of gold and materially affected the market for it. The demand for gold was strengthened in a world already inadequately supplied with it and the burden of reparations became much heavier than originally intended. The increased price of gold would also have made much heavier all world debts contracted in gold

(8) Angell, *The Recovery of Germany,* pp. 3–16.

and in many cases would have completely undermined the solvency of debtors, both public and private. It was simply unrealistic to require such huge sums of gold for reparations, when more than one-third of existing world monetary stocks had already been shipped to the United States and would not return.[9] Yet the French were adamant. They were obsessed with memories of the war indemnity they had paid in 1871, the security of the reparations payments now owing to them, and the need to enhance the value of gold already held in French private hoards, to restore its prewar purchasing power against other commodities. For the next few generations the world would struggle to recover from the mistakes made at Versailles in 1919.

The German Army had been reborn within weeks after signature of that Versailles *Diktat*. In retrospect it seems inevitable that Ebert's government had felt compelled to seek Army support. On July 19, 1919, Colonel–General Hans von Seeckt had been named First Chief of the *Truppenamt* at the German Defense Ministry. Thus in disguised form the German General Staff had been reformed. Under the very noses of the Allied Control Commission the training of staff officers had begun in all seven *Wehrkreise* of Germany. When the forlorn German delegates to the Versailles conference had returned to Berlin, they had found themselves the sorry objects of universal loathing. The end of hostilities had restored some calm to the foreign-exchange markets. But when it had become obvious that the Allies intended to impose a punitive peace, the mark had begun to depreciate. Speculators had hastened to dump their holdings, and by the end of 1919 the mark had depreciated to 10 percent and the Austrian crown to 5 percent of their prewar gold parities on the Geneva exchange. Each new application of Allied pressure on Germany caused further depreciation.

Uncertainty about the total indebtedness the Allies would eventually impose was also a serious obstacle to the resumption of Germany's foreign trade. Foreign suppliers were understandably reluctant to provide even the staples Germany needed so badly when paid in marks that depreciated so steadily. Within Germany the illegal speculation in foreign currencies needed to pay for imports caused one public scandal after another. Yet the German government was making strenuous efforts to restore order in its domestic finances. On July 21, 1919, it had introduced the collection of customs duties in gold. On September 10 the first of a series of special taxes had been approved. Belatedly war profits were severely taxed, and provisions were made for more rapid collection and the anticipatory payment of taxes, in the hope that the revenues of the state would keep pace with the depreciation of the mark. On April 8, 1922, a comprehensive revision of all existing taxes was introduced, and many were increased. Yet the results of those efforts proved inadequate.

[9] See Appendix.

From 1919 to the middle of 1922 Germany paid out an estimated 11 billion gold marks to meet international obligations. Of that sum 1.25 billion marks were in gold, and the balance in varied types of securities. That was not enough. And the political, economic and fiscal menaces under which the German government was laboring frustrated all efforts to revive the German economy. Desperate though they were, all fiscal measures taken failed to stop further depreciation of the mark. As its deterioration became progressive, the public expenditures of Germany continued to exceed its revenues. By May 1, 1921, when the total reparations bill was presented, the exchange rate had fallen to 60 marks to the American dollar. The Reichsbank began to pay a premium for gold coin purchased from private citizens and thus acknowledged for the first time the existence of inflation. An astonishing 2 billion old gold Reichsmarks were dishoarded in response to that premium. Yet Germany's inability to raise as they came due all the cash payments owing to the Allies led, on December 14, 1921, to its request for a moratorium. On the foreign exchanges the mark immediately fell to 140 to the dollar.

An international conference was held in Cannes at the beginning of January 1922. For the first time there appeared to be some recognition by other governments that Germany simply could not pay. Unhappily the assembly in Cannes was disrupted by the fall of Briand's Cabinet in Paris and his replacement by Poincaré. A native of Lorraine, that new Premier had been President of France from 1913 until 1920. He had never been known to show any sympathy whatever toward Germany.

RECOVERY ENSNARLED IN DEBTS AND REPARATIONS

During the Versailles Conference, President Wilson had made it quite clear that the United States would not be a party to the German reparations settlement and would not ask for any enemy territory. Americans had outgrown their brief flirtation with imperialism. Wilson had also emphasized that the United States would not consider cancellation of war debts, the loans it had advanced to all its Allies. Recalling centuries of American indebtedness to Europe, the prevailing American opinion was later summarized by the Yankee Calvin Coolidge, who exclaimed: "They hired the money, didn't they?"

When President Wilson returned to Washington, he found that both the Republican majority in the Senate and the American people generally had become hostile toward the entire Versailles Treaty and the League of Nations it had founded. The European animosities and vindictiveness displayed at Versailles had estranged Americans of all shades of opinion. Their attitude toward Europe had become "a plague on all your houses." There was a pronounced unwillingness to participate any further in the apparently intractable problems of Europe and a strong desire for "a return to normalcy" in the United States itself. During 19 months of war domestic prices had doubled. Peace had brought industrial as well as military demobilization and with it both uncertainty and a loss of business confidence. Commodity and security prices had slumped. Then from February 1919 through June 1920 Americans indulged themselves in a postwar buying and speculative spree. Wholesale prices rose almost 30 percent and retail prices still more. Supporting that price inflation was an expansion of the money supply, both in credit and in cash, without parallel in any earlier period. From June 1918 to June 1920 American bank loans increased from $22.4 billion to $30.8 billion, a 40 percent expansion in a mere 2 years. Currency in circulation increased from $4.5 billion to $5.5 billion.

The Federal Reserve Board made no effort to restrain that boom, which was followed by a brief slump in the spring and summer of 1920. Therefore it was sharply criticized for both the earlier inflation and the later recession. The wholesale price index fell 45 percent, industrial production 30 percent and factory employment 25 percent. The Federal Reserve System's gold position and prevailing monetary conditions abroad also enforced recognition of the differences between its current problems and those of earlier central banks. It was compelled to face the need to develop policies and practices to replace the quasi-automatic operation of the international gold standard Great Britain had managed until 1914. Though the Federal Reserve System had subsequently become more free, it had also acquired more problems. One result was a deliberate effort, for the first time in monetary history, to preserve balance in international payments and to prevent or moderate financial crises. That was a major step toward assumption by the American government of responsibility for economic stability. We now simply assume that in both good times and bad the Federal Reserve Board will use the monetary tools at its disposal to affect business cycles. In 1920, however, those techniques had not yet been developed.

Recovery from the postwar slump began toward the end of 1921, owing in part to an underlying factor new in American experience. By 1920 the monetary gold stock of the United States had risen to $2.8 billion. As more European capital fled to the safety of the United States, as Europeans began to liquidate some of their wartime debts, and as they continued to purchase commodities only the United States could supply, its gold stock jumped to $4.5 billion in 1924. That increase, of some 250 percent since 1914, symbolized the basic change that had occurred in world power relationships. Because of changes since 1914 in the banking system of the United States, which permitted a greater credit expansion for a given amount of gold, that increase in its gold stocks would give the United States a decade of comparatively easy money and low long-term interest rates.

On June 9, 1919, the United States had removed its prohibition on gold exports. Though some gold had been exported thereafter, Treasury and Federal Reserve officials considered resumption of gold payments politically and financially expedient, to make known the enhanced power of the United States. Unhappily, when Governor Strong of the New York Federal Reserve Bank visited Europe that summer, he was disconcerted to find no gratitude for the help the United States had given. Instead he learned that American assistance had been taken for granted, and more was expected. He reported to Washington that he discerned

> a feeling that the Allies have made the great and most vital sacrifices in the war, both of men and finance and in material damages suffered; that our losses have been slight and our profits immense, and that the existence of this great debt due on demand is a sword of Damocles hanging over their heads.

On every European exchange, including those in Geneva and Zürich, the dollar commanded a premium. Distraught Europeans had begun to believe that only the dollar was a real gold currency, with free coinage provided and no restrictions on either import or export of gold. Since the United States had resumed specie payments in 1879, gold's price had appeared to be a constant $20.67183 per fine ounce.[10] Therefore the American dollar seemed to be the hardest and most desirable of currencies, and until 1925 it would serve as the worldwide standard against which other currencies would fluctuate in varying degrees.

Those years of dollar supremacy displeased the bankers of London, who were anxious to regain the dominant position in world finance they had held until 1914. British policies had therefore been assuming a return to the gold standard at the earliest possible time as an essential step in the restoration of British prestige and trade abroad. Before retiring as Governor of the Bank of England, Lord Walter Cunliffe had chaired a committee appointed by the British Treasury in January 1918 "to consider the various problems which will arise in connection with the currency and the foreign exchanges during the period of reconstruction and report upon the steps required to bring about the restoration of normal conditions in due course." Throughout that committee's discussions it had simply assumed that Great Britain would return to the gold standard at the prewar parity of the pound. No one had questioned that assumption or had proposed alternative gold-standard parities or gold-standard policies.

The Cunliffe committee had expected the transition to normal monetary

---

[10] That was deceptive. Increased wartime production costs had caused clamor by American producers for passage of the McFadden Gold Bonus Bill of March 1920, under which a premium or bonus of $10 per ounce was paid thereafter to American producers upon delivery of their newly mined gold at the mint. Brown, *England and the New Gold Standard,* p. 23.

conditions to take some 10 years. Its concern had been to recommend means for successfully concluding that period with the exchange rate of the pound at its prewar gold parity and with the operation of the Bank Act of 1844 restored in its essentials. That meant amalgamation of the Treasury note issues with those of the Bank of England and a central reserve of some £150 million in gold. Both the committee and the expert witnesses it had summoned had accepted the need for postwar deflation to some unknown extent. They had also recognized that the process of deflation would be difficult, with the need for postwar conversion of industry and the pressures for changes in social policies. Nevertheless they had hoped that restoration of the pound's prewar parity might be eased by further inflation in the United States. Subsequently they were quite disappointed to observe that the Federal Reserve Board was not following prewar British gold-standard rules. The United States did not expand credit or experience consequent domestic inflation as much as it could have with the increased gold reserves at its disposal. Instead the Federal Reserve Board continued its unorthodox, ungentlemanly practice of calculating the extent of credit expansion desired and "freezing" excess gold reserves.

The Cunliffe committee had not considered the radical political changes that had occurred since 1844 while Great Britain's creditor classes had been gradually losing control. Creditors have always been pleased and served by mild deflation. By 1918, however, British debtors had not only gained the vote but had also lost their subservience toward creditors. Nor had the blundering of British governments throughout the First World War enhanced their prestige among workmen, who had learned to observe and think for themselves. Though deflationary policies were recognized and accepted as necessary by trade unions in other countries, such as Sweden, they were hotly resented by British workers. Increased direct taxes had also made the British public aware for the first time that the costs of Empire were high and had previously been paid by indirect taxation that fell most heavily on the poor. Some postwar conditions were foreseen by the Cunliffe committee. They were aware that the pound had become overvalued, but they were uncertain by how much. They were also unsure about how long it would take to convert from a wartime regime of pegged exchange rates maintained by foreign borrowing, official restrictions and intervention to a system based on gold and no controls. Only time and experiments could determine the correct decisions, and the first few tests were discouraging.

On March 20, 1919, when official exchange support ended, the pound began to depreciate from its wartime pegged rate of $4.76 until it reached a low of $3.40 in February 1920. British national pride was severely jolted, and London's newspapers were indignant about the seeming loss in prestige. On April 1, 1919, official regulations under the Defence of the Realm Act had prohibited gold exports without official permission, and for the first time the public had become aware that Great Britain had in fact left the gold standard. In July 1919 the Bank of England had also held a trial sale of 50,000 ounces of gold on the London market, where it had fetched £4.13s.4d. per ounce, roughly a 20 percent premium over the official price of £3.17s.9d. Finally, in the course of 1919, most of the remaining economic controls were removed, and Great Britain enjoyed a brief postwar boom that broke in the spring of 1920. The recession that followed caused severe discontent not only among workers but also among those British whose sympathies had been strongly stirred by the difficulties war veterans were experiencing in their efforts to readjust to civilian life. Because their complaints were not heeded by the Bank of England, resentment grew toward its private owners. By December 1922 the wholesale price index stood at 64.5 percent of its 1918 level. The cost-of-living index had fallen to 79.1 percent. Unemployment among trade union members had averaged 2.4 percent in 1919 and 1920 and then jumped to 15.2 percent in 1922. Labor unrest began that has disturbed the British economy ever since. In due time it would play a part in the disintegration of the British Empire.

That postwar recession persuaded many British economists and most Labour or Liberal politicians that deflation was an unmitigated evil and that inflation must always be tolerated, to benefit the least skilled workers and the least provident citizens of Great Britain. Among those poor the illusion was spreading that the British Empire was so rich it could and should provide for all the needs of all its citizens. Nevertheless by 1922 the British government had achieved some significant improvements in its financial position. Its expenditures had fallen almost 60 percent, while its revenues had risen 27 percent. The deficit of £1.7 billion in financial year 1918–1919 had been transformed into surpluses of £238 million in 1920–1921, £46 million in 1921–1922, and £102 million in 1922–1923. By 1922 the Bank of England had also regained control of London's financial markets, and limitations had been imposed on its issues of fiduciary notes. At the end of 1922 the exchange rate of the pound rose to $4.63, a cheering improvement that lifted the spirits of London's bankers, proud that their currency could once again "look the dollar in the eye." Yet Great Britain had almost reached the limits of "self-help." The Bank of England was forced to await settlement of war debts and reparations claims, which were troubling all European exchanges. They strongly affected sterling, because a large part of the payments to the United States passed through the London exchange.[11]

Those war debts were severely worsening relations among all the former Allies. The largest owed £1.67 billion to the United States, including £800

[11] Moggridge, *British Monetary Policy 1924–1931,* pp. 17–28.

million by Great Britain, £485 million by France and £275 million by Italy. In turn a total of £1.45 billion was owed to Great Britain, including £390 million by France, £390 million by Italy and £520 million by Russia. The Kerensky government had lightened Russian indebtedness by shipping 200 million gold rubles to London in July of 1917, but that had been the last. And a total of £365 million was owed to France, including £160 million by Russia, £90 million by Belgium and £35 million by Italy. The British and French official indignation aroused by the advent of Lenin's Bolsheviks should be quite understandable. It appeared doubtful that those creditors of Russia would ever recover a penny of the sums they had lent. And there had been many pleas by the small Allied and Associated powers for the forgiveness of all war debts. The United States and Great Britain would then have become the losers in a major way. All others, including France, would have gained. Needless to add, neither the United States nor Great Britain was disposed to forget those debts. By stalling, however, the debtor nations did make it obvious that disentanglement and settlement of that network of inter-ally indebtedness would depend on receipts of reparations payments from Germany. If Germany could not or would not pay, neither would France, Italy and many lesser powers.

When Germany requested a moratorium, in December 1921, the world's financial relations reached deadlock.

RETURN TO A REVISED GOLD STANDARD

The most heated of those war-debt disputes had arisen between the British and the French on the settlement of wartime gold transfers and postwar dollar balances. To the British government it seemed that only the United States could cut that Gordian knot, because it had become the world's largest creditor. There were many private appeals to Washington, to apply some common sense with a heavy hand.[12]

On February 9, 1922, the United States Congress created the American Debt Funding Commission, which functioned for the next 5 years. It was chaired by the conservative Republican Andrew Mellon, Secretary of the Treasury. Though a rich man who regarded inflation and speculation as equally distasteful diseases, Mellon had never been a student of economics. Strong had been obliged to brief him thoroughly on the mechanics of the prewar gold standard. Neither Mellon nor Strong chose to respect the ancient traditions of the Bank of England and the Bank of France. The remaining members of that Commission were the Secretary of State, Charles Evans Hughes; the Secretary of Commerce, Herbert Hoover; and five Senators and

[12] Harris, *Monetary Problems of the British Empire,* pp. 301–324.

Congressmen. Late in 1922 Stanley Baldwin, then Chancellor of the Exchequer, arrived in Washington. An agreement was reached to convert Great Britain's entire debt into bonds totaling $4.6 billion, bearing interest at 3 percent for the first 10 years and at 3½ percent thereafter. Both in Great Britain and in the United States British sympathizers began a long, unsuccessful campaign to cancel those debts.

French resistance to repayment was more stubborn. It extended even to payment of some $400 million the French owed for surplus war materiel bought from the United States after the war. Every device was used by the French government to evade all payments to the United States. The entire French Chamber of Deputies rose to applaud when one of its members angrily protested that: "While war still raged, statesmen in every country appealed to the common cause. Some gave their ships, some their money, and today only those who gave money come saying to us: 'Give us back what we loaned.'" The Department of State, not impressed by such emotional appeals, banned any further American public or private loans to France until those debts were settled.[13] Much subsequent grief would have been forestalled if that department had permanently banned all further American loans to France. However, on April 29, 1926, earlier French debts to the United States were at last funded at $4.025 billion, with annual payments ranging from an initial $20 million to $113 million in the final 62nd year. By February 1927 Mellon's Commission had compounded the original debts of some $11.5 billion with the thirteen principal wartime debtors of the United States. All those agreements were later ratified by their governments.

The Department of State was conducting many sensitive negotiations in those years. Because the United States Senate had refused to ratify the Treaty of Versailles, the immediate problem had been peace. Separate American treaties had been signed with Austria on August 24, Germany on August 25 and Hungary on August 29, 1921. All had accepted American war claims. More far-reaching had been the problem of naval armaments. Though the German and Russian fleets had vanished, both Great Britain and Japan had been maintaining large, growing navies that did not appear to have any potential enemies anywhere. Secretary Hughes had therefore sought a conference on limitation of naval armaments that had begun in Washington on November 12, 1921. The naval treaty that had followed had temporarily ended competition among the major powers in the construction of capital warships. Relations with the Soviet Union had also received considerable attention.

Because the United States had not become a member of the League of Nations, it declined to participate in the League's Genoa Conference, held in

---

[13] Feis, *The Diplomacy of the Dollar,* pp. 18–24.

the spring of 1922 primarily to seek a basis for recognizing the Soviet Union. Many Europeans had been vainly hoping that somehow it might be possible to reconstruct their ravaged Continent by improving trade with the Soviet Union. Few who attended that Conference had sufficient common sense to ask how a Soviet Union ruined by war and revolution could be expected to pay for imports of Europe's manufactures, either with cash, securities or its former agricultural surpluses, when the Russian people were not only bankrupt but starving. However, in nearby Rapallo, the Germans and the Russians did agree to resume normal relations and to cancel all claims against each other. In exchange for German technology and equipment the Soviet Union also began secretly to provide the German Army several training areas for testing tanks and techniques of armored warfare.

On monetary questions, resolutions presented at the Genoa Conference served as the basis for reconstruction of monetary systems in years that followed. It is a curious characteristic of human behavior that institutions functioning reasonably well are taken for granted until they have decayed or been wrecked beyond repair. Then there is a public outcry, and frantic, futile efforts to rebuild them. So it was in the 1920s with the international gold standard. The mass of literature on that monetary standard, describing it with lavish praise and attention to detail, was published in the 1920s. The theory could be simply stated. If prices rose unduly in one country, its balance of trade would become unfavorable. Then it would be exposed to a drain of gold reserves, with consequent contraction of domestic credit and currency in circulation. Those pressures on price levels would be sufficient to restore the old price equilibrium. On the other hand a country receiving gold imports on an unduly large scale would experience a rise in prices that would tend to counteract the import of gold. Thus the system would promote general stabilization, including both a suitable adjustment of the price levels in the different countries and a rational distribution of the world's monetary stock of gold. Moreover those results would be attained by machinery working automatically and in no need of being "managed."

This automatic functioning of the gold standard was looked upon both by experts and by the public as its principal strength, because exclusion of all kinds of political influences on the monetary system was held to be of primary importance. Central bankers have always distrusted politicians, having so frequently been given sound reasons to do so. Nevertheless the experts assembled in Genoa should have been reminded of Walter Bagehot's famous remark: "Money will not manage itself." Someone must do it. Far better that it be managed in the full light of day, rather than in the shadows inhabited by central bankers. In reality the prewar gold standard had never functioned automatically. Before 1914, central banks had frequently intervened in the markets to affect the exchange rates of their currencies and to control the import or export of gold. The supposed "automaticity" of that gold standard was merely a pretext used in 1922 by central bankers anxious to foil the politicians who were seeking to interfere with their deflationary policies.

Where nostalgia was so strong for the era of easy international relations that had ended in 1914, it should be understandable that the merits of the old gold standard were exaggerated. After a decade of political and economic turmoil, both the rich and the poor of Europe were frantic. They grasped at every straw of hope, and every quack offering a panacea found a ready audience. Most Europeans were convinced that their sadly depreciated national currencies would somehow miraculously regain lost purchasing power if only the gold standard could be revived. A few experts pointed out the weaknesses of that prewar system and explained the difficulties of constructing any system based on gold when its distribution among the central banks of the major trading powers had changed so radically. Theoretically it had become possible to form a new system based entirely on paper. However, after a decade of excessive inflation in their national currencies, the peoples of Europe would not have accepted it. Both public and private bankers urged return to gold, and British politicians such as Winston Churchill valued it for political purposes, because gold had knitted together the power and prestige of the British Empire.[14]

The Genoa Conference, whose monetary committee was led by the British delegation, therefore recommended that all nations should return to a gold standard. Only two caveats were recorded, namely, that suitable gold parities be chosen and that a "gold-economizing program" be employed. Most experts at Genoa agreed on a "gold-exchange standard" that would permit both gold and currencies directly convertible into gold to be used as national reserve assets.[15] Thus the British obtained international acceptance for continuing the circulation of sterling notes beyond the borders of the British Empire. The official concern of the United States was later expressed in a letter Governor Strong wrote to Secretary Mellon on May 27, 1924. He emphasized that

> Our own interests demand that no effort be spared to return to the gold standard, and so arrest the flood of gold which threatens in time to plunge us into inflation. We now hold one-half of the world's monetary gold, and our holdings increase steadily.

Strong knew how to stir Mellon into action.

Intervening political events in Europe had drastically increased the need to restore some stability in the exchange rates of its currencies. When Germany

[14] Grigg, *Prejudice and Judgement,* p. 184.
[15] Cassel, *The Downfall of the Gold Standard,* pp. 26–34.

had defaulted on its reparations payments to France, its credit abroad had vanished and the mark had begun to depreciate at a rate that became astronomical. To collect the payments France claimed, in January 1923 Poincaré had sent the French Army into Germany to occupy the Ruhr, the heart of German industry. In the Rhineland the Director of Finances of the French High Commission was young Edmond Giscard, who had considered it politic to take the name of the ancient, extinct family Estaing. Giscard busied himself on behalf of French interests, urging Rhineland separatists to establish a note-issuing central bank of their own, independent of the Reichsbank and supported by a French banking syndicate led by the Banque de Paris et des Pays-Bas.

Those events proved to be the turning point. Though the French public continued to believe Poincaré's rash promises that Germany could and would be compelled to pay, the spectacle of French troops committing armed robbery on German banks swung world opinion against France. Bad winners cannot command lasting respect. Nor were the Germans themselves slow to exploit their new advantage. In the winter and spring of 1923 there were many private talks between the Germans and the British, and gradually Great Britain began to withdraw its support from France. The British had been among the first to grasp what became known as the "transfer problem." Though it was easy to demand that Germany should pay up, it could do so only by taxation within Germany. The sums thus raised could be transmitted to other countries only in gold or in goods. German marks could be spent only in Germany, and vast exports of German products meant more severe competition for all other exporting countries. The higher the reparations payments France and Great Britain demanded from Germany, the more harshly they penalized their own manufacturers, and damaged the French and British workers who produced their own exports.

In November 1923 Hjalmar Schacht was appointed a special Currency Commissioner by the German Finance Ministry and given the responsibility for achieving stabilization of the mark. Since 1919 many reform schemes had been proposed. Schacht's had varied merits, which included shrewd presentation at the right time to the right people. At the height of the unrest and disorder accompanying hyperinflation, on November 8 an obscure Austrian housepainter and former corporal named Adolf Hitler attempted a "beerhouse revolt" in Munich. Schacht proposed a monetary system related to gold, on grounds that in the peculiar circumstances of 1923 Germany could obtain the commodities it needed from foreign suppliers only by payment in gold or in strong currencies. To finance that foreign trade, he therefore proposed formation of a new bank, the Gold Discount Bank, to be managed by the Reichsbank. Part of the Gold Discount Bank's initial capital consisted of foreign currencies raised within Germany, and Schacht also obtained a sterling loan from the Bank of England at the generous interest rate of 5 percent. He never forgot that friendly gesture by Montagu Norman, its new Governor. Until 1945 the Gold Discount Bank continued to serve as Germany's central bank for financing international trade.

To meet domestic monetary needs, Schacht devised the Rentenmark, backed by mortgages on the whole of German landed property, so that in theory any given sum in Rentenmarks could be exchanged at any time for an equal sum in mortgage bonds. At the time he commented

> The issue of money on the security of the soil is, in fact, a phenomenon which recurs at intervals in the economic history of the world. The paper money of John Law based on the soil, the *mandats territoriaux* of the French Revolution, and the attempt to underpin the Danish Reichsbank by the handing over of a 6 percent charge on the value of all immovable property in the year 1813, constitute the principal—all more or less unsuccessful—forerunners of the Rentenmark.

Though Schacht's knowledge of history was imperfect, his understanding of the German people was sound.

To the chagrin of the French the new Rentenmark was an immediate success. All German officials concerned cooperated fully to establish it, and therein lay one of the primary reasons for their successful accomplishment of so vital a reform. Theoretically the Rentenmark was equivalent to the gold mark, though the latter was available only at the Gold Discount Bank for officially approved payments abroad. Payments in Rentenmarks were therefore calculated at the current exchange rate of the gold mark or the American dollar on the Berlin Bourse. By a useful coincidence, on the day that reform was inaugurated, November 20, 1923, the official rate was 4 trillion 2 billion (4,002,000,000,000) marks to one American dollar, whereas the pre-1914 exchange rate had been 4.20 marks to the dollar.

With the Rentenmark's prestige enhanced by its supposed relationship to gold and the dollar, the conversion of old marks into new Rentenmarks began at the rate of 1 trillion old to 1 Rentenmark. On German exchanges the Rentenmark was publicly quoted at 1 gold mark or $10/42$ dollar. At the time there were 133 printing offices and 1783 machines that had been producing notes for the Reichsbank or the German Printing Office. More than thirty paper factories had been working full time, exclusively for the Reichsbank. Issue of the new Rentenmark was rigorously controlled, the Reichsbank recovering the exclusive power to issue notes in Germany. Thereafter all issues of *Notgeld,* or emergency money, were forbidden. Concurrently the Finance Minister, Hans Luther, began the task of balancing Germany's budget and ceased to demand credit from the Reichsbank. Those government demands for credit had always been by far the largest source of inflation. Germany's money, its credit, and its commerce at home and abroad, began to recover. [16]

Because Germany had apparently returned to a stable mark based on gold at the prewar parity, it seemed important not only to immediate neighbors and trading partners but also to all major world competitors that they should do so too, if only for reasons of national prestige. Within the next few years most countries therefore returned to a gold standard, though in forms quite different from that known until 1914. In 1923–1924 even Russia successfully stabilized its currency and hypothetically related it to gold. Yet the decisive step to exclude gold coinage from further circulation was taken when Great Britain hastened in April 1925 to return to gold, much earlier than the Cunliffe committee had anticipated. British notes were restored to their pre-war gold parity, and rules were drafted to guarantee that parity thereafter. However, the centuries-old obligation of the Bank of England to redeem its notes in gold coin was discarded. Instead that Bank's obligation was to sell gold bullion at a fixed maximum price. Anyone who wanted gold from the Bank of England had to arrange considerable transport and insurance, because the minimum conversion permitted was 400 ounces. That did indeed deter domestic demand and discouraged runs on the Bank's gold reserves by the average British citizen or foreign depositor in London. More than a century late, Ricardo's advice had been taken.

Because most nations had habitually looked to London for guidance on monetary policies, the new British rules provided a model for many others to follow. Only Switzerland continued to argue in international conferences for restoration of gold coinage, primarily to reassure those disgruntled Swiss citizens who had been damaged by wartime inflation or by loss of investments in sadly depreciated currencies such as the German Reichsmark or the Austrian crown.[17]

After the Genoa Conference the French franc had also begun the familiar, progressive deterioration. Finding themselves in constant financial embarrassment, successive French governments had resorted to deliberate inflation of their currency. The note circulation of the Bank of France had increased from 36.4 billion francs at the end of 1922 to 56 billion in July 1926. The general price index rose from 327 in 1922 to 703 in 1926. It reached a high of 837 in July of the latter year. That domestic deterioration of the franc was reflected in its value on the foreign exchanges. The annual average quotation in New York fell from 8.20 cents in 1922 to 3.24 cents in 1926. In July 1926

[16] Schacht, *My First Seventy-Six Years,*, pp. 177–206.
[17] See Cassel, *Postwar Monetary Stabilization;* and Jack, *The Restoration of European Currencies;* passim.

it dropped to a low of 2.06 cents. After that collapse Premier Poincaré forced through the recalcitrant Chamber of Deputies new measures to stabilize the franc at a rate of 3.92 cents. And in June 1928 France returned to a "gold-bullion standard" at that parity. Thus the franc's par was reduced to only slightly more than 20 percent of its prewar value.

So radical a cut in the parity of the franc was received with intense dissatisfaction by a nation of habitual savers. Hundreds of thousands of the French bourgeoisie lost 80 percent of the value of their wartime investments in the *bons pour la défense nationale* and became embittered toward their republican governments. Poincaré was compelled to promise them that subsequently the gold value of their paper franc would be increased. Patriots had been penalized and suspicious hoarders of gold rewarded, because its value in francs had quintupled. The French propensity to hoard gold became intense. As a symbol of national prestige, the franc had been badly battered. Chauvinists were outraged, because the mark, the pound and the dollar appeared to retain their pre-1914 value, whereas the franc had not.

Yet in Great Britain exporters were complaining that they had been unnecessarily burdened by return to the gold standard at the old parity of the pound, whereas the French had gained an export advantage by undervaluing their franc. British manufacturers began to demand protection. To all appearances the international gold standard had been strengthened by the return of France. Yet the actual result would be the contrary. The old easy cooperation among European central banks had disappeared. The French yearning for security caused a greedy pursuit of gold by the Bank of France. Huge and growing national gold reserves reassured not only French citizens but also French bankers and monetary experts that their economy was still strong and could rank with the German and the British. Such appearances had so often proved frivolous that foreign observers were mystified by the faith the French so solemnly placed in them.

In the Far East there had been similar though lesser disorders. In 1917 Japan had imposed an embargo on gold exports. Like so many former debtor nations, it had concerned itself solely with importing far more gold than it needed. Loyal to the prewar rules of the international gold standard, it had hugely expanded domestic credit, and the natural consequence had been severe inflation. Even after the earthquake of September 1923 had compelled harsh reviews of Japanese monetary policies, that embargo had remained in place. The gold reserves of the Bank of Japan rose to an excessive 1.1 billion yen. At length Japan returned to the gold standard in 1929 and relaxed its embargo on gold exports. More placidly the Chinese had continued to cling with the utmost conservatism to their ancient silver standard. For several millennia their tradition had been to settle transactions once a year, at the end of the year by the lunar calendar. The accounts thus settled at the

Chinese New Year, and consequent Chinese demand for silver, were so large that its price tended to rise all over the world at that season. Because China produced no silver of its own, it was entirely dependent on foreign suppliers.

BREAKDOWN

At an annual meeting of the American Historical Association, in December 1922, Secretary of State Hughes had presented a plan for solution of the reparations problem. He had suggested that it be turned over to financial experts and thus divorced from politics as much as possible. On September 12, 1923, the governments of Great Britain, Belgium and Italy had accepted, but France had hesitated for some time. Though willing to discuss Germany's ability to pay, Poincaré was not willing to discuss French occupation of the Ruhr or to allow French rights and claims under the Treaty of Versailles to be questioned. Eventually, however, the Allied Reparations Committee agreed in November 1923 to name two committees of experts. The first was to study balancing the German budget and restoring its currency, and the second was to evaluate German wealth abroad and its possible recovery. Charles G. Dawes was the American member named to the former committee, and Owen D. Young to the latter.

The Dawes Report subsequently accepted by both Germany and the former Allies provided among other features that Germany should pay on a progressive basis, beginning with 1 billion marks in the first year. A foreign loan of 800 million gold marks was also provided, to establish a gold reserve for the new German currency and to enable Germany to meet its immediate obligations abroad. Thus began the extraordinary practice that would continue throughout the 1920s, as the United States and others loaned to Germany most of the funds it then paid in reparations to France and to lesser beneficiaries of the Versailles Treaty. That had appeared to be the only way to disentangle the problem of war debts and reparations. Considerable efforts were made by the Dawes Committee to reconcile French and German animosities, and eventually France also agreed to withdraw from all occupied territories. The Dawes Plan reached its maximum payments schedule in 1928 without any serious difficulties, primarily because of those loans Germany was receiving from the United States. Nevertheless Germany continued to argue for its modification.

In February 1929 another committee therefore met in Paris and recommended a revised reparations program, the Young Plan. German payments were set at $9 billion, to be funded over a 58-year period. Annual installments were to rise from an initial $405 million to $524 million at the end of 10 years. The Bank for International Settlements was founded, in a shabby, bankrupt hotel in neutral Basle, to handle the instruments of settlement.

That was the beginning of formal, institutional banking cooperation among governments. The Young Plan was adopted in January 1930, and Germany also secured the evacuation of French troops from the Rhineland. Yet those disputes had been searing experiences, from which neither the Germans nor the French would recover. [18]

In October 1925 Gustav Stresemann had signed the Pact of Locarno, which had guaranteed the Franco–German border and had admitted Germany to the League of Nations. Hopeful Europeans had at last relaxed. As the major postwar battles of Europe were resolved one by one, there should have been a return to something approaching normal political and economic conditions. Yet that never occurred. Throughout the 1920s the economies of Central Europe were sustained by private American loans that were extended carelessly and used imprudently. The native investors of Central Europe had become either too impoverished or too cautious to employ their own funds for the revival of their economies. With their restraining hand removed, speculative excesses had become prevalent both in Central Europe and in New York.

By the spring of 1927 postwar growth of the American economy appeared to be nearing an end. The Federal Reserve Board therefore undertook to stimulate it by pursuing a vigorous policy of cheap money in the United States. Great Britain and France were also in need of constant help, to remain on their new gold standards. By lowering the "call rate," whose international importance had been significantly increased by the return to gold parities, the Federal Reserve Board tried not only to stimulate the American economy but also to encourage export of its excessive gold reserves. That inflationary policy succeeded only too well. Domestic recession was averted. Both American industrial production and the price of stocks on the New York markets rose. Great Britain and France were assisted.

Then the situation got out of hand. The speculation in New York became frenzied, and neither private warnings nor increases in the discount rate served to restrain the company promoters and speculators who had seized control of the New York markets. The situation worsened with the death of Governor Strong in October 1928. A struggle for power began within the Federal Reserve System, with control of speculation the principal dispute among its senior officials. A British observer of the international money markets would later comment: "With resignation the best men in the system looked forward to the inevitable smash." Their overriding concern was to deflate the American economy.

The long, postwar boom of the 1920s finally burst in October 1929, with the first of several successive crashes on the stock markets of New York. Then

[18] Dawes, *A Journal of Reparations*, passim.

began the most severe contraction of credit in American history, as both foreign and domestic investors either lost or liquidated their holdings. The extension of further American loans to Europe had already begun to slow, and it came to an abrupt halt. American balances held abroad were withdrawn, and financial conditions in European cities became difficult. An English economist named John Maynard Keynes, whose opinions had begun to receive wide circulation through the Beaverbrook newspapers, complained that Great Britain's economy should not be dependent on "that casino," the New York stock exchanges. By 1929 Great Britain should have become independent of American loans. It had not.

European banks had been holding abnormally large amounts of international short-term capital that moved from one to another as conditions of risk and opportunities for profit changed. By May 1931 Vienna had become the highest risk. There the withdrawal of capital caused by the slump had so crippled the Kredit Anstaltbank that it became unable to meet its liabilities. Its collapse was the beginning of a worldwide financial crisis. Deflation, with the growing political tension that accompanied Adolf Hitler's rise to prominence in Berlin, pointed to that city as the next highest risk. Runs began on its banks, and both American and French depositors hastened to withdraw their deposits. Vain efforts, a moratorium declared by President Herbert Hoover being only the most conspicuous, were made to stop that disintegration. On the morning of July 13th Berlin's Danat Bank closed its doors forever. The Danat had been Hjalmar Schacht's former employer, and he promptly, loudly accused its French depositors of seeking personal revenge for his many years of opposition to the reparations claims of France. The next day all the banks in Berlin except the Reichsbank were closed by decree.[19]

That foreign crisis would have had severe repercussions in London even if the domestic economy of Great Britain had been in the best possible condition. But when the run on Berlin's banks began, Great Britain's economy was already in the doldrums. Having enjoyed more than a century of the consumption habits of a creditor nation, the British had been neither willing nor able to adapt to their new status as debtors. Nor have they ever done so. And London's bankers had been slow to follow their American and French colleagues in withdrawing funds from Berlin. Thus many were caught, their assets frozen, when Berlin's banks were closed. Important London banking houses were believed to be heavily involved, international confidence in their competence having been ebbing for many years. London's foreign creditors became exceedingly nervous, and a run on sterling began. The Directors of the Bank of England were unable to stop it, because they had become part of

---

[19] Friedman and Schwartz, *A Monetary History of the United States,* pp. 240–419; and Robbins, *The Great Depression,* passim.

the rot. Montagu Norman, its Governor, was descended from long lines of Bank directors during its Victorian supremacy. Nothing had persuaded him that its importance and prestige abroad had in any way diminished. Like his grandfathers he had continued to base his decisions on intuition, rather than on statistical evidence.

The cooperation among central bankers that had become essential to the Bank of England had begun to collapse as early as 1927, when Governor Strong of the New York Federal Reserve Bank had become concerned about the singularly self-serving, shortsighted practices of Émile Moreau, who had become Governor of the Bank of France in June 1926. In the subservient tradition of Colbert, Governor Moreau was an intensely patriotic subordinate of Premier Poincaré and never hesitated to use French deposits abroad as tools with which to apply pressure on other governments. That leverage was always discreet and carefully coordinated with the political maneuvers undertaken by Poincaré. Thanks largely to the undervalued franc, France and the United States were the only major countries consistently earning large payments surpluses through those years. Therefore Moreau could and did accumulate gold and could manipulate large sums held abroad by French banks. He used the French balances in Berlin to coerce the German government whenever it became especially stubborn about reparations payments. And in July 1931 the Bank of France did encourage the withdrawal of French balances from Berlin in a deliberate effort to topple the Brüning government. Schacht was correct. Thus the Bank of France wittingly assisted Hitler's rise to power. For many years the Bank of France had also regarded French deposits in London as means with which to bind British governments to French policies and French ambitions.

Then and ever after, the New York Federal Reserve Bank would watch with suspicion and dismay that political use of French banking power. Cooperation among central banks had been close when Europe needed American help for postwar reconstruction. It had continued to exist through the prosperous years. At the first sign of serious trouble it disappeared. London had begun to suffer from heavy, frequent gold losses to Paris toward the end of 1929, and these became regular in the spring of 1930 as London's interest rate advantage lessened. The Federal Reserve Board became loath to lend further sums of gold and currencies to the Bank of England, because they would simply have been drained from it by France. While all others were striving to stop the progressively more damaging financial crises, the Bank of France was encouraging them, to serve its own immediate, political purposes.

The final attack on sterling began in late August 1931. Disturbances in the British Navy, caused by pay cuts under an emergency budget, had been magnified by the press at home and abroad into a serious mutiny. To foreign creditors the government of Great Britain appeared to be collapsing, as the republican regime of Germany indeed was. In the days following the announcement of that naval mutiny, prices on the London stock exchange began to fall sharply and continuously. Only a small part of the pressure against sterling was on official foreign account. Though central bankers were nervous, most of them refrained from withdrawing the bulk of their sterling balances. Early in September the Netherlands Bank asked the Bank of England for a gold guarantee of its sterling balances and was refused. Instead it was offered gold then and there but decided not to withdraw its funds. To the last, British officials firmly declared that sterling's gold parity had been guaranteed forever. The Dutch were therefore caught like so many others when Great Britain abandoned the gold standard and the pound began to depreciate from its gold par of $4.86. The confidence of Continental central bankers in sterling as a national reserve asset has never recovered from that shock.

As the Labour Chancellor of the Exchequer would later record, the end came "with appalling suddenness." The balancing of the British budget for which he had worked so long and had sacrificed so much support among Labour voters had been considered the key to the defense of sterling's gold parity. Yet it had been in vain. British officials were compelled to approach Paris and Washington for further loans, and hoped also to obtain permanent cancellation of war debts and reparations. From both Paris and Washington the replies were not merely discouraging but chilly. The British believed there was nothing more they could do to help themselves.

To conserve the Bank of England's remaining gold reserves, which had dwindled to £136 million by September 16, Governor Norman advised the Cabinet that the Bank should be relieved of its obligation to sell gold at a fixed price under the provisions of the Gold Standard Act of 1925. That was accepted on Sunday, September 20, and "suspension" of the gold standard was announced to the British people that same evening. Foreigners who continued to hold sterling balances in London would see their gold value reduced 30 percent by the depreciation in the exchange rate value of the pound between September 20 and the end of 1931. Others converted their pounds into dollars to obtain gold in New York.

Between September 16 and October 28, anticipating that the United States would also abandon the gold standard, both private citizens and the central bankers of France, Belgium, the Netherlands, Switzerland and Sweden began to convert their dollar assets into gold. The dumping of bills onto the New York Federal Reserve Bank assumed panic proportions. Its gold stock declined $725 million in those 6 weeks, even though it promptly raised its discount rate to 3½ percent, the sharpest increase in so brief a period that the Federal Reserve Board had ever directed. Though the United States was not compelled to leave the gold standard, cooperation between the Federal Reserve Board and the Bank of France ended abruptly. In the last 4 months of 1931 the gold reserves of the United States declined 11 percent, to their legal minimum.[20]

Both at home and abroad British prestige had received an awful jolt that has been vividly remembered ever since. Yet in Great Britain the public outcry soon disappeared as economic conditions perceptibly eased. British exporters gained a substantial competitive advantage as the pound depreciated, and unemployment lessened as exports increased. With the advantage of hindsight it is obvious that throughout the 1920s only the United States had held sufficient gold stocks, investments abroad and annual payments surpluses to manage successfully an international monetary system based on gold. Yet the United States had neither the central banking skills nor the political willingness to accept that responsibility. Nor would the Bank of England or British governments of any party have been willing to resign to New York that commanding position in world finance.

Almost three decades later a neutral Swede would comment:

> The events of 1931 and the long-drawn-out depression of the 1930s so influenced the minds of men that this period stands out as the Great Modern Divide in economic thinking, and thus also in the evolution of economic and financial policies.[21]

---

[20] See also Clarke, *Central Bank Cooperation 1924–1931*, passim.
[21] Jacobsson, *Towards a Modern Monetary Standard*, p. 1.

5 = Resort to Barter
1931–1944

Rather than admit their own follies and failures, the feckless governments of France have had a nasty habit of blaming foreigners. Though they have not been the only ones to do so, that practice explains why the French have so often found themselves friendless in times of dire need. In July 1926 an American journalist in Paris had observed that the French Treasury was empty. Billions of francs in short-term loans had fallen due and could not be paid. The franc had fallen to 50 to the American dollar, and a mob was howling outside the Chamber of Deputies, angrily criticizing the Republic for that most recent of many crises.

> Some of the rioters across the Seine on the Place de la Concorde were stoning buses full of Yankee tourists, who were held responsible, with their compatriots at home, for plotting the currency's fall (and cursed for taking advantage of it by living it up in Paris on devalued francs).[1]

THE POLITICAL DEBILITY OF FRANCE

In fact many American officials had been quietly trying to help France. They had erred only in providing the assistance specifically requested by the French, who did not know how to cure themselves and would not have taken the cure if they had known it. In 1927 the Deputy Governor of the Bank of France, Charles Rist, had visited Governor Strong in New York and the Federal Reserve Board in Washington to ask for an "easy-money policy" in

[1] Shirer, *The Collapse of the Third Republic*, p. 163.

113

the United States "as another step in their joint program of restoring and maintaining sound currencies." Low interest rates in New York encouraged capital movements to Paris, seeking higher returns there. Though that stimulated the speculative excesses in New York that would later lead to the crash in October 1929, it helped France return to the gold standard in 1928.

The Federal Reserve Board had also been urging Premier Poincaré to begin taxing the rich of France. "Why not turn to those who have more than ten billion francs in securities or gold abroad? Why not turn to your own Frenchmen?" Yet neither then nor since have French governments dared to seek substantial revenues "where the money was." Poincaré had been an exceptional figure in French history, and his massive reputation enabled him to push through the Chamber of Deputies the first tax on capital, a 7 percent levy on transfers of real property. He also gained approval for several additional, minor tax increases. But he was the lonely exception to the rule that French governments have always had to rely heavily on indirect taxation and loans to meet state expenditures. Consequently, whenever those expenses have been extraordinarily heavy, French governments have been prone to use without restraint the printing presses of their mint. Subsequent inflation, accompanied by devaluation or depreciation of the franc, has estranged conservative support at home and friends abroad.

Whenever threatened with direct taxation by any premier except Poincaré, the French bourgeoisie either buried their capital in secret hoards of gold, or smuggled it abroad, or sought to destroy their government. During the 1920s and 1930s only the application of harsh, rigid controls to banking and exchanges could have prevented those capital flights. But such controls were regarded as sacrilege by the Bank of France, whose ownership had remained in private hands. The "assembly" of its 200 largest stockholders was described by the liberal and radical press as "The Two Hundred Families of France." They were invariably successful in defending their private interests, even though they so frequently conflicted with the national interests of France.

The short-lived Poincaré recovery was therefore accomplished, not by fiscal reforms, but rather by monetary measures alone—high interest rates and an undervalued franc. Those were mere palliatives, not cures. And they harmed the neighbors of France. In the time-honored tradition of earlier French bullionists the Bank of France then used foreign trade surpluses for the single-minded purpose of building its gold reserves. On August 18, 1930, *Le Temps* exulted that "Whatever the causes of the world depression, France can face it with serenity." French gold reserves had been rising rapidly, from 5.9 billion (pre-devaluation) francs in June 1928, to 36.6 billion in June 1929, 43.9 billion in June 1930, 56.3 billion in June 1931, and 81.2 billion in June 1932. They reached a high of 83.2 billion francs in December 1932. As all

Frenchmen had known since their school days, those gold reserves were the only true measure of the financial greatness of a nation. The French were not disturbed by the outcry abroad that their obsession with gold reserves and their unwillingness to invest those surpluses abroad in long-term projects were contributing to the severe deflation in other countries.[2]

France had remained primarily an agricultural society and therefore did not suffer as severely from the depression of the 1930s as the United States, Great Britain and Germany. Nor was France dependent on exports, as Great Britain was. The undervalued franc protected French industries by discouraging imports and by giving them a competitive advantage in world markets. During the depression years unemployment seldom exceeded a half-million, and the French people continued to ignore most events abroad. Many were quite pleased by the economic plight of their erstwhite allies and enemies. When Great Britain left the gold standard in September 1931, all the Commonwealth currencies adhered to the gradually depreciating pound. World commodities, priced in sterling, began to fall. French imports became cheaper. Another twenty-five currencies left the gold standard and were devalued within the next year, including the Scandinavian crowns and the Japanese yen.

After September 1931 only France, Belgium, the Netherlands, Switzerland, Italy, South Africa and the United States retained their classic pre-1914 gold parities and freedom of foreign exchange markets. French monetary experts and the French public therefore believed themselves to be among the small minority of those who had remained "pure," untainted by monetary heresies that had probable Bolshevik origins. French commentators described themselves as "salamanders who might walk through fire with impunity," because they had continued to defend the gold standard stoutly. On September 22, 1931, Le Figaro commented:

> The national pride of Great Britain is certainly humbled. The prestige of the City has been weakened . . . The English crisis enhances the prestige of the franc.

And that same day, Le Temps exulted:

> Because of the fortunate equilibrium of the French economy, and the virtues of our people . . . France has become one of the two pillars that now sustain the world economy.[3]

Harking back to Napoleonic traditions, many of the French had become absorbed in Central European affairs. In those years France was not led by its elected representatives and the unstable governments they so often overturned. The elections of 1928 had returned a conservative Chamber of Depu-

[2] Wolfe, *The French Franc between the Wars 1919–1939*, pp. 83–102.
[3] Sauvy, *Histoire économique de la France entre les deux guerres (1918–1939)*, vol 2, pp. 15–27.

ties, and Poincaré's resignation in July of 1929 had ended an era of political stability. In the 17 months that had followed, five cabinets had been overthrown. There was no consistent parliamentary majority for any policy or any cabinet, and any pretext served the Chamber or the Senate to throw out any government that pretended to have any ideas of its own. None of them remained in office long enough to cope with any crisis.

Continuity in French policies was therefore provided by the conservative, permanent officials of the Finance Ministry, the Foreign Ministry and the Bank of France—men such as Edmond Giscard, who had just published a rash book on *Capital*. Chastened by events he had not foreseen, he was writing an unhappy sequel entitled *La maladie du monde*, to be published in 1933. Somewhat more mature, and much less revolutionary in his aims, he now had a son named Valéry, born in Koblenz during French occupation of the Rhineland. He also had a daughter, Sylvie, whom he would later marry to a descendant of the first Napoleon's biographer on the isle of St. Helena. Like the Bonapartes, Giscard was fascinated by the wreckage of the old Holy Roman Empire of the Habsburgs. Before and after declaration of the Hoover Moratorium in July 1931 there had been a wave of bankruptcies throughout Central Europe. In those "succession states," central banks had been drained of gold and foreign currency reserves. Exchanges had been paralyzed, and agricultural prices had collapsed. Debtors were defaulting on loans from Parisian banks. Economic disorders had been quickly followed by political agitation. French officials therefore asked the British government to convene an international monetary conference, to devise concerted measures for salvaging French interests in those Central European and Balkan nations where so many earlier troubles had begun.

The French finance minister of the day, a conservative Anglophile named Flandin, would later describe French plans in some detail:

> France, friend and protector of the Little Entente (Czechoslovakia, Rumania and Jugoslavia), relied upon the political statute created by the Treaties of 1919. Faithful to its policy of consolidating the Treaty of Versailles, it sought to reinforce the territorial *status quo* in order to re-establish the confidence necessary for capital investments. . . . It proposed to revive the commercial exchanges among the Danubian states by a preferential customs system. . . . But the essential assumption of the problem being political as always, it was necessary first to give a political base to financial and economic solutions.[4]

For the first time since 1918 French ambitions in Central Europe were being challenged. Mussolini's Italy had become a rival with pronounced imperial intentions. Since 1925 Mussolini had also been spending Italian gold reserves abroad to buy the most modern weapons and munitions. In those Danubian

[4] Flandin, *Politique française 1919–1940*, pp. 97–99.

"protectorates" of France the Italians were "prudently" supporting the clamor for revision of the Versailles Treaty. France therefore needed not only
the financial cooperation but also the political support of its former allies,
Great Britain and the United States.

Because the United States had never signed the Versailles Treaty of 1919,
it had never recognized the legality of French "protection" and direction of
the policies followed by the governments of the succession states. Both Flandin and the French Foreign Ministry had been quite displeased to observe
the growing American sympathy and support for the Central Europeans who
had been urging revision of that Versailles Treaty.

DEVALUATION OF THE DOLLAR

To oblige the French, in May 1932 the British government approached the
United States to ask for its views of the proposed monetary conference. The
reply from Washington was favorable, provided always that war debts to the
United States were not included in the discussions. In reality, however, the
circumstances had turned against diplomacy. Effective monetary cooperation
between the United States and Great Britain was impossible while the former
remained on the gold standard and sought salvation in continuing deflation,
and the latter adapted itself to a depreciating sterling standard. Moreover
President Hoover no longer had any sympathy whatever for the ambitions of
France.

There was no doubt about Hoover's steadfast loyalty to the gold standard
or about his thorough understanding of Europe. As a prominent mining engi-
neer, in 1917 he had helped a young Englishman named Ernest Oppenheimer to obtain from Messrs. Morgan of New York the financing needed to found
the Anglo American Corporation, which would later become the largest producer of South African gold. Oppenheimer had been introduced to Hoover
by British Treasury officials, who had found J. Pierpont Morgan their most
loyal ally among the bankers of New York.[5] In 1918–1920 Hoover had seen
Europe at its worst, through his work for the American Relief Administration
and his attendance at the Versailles Conference. Later he had carefully read
Keynes's tract on *The Economic Consequences of the Peace.* Both as Secretary of
Commerce and as a member of the American Debt Funding Commission, he
had obtained first-hand experience with the problem of war debts and reparations.

In 1932, however, Hoover was not in command of American monetary
policies. He had inherited Mellon from two earlier Republican administrations. As Hoover would later describe that situation:

[5] Gregory, *Ernest Oppenheimer,* p. 87.

the "leave-it-alone liquidationists" headed by Secretary of the Treasury Mellon
. . . felt that government must keep its hands off and let the slump liquidate
itself. Mr. Mellon had only one formula: "Liquidate labor, liquidate stocks,
liquidate the farmers, liquidate real estate." He insisted that, when the people
get an inflationary brainstorm, the only way to get it out of their blood is to let
it collapse. He held that even a panic was not altogether a bad thing. He said:
"It will purge the rottenness out of the system. High costs of living and high
living will come down. People will work harder, live a more moral life. Values
will be adjusted, and enterprising people will pick up the wrecks from less competent people."[6]

Within limits Mellon was right, but he had become an extremist. His haugh-
ty disregard for the economic distress of so many millions of his fellow citizens
was souring an entire generation of young American economists on the merits
of prudence in public finance. Quite unlike the French, when the American
rich became overbearing and ignored the welfare of the less fortunate, they
could simply be voted out of office.

President Hoover had additional reasons for being wary of any monetary
conference with France. In 1930 Henry Stimson, his Secretary of State, had
headed the American delegation to a naval disarmament conference at which
French intransigence had been notably troublesome. Though Stimson was a
calm, patient man, Hoover was not. A recent French historian has commented: "Disconcerted by the impulsive character and by the finesse of Briand,
Hoover manifested the most total incomprehension of the French attitude."[7]
It would be more accurate, if less diplomatic, to say that Hoover compre-
hended the French only too well and considered them stubborn fools. He had
been further exasperated when he had proposed the debts-reparations moratorium on June 20, 1931. Then the immediate problem had been to obtain
the agreement of France, which had been receiving 52 percent of all German
reparations payments. It had taken more than 2 weeks, in the heat of summer, to placate the French. The most delicate negotiations in Paris and hectic
discussions in Washington had been required. Under Secretary of State Castle and Under Secretary of the Treasury Mills had lost their tempers with
each other, and Hoover had raged against both of them. At last, on July 6,
the 17th day of negotiations, the French had signed, and a 1-year suspension
in payment of all debts and reparations had gone into effect. Largely because
of French delays that measure had been almost too late. The German banking system had moved on toward disaster, and only imposition of the most
stringent exchange controls had prevented another collapse of the German
mark.[8]

[6] Hoover, *Memoirs,* vol. 3, p. 30.

[7] Duroselle, *De Wilson à Roosevelt,* p. 220

[8] Bemis, *The American Secretaries of State and Their Diplomacy,* vol. 11, pp. 205–218.

Moreover, at the Lausanne Conference held by the League of Nations in June and July 1932, which the United States did not attend, the European creditors of Germany magnanimously agreed to write off more than 90 percent of Germany's $25 billion in reparations owing to them, contingent upon corresponding cuts in their war debts to the United States. Well aware that Congress would be furious, Hoover bluntly refused. Europeans then blandly ignored him. To his considerable shock Hoover found that the Federal government was not the only victim of that European hostility. American private investors were losing approximately $2.225 billion in loans to Germany, and American private bankers were losing another $1.7 billion in Central European trade bills. By 1934 there would be total or partial defaults on 32 percent of American-owned foreign bonds.

Beginning in December 1932, at a politically opportune moment, the nations that had owed war debts to the United States began to default. France was the first to do so. The Herriot government, which had intended to continue payment of those French debts, was overthrown on that question even though it otherwise had a large majority in the Chamber of Deputies. Great Britain also made its last debt payments. The United States Attorney General rejected as a breach of treaty the British offer to continue only token payments. After December 1932, tiny Finland was alone in continuing to pay its debts to the United States. Ever after, the Finns would be honored guests at the United States Treasury. Americans became firmly convinced that Europeans were corrupt and immoral.

So long as Herbert Hoover remained President, neither the French nor the British had the slightest chance of obtaining any financial or political concessions from the United States. Between August 1931 and March 1933 the index of American prices fell from 72 to 60. Regardless of that severe deflation at home, officials in Washington became convinced that the British were gaining an unfair trading advantage from the continuing depreciation of the pound. The pound–dollar exchange rate had fallen from the old gold parity of $4.86 to $3.28 by November 1932, when the do-nothing Mellon was swept from Washington by a landslide defeat of the Republican Party. President Hoover followed him into oblivion.

The new President-elect was Franklin Roosevelt, a patrician New Yorker who owed nothing to its bankers. One of his first diplomatic gestures was to send a smiling invitation to Ramsay MacDonald, the British Labour Prime Minister, to visit Washington for preliminary discussion of matters that might arise at a world economic conference. As usual the British were tardy. Surrounded by his "brains trust," Roosevelt also began privately in December 1932 to discuss devaluation of the dollar with a wide variety of interested parties. He persisted, regardless of an open letter from twenty leading American economists, who instructed him that "The gold standard of the present weight and fineness should be unflinchingly maintained. . . . Agitation for experiments would impair confidence and retard recovery." New York's bankers, quite worried about "tinkering with the currency," voiced their opinions through their pet academics. Speculative movements in capital were widely reported in the American press, because currency speculation had once again become a profitable pastime for those skilled in it. An English economist named Keynes was gaining from his foreign-exchange dealings the spare cash needed to form an interesting collection of rare books and pictures.

Roosevelt was irreverent toward the orthodoxies of the financial world. A product of Groton and Harvard, whose professors advocated economic reforms, he had been taught that any economic system should not be judged on abstract principles alone. Instead it should be evaluated on its performance and its contribution to human welfare. His thinking was therefore eclectic, opposed not only to the self-serving philosophy of fellow millionaires like Mellon but also to the gold "orthodoxy" of France. On January 31, 1933, one of his agricultural advisers leaked to the press Roosevelt's opinion that "The smart thing would be to go off the gold standard a little farther than England has. The British debtor has paid off his debts 50 percent easier than the United States." During the first 2 weeks of February, the flight from the dollar therefore increased enormously. Gold exports for those 2 weeks alone totaled $114 million. Domestic hoarding had also become pronounced. In the week ending February 11 it rose to $149 million, of which $24 million was in gold and gold certificates. An even greater danger was that large banks in central cities and nationwide corporations were withdrawing funds held in the interior and in small correspondent banks, thus weakening the banking structure throughout the country. When Roosevelt took office on March 4, 1933, he was compelled to act swiftly and radically.[9]

Because of his disregard for formal doctrines of all kinds President Roosevelt has remained an enigma to the French. He regarded those he met as pedantic or frivolous, traits for which he had veiled contempt. He was astonished by the French claim that any departure from their gold-standard rules would be "immoral," and he saw no reason why he should consider the welfare of French interests while seeking to revive the foundering economy of the United States. Where the French bitterly opposed any kind of innovation, Roosevelt thoroughly enjoyed experiments of all kinds. But in his plans for devaluing the dollar there were essential difficulties. He did not have legal authority from Congress, and he could not afford to disclose his intentions to speculators. To do so would only have increased the flight of gold and dollars that was already adding to deflationary pressures in the United States. Moreover, only France, Belgium, the Netherlands, Switzerland, Italy and South Africa retained gold parities. There was scant advantage to be gained by

---

[9] Myers and Newton, *The Hoover Administration*, pp. 329–367.

devaluing the dollar against those few currencies. Rather than a sudden, overnight devaluation, Roosevelt and his leading financial adviser, Henry Morgenthau, were compelled to contrive a slow depreciation that would eventually achieve a more realistic, competitive exchange rate for the dollar against the world's major trading currencies—the pound, the mark and the yen. As a former Secretary of the Navy, Roosevelt was keenly aware that in 1931 the Japanese had begun their imperial adventures on the mainland of Asia.

In 1933 not only laymen and politicians but also many businessmen and economists believed that depressions were simply the result of a collapse in prices. Those who argued that all commodity prices were directly correlated with the price of gold had concluded that American recovery would follow an increase in the official price of gold. In 1933 that was by no means a radical idea among Americans. Farmers and other debtors had been calling loudly for a variety of inflationary programs, ranging from excessive issue of paper currency in the French and German pattern to increased use of silver as a base for currency, a panacea that had frightened most American bankers for generations. By comparison, increasing the official price of gold seemed a conservative measure. When Roosevelt and Morgenthau began to act, they therefore described their decisions to the public as ways to raise domestic prices. On March 6 and 9 gold exports were forbidden except by Treasury license, though it continued to use monetary gold reserves to support the dollar in foreign-exchange markets. In April domestic hoarding of gold was forbidden, and all gold in private hands was called into the Federal Reserve Banks. By executive orders, on April 19 and 20, Roosevelt then prohibited all gold exports.

When Ramsay MacDonald arrived in Washington on April 21, entirely unprepared for that American departure from the gold standard, "a little strain was evident at first as a result of this occurrence." The dollar had immediately begun to depreciate against the pound. However, MacDonald was not a monetary expert and was soothed by Roosevelt's explanation that he sought to inflate domestic prices, a measure that had so often been urged on Americans by the Bank of England. Concurrently the prices of American commodities and securities did begin to rise, and speculative price increases continued through June. To many of the American rich, abandonment of the gold standard seemed the end of Western civilization. More perceptive bankers such as J. Pierpont Morgan welcomed Roosevelt's action. Morgan had become somewhat embittered toward his friends at the British Treasury after their default on those American wartime loans to Great Britain, so many of which he himself had arranged. The prestige of Morgan Brothers had been damaged beyond repair.

The long-awaited World Economic Conference opened in London in June

1933 amid the fossils of the Geological Museum in South Kensington. Having allowed the pound to depreciate since September 1931, Great Britain was now willing to stabilize it at an advantageous exchange rate. But the United States was not ready, and Roosevelt was keeping his intentions to himself. Until August 16 he did not tell even Morgenthau that he wanted to begin buying gold in the open market at prices higher than those prevailing. When finally told, Morgenthau was aghast. A Hudson River Valley apple farmer with a nice regard for legalities, he reminded Roosevelt that he had no legal authority to do so. Roosevelt cheerfully answered his elaborate circumlocutions by saying: "I have a method of my own to break the law which I think is much simpler." In those days Roosevelt had an obliging Congress. They demanded action and got it. A subsidiary of the government-owned Reconstruction Finance Corporation was used to buy gold in New York. Thus the price in New York usually exceeded the price in London at the prevailing exchange rate. That encouraged arbitragers to buy gold in London with sterling, to sell in New York for dollars. Consequently sterling's exchange rate rose against the dollar and other currencies, weakening the competitive position of British exporters. Is anyone still surprised by Roosevelt's unwillingness to confide those intentions to Ramsay MacDonald and to the world monetary experts assembled at the Geological Museum in South Kensington?

Beginning October 25 Morgenthau and two other advisers met in Roosevelt's White House bedroom each morning to set the price at which gold would be bought in New York that day. While the President breakfasted on his habitual soft-boiled eggs, the others reported on the behavior of gold and commodity prices. The new gold price they established on any given day was not related to those commodity price changes. Random numbers were chosen to foil speculators. By January 15, 1934, Roosevelt was able to send a message to Congress, requesting an upper limit of 60 percent for his authority to devalue the dollar against gold. On January 30 both Houses passed without demur the Gold Reserve Act of 1934, which set the price at $35 per ounce. That was 59.06 percent of its pre-1933 gold content.

For all its faults that American gold-buying program exemplified the spirit of Roosevelt's "New Deal." Later Morgenthau's biographer would write: "The luxury of self-searching had to await a quieter time. In 1933 those with power had to use it fast and joyously." [10]

THE LONDON CONFERENCE AND ITS AFTERMATH

Cooperation among the United States, Great Britain and France having disintegrated, there was no hope that the French could have obtained at the

---

[10] Blum, *Roosevelt and Morgenthau*, p. 53.

World Economic Conference of 1933 either restoration of a regime of fixed gold parities or support for their political ambitions in Central Europe. That London Conference had been doomed to failure before it began.

Two irreconcilable monetary positions appeared. Countries committed to paper currencies wanted first a rise in their domestic price levels before stabilization of exchange rates. They believed that stabilization was feasible only when price levels had risen far enough to make it possible to establish certain equilibrium rates. Therefore they considered an eventual return to the gold standard as the final stage in a long series of steps. In contrast countries committed to the gold standard insisted on immediate return, with at least a provisional agreement on gold parities. The French delegation led those gold interests in the most arrogant manner, because in 1933 they were certain they had "the strongest currency in the world." The entire French financial community had rallied around the gold standard and had urged French delegates to remain steadfast. On April 24, *Le Temps Financier* had proclaimed:

> France . . . will maintain the gold standard. In the midst of universal upheaval, Marianne will cling to the solid ground offered by monetary order, and her money will show other nations the sole road to follow and the sole goal to aim at in order for the world to recover normal activity and future security with sane currencies.

It is curious that French financial writers so often refer to France as Marianne, inviting rape.

After many weeks of discussions, in which the British sought to appease the French, a provisional plan for stabilization in terms of gold was transmitted to the governments represented at the London Conference. President Roosevelt exploded in anger. On July 5 he replied:

> I would regard it as a catastrophe amounting to a world tragedy if the great Conference of nations, called to bring about a more real and permanent financial stability and a greater prosperity to the masses of all nations,[11] should, in advance of any serious effort to consider those broader problems, allow itself to be diverted by the proposals of a purely artificial and temporary experiment affecting the monetary exchange of a few nations only. Such action, such diversion, shows a singular lack of proportion and a failure to remember the larger purposes for which the Economic Conference originally was called together. . . . Old fetishes of so-called international bankers are being replaced.

[11] Roosevelt's gold-buying program would have the incidental, friendly effect of providing a bonanza for Joseph Stalin's Russia. Soviet indebtedness abroad had reached a peak of 1.4 billion rubles in 1931. By the end of 1935 that would be reduced to 120 million rubles, thanks partly to the increase in the official price of gold exports. Between 1931 and 1934 Soviet gold production rose from 1,655,725 fine ounces to 3,858,089. It would reach a prewar high of 5,358,982 fine ounces in 1937.

Via the Department of State, but more quietly, he also made known his distrust of French political designs on Central Europe. Stung by plain talk, the French delegation headed by Flandin protested "the President has ruined the Conference by his rough message." Parisian newspapers trumpeted: "Roosevelt torpedoes the London Conference." The gold-standard countries led by France announced that it was impossible for them to take any part in any further discussions on monetary questions. France staged a solemn retreat into golden isolationism. If those "Anglo-Saxons" would not play money games by French rules, Paris was confident that it could and would become the banking capital of the world.[12]

Thus the Western democracies publicly, abruptly split into a gold bloc, a sterling bloc (the British Commonwealth and its close trading partners, such as the Scandinavian kingdoms), and a dollar bloc (the Americas). As each sought to protect its own interests more rigorously, the bickering among them became tragic. Adolf Hitler had been named Chancellor of Germany in January 1933. In March he had invited Hjalmar Schacht to resume office as President of the Reichsbank. Schacht also became Minister of the Economy on July 20, 1934. In September of that year he announced his "New Plan" for foreign trade. Seeking "autarchy," complete German self-sufficiency in essential foodstuffs and raw materials, he reserved gold and foreign currencies for the most vital foreign purchases and for war. Rigid exchange controls were accompanied by the invention of a variety of "blocked marks" that provided favorable exchange rates for foreign tourists and foreign buyers of designated categories of exports. Jewish and other German emigrants were required to surrender their gold holdings. Germany began a trade invasion of the Danubian basin, offering barter deals with which the French could not compete to those nations of the Little Entente that had become deeply indebted to Paris and were unable to pay those debts. The consternation of Flandin and his Parisian friends only revealed French futility.[13]

Challenged in Central Europe by both Germany and Italy, France began desperately to need allies. By remaining on the gold-bullion standard of Poincare and seeking to reestablish the Latin Union of Napoleon III, France had retained a shallow prestige and fair-weather friends in Belgium, Switzerland and Italy. The price paid was diplomatic failure abroad and severe deflation at home. Between 1932 and 1935, while industries in other countries were beginning to recover, France remained in a state of unrelieved depression. All other major powers had reached their lows in 1932 and thereafter increased their industrial production each year until 1937. All five major Western powers had increased that production in 1933, and only France declined in 1934

[12] Cassel, *The Downfall of the Gold Standard,* p. 154.
[13] Guillebaud, *The Economic Recovery of Germany,* pp. 61–100.

and 1935. By 1935 all economic indicators demonstrated that France was in one of the worst industrial depressions it has ever experienced. The index of new construction starts fell from 100 in 1928 to 90 early in 1934, then plunged to 66 in the spring of 1935. Though advised to invest in more modern plant and equipment, French industrialists refused to do so because of the lack of profit incentives and the uncertain political and social situation. Wholesale prices fell from 400 in 1933 to 322 in July of 1935. And the Paris Bourse had fallen into a stagnation from which it has never fully recovered. By the end of the 1930s, French industry would drop even farther behind its foreign competitors than it had been in 1929.[14]

In March 1935, confident that France had forfeited the support of its former allies, Adolf Hitler abrogated the military clauses of the Versailles Treaty and openly introduced conscription in Germany. The Reichsbank had been working closely with the economic planners of the new German Army since 1918. Both had made the classic error of believing they could control and restrain a leader whose ambitions were Napoleonic. With astonishing gall the French governments of Laval and Flandin were loudly blaming the United States for the failure of the Versailles Treaty. In Washington Congress passed the first of several Neutrality Acts. And in Moscow the Russians ceased to publish statistical reports on their gold production and reserves, rather than disclose them to potential enemies.

Unemployment in France was still less than 5 percent, whereas in the United States it had reached 25 percent in the depths of those depression years. Yet French conservatives remained highly alarmed about the supposed dangers of Bolshevism. Unrest was widespread among both liberals and conservatives. Armed demonstrations and street fighting between rival political gangs had become frequent. In Brussels a descendant of King Louis-Philippe was plotting restoration of a French monarchy. There was widespread distrust of the corrupt, incompetent governments of the Third Republic, as one scandal after another was announced in Parisian newspapers, the most venal in Europe. The political leaders of the Third Republic seemed interested only in continuing their profitable game of musical chairs. Marshal Pétain, known to be disdainful of those republican politicians, began to appear a possible savior to the rich Right. Authoritarianism was believed by many to be the only antidote for the permissive excesses and weaknesses of France. And in 1935 Edmond Giscard became President of the *Société financière pour la France et les pays d'outre-mer*, a post he would hold for the remainder of his active years. He began to fade into the anonymous financial shadows behind reactionary movements such as the *Croix de Feu* and *Action Française*.

In March 1936 German troops reoccupied the Rhineland without arousing

(14) League of Nations, *Production mondiale et les prix, 1936–1937*, passim.

anything more than a timid flutter of protest from the French Foreign Ministry of Flandin and the British Foreign Office of Anthony Eden. In London the Royal Institute of International Affairs had been trying to invent magical monetary schemes that might somehow hold together the decaying British Empire, even though its peoples were no longer willing to pay for the armies, navies and air forces required.[15] Some Frenchmen did try to stop their country's headlong descent into ruin. For 30 years the Socialists had consistently refused to take part in any "bourgeois" government. Yet in the April elections of 1936 they became the largest party in the Chamber of Deputies. French voters no longer trusted the conservative parties and their leaders to cope with the threat of a revived, rearmed Germany. When Léon Blum announced that his Socialists were willing to form a government, the French rich panicked. They could not see any difference between Blum and Stalin. French government bonds fell sharply, and shares in the Bank of France fell to a new low. French capital fled abroad, and intensive buying of gold by hoarders began to push France from its cherished gold standard.

Within a week after those elections the Bank of France lost 2.5 billion francs from its gold reserves. Financial disorders continued until September 25, when Blum announced that he had signed a Tripartite Agreement with Great Britain and the United States. Both had agreed to a 30 percent devaluation of the franc against their currencies. The gold bloc was shattered. There was a certain sympathy between Blum and Morgenthau, because both were liberal Jews. On September 25, the franc was officially devalued for the second time in 8 years. French popular confidence in paper currencies ended then and there. Because of the absence of any fixed relationship to gold the new franc was officially described as "elastic." A chronicler of the Paris Bourse wailed that it had been "beheaded." Private owners of gold were supposed not to benefit from that devaluation of the franc and were therefore given a choice between selling their gold to the Bank of France at the predevaluation price or holding it by paying to the government a sum equal to the increase in the franc value of their gold holdings. Gold exports were forbidden, without specific permission from the Bank of France. Any gold not declared was liable to confiscation. In practice, however, those provisions of the Law of October 1, 1936, were simply ignored.[16]

Laws that cannot be enforced merely discredit governments that promulgate them. Rather than unite France, Léon Blum further divided it. Though popular in London and in Washington, he had become anathema to rich French conservatives. Anti-Semitism had been growing in France and began

---

[15] See an odd Chatham House publication entitled *The Future of Monetary Policy* that appeared in 1935.

[16] Sédillot, *Le Franc*, pp. 289–304.

to be as fashionable as it was in Nazi Germany. Today students at the University of Paris are taught that "A curious phenomenon appeared on the Right—the birth of a bourgeois pacifism. One could say that their obsession with the communist success . . . in the elections of 1936 led a part of the Right to forget the danger of Hitler."[17] It would be more accurate, if less diplomatic, to say that many of the French rich were less frightened of Hitler than of Blum. Yet economic conditions in France did begin to improve. In 1938 approximately 14 billion francs were repatriated, partly because the Bank of France frequently planted rumors in the Parisian press that the pound or the dollar would soon be devalued again. That Bank's gold reserves increased by 10 billion francs between the end of 1938 and the end of 1939. As Finance Minister, Paul Reynaud proudly announced over French radio that the franc was "the first money of Europe." In 1939 the Bank of France was able to lower its discount rate to 2 percent, and improved conditions in the Paris money market eased the placement of new national defense bonds. Nonetheless the conservatives of France had ceased to oppose Hitler and Mussolini, and were consistently disobeying their own governments.

Recurring war scares and political upheavals in Europe had been causing repeated flights of capital to the United States. The price of $35 per ounce had served as a magnet that had attracted more than $5 billion in gold between 1934 and 1938. That price had also stimulated a boom in South African gold production, for the first time since 1915. Improvements in American foreign trade accounts had also been encouraging. On October 12, 1936, the United States had therefore resumed selling gold at $35 per ounce to the exchange equalization or stabilization funds of those countries willing to agree to the terms, rates and conditions established by the United States Treasury. By refusing to permit American citizens to resume private ownership of monetary gold, the Treasury prepared the groundwork for eventual demonetization. Yet gold once again became useful as a national reserve asset with Blum's Tripartite Agreement. The United States, Great Britain and France began to use gold to manipulate exchange rates in world money markets. Belgium, Switzerland, the Netherlands and even Italy applauded that agreement, soon accepted its principles, and joined the new "currency club." Though it was impolitic for Roosevelt to say so in an election year, because American voters remained so thoroughly disgusted with Europe, relations among Washington, London and Paris began to improve.

The benefits of that Tripartite Agreement, though essentially technical, had broad implications. For the first time the Western democracies had accepted the American price of gold as the basis for their exchange rates. In international finance their stabilization funds became the successors of cen-

---

[17] Duroselle, *Les relations franco-allemandes de 1914 à 1939,* Part 3, p. 115.

tral banks. A degree of comity was restored, where there had been only
hostility and suspicion.[18]

MONETARY CONTROVERSIES OF THE THIRTIES

Until the world economic depression of the 1930s the *laissez-faire* philosophy
had remained dominant in Anglo-American economies. Bankers, industrialists and foreign traders had strenuously resisted all governmental and academic attempts to meddle in their affairs. The depression years shattered the
self-confidence of those entrepreneurs and the trust the public had placed in
them. It was quickly perceived that the old order was passing, and the essential question in everyone's mind was what could and should replace it.

Fortuitously, in 1930 John Maynard Keynes had printed *A Treatise on Money* and in 1936 he followed it with *A General Theory of Money, Interest and Employment*. Those studies became the banner and intellectual justification for economists who argued that the old economic order should be overthrown and
replaced by government intervention in the economy, by means of budget
policies that would compensate for any shortcomings in the private sector.
Disillusioned by Anglo–American experience with unrestrained capitalism,
yet wary of the examples of Fascist and Marxist socialism provided by Germany, Italy and the Soviet Union, many British students were closely watching the experiments in Sweden. There government control of trade cycles
within an otherwise free-market economy was being most carefully and successfully practiced. In September 1932 a new Swedish government had begun
to pursue an active, planned inflationary policy, assisted by deliberate undervaluation of the Swedish crown against sterling. Between 1932 and 1935
Swedish interest rates were gradually reduced and public works programs
continued to alleviate unemployment. To counteract a decline in private
investment, government loans were issued. Sweden's economy had begun to
revive in 1933, and many British economists attributed that recovery largely
to reliance on increasing exports.[19]

British governments had never heeded academic advice as the Swedes had.
Throughout the 1930s British economists were unable to persuade successive
Labour and Conservative governments to adopt domestic measures similar to
those being tried in Sweden and the United States. The opinions of London's
laissez-faire bankers and businessmen continued to be dominant, and domestic
policies remained mostly orthodox. British government intervention remained steadfastly intent on providing suitable conditions for the recovery of
private enterprise. Thus Keynes would never live long enough to observe for

[18] Paris, *Monetary Policies of the United States 1932–1938*, pp. 19–41.
[19] Arndt, *The Economic Lessons of the Nineteen-Thirties*, pp. 207–220.

himself the application and effects of the remedies he recommended for his own country, based on his first-hand knowledge of its peculiar economic traditions and conditions. Nor was he knowledgeable on economic systems outside the British Empire. Yet he became a hero among less articulate academic colleagues, perhaps because he was regarded as the archvillain by bankers in London and New York.

The slump in Great Britain had so closely followed the collapse of its export market in the United States that British banking opinion in the 1930s tended to associate the two directly. Moreover Great Britain's domestic depression was milder than that in the United States. It therefore appeared entirely logical to British governments that their policies should be directed toward foreign trade. Manipulation of the pound's exchange rate was their primary effort. It had begun in 1932, with establishment of an Exchange Equalization Account armed with £150 million. That had been supplemented by £200 million in 1933 and by another £200 million in 1937. With experience gained during the First World War that Exchange Equalization Account was operated to prevent any appreciation of the pound that might have lessened the trading advantage Great Britain had gained by its departure from the gold standard. The United States countered by forming its Exchange Stabilization Fund in 1934.[20]

In March 1932 another spectacular yet logically sequential step had been taken. Free trade had been abandoned in favor of a general tariff and "imperial preference." British domestic producers had thus been further guarded against foreign competition, and their export markets in the dominions and colonies had been defended with those new preferential duties. By making it more difficult for other countries to export to British colonies, the access of foreign competitors to British raw materials had been restricted. American exporters had been angered, and Hjalmar Schacht had been given a propaganda weapon with which to batter the British for having deprived Germany of its own colonies. Though British exporters had benefited, and West Indian sugar producers were pleased, native populations in parts of the British Empire such as India became convinced that their living standards were being reduced for the benefit of the English.

British investment in that Empire and throughout the world had virtually ended in 1931, and the United States had become the leading creditor nation to which Australians, South Africans and Canadians had begun to look for new development capital. In Great Britain the unofficial embargo on new foreign issues had not been relaxed until January 1933 and then only in favor of Empire borrowers. As a banking center London would never fully recover. Throughout the 1930s the British Treasury would grant permission for other foreign loans only in exceptional circumstances, yet those restrictions would

[20] See also Henderson, *The Inter-War Years*, pp. 28–161.

not stimulate investment at home. For the first time many British investors began to emigrate bodily to excape the new taxes and controls. For those who remained in Great Britain anticipated returns on traditional types of invest-ment had become so meager that they increasingly consumed or sought other, more profitable ways to place their money—including speculation in com-modities, such as gold and silver.

No history of money would be complete without a description of the agita-tion for remonetization of silver that troubled so many national economies throughout the 1930s. Roosevelt's exasperation with the inherent difficulties of metallic forms of money was responsible for the decision of American Treasury and Federal Reserve officials to eliminate eventually all but token coinage from the monetary system of the United States. The old bimetallic arguments had never entirely disappeared. Agitation had continued, support-ed by the silver producers, and during the postwar troubles of the gold stan-dard they had once again urged their case. They had won the support of other silver-producing countries, of which the largest was Mexico. They had also been helped by some merchants engaged in the Oriental trade. Between 1925 and 1930 the net imports of silver by India and China had averaged approximately 200 million ounces per annum, from a total world production of approximately 255 million ounces. Obviously there were traders who could have profited handsomely if the silver used for their payments to Indian and Chinese merchants had increased in price. The activities of those silver agita-tors had become pronounced after 1928, when the world price of silver had begun to decline sharply, from an average of 58 cents per ounce in that year to a low of 31 cents per ounce in 1931. That sharp fall in the price of silver had caused a rise in the price of goods wherever silver was the monetary standard. Of those nations China had continued to be the most important. By 1929 China had begun to experience severe inflation.

The strongest argument of the silver producers had been that the world supply of money was inadequate and that gold should therefore be supple-mented with silver. Wherever the public had been taught to believe in the necessity of a metallic base for money, that had appeared to be a compelling argument. The silver producers had also claimed that a rise in the price of silver would increase the purchasing power of countries that used silver coin-age. Behind that eloquent benevolence toward the Orient there had been solid, unenlightened self-interest. Nevertheless, in September 1931 the China Association of London had unanimously recommended an increase in the price of silver, and its remonetization, as "the quickest and most effective remedy to the present disastrous fall in prices." And at the London Confer-ence of 1933 the only tangible accomplishment had been an agreement se-cured by American silver interests. The five leading producers (the United States, Mexico, Canada, Peru and Australia) had undertaken to absorb 35 million ounces per year, the American share of that total being 24.4 million. Roosevelt was coerced by Congress into "rehabilitation" of silver; on June 19, 1934, he reluctantly signed the Silver Purchase Act of that year. It was described as a "compromise" with the extreme proposals of the silver producers. Because he had "done something for gold," the silver interests were determined that he should also raise the price of their product.

The result was a disaster. There are times when a so-called compromise is in fact the worst of all possible choices. The mints of the United States were required to buy newly mined domestic silver at an official price of $1.2929 per ounce, with a deduction of 50 percent. Thus the actual buying price was approximately 64.6 cents, which was nevertheless double the price that had prevailed in New York before that otherwise unprofitable London Conference. American taxpayers were subjected to a massive swindle. Treasury officials must have been daydreaming of some eventual world bimetallic system, but that delusion would not last long. Silver certificates were issued at the official price of $1.29 per ounce. Thereby silver was reinstated at the old American ratio to gold of 1–16, based on the pre-1933 official price of gold. A silver-buying program was proposed that would have required the Treasury to purchase 1.6 billion ounces at the exorbitant price of $1.29 per ounce. By the end of 1934 the international silver acquisitions of the United States for that year alone totaled 317.4 million ounces, and speculation had become intense.

The practical effect of that American support program was to drain the silver coinage from China, Mexico and many other countries. For the first time in history even India began to disgorge part of its ancient hoards. By the autumn of 1935 the insecure Nanking government of Chiang Kai-shek was compelled to call for surrender of all silver in China, in exchange for paper notes. Throughout the remainder of his regime China would never be able to develop a stable monetary system. Its ancient foundations had been shattered permanently. Unwittingly the American policy of supporting a high price for silver thus forced countries off their silver standards and drove silver out of circulation. That was the opposite of its announced purpose, "to restore silver to its time-honored place in the world's monetary system." For decades thereafter, to the embarrassment of the United States Treasury, it would continue to hold a large, useless stock of that metal, supposedly as a strategic reserve for wartime needs.

The real wealth of a nation lies in its human, industrial and agricultural capacity to produce efficiently the most advanced goods and services.[21] Be-

[21] For the gold reserves reported to the Bank for International Settlements in 1938, see the Appendix. Not only the Soviet Union but also Germany, Italy and Japan had declared that information secret.

tween 1932 and 1937 the industrial recovery of Great Britain had been remarkable, even though it had been predominantly a recovery in the domestic
market. By 1937 most indices of economic activity demonstrated that economic conditions in Great Britain were improving more rapidly than in
France or the United States. Unemployment still affected 10 percent of British workers on the insured list, but the number of those employed had risen to
a new high of 11.5 million. The volume of industrial production was 20
percent higher than in 1929 and 50 percent higher than in 1932. Nevertheless
by 1938, there were many in the Western democracies who recognized that
the combined weight of Great Britain and France could not equal that of the
revived Germany. British and French leaders therefore sought to appease
Hitler, to buy time for their own tardy rearmament programs. History will be
kinder to Neville Chamberlain and Edouard Daladier than their belatedly
awakened contemporaries were.

Hitler's occupation of the "rump" of Czechoslovakia, on March 15, 1939,
destroyed the "cordon sanitaire" of Central European alliances the French
Foreign Ministry and Finance Ministry had so laboriously constructed to
restrain Germany. There remained only the apparently impregnable defenses
of the Maginot Line to defend Paris itself. Having spent so many billions of
francs on those elaborate fortifications, the citizenry of France had persuaded
themselves that at last they were secure from any further invasions by the
Hun. Yet when Germany invaded Poland, on September 1, 1939, many
French conservatives were bitterly opposed to assisting that traditional ally.
Neither French nor British troops cheerfully advanced to seek combat with
the German armies, as they had in 1914. This time they waited, to be attacked at Hitler's convenience.

RENEWED WAR, AND NEW POSTWAR PLANNING

This time the major belligerents understood the economic demands of prolonged warfare. During the interwar years much had been written on the
"political economy of war," or *Wehrwirtschaft*. In May 1939 the British and
French governments had also signed a far-reaching agreement for full cooperation in every dimension of warfare, a commitment many of the British had
opposed and would continue to resist. So ended the ancient British concept of
"limited liability" when allied with Continental powers. One of the British
contributions would be a land army of 32 divisions.

In France five sets of monetary controls were introduced when hostilities
began. All operations in foreign currencies became a monopoly of the state.
French citizens were offered the choice between declaring or repatriating
capital held abroad, and 24 billion francs returned during the first 3 months
of war. Capital exports in any form were forbidden, and foreign deposits in

France were blocked. The state assumed, not a monopoly, but rather the direction of all imports and exports, for which licenses were required in every instance. To the 1936 embargo on gold exports was added a prohibition against trading in any form of gold without the authorization of the Bank of France. By offering a premium for gold, that Bank was able to persuade French citizens to surrender 10 billion francs in gold and foreign currencies by the end of 1939. All nonagricultural wages and prices were frozen at their September 1 levels. As always French farmers had obtained preferential treatment. All the belligerents understood that their financial policies would have to be reinforced by appropriate fiscal measures and by direct controls on prices, wages and supplies of scarce commodities. Yet in Germany, for the first 4 years of war, the taxes and rationing imposed would be less rigorous than in France and Great Britain, because of the need to reassure the German people that their beloved *Führer* would indeed win. Many had been doubtful.[22]

Neither Russians nor Americans wanted any share in another stupid brawl among Europeans. Before addressing the reconvened United States Congress on September 21, 1939, President Roosevelt was privately warned by the leaders of both political parties that they would repeal the American embargo on arms exports only if the sale of munitions was limited to "cash and carry" and American credits were forbidden to all belligerents. Required to accept those conditions, Roosevelt privately warned the British government to appoint a purchasing mission. The British Treasury had been planning to negotiate procurement of American supplies through the Chase National Bank and the Rockefellers, as they had used Morgan Brothers during the First World War. Morgenthau candidly explained to the British that many Americans had held J. P. Morgan personally responsible for getting the United States into that earlier war, to save his investments in Great Britain and France. This time British and French attempts to deal through private bankers and thereby to evade the explicit wishes of the President and the Congress would not be tolerated. The British Treasury reluctantly agreed on October 30, and the French still more grudgingly in December, to open special accounts at the New York Federal Reserve Bank. Jean Monnet was named Chairman of the Anglo–French Coordinating Committee in London, and its purchasing mission in the United States was assigned to a Canadian who had no personal ties to the New York financial community.

According to estimates of the United States Treasury, in 1939 British and French nationals owned approximately $15 billion in gold, American securities and American properties whose value might have been realized within the first 2 years of war. Roosevelt kept at hand an inventory of those proper-

---

(22) See also Hancock and Gowing, *British War Economy*.

ties. Only by selling them could Great Britain and France obtain funds to purchase American goods. Both had consistently had deficits in their trade accounts with the United States, and now neither had substantial amounts of goods and services available for export. Moreover both were doubly barred from American credits—by the Johnson Act, because they were defaulters on earlier American loans, and by the Neutrality Act, because they were belligerents. Morgenthau was also concerned to prevent disturbances in the New York markets, which the sudden dumping of Anglo–French gold and securities might have caused. He therefore asked Ambassador Joseph Kennedy to obtain accurate data on British financial assets.

From the beginning the British Treasury cried that it was too poor to be able to pay anything. By cable Kennedy informed Morgenthau that "England is busted now." At the Bank of England the aged Montagu Norman wailed that, whether Great Britain won or lost the war, all the world's gold and currencies, all European assets, would go to the United States. "There will be no hope for the world . . . at least none for Europe." Norman's gloom was deepened by the indecisiveness of Sir John Simon, then Chancellor of the Exchequer. Every effort was made to avoid selling any Anglo–French gold or securities abroad. Throughout the months of "phony war," until May 1940, Allied purchases in the United States were restricted to the bare minimum. Both Great Britain and France bought everything they could from sources within their empires.

On February 8, 1940, the British government at last announced the first sale of American securities owned by British subjects. It took place without disturbing American markets. In April a second requisition and sale occurred, Great Britain's increasing need for dollars compelling it to increase sales of gold. Morgenthau and many Americans feared that Germany would win the war and then demonetize gold. The United States would be caught with a huge, worthless hoard of that metal. Kennedy therefore urged President Roosevelt to ask Congress for legislation prohibiting further purchases of gold. Yet Morgenthau, concerned to protect the value of existing American gold stocks, insisted that the United States continue to buy at $35 per ounce all gold offered to it.

When Hitler invaded Denmark and Norway in April 1940, $267 million of their assets in the United States were frozen. The need for further American controls widened in May, when the German armies turned to the Netherlands, Belgium and France. Effective control was established over the funds of citizens from all countries conquered by Hitler, to protect them for their rightful owners, though German-owned funds were not controlled. The United States began to rearm, and by the last week in May the British requests for supplies were arriving faster than General George Marshall, Army Chief of Staff, could find surplus materiel for sale. After the British Army completed its evacuation from Dunkirk in June, they asked for everything on his surplus list—"the whole damned lot." And they eagerly contracted to pay for everything "as is" and "where is." [23]

Though German propaganda scorned gold, as "a Jewish–capitalist folly," Europe's central bankers had noted with alarm that the Reichsbank had been anxious to seize the gold reserves of the Austrian and Czechoslovak national banks. Therefore the Bank of the Netherlands had transferred its gold abroad at the beginning of the war, and the Swiss National Bank had hidden its reserves in secret vaults dug into the Alps. The Poles had been able to evacuate their gold reserves in September of 1939, via Rumania, the Black Sea and Syria.

Between September 1939 and June 1940 the Bank of France had also been able to transfer most of its own gold. Those French stocks took strange and troubled journeys. Not counting the remnant of 190 tons in its Exchange Equalization Fund as of June 1940, the Bank of France had officially retained in Paris 1777 tons, valued at 84.6 billion francs. When that Bank moved its operations to Bordeaux, just before the fall of France, the last of those French gold reserves began their odyssey. Some 756 tons were loaded into 14,000 gray sacks, each weighing 60 kilograms, and were transported by trucks to Brest. There they were quickly loaded aboard the cruiser *Emile-Bertin,* which had just escaped from the destruction of the Anglo–French expeditionary force sent to Norway. On June 12, that warship left port with orders for Canada, which were changed in mid-Atlantic. Delivered instead to Martinique, that portion of French gold reserves was deposited for the duration of the war in the casements of Fort Desaix, which dominates the bay of Fort-de-France. President Roosevelt quietly instructed the United States Navy to watch it carefully, lest it fall into German hands. Additional quantities of French gold had already been shipped to London, Ottawa and New York, where a deposit of 13 billion francs was held for settlement of French purchases of war materiel. And in Africa some French gold reserves were held at Dakar and Rabat. The Bank of France meticulously recorded that, in the course of all those hazardous transfers, only a small fraction was somehow lost. [24]

Shocked by the collapse of France, the United States Congress began to provide unprecedented appropriations for rearmament and to consider a draft of men. Both British and American leaders were compelled to reassess their national prospects in conditions of unusual tension and confusion. The American Congress and the American people remained totally opposed to lending any money to Great Britain. Nonetheless Roosevelt and Morgenthau

---

[23] Blum, *From the Morgenthau Diaries,* vol 2, pp. 43–277.
[24] To be precise 18,827,286 francs and 19 centimes. Sédillot, *Le franc enchaîné,* pp. 89–97.

answered Winston Churchill's impassioned pleas for help with private assurances that somehow ways would be found. In July 1940 Morgenthau was told that Great Britain expected a payments deficit of some £428 million during the following year. To meet it, so much gold and securities would have to be sold that useful British dollar assets would shrink to the equivalent of £400 million. Roosevelt was persuaded by Churchill's willingness to make such sacrifices that the British would indeed persevere. That question had been uppermost in the thinking of American leaders. Kennedy's reports from London had become quite pessimistic, and Morgenthau had told Roosevelt that he considered British Treasury estimates too optimistic. Privately Roosevelt had therefore been given American Treasury estimates that the scope of British purchasing plans would reduce British gold reserves to a minimum by the end of 1940 and its liquid dollar assets to some $600 million within a year, a dangerously low reserve for Great Britain. By June 1, 1941, Morgenthau anticipated a British payments deficit for the intervening year of at least $2 billion.

For years thereafter members of the United States Congress continued to doubt the severity of the British financial crisis at that time. The British themselves had long fostered public belief in the richness of their Empire, and suspicious Congressmen were convinced that *perfide Albion* must have hidden billions of dollars worth of assets somewhere. Roosevelt and Morgenthau were compelled to talk brusquely to the British in public and to act with circumspection. Their first resort to barter was an exercise in camouflage. In August 1940 arrangements were made to transfer fifty obsolescing American destroyers to Great Britain in trade for the lease of bases in Newfoundland, Bermuda and Trinidad that were useful to the United States but not essential. After careful thought Roosevelt decided to authorize that trade himself and then afterward tell Congress it had been done. He began slowly to prepare their thinking for a far more radical idea. By the summer of 1940 Great Britain's friends in the United States were well aware of its plight and had begun noisily to urge American gifts or loans. Roosevelt therefore knew he could obtain some public support.

Returning refreshed from a vacation aboard the cruiser *Tuscaloosa* on December 17, Roosevelt began one of the most difficult political maneuvers he had ever undertaken. First he informed Morgenthau:

> I have been thinking very hard on this trip about what we should do for England, and it seems to me that the thing to do is to get away from the dollar sign . . . I don't want to put the thing in terms of dollars or loans, and I think the thing to do is to increase our productivity, and then we will say to England, we will give you the guns and ships that you need, provided that when the war is over you will return them to us in kind, the guns and ships that we have loaned you, or you will return to us the ships repaired and pay us, always in kind, to make up the depreciation. . . .

Assured that Morgenthau agreed and would support him fully, that afternoon Roosevelt told the American press that he was trying to get rid of
"the silly, foolish old dollar sign" and to substitute "a gentleman's obligation
to repay in kind." The concept of Lend-Lease was born. Yet it would take a
massive, sustained effort to gain its acceptance by an unwilling Congress.
Without it the United States could not have financed Allied efforts so easily
throughout that Second World War. Yet it also had some unfortunate effects
that would linger for decades. Both Americans and Britons became accustomed to the comforting but perilous illusion that balance in international
payments was no longer important. Europeans also began to believe that
somehow the United States would always be obligated to rescue them from
their follies, no matter how disastrous.

Meanwhile the French franc had become "the vassal of the mark." With
typical thoroughness, when the invading German armies had got no farther
than Sédan, their first monetary proclamation had appeared. Whenever occupying enemy territory, German policy had been to overvalue the mark, to
maximize the quantity of goods and services it could purchase in those subject economies. In Austria its exchange rate had therefore been fixed at 1.50
schillings, in Bohemia at 10 crowns, and in Poland at 2 złotys. In France, on
May 17, 1940, its official exchange rate was established at 20 francs. That so
overvalued the mark that German occupation troops became welcome guests
in the shops and *boîtes* of conquered Paris. They also became profiteers in
ways reminiscent of the behavior of French troops in the occupied Rhineland
prior to 1930. Typically the French considered themselves humiliated by that
undervaluation of the franc, yet many hastened to ingratiate themselves with
the winners.

The new Vichy regime of Marshal Pétain spoke humbly. On October 3,
1941, his Minister of Finance commented sadly:

> Without trying to base our economic policy on doctrinal justifications, we simply
> recognize that it was born of unfortunate circumstances. The experience was
> empirical. Each must adapt himself.

Stripped of gold reserves, the Vichy regime had been unable to convince the
defeated French that its paper currency had any real, lasting value. And in
Berlin the grand scheme of the Third German Empire was to replace international settlements in gold and currencies by payments in checks. Debts and
credits, commercial and otherwise, were to be centralized in one clearing
house for multilateral compensation among all the countries under German
control. Throughout the Second World War representatives of the belligerent
central banks continued to appear in neutral Basle for the regular, useful
meetings at the Bank for International Settlements, the prototype for that
German planning.

In 1940, quite early in the war, those Europeans had been informed by publication in New York of William Adams Brown's *The International Gold Standard Re-interpreted* that the United States Treasury and Federal Reserve Board could foresee a situation in which the United States would become not only the world's largest creditor but perhaps the only one and would therefore be obliged to accept full responsibility for managing a gold-exchange international monetary system using a convertible American paper dollar as the only currency acceptable throughout the world. That book was carefully read, not only in London but also in Basle and Zürich. When the triumphant German armies invaded the Soviet Union in June 1941, both the United States and Great Britain recognized that the time had come to define publicly their common objectives in international economic affairs.

In August President Roosevelt and Prime Minister Churchill therefore met at a secret conference aboard warships anchored in Placentia Bay, Newfoundland. Political and economic considerations were entangled in their thinking. Roosevelt believed there should be an authoritative declaration of principles "to hold out hope to the enslaved peoples of the world." The joint statement emerging from that conference became known as the "Atlantic Charter." Its fourth paragraph declared that the United States and Great Britain "will endeavor to further the enjoyment by all peoples of access on equal terms to the markets and to the raw materials which are needed for their economic prosperity." Specifically Roosevelt intended to end the British system of "imperial preference." Though Churchill was no longer in a position to defend that tariff system, many of his Tory supporters would fight bitterly to keep it. The concluding fifth paragraph added that the signers: "desire to bring about the fullest collaboration between all nations in the economic field with the object of assuring, for all, improved labor standards, economic development and social security." Thus that first public statement of Anglo–American postwar economic goals embodied the multilateral, global approach that dominated their thinking thereafter.

The American Congress and the American people had remained so firmly opposed to entering the war that the British had every reason to despair of its outcome. Then December 7, 1941, at Pearl Harbor, the Japanese Navy informed all Americans in unmistakable terms that they no longer had a choice. Anglo–American planning for the postwar reconstruction of Europe and the Far East began within weeks after that explosive change in American intentions. This time officials at Henry Morgenthau's Treasury and Cordell Hull's Department of State were determined not to repeat past errors. Despite the objections of his juniors at State Hull was willing to let Morgenthau take the lead in international economic planning. Recalling the interwar years, he stipulated only that there must be no repetition of the "reckless international lending and borrowing" that had ended in the crash of 1929 and in the subsequent defaults on American loans to Europe.

In London *The Economist* described the first few American planning studies as "revolutionary":

> Let there be no mistake about it. . . . It is a genuinely new conception of world order. It is an inspiring attempt to restate democracy in terms of the twentieth century situation, and to extend its meaning to the economic and social sphere.

Yet neither the American Congress nor the British Parliament were ready for close international cooperation. The political groundwork was therefore prepared slowly and with care. Governments themselves remained uncommitted, while discussions among the Allied and Associated Powers were conducted at the level of technical experts.

Secretary Morgenthau assigned preparation of the American monetary plan to Harry Dexter White, a career civil servant at the Treasury. Born in Boston, of poor Russian–Jewish immigrant parentage, with limited education but ample imagination, the aggressive White was Director of the Division of Monetary Research. He was also responsible for handling Lend-Lease negotiations and had therefore become one of the few Americans who were fully informed on inter-Ally finance. Concurrently, at the British Treasury, to which John Maynard Keynes had volunteered his wartime services, a similar plan was being prepared. Naturally the British were using their wits to maximize their few remaining advantages and to minimize their increasing distress. Great Britain was nearing bankruptcy and subsequent collapse of the British Empire.

The prospect that London might lose forever its leadership in world finance was shattering to men who had devoted their lives to preserving it. Every effort was made to secure continuing acceptance of sterling as an international reserve asset, and thus a medium of international payments, even though Great Britain would no longer have any gold to back it. Nor could the British easily obtain new stocks of gold from the dominions to which they were becoming so deeply indebted. The choice of Keynes as the public author of the British plan was therefore brilliant. Firmly established at Cambridge University, where he commanded a large, intensely loyal academic following, he also had the support of the staunchly imperial Beaverbrook press. Skilled in the arts and trickery of public debate, Keynes could be relied upon to defend essential British interests ardently. White's credentials were not so impressive, and he had no public standing. He had only the full confidence of Secretary Morgenthau, which sufficed to give him strategic if not tactical advantages in his arguments with Keynes.

The White and Keynes plans for the postwar monetary world were unveiled in April 1943. Morgenthau himself presented the American plan to the appropriate committees of Congress, and both were discussed in Parliament. In Washington, New York and London, press and banking reactions were unfavorable. On September 29 *The New York Times* rejected both plans and called for a return to the gold standard as rapidly as possible. By contrast British press comment revealed a strong determination, shared by all classes, to avoid "the straitjacket of the gold standard." On August 24 the *Manchester Guardian* had commented: "Let it be said at once that no British government could accept anything remotely like these proposals and remain in power beyond the first post-war election." The Keynes plan, which minimized the role of gold, was more favorably received in Great Britain.

It had always been obvious to Keynes himself, and to the British Treasury, that for political reasons alone it would have been impossible at that time to eliminate gold from the world's monetary system. British Empire producers remained the world's largest, and the United States was the largest repository of that metal. South Africa, Australia and Canada would have been outraged if gold had been demonetized, removing British Treasury support for one of their major exports. And there was not the slightest chance that the United States Congress would obligingly have jettisoned its hard-earned hoard of $20 billion in gold. Yet the scorn Keynes publicly and so eloquently cast upon gold should be understandable. By 1945 the British Treasury's gold reserves would be reduced to a nominal $1, while the United States would own more than half of the world's declared monetary stocks.[25] Only British academic economists, for obvious reasons, would ever seriously consider Keynes's proposal for the creation of a new international reserve asset to be called the "bancor," to be distributed *gratis* to Great Britain and other debtor nations. Both Keynes and the British Treasury were merely maneuvering for position, to gain every possible world trading advantage for the pound inconvertible into gold. Those public debates and subsequent hearings by Congressional and Parliamentary committees also served gradually to secure acceptance for the idea that some kind of international monetary organization would be required, to avoid past errors and to secure international financial cooperation in the postwar world.

Though much has been written about the White and Keynes plans, a curious characteristic of the many American and British commentaries is their failure to mention the effects of Continental thinking on the international agreements and institutions that would eventually emerge.[26] In several respects those Continental opinions would prove decisive. A French plan had also been prepared and had been published in *The New York Times* for May 9. 1943. Its authors had been Hervé Alphand, former French financial attaché in Washington, and André Istel, former financial adviser to Premier Reynaud and a negotiator of the Franco–British financial agreement of 1939.

[25] See Appendix.
[26] See especially Williams, *Post-War Monetary Plans;* Halm, *International Monetary Cooperation;* and Gardner, *Sterling-Dollar Diplomacy.*

Well informed on the dire monetary conditions in occupied France, they had warned quite plainly that no French government could agree to participate in any international agreement that did not provide official support for the gold owned by French citizens. They also cast doubt upon the practicability of any global monetary organization and recommended instead that planners "begin small" by using the Tripartite Agreement of 1936 as the basis for postwar international monetary cooperation.

For the first time the Swiss National Bank had also begun to take a serious interest in Anglo–American monetary thinking. Since 1938 its gold reserves had almost doubled. Moreover gold had remained the favorite form of personal savings for Swiss citizens, who recalled only too well the losses incurred by investing in paper currencies and paper securities during the First World War. It was unthinkable that gold might lose its monetary role, depriving them of the security provided by that official floor price of $35 per ounce. By no coincidence Friedrich Lutz therefore appeared in the first of Princeton University's "Essays in International Finance." He deplored both the White and the Keynes proposals, and concluded with obvious anxiety that "Gold is quite unnecessary or even a nuisance under both schemes." In 1944 there was no possibility that widespread international agreement could have been obtained for any monetary plan that did not defer to the world's many gold interests. The White and Keynes plans were filed in libraries, to await another day and a radical change in circumstances.

On May 26 President Roosevelt announced that a formal international monetary conference would meet in the peaceful resort of Bretton Woods, New Hampshire, beginning July 1. Morgenthau presented to the several intensely interested Congressional committees a new draft plan that allayed their worst fears. He also assured them that the President would name Senators and Congressmen to the American delegation, to guarantee that no harebrained schemes could be secretly concocted by crafty bureaucrats. In the flush of confidence that followed successful Anglo–American landings in Normandy on June 6 the delegates of forty-four nations assembled in Bretton Woods were prepared to accept the wishes of the coming victors. On July 22 they unanimously adopted projects to found an International Monetary Fund and a Bank for Reconstruction and Development. The "Final Act" of that conference, embodying the revised Anglo–American plans, concluded with the statement that "proposals formulated at the Conference . . . are now submitted, in accordance with the terms of the invitation, for consideration of the governments and peoples represented." Thus the next and decisive phase, so far as the democratic countries were concerned, was to be legislative action. No one could have foreseen what decisions would be taken by the Soviet Union, which was becoming not only the dominant power in Eastern Europe but also influential in the Middle East.

Behind that public display of harmony among so many Allies their negotiations could not have been described as amiable. It had been particularly difficult to obtain the signature of the Gaullist French representative, Pierre Mendès France. An astute student of the tactics used two decades earlier by Poincaré, Mendès France had resorted to the time-tested French methods of excessive demands and obstreperous delays to gain every possible advantage for his Free French Committee. Secretary Morgenthau had been compelled to "get tough," simply to obtain his eventual signature to that Bretton Woods accord. And the price had been high. General Charles de Gaulle was at last recognized by the United States and Great Britain as the only legitimate leader of the Free French liberation forces. He had made a triumphal visit to Washington while the Bretton Woods Conference was in session. As the battles in Normandy also progressed, his cooperation was becoming essential. Yet to attract attention and to enhance his own importance, rather than cooperate he had been deliberately hindering those Anglo–American operations. General Marshall, normally circumspect and self-controlled, had been enraged.

Intent on upholding the shattered national prestige of France, de Gaulle even provoked a diplomatic crisis over the American engraver's design for franc-denominated military occupation currency to be used by American and British troops. It bore the American and British flags, not the French alone. And the Free French refused to agree that France, an ally, could be "occupied" by the Allies. So many concessions had already been made to French vanity and interests, such as an exchange rate that seriously overvalued the franc (50 to the dollar, 200 to the pound), that not only Marshall but also the American Secretaries of War, of State and of the Treasury would gladly have discarded him. Yet Anglo–American indecision had lasted too long, and in Charles de Gaulle his French followers had found the firmly anti-German, authoritarian leader they had craved for so many years.[27]

A reluctant, resentful President Roosevelt therefore agreed on July 7 that only de Gaulle's Free French Committee should have the "de facto authority" to issue currency in France. Roosevelt also approved an agreement that recognized de Gaulle as the civil administrator in France, "pending selection of a French government by the free choice of the French people." Moreover, before de Gaulle would authorize Mendès France to sign that Bretton Woods Agreement, he and Jean Monnet were given assurances that he would receive from the American Export–Import Bank credits of at least $550 million for the reconstruction of a France that had not yet suffered any substantial physical damage by war. The price for the favors of Marianne has always been high. Often it has been excessive.

[27] See also Blum, *op. cit.*, vol 3, pp. 165–177.

6 = Gold Versus Paper
1944–1956

Adolf Hitler's methods of handling the French had been quite different. During the Second World War, France had been the only country that had signed an armistice with Germany. To remind them forcibly of that most recent German victory in their running feud, in 1940 French representatives had been compelled to sign the formal instruments of surrender in the same railroad car, in the same forest of Compiègne, where the Germans themselves had admitted defeat in 1918. For decades thereafter that event would scorch the memories of the Frenchmen who witnessed it.[1]

FRANCE OCCUPIED, FRANCE LIBERATED

By the end of 1942 German domination was complete throughout France. It became a milch-cow whose resources were fully exploited for German wartime needs. Recalling French rapacity after the armistice of 1918, few Germans felt any compunctions whatever about forcing Marshal Pétain and his ministers to deliver huge war reparations. Hitler's ambassador to France had reported to Berlin that:

> Labor Minister Belin and Finance Minister Bouthillier have assured me several times in the course of conversations that the French Government was perfectly aware that a defeated nation must expect from its conqueror extreme economic and financial demands. French industry, in both the occupied and unoccupied

[1] See Alphand, *The Financial and Economic Situation of France,* published in 1942.

143

zones, will be disposed to carry out German orders, even for products that directly serve the German war effort, conditional only that the necessary raw materials and means of transport are placed at its disposal. Government circles and French industrialists also understand the fact that the centers of French heavy industry which might someday produce war materiel against Germany, the French chemical factories which partly use German inventions stolen by the Treaty of Versailles, and other branches of industry that compete with German production, will be destroyed by the victorious power, or severely limited in their productive capacity[2]

That plan for the postwar destruction of French industrial power was never implemented. Until his own bitter end Hitler continued to need all the goods and services that could be squeezed from France and its workers. After the British naval attack on French warships at Dakar, Marshal Pétain and his Cabinet had even offered to declare war against their former allies, those British who had hastened to the aid of France in 1914 and again in 1939. French pride and prestige had sunk to a new nadir. When Reichsmarshal Hermann Goering had demanded all the shares in the mines of Bor, Premier Laval had promptly delivered them, on November 26, 1940. Then the Reichsbank had insisted on surrender of 200 tons of gold that belonged to the Belgian National Bank and had been shipped to Senegal for safekeeping. On November 29 Laval had complied with that wish. December 15 was the hundredth anniversary of the return of the first Napoleon's body from St. Helena, and a triumphant Hitler had devised a gesture he considered gracious in a conqueror. The ashes of Napoleon's son, that King of Rome whom the Austrian Habsburgs had degraded to mere Duke of Reichstadt, had long reposed in Vienna's Capuchin Church. Hitler ordered them disinterred and shipped to Paris for reburial beside Napoleon. He believed that would unite the Germans and the French and would disguise his own exactions. The aged Marshal Pétain, given only 48 hours' notice of that propaganda feat, made his excuses and remained in Vichy. He did not want to return to Paris for the first time merely to preside over a demonstration of Franco–German solidarity.[3]

"At that time, France was a mist agitated by contradictory currents in which fear, hope, egotism and devotion to duty conflicted with each other."[4] The Pétain regime nominally administered not only both zones of metropolitan France but also those colonies that had not declared their independence. Extensive propaganda spread the belief that collaboration between Vichy and Berlin was freely undertaken, and the economic structure of France

[2] Abetz, *Pétain et les allemands,* pp. 18–19.
[3] Bouthillier, *Le drame de Vichy,* vol 1, pp. 159–253.
[4] Soustelle, *Envers et contre tout,* vol 1, p. 180.

became a field in which Germany experimented with ways to transform conquests into dutiful servants of the Third Reich. Despite diminished revenues the Vichy regime was forced to support both its own budgets and the war indemnities and did so by resort to extensive borrowing and excessive issues of paper currency. In May 1941 payments to Germany for occupation costs were fixed at 300 million francs per day. Total French government expenditures, a mere 66 billion francs in 1939, therefore rose to 125 billion in 1941 and to 140 billion in 1942. Yet the revenues of the French state were an inadequate 95 billion francs in 1941 and 105 billion in 1942. Those deficits could be covered only by advances from the Bank of France or by issue of Treasury bonds. Consequent inflation was partly avoided by increasingly severe state controls on exchanges, credits and prices. Private capitalism almost vanished, and ever since, France has retained the most rigorous exchange controls found anywhere in Western Europe. Compulsory savings absorbed a portion of workers' wages, and distrust of paper currency and paper securities prevailed throughout all classes.

Note circulation of the Bank of France had been 109 billion francs at the end of 1938 and 151 billion at the end of 1939. By August 1940 it had reached 200 billion; by August 1941, some 245 billion; and by February 1942, an excessive 271 billion. The old and familiar progressive inflation had begun. Controls did keep the price of bread low. A kilogram cost 315 francs in May 1940 and only 370 in August 1944. But the price of a dozen eggs rose from 1250 francs to 4320 during those years. Whereas the average hourly wage in the Paris region increased from 10.80 francs to 18.15, agricultural wages more than doubled. Controls dampened currency speculation, but black markets flourished. Between August 1939 and November 1942 the gold louis d'or jumped 2000 percent in price, to 5200 francs. American gold coins commanded a 10 percent premium, in the superstitious belief that they were related in some way to the growing power of the United States. Black market prices for gold began to fall only when the United States agreed that the Free French Committee in Algiers could fix its franc at 50 to the dollar. A chronicler of the Paris Bourse cynically observed:

> The Frenchman is born undisciplined. He enjoys watching Guignol beat the police. Restrictions on supplies and prices excited his native ingenuity. That is why he made false declarations, hid his reserves, and played tricks with the law. . . . The rich made fortunes; the poorest sold their ration tickets. All succumbed to temptation or to adversity.[5]

Another measure of the paper franc's deterioration during those occupation years was its exchange rate against the Swiss franc. From 1850 to 1914

[5] Sédillot, *Du franc Bonaparte au franc de Gaulle,* pp. 89–163.

they had been equals, exchanged one for one. In May 1940 the parity of 100 French francs had still been officially maintained at 10 Swiss. By August the rate had dropped to Sfr 9.65, and by December to Sfr 8.80. At the end of 1942, after the German occupation of Southern France, the exchange rate for 100 francs abruptly slumped to Sfr 3.22. In 1943 measures were taken to strengthen the French currency, but by December 100 francs had risen no farther than Sfr 6.34. Not until the summer of 1944, when an Allied victory appeared certain, would 100 French francs rise to almost 8 Swiss. When Anglo–American forces landed in Normandy that June, their Allied Military Government (AMGOT) paper currency was willingly accepted by French citizens in every town they freed. Yet it had aroused the worst suspicions of General de Gaulle's hypersensitive Free French Committee, who regarded it as a calculated, subversive attack on French sovereignty. By radio from London de Gaulle therefore warned the French people on June 10 that "The issue in France of a so-called French money without any agreement and without any guarantee by the French authority can only lead to serious complications." He did not rest until, firmly installed in Paris, he obtained withdrawal of all 23 billion AMGOT francs that had been put into circulation and their replacement by notes of the Bank of France. The entire issue of 82 billion tricolor AMGOT francs that had been the cause of so much Franco–American diplomatic heat in Washington then vanished in smoke, consigned to the fire.

Though the gold reserves of the Bank of France had remained almost intact, the quantity of paper notes in circulation had increased by 450 percent since 1939. Official prices had risen by 200 to 300 percent, and black market prices (a quarter or perhaps a third of all transactions) by 300 to 400 percent. Controlled wages had risen 70 percent and rents 30 percent. A turbulent readjustment was at hand. Workers demanded higher wages, while consumers eagerly grabbed any goods that appeared in shops. On June 15, 1945, the Provisional Government of Charles de Gaulle began what was described as a "purification" of the currency. All notes in denominations higher than 20 francs were withdrawn and replaced by a new issue, yet without any restrictions. That cancelled all notes destroyed during the war or taken from France by the retreating German armies. It also permitted an inventory of personal fortunes, for tax purposes. But it did not solve the problem of the excessive quantity of money in circulation. New expenditures by de Gaulle's government would also be financed by the printing press. At the end of 1945, as at the end of 1944, the total of notes in circulation therefore remained approximately 400 billion francs. That basic monetary problem would remain unsolved. Premier René Pleven made a start, by proposing to the Constituent Assembly that the Bank of France be nationalized, with full compensation to its stockholders. On December 2, 1945, that law was approved by a vote of 521 to 35. The incredible, the absolutely unthinkable, had occurred. "The masses dispossessed the first families of France." Recent admirers of de Gaulle have conveniently forgotten that, whenever it served his purposes, he could be at least as radical as any of the French communists he publicly opposed. Then and ever after, Gaullists would seek the support of the French electorate by claiming that they were the only real alternative to a Bolshevik conquest of France.

In private, relations between General de Gaulle and Russian communists had often been cordial. On September 26, 1941, the Soviet Union had been the first to recognize him formally as "the leader of all the Free French." Ivan Maisky, the Soviet ambassador in London, had also offered to grant the Free French "aid and assistance in the common struggle against Hitlerite Germany and its allies." The Soviet government had declared its determination to seek "the full and entire restoration of the independence and grandeur of France." They understood de Gaulle and the ways to flatter him. Privately he had replied that he felt closest to the Russians because, unlike the "Anglo–Saxons," the Soviet Union had not maintained diplomatic relations with Vichy. Those Anglo–American Allies, his near neighbors as the Russians were not, had remained suspicious and often hostile toward him. Though Great Britain and later the United States had armed, equipped and supplied the Free French forces in North Africa, the Free French had not been given any significant role in the Normandy landings. Correctly General Marshall had doubted their willingness to obey the orders of General Dwight Eisenhower, the Supreme Allied Commander. After beachheads had been secured and exploitation of the first Allied successes had begun, a French division had been given the honor of recapturing Paris. But in the invasion of Germany itself the role of French forces was carefully circumscribed.

Among Allied leaders at the time the American Secretary of War, Henry Stimson, had been almost alone in foreseeing that the French could not be permitted to impose on Germany another vindictive peace comparable to the Versailles Treaty of 1919. At the United States Treasury, Henry Morgenthau and Harry Dexter White had been preparing a plan not only for demilitarization of Germany but also for elimination of all German industry that was in any way related to the production of war materiel. Morgenthau had the hesitant support of Secretary of State Hull. President Roosevelt himself had been maintaining an ambiguous silence, listening to all proposals, as was his wont while awaiting the right moment to act. At the Quebec Conference, in September 1944, Morgenthau believed he had obtained the wholehearted concurrence of Churchill and the British government for his proposals to destroy forever the warmaking potential of the Ruhr and the Saar. Yet Stimson continued steadfastly to oppose the entire concept. He attacked the Morgenthau plan as vengeful toward the German people and dangerous for the economy of Europe. He regarded the Morgenthau and White proposals as a product of Jewish hatred and nothing more. Roosevelt therefore remained cautious, until Churchill too began to change his opinions. The Russians had started to demand reparations from current German production. British and American press reactions to the Morgenthau plan were unfavorable, and the Republican presidential candidate opposed it. Powerful opposition had also arisen in Congress. Eventually Stimson prevailed and assigned to John J. McCloy the responsibility for the formation of American policy in occupied Germany. When Morgenthau saw that his postwar plans for Germany were defeated and discredited, he resigned office in July 1945.

A new crew had begun to occupy Washington's seats of power. The exhausted President Roosevelt had died on April 12. One of his last acts had been to send a message to Joseph Stalin, accepting the Russian explanation for recent "allegations," "misrepresentations" and other growing "recriminations" among those wartime Allies. Roosevelt had added: "There must not, in any event, be mutual distrust, and minor misunderstandings of this kind should not arise in the future." In a parallel message, his last to Churchill, Roosevelt had expressed a desire to "minimize the general Soviet problem." His concluding sentence had read: "We must be firm, however, and our course thus far is correct." Within 24 hours he had been succeeded by the more plainspoken Harry Truman, a mulish Missourian and a veteran of the Senate whom Roosevelt had foreseen would be both firm and correct. Nor had Roosevelt mistaken his man. Truman had served as an artillery officer in France during the First World War and had chaired a Senate committee responsible for investigating the excessive profits of many American companies engaged in war contracts during the Second. Within days he was embroiled with the French. Of de Gaulle himself Truman would later comment:

> One of the tragic aftermaths of a world war is the harvest of little Caesars and their acts of aggression. When the great powers are in conflict, pent-up fanatical nationalisms begin to stir everywhere.

Such candor would not endear him to the French.

Truman agreed with Stimson on Allied occupation policies for Germany, Italy and Japan. An avid student of history, he:

> opposed any plan that would deprive Germany of the means of building up a contented Germany interested in following non-militaristic methods of civilization . . . a solution had to be found for the future peaceful existence of the Germans. It was to the interest of the whole world that they should not be driven by the stress of hardship into a non-democratic and necessarily a predatory way of life.

Hence he found himself in fundamental disagreement with Charles de Gaulle from the very beginning. French troops had seized Stuttgart in April 1945 in an effort to take by force a French occupation zone in Germany. Neither General Eisenhower's personal intervention nor a May 4 message from Truman moved de Gaulle. Promptly Truman ordered all American supplies to French troops discontinued. Only then did the French evacuate Stuttgart.

A more troublesome incident occured in Italy, for de Gaulle too was a student of history. The Italian Val d'Aosta appeared to him not only a rich prize of war but also symbolically most important. It had been one of the original principalities from which the defeated Italian royal house of Savoy had arisen centuries before. Annexation would have displayed French participation in the Allied victory, and de Gaulle therefore ordered his troops to occupy that valley. Its Italian people were invited to declare for France and were required to accept French currency. His commander even threatened to open fire against any Americans who might enter. When Truman protested, "de Gaulle's attitude in reply was one of injured dignity. France, he said, was only asking what was her due." Nor was de Gaulle deterred by the warning that he was violating the Atlantic Charter's pledge against "territorial aggrandizement." When the American ambassador in Paris tried to reason with him, the only subjects he was willing to discuss were the supposed "humiliations" to which he claimed the French were being subjected. Once again Truman threatened to stop further shipment of American supplies to French troops. Then, at last, de Gaulle withdrew them from the Val d'Aosta.

The independence of Syria and Lebanon, mandated to France by the League of Nations in 1919, had already been recognized by the United States and Great Britain. Nevertheless, in May, de Gaulle also landed troops there. They shelled Damascus and other towns in an attempt to enforce submission to French rule. By doing so, de Gaulle disrupted the San Francisco Conference, where the United Nations Organization was slowly taking form. Churchill cabled Truman that he considered de Gaulle:

> one of the greatest dangers to European peace. No one has more need than Britain of French friendship, but I am sure that in the long run no understanding will be reached with General de Gaulle.

Truman later observed: "Once de Gaulle got involved, the question of prestige kept him there until he was forced out." In Lebanon and Syria the British Army intervened and ordered de Gaulle's troops to cease fire. Grudgingly they did so. Yet order in the Middle East was not restored until the British government guaranteed that the new governments of Syria and Lebanon would not be subjected to any further pressures from the French.[6]

Lasting bitterness had begun, among recent allies. To their long list of enemies French Gaullists were adding the United States and Great Britain.

[6] Truman, *Memoirs*, vol. 1, pp. 155–162.

Decades of American and British generosity to France would be quickly forgotten.

THE AFTERMATH OF WAR

President Truman had his first face-to-face encounter with the Russians at the Potsdam Conference in the summer of 1945. Elated by their conquest of Berlin, they underestimated the forthright little gentleman from Independence, Missouri. Truman was determined not to repeat the mistake of permitting huge reparations payments to be extracted from a defeated Germany, for which American citizens would then pay by lending dollars to the Germans. He believed he had succeeded during that first meeting with Joseph Stalin. Yet he also concluded that the Russians, fearful of a later revival of German vindictiveness, would never relax their new hold on Eastern Europe. He therefore decided not to permit any Soviet participation in the Allied occupation of Japan.

Soviet intentions at that time were essentially defensive. The Russians sought to surround themselves with friendly buffer states and occupied any neighboring territories where they encountered little or no opposition. After 4 shattering years of war the Soviet Union lacked the resources for any further expansion against organized opposition. Yet Truman became convinced that Russian designs were imperial, and that belief was urged on him by many European leaders. British and French conservatives were thoroughly frightened, certain that the Soviet Union was planning nothing less than world conquest. They were determined to prevent any further Russo–American cooperation, and to retain American troops in Europe for their defense, at American expense. The victorious saber-rattling of Soviet marshals and generals did nothing at all to lessen their anxieties. Thus the tensions and rivalries that would soon be described as the "cold war" began to appear at that Potsdam Conference. Truman also considered it "clear that the Russian foreign policy was based on the conclusion that we were heading for a major depression, and they were already planning to take advantage of our setback." Perhaps he gave the Russians credit for more foresight than they had. In June 1945 there was a widespread belief in the United States that a severe postwar recession would soon follow, paralleling American experience after the First World War. Nevertheless those first impressions of the Russians deeply affected Truman's thinking and shaped American policies for the decade that followed.

In Washington, Truman's fresh views on Europe, the Soviet Union and the Far East received full support from a former colleague in the Senate, the Republican Arthur Vandenberg of Michigan. A conservative Dutchman and

former editor of the Grand Rapids *Herald,* Senator Vandenberg had originally been an ardent opponent of the League of Nations, had advocated
nationalism rather than international cooperation and had urged American
neutrality throughout the interwar years. He had described his position as
"insulationism" rather than "isolationism." However, the Japanese attack on
Pearl Harbor had instantly converted him into a supporter of Roosevelt's
policies abroad. Thus the man who had been the leading isolationist choice
for the Republican presidential nomination in 1940 had become the champion in the Senate of a "nonpartisan" foreign policy. The tradition began that
American policies abroad should be bipartisan, because they could be fully
effective only if they had the support of both parties in Congress. Truman
returned from Potsdam to find Vandenberg, ever suspicious of foreigners,
eager to cooperate:

> The United States has no ulterior designs against any of its neighbors anywhere
> on earth. We can speak with the extraordinary power inherent in this unselfish-
> ness. We need but one rule. What is right? Where is justice? There let America
> take her stand.

Such sentiments would later sound naive. Yet in 1945 they were the authen-
tic driving purpose behind American efforts to assist the postwar recovery of
Europe and the Far East.

The worst fears of Truman and Vandenberg were confirmed when the
Soviet Union continued to demand reparations from Germany, Italy and
Japan. A year after the end of hostilities they were outraged by Stalin's
insistence that he should receive $100 million in reparations from Italy, with
which the Soviet Union had been only nominally at war. During that intervening year the United States had already given $650 million to Italy for
reconstruction purposes and had channeled another $330 million in aid to
the Italians through the United Nations Relief and Rehabilitation Administration. Great Britain had provided an additional $120 million, a magnani-
mous gesture it could ill afford. The Soviet Union's misunderstanding of
Anglo–American purposes, and its mishandling of relations with those recent
allies whose help it still sorely needed, had never been more blatant. Truman
and Vandenberg interpreted it as deliberate provocation.

Vandenberg's cooperation would soon become essential to Truman. In
November 1946, after more than a decade of Democratic majorities, the
Republicans gained control of both Houses of Congress. Vandenberg became
not only Chairman of the Senate's Foreign Relations Committee but also its
President Pro Tempore. Truman heeded carefully his insistence on "firmness
with Russia." And Vandenberg had a new protégé. After the San Francisco
Conference he had noted:

I think the most valuable man in our entire American setup has been John Foster Dulles. . . . He knows more of the foreigners here personally than any other American. Incidentally, he has perfect poise and patience and good nature. He would make a very great Secretary of State.

Truman soon asked Dulles to negotiate a peace treaty with the Japanese. His brother, Allen Dulles, began to form the first unified American intelligence service. Their sister, Eleanor, occupied the German desk at the Department of State. For the next decade and more the name *Dulles* became almost synonymous with American foreign policies. The Presbyterians of Princeton returned to Washington in force, and they arrived well armed with costly Wilsonian ideals.[7]

The war years had wrought both an economic and a social revolution in the United States. Many of the rich had become very rich. New industrialists had brusquely swept aside the old ruling class of professionals—the ministers, professors, lawyers and physicians—who had provided local leadership since early colonial times. Industrial workers and farmers had prospered, and many of them had turned conservative. The Democratic Party had not been able to hold their loyalties. War work in factories had been patriotic, and suddenly it had become respectable for women. By the millions they had donned overalls. For the first time minority groups such as the blacks had obtained a share in the war effort and in its prosperity. Roosevelt and Truman had encouraged their aspirations. Price controls had kept inflation within tolerable limits. Between September 1939 and the peak in August 1948 wholesale prices had more than doubled, the stock of money in circulation had almost tripled, and money income had multiplied more than two and a half times. Though the sorrows of the depressed 1930s had so swiftly vanished, they were not forgotten. Both Truman and Vandenberg were determined to perpetuate that wartime prosperity, by unorthodox methods if necessary. Yet they faced growing opposition by the American people to further spending abroad.

In May 1945, on the very day Admiral Doenitz had signed at Flensburg the unconditional surrender of Germany, Truman had ended American Lend-Lease aid to Europe. Though vilified by Europeans for doing so, he had been obeying the explicit instructions of Congress. So many Americans rightly believed they had been bilked by the Lend-Lease programs that Truman would face increasing opposition to his reelection in 1948. Between July 1, 1940, and July 1, 1945, total American assistance (net of reciprocal assistance and repayments) to all foreign countries had approached $41 billion. Though the gross amount had exceeded $49 billion, returns to the United States in the form of reverse Lend-Lease had exceeded $8 billion.

(7) Vandenberg, *Private Papers,* passim.

Throughout those Lend-Lease operations the question of gold and dollar reserves had been the principal consideration in determining the presumed ability of countries to pay for Lend-Lease supplies. The few Allied and Associated nations amply endowed with such reserves had been asked to pay. Invariably they had refused. A second problem, almost equally important because of its significance in Anglo–American relations, had been the policing of the exports of countries that had received Lend-Lease assistance. If they had not been forbidden to export products identical with or similar to the supplies they had received via Lend-Lease, American taxpayers could have been fleeced more flagrantly than they were. Yet that interference in the internal affairs of other countries had been sensitive everywhere. The third difficulty that had arisen affected the classification of Lend-Lease items into those expended during the war and those whose benefits lasted into the postwar period. The latter were supposed to be (but often were not) involved in later, final settlements under the Lend-Lease Act, which had automatically expired with the end of hostilities. Disputes over those final settlements continued for decades thereafter.

Great Britain had been the largest beneficiary of that Lend-Lease assistance. Consistently the British had also spent a higher proportion of their national income on their war effort than either the United States or the Soviet Union. Therefore it had become an ingrained belief among the British people that the United States was somehow obligated to continue aid to them into the postwar recovery years. By 1945 British production of civilian consumer goods had fallen to 50 percent of its 1939 output. The volume of British exports had dropped to less than one-third of the prewar level. By 1945 more than $4 billion in British assets abroad had been sold, yet its external liabilities had risen to more than $12 billion. Because so many American troops had spent so much of their pay in the sterling area, British dollar reserves had risen to $1.5 billion. But as American troops were withdrawn and returned to the United States, that source of dollars had begun to disappear.

The ratio of British reserves to liabilities abroad became frightening, at a time when the British Treasury was forecasting with some accuracy that its international payments deficit would total at least $5 billion for the first 3 postwar years. Not only Lend-Lease but also most of the international operations of the American Reconstruction Finance Corporation had ended with the war. Great Britain's friends in the United States were arguing that new American assistance programs were essential, and elaborate propaganda campaigns were launched to obtain them, but Congress remained firmly convinced that gifts should be succeeded by loans. The operations of the American Export–Import Bank and the United Nations Relief and Rehabilitation Administration therefore began to increase massively but the recovery of Western Europe remained slow and hesitant, partly because European investors were unwilling to place their own capital in the industrial reconstruction of their own countries. Most Europeans preferred to deposit their funds in Swiss or New York banks while awaiting restoration of orderly political and social conditions.[8]

Thus the gold reserves of the United States had continued to grow and reached $24 billion in 1948. That represented more than 60 percent of total world monetary stocks, an obvious maldistribution of gold reserves in any monetary system supposedly based on that metal. There appeared to be no way to end that drain of gold from the rest of the world. The export trade surplus of the United States, $8.2 billion in 1946, rose to an embarrassing $11.3 billion in 1947. The principal source of that disequilibrium was Europe, whose trade deficit with the rest of the world reached $5.8 billion in 1946 and $7.5 billion in 1947. Both American Treasury and Federal Reserve officials were anxious to stop further imports of gold and supported proposals for additional American aid programs that might help a revived Europe earn surpluses in its trade accounts. The Departments of State and the Treasury were also convinced that postwar political difficulties in Europe would begin to ease only when unemployed European workers were given jobs, not only on reconstruction projects, but also in export industries. If only for that political reason they began to urge European governments to undervalue their currencies against the dollar, to encourage their export industries.

The United States was the only remaining market of consequence. Though American consumers might become spoiled by cheapened European products, neither American labor nor industry protested. They were already working at full capacity, to satisfy both the postwar boom in American consumer spending and the continuing foreign demand for goods and services only the United States could now supply. An era of increasingly free world trade began.

IMPLEMENTATION OF THE BRETTON WOODS AGREEMENTS

Planning is an art, not a science. At best it provides crude guidelines into a future that might otherwise become anarchic. At worst it can be so unrelated to reality that impossible expectations are aroused among the public. Then planners themselves become such obvious targets for their critics that adverse reactions can be developed into counterplans.

Early in 1945 President Roosevelt had sent the Bretton Woods Agreements to Congress, recommending that they be approved "as cornerstones of post-

[8] Brown and Opie, *American Foreign Assistance*, pp. 47–81.

war international cooperation." In the spring of that year Harry Dexter White had taken the lead in maneuvering attendant legislation through the Senate and the House, and had appeared before the responsible Congressional committees. The impending defeat of Germany and Japan, and the idealistic fervor that had accompanied creation of the United Nations Organization, had combined to raise liberal hopes that American isolationism was dead at last and that a new age of world peace was at hand. In New York a "World Federalist Movement" was being formed. It attracted not only starry-eyed dreamers but also many very practical men who sought money from Congress for a wide variety of foreign causes.

Nevertheless opposition to the Bretton Woods Agreements was widespread throughout the United States. It arose not only among conservatives but also in the financial community. Most of the New York press opposed those agreements, largely on grounds that the new international institutions to be created would favor debtors rather than creditors, and would not adequately protect the financial interests and bargaining power of the United States. Many of the planners' assumptions were rigorously challenged, as they should have been. It had been assumed that the International Monetary Fund and the International Bank for Reconstruction and Development (soon popularly renamed the World Bank) could and would relieve the United States of most of the postwar expense and responsibility of lending or otherwise paying the dollars needed for the postwar reconstruction of Europe and the Far East. Therefore it had also been assumed that the dollar would remain a "scarce currency." By approving the British pound as the second "key currency," virtually coequal with the dollar as an approved national reserve asset, planners had assumed that Great Britain would retain its Empire, would remain a major trading power and would fully share with the United States the responsibility for maintaining political order throughout most of the world during the postwar recovery period. No one could have foreseen that the British Empire would so quickly collapse, because its taxpayers and Labour governments would refuse to bear the costs of the armed forces needed. Nor could anyone have foreseen that British governments would begin to shirk all responsibilities abroad. Nor would anyone have dared to predict that the British share in world trade would steadily dwindle.

Throughout 1944 and 1945 the United States Treasury had paid for a powerful public relations campaign to secure passage of the Bretton Woods legislation. Articles had appeared in publications as diverse as *Foreign Affairs* and the *Reader's Digest*. The case for the Bretton Woods Agreements had also been presented to the public through many organizations that had worked on war bond campaigns. Later Morgenthau's assistant for public relations would comment:

The battle in Congress was won only because the issue was taken to the people who in turn applied the pressure to Congress. . . . Parenthetically, the Treasury also had the money to finance this program—it controlled the Stabilization Fund from the devaluation of the dollar and its use was not subject to scrutiny or audit by any other authority. I am not suggesting that the Treasury bought public opinion, but it had no budgeting problem in turning Bretton Woods into a War Bond drive.[9]

The most important of the Congressional committees reviewing that legislation was the Senate Committee on Banking and Currency. Chaired by Senator Wagner of New York, its members included the conservative and quite skeptical Senators Tobey of Vermont and Taft of Ohio. The younger, liberal Senator Fulbright, a former Rhodes scholar from Arkansas, deftly diverted their most dangerous questions and firmly steered the Bretton Woods Agreements Act (H.R. 3314) toward passage on June 21, 1945. Senator Taft was only one of many millions of Americans who were worried about the prospect of postwar American lending abroad. During those hearings he had asked an expert witness:

What I really have in mind was that I have at times used this same figure, three billion to the British, and I thought that about three billion for all the rest of the world would take care of—well, we could be fairly well said to have started things going again.

Cautiously that witness had replied: "Yes, I certainly think it would help a great deal." Senator Taft would have been appalled if he had been told that he had been underestimating the need abroad, and subsequent American gifts rather than loans, by an order of magnitude[10]

Opposition to the Bretton Woods Agreements was not confined to the United States. In Great Britain the Tory Opposition was fighting a bitter rearguard action to protect its trade with a crumbling Empire. Tories were livid with rage when informed that the Labour government of the deceptively mild-mannered Clement Attlee had meekly accepted the Bretton Woods Agreements as one of the terms for the first postwar American loan of $3.750 billion to Great Britain. Nor were they grateful for its generous terms—an interest rate of 2 percent, and a period of 50 years in which to repay both principal and interest. Instead those Conservatives accused the United States of "wrecking the world" after the First World War by refusing to sign the Versalles Treaty and now by deliberately seeking to dismember the British Empire.

Angrily opposed to restoration of free trade, a Tory spokesman charged that the United States was attempting:

[9] Rees, *Harry Dexter White,* pp. 342–349.
[10] Williams, *op. cit.,* p. 354.

to force the whole life of our country and of the British Commonwealth into a pattern dictated by the out-of-date theories of the present American Administration and by short-sighted American exporting and financial interests.

He added that the united States was trying:

to compel our Government to join, as satellites, in the task of persuading other nations to fall in line. The object of American policy is perfectly simple. It is to clamp upon the world, and in particular upon the British Empire, the obsolete economic system of the last century. . . . This time we are to have *laissez-faire* in a strait-jacket. In 1931 we were free to cast off completely from the gold standard. We were free to abandon the foolish pedantry of free imports. We were free to develop Imperial Preference, which stood us in such good stead. That freedom we have now been ordered to abjure. We are to sacrifice sterling, the finest monetary system yet devised, in order to hand over all control of our monetary policy to an international committee sitting in America, from whose decisions there is to be no appeal.

Then he heaped scorn upon:

poor Lord Keynes, a brilliant, versatile and ingenious economic specialist, with no political authority or responsibilities, and, in so far as he was a politician at all, at heart an old-fashioned internationalist Liberal.[11]

Though that romantic, old-fashioned imperial Tory did not relish the prospect of commercial competition with his American friends, in private he was insistently urging them to subsidize resistance movements in Eastern Europe, "to roll back the Communist hordes." Great Britain's Conservatives were demanding complete protection from all the perils of this world. Their adventurous spirit was spent.

On the Continent of Europe, conservative nationalists were more willing to accept the Bretton Woods Agreements, precisely because they did provide a guaranteed floor price of $35 per ounce for private gold holdings. That was a security their own governments could not offer. So long as the American paper dollar was readily convertible into gold and was therefore "as good as gold," they were quite willing to look to the United States not only for defense against external enemies but also against internal disorders they could no longer control. The aging Charles Rist, now an "Honorary Governor" of the Bank of France, would write in 1948 that:

after two years of financial management in which for the most part good intentions have had to give way to political passions, France faced a monetary situation completely dominated by an inflation which had been increasing for six years, first because of the malice of the enemy and then, following the Liberation, because of the ignorance of those who took over the reins of government.[12]

(11) Amery, *The Washington Loan Agreement*, pp. v–viii, 102–103.
(12) Dieterlin and Rist, *The Monetary Problem of France*, p. x.

Charles de Gaulle's ignorance of economics had become only too clear, soon after the establishment of his government in Paris.

Those European conservatives were also alarmed by many American officials, whose radical suggestions for the reconstruction of Europe were threatening many long-established interests. Harry Dexter White became their primary target. His apparent largesse to foreigners, as a negotiator of Lend-Lease, had also attracted hostile attention in the United States. Late in 1945 the Federal Bureau of Investigation had therefore initiated inquiries into accusations by several of its anonymous informants that White had been committing espionage on behalf of the Soviet Union. In American law there was no well-defined line of demarcation between legal and loyal cooperation with a wartime ally and illegal and disloyal espionage on behalf of that ally. Almost overnight the mass of American officials in Washington were being intimidated by the fear that they too might be charged with Bolshevik sympathies, as traitors to capitalism. To safeguard their careers, many became eager collaborators with the most reactionary interests of Europe.

White himself escaped prosecution, because there was no legally admissible evidence against him. But he no longer enjoyed the protection of Secretary Morgenthau. By February 1946 sufficient doubt had been created in the mind of President Truman to stop White's appointment as the first Managing Director of the International Monetary Fund. Instead that post went to an obscure Belgian named Camille Gutt. A fervent admirer of Charles de Gaulle, Gutt's conservative reputation and credentials were impeccable. In 1940 he had been the Belgian Finance Ministry official who had recommended entrusting to the Bank of France the 200 tons of Belgian gold that had aroused the cupidity of the Reichsbank. Early in 1941, at the most critical time in British finances, before American Lend-Lease programs had begun, Gutt had lent another $300 million from Belgian gold reserves to the British Treasury.[13] Quietly the tradition began that the senior official of the International Monetary Fund must always be a European jointly nominated by France and Great Britain. As a direct consequence the United States Treasury would remain reluctant to trust any of them.

The inaugural meeting of the Fund, at Savannah, Georgia, in March 1946, was also inauspicious. It was not the "pleasant party" Keynes had anticipated. The Soviet Union neglected to send representatives. It was becoming clear that, rather than ratify the Bretton Woods Agreements, the Russians would seek to divide the world into rival camps of capitalist and socialist powers. Disputes also appeared between the United States and Great Britain. There were involved arguments about the sites for the new

---

[13] Gutt, *La Belgique au carrefour 1940–1944,* passim.

Bretton Woods institutions and the functions of their executive directors. Were the Fund and the World Bank to be purely financial institutions, whose direction could safely be entrusted to international civil servants, or would their operations have such political and economic significance that they would require close control by member governments? White stated the American view that:

> It has been our belief from the beginning that the Fund constitutes a very powerful instrument for the coordination of monetary policies, for the prevention of economic warfare, and for an attempt to foster sound monetary policies throughout the world. As part of the necessary machinery to implement those objectives, it was regarded by the United States and others as essential that there should be large resources available to the Fund. But I should like to call attention to the fact that those large resources were regarded as one of the instruments to make possible the broader purposes of the Fund.

In that last argument with the dying Keynes, White again prevailed.

When the International Monetary Fund began operations in May 1946 from the drab Hotel Washington on Pennsylvania Avenue, its international civil servants were not allowed to allocate its considerable dollar resources freely to a world that was experiencing an acute dollar shortage. There was no certainty that such loans could and would have been repaid on schedule. Defaults would have discredited a new and untried institution that already had too many opponents. Its first loans would be directed toward founding currency stabilization programs rather than toward financing reconstruction of Europe and the Far East. By December 18, 1946, the Fund was able to publish official parities for thirty-two currencies, against both the dollar and gold, in the first formal effort since 1939 to reestablish fixed exchange rates. By the end of 1947, after its first 18 months of operations, it had been able to lend its 45 member nations no more than $435 million and £1.5 million. Those figures also indicate the comparative demand for the two key currencies of the Bretton Woods system in those first few postwar years.[14]

THE RECONSTRUCTION OF EUROPE

In Western Europe two schools of economic thought had emerged. One believed the only way to obtain maximum performance from an economy was to stimulate production aggressively with full use of credit, large government expenditures, and strong central planning of investment and foreign trade. Its proponents argued that the inflationary effects of expansionary and full-employment policies could be restricted by price controls, rationing, and extensive regulation of both foreign exchange and trade. Combined with sharply

[14] *United Nations Bulletin,* January 1, 1948.

progressive taxation, those measures were also expected to serve social purposes—"fair shares for all," social security and the abolition of unemployment. British and Scandinavian economists were the foremost exponents of
that school, while the far more conservative Belgians were the first to develop
opposed economic policies. They were less interested in encouraging production and employment, and more concerned with improving the economic
machinery of their nation and preventing inflation. Consequently they urged
abandonment of controls, stable currencies and freer foreign trade. Less worried about "social values," they were willing to accept inequalities of income
and consumption. American Democrats tended to sympathize with the former school, and American Republicans with the latter.[15]

In Great Britain a quiet revolution had occurred. Its debtor classes had
seized political control. In 1944, after 5 enervating years of war, the coalition
government nominally headed by Winston Churchill had been eager to
promise anything to anyone, to persevere until victory could be achieved.
Both governing parties had sought to spur workers at home and troops
abroad by pledging themselves to postwar full employment and a higher
standard of living for everyone. That had placed the British Treasury in an
awkward dilemma. It could not contemplate repudiation of wartime debts
and cancellation of excessive currency issues, as the Free French and the
Belgians had been planning. British credit abroad would have been destroyed, at a time when it needed more foreign credits than ever before. The
only recourse, to fulfill the political promises of British leaders and to manage
the now staggering British national debt, was to permit inflation of sterling to
extremes that had previously been considered intolerable. After the death of
"poor Keynes" his prewar writings would be used as intellectual justification
for deliberately inflationary policies, in entirely new and different economic
circumstances. A second essential step was to subordinate the Bank of England to the new Labour government.

Hoping to sweeten that bitter pill, Clement Attlee had named as Chancellor of the Exchequer an Old Etonian, the son of a tutor and chaplain to King
George VI. Later Hugh Dalton would gently complain that he was now
treated as a renegade and was no longer received at Court. Yet his chagrin
could have been anticipated. In October 1945 he had pushed through the
House of Commons a bill to nationalize the Bank of England. It was becoming one of the most inflationary printing presses in the Western world. Centuries-old barricades between British creditors and debtors disappeared, without bloodshed. In those days there was much wishful thinking in Great
Britain. Both the press and political leaders spoke hopefully of "further rises
in the productivity of our industries." There were pious pleas for "a substitu-

(15) Wallich, *Mainsprings of the German Revival,* p. 13.

tion of the idea of partnership in effort for the old idea of boss and worker."
Yet most of the British people were convinced that they now deserved peace
and plenty, without having to work any further for them. Great Britain's
creditors abroad ceased to believe anything told them by the British Treasury
and its newly faithful servant, the Bank of England.[16]

To recover the prewar prestige of the London money market, British bankers had been eager to restore the convertibility of sterling. Both the British
Treasury and the Bank of England considered that step not only feasible but
highly desirable. It proved to be a classic example of official overconfidence
and misunderstanding of market realities. When convertibility began, on
July 15, 1947, most of the first postwar American loan of $3.750 billion was
immediately drained away as foreign creditors hastened to exchange their
blocked sterling for dollars. A Canadian loan of $1.250 billion proved equally
inadequate, and the Bank of England hastily stopped convertibility on August 20. Ever after, it would maintain rigorous controls. Before December
1946 the second largest component of American lending abroad had consisted of $2.3 billion extended by the Export–Import Bank. France had received
$1.2 billion, which represented one-third of the resources at the disposal of
the Bank of France. The Netherlands had borrowed $300 million, Belgium
$100 million, Norway $50 million, Poland $40 million, Finland $35 million,
Turkey $28 million and Greece $25 million. Outside Europe the Export–
Import Bank had authorized credits of $100 million to the Netherlands East
Indies, $67 million to China and $25 million to Saudi Arabia. South American allies had received less than $100 million. As of December 1946, rather
than the $6 billion Senator Taft had hopefully forecast, known postwar lend-
ing by the United States to foreign countries had totaled approximately $9
billion. That had been only an inadequate beginning.[17]

The economies of the liberated countries on the Continent of Europe had
been so disrupted by 4 years of German occupation that for the first 2 years
of peace it proved impossible to calculate realistic exchange rates for their
currencies. Discussion of purchasing power parities was academic when applied to countries that had been totally cut off from world trade and had had
their currencies grossly inflated by German occupation authorities. Moreover, though restoration of their foreign trade would have been helped by
undervaluing their currencies, the practical effect would have been to encourage American and British troops to strip European shops of the scanty
consumer goods that had remained. Therefore the first postwar rates chosen
for the French franc, the Belgian franc (44 to the dollar, 177 to the pound)
and the Dutch florin (2.65 to the dollar, 10.69 to the pound), though substan-

[16] Cooke, *The Life of Richard Stafford Cripps*, pp. 316–404.
[17] Kriz, *Postwar International Lending*, passim.

tial devaluations from prewar parities, had nevertheless overvalued those currencies.

Next currency reforms had been undertaken. Belgium had been the first, in October 1944, to push through a drastic purge. All holdings of currency and bank deposits in excess of their prewar size had been blocked. Existing notes had ceased to be legal tender and could be exchanged for new notes only to declared limits. Thus each member of a household could obtain new notes for old to a limit of 2000 Belgian francs. The quantity in circulation was abruptly, compulsorily reduced from 164 billion Belgian francs to 57.4 billion. All currency holdings and bank deposits in excess of that amount were blocked, and by 1947 only 40 percent of that balance would be released to owners. The remaining 60 percent was converted into a forced government loan at 3½ percent, which was nonnegotiable but could be used for payment of certain taxes. There was also a capital levy of 5 percent and a new excess profits tax of 70 to 100 percent. The confiscatory rate of 100 percent applied to profits earned from wartime trading with Germany. By those Draconian measures the Belgian government not only eliminated excessive purchasing power but also punished wartime collaboration with Germany. Moreover they charged the United States and Great Britain approximately $1 billion for expenses incurred by American and British troops on Belgian soil, and thereby obtained a tidy increase in their national reserves. Belgium therefore got a good start in its economic recovery program, and the exchange rate of the Belgian franc remained the same until 1949.[18]

At first the French provisional government of General de Gaulle had not adopted such severe measures, because it needed the support of French conservatives against the communists. Thus many of the French rich had been able by diverse, obscure methods to perserve their wartime gains intact. The first serious objections to the "brutal" handling of the French economy by de Gaulle's lieutenants began in December 1945, when the franc was devalued to 119 to the dollar and 480 to the pound. Concurrent with nationalization of the Bank of France Premier René Pleven also proposed measures described as "structural reforms," which included nationalization of the four principal banks of deposit and credit. A chronicler of the Paris Bourse moaned that "The franc had escaped from the German prison only to fall into the jails of the octopus State." Then occurred the greatest horror of all. By Law of December 26, 1945, requisitions were imposed on all private holdings of gold and "strong moneys" (the dollar and sterling) both at home and abroad. French conservatives were not grateful for that tardy Christmas gift. Thoroughly disillusioned, they began to agitate in the Constituent Assembly against Charles de Gaulle himself. Within weeks he had become exasperated by those *politichiens*. To the astonishment of his followers he abruptly quit

[18] Crump, *The ABC of Foreign Exchanges*, pp. 211–218.

office on January 20, 1946. Petulantly he simply walked away from the government of France, without a word of explanation. Confident that the Constituent Assembly would recall him within a week, on his own terms, he retired to his country house at Colombey. There he would remain, "in the desert," for the next 12 long and bitter years.

Like schoolboys when the master has left the room, the politicians of the Fourth Republic resumed the games that had brought so much misery to France during the Third. Political disorders were accompanied by economic distress until 1948, when the natural strength of the French economy began to reassert itself regardless of soaring inflation caused by excessive government expenditures. The general budget alone increased from 532 billion francs in 1945 to 1593 billion in 1948. Meanwhile the inadequate revenues of the state had increased from 294 billion francs to 1023 billion. As so often before, French politicians were unable to increase taxation but sought popularity by saying yes to every demand for public spending.

By 1949 the printing presses of the Bank of France had put into circulation the first trillion francs. By September 1952 the circulation exceeded 2 trillion. If December 1938 is taken as the base of 1, the index of consumer prices had risen to 5 by December 1945, to 19.5 by December 1948, and to 26.9 by December 1951. That was accompanied by further, frequent devaluations of the franc, until it fell to 545 to the dollar and 1650 to the pound in December 1948. Concurrently the price of the gold Napoleon so fondly cherished by the French rose sharply. Its parity had been 20 francs as recently as 1914, and only 225 francs 75 centimes in 1938. Then it had soared to 3700 francs in September 1944, to 4850 in December 1946, and to 5975 in December 1948. Though a stabilization program was sadly needed, accompanied by the most rigorous fiscal reforms, Pierre Mendès France tartly reminded American critics that "American aid prevented France from drowning herself. It was not supposed to teach her how to swim as well." The only possible rejoinder is that when Marianne is determined to drown herself, it is prohibitively costly to stop her from doing so.

The American Military Governor and High Commissioner had found economic conditions in Germany considerably worse. Decades later he would remind West Europeans:

> It is well to recall that in the immediate post-war period there was not a single nation of Western Europe remotely disposed from a security point of view to go it alone. The emphasis then was upon collective effort and very little upon individual national aspirations and objectives. European nationalism had become largely discredited in the wake of a second disastrous European war growing out of a fragmented Europe of separate nation states.[19]

(19) McCloy, *The Atlantic Alliance: Its Origin and Its Future,* p. 29.

In May 1945, organized economic activity in Germany had almost ceased. Throughout large areas there was neither electric power, nor gas nor water. There was neither telephone nor postal service. Millions of refugees were roaming the highways in search of food and shelter. Widespread starvation was averted only by the intervention of the occupying American and British armies. All German public authorities having vanished at the time of surrender, essential functions were gradually restored by Allied military administrations.

The inflationary wartime financing methods of Hitler's government had caused excessive issues of currency, but the exact total will never be known. It must have exceeded by far the 118.7 billion Reichsmarks that would be registered by private owners when the currency reform program finally began in 1948. Curiously, during those first few postwar years, black markets had been slow to develop. At first most Germans had been inhibited by habits formed during a decade of life within the rigorous framework of Nazi wage and price controls. The Allies had resumed its operations, and for a time most goods had continued to move through legal channels, though not in adequate quantity.

Anglo–American aid to West Germany had totaled $64 million in 1945, $468 million in 1946 and $600 million in 1947. In July of 1947 when the Soviet Union refused to participate in combined efforts to revive the German economy, the United States and Great Britain abruptly ceased to consider all of the varied Franco–Russian proposals for further reparations, forced coal exports, dismantling, limitation, decartelization or deconcentration of German industry. American and British taxpayers were being forced to subsidize, via Germany, the reconstruction of the Soviet Union. Preparations began for full West German participation in the European Recovery Program. Though a group of American economists had designed a currency reform program as early as the spring of 1946, protracted negotiations with the Soviet Union had got nowhere. Like the French in 1919, the Russians were determined "to bleed Germany white," not only to assist their own recovery but also to prevent any revival of a German threat to their security. They continued to insist that they be given engraver's plates for any new currency to be used in the Western zones, so that they might issue identical notes without any centralized control over quantity. Thus they hoped not only to finance their occupation costs but also to gain the power to wreck at will the entire currency reform program, by excessive issue.

In June 1948, when that reform program at last began in the Western zones, without their concurrence, and new notes were put into circulation in West Berlin, the Russians promptly began an economic blockade of that city. It was breached only by a novel device, the Anglo–American airlift. Then the so-called cold war became very real indeed, its most immediate cause being the question whether German economic recovery should be permitted by the introduction of a sound currency. Delays in that reform had already stalled revival in every other sector of the economy. Once the Anglo–American decision was made not to allow any further Soviet participation in the monetary decisions and currency issues of West Germany, a spectacular recovery began. Contraction of the money supply was the most conspicuous element in that reform program. All old currency and bank deposits owned by individuals and firms had to be registered and were converted into new Deutschmarks at a ratio of 100–6.5. Though that caused much bitterness and distress at the time, the quantity remaining in circulation proved adequate to enable all West Germans to begin afresh. The next day, June 21, goods began to reappear in shops. With restored confidence in their money the West Germans went to work to rebuild their shattered country. They have never looked back.

By the summer of 1947 the United States Congress had become thoroughly alarmed, not only by the size and probable misuse of American loans to Europe but also by the lack of any tangible signs of European recovery. The Department of State was compelled not only to defend the loans already made but also to devise novel approaches to the problems of European revival, which Europeans themselves seemed unable to solve for themselves. The difficult winter of 1946–1947 had worsened already dire conditions, especially in Great Britain and France. On May 7, 1947, Dean Acheson, an Anglican lawyer then serving as Deputy Secretary of State, had therefore sent up a "trial balloon" in a speech delivered at Cleveland, Mississippi. He had stated quite baldly: "We now know that further financing, beyond existing authorizations, is going to be needed. . . . It is necessary if we are to preserve our own freedoms and our own democratic traditions." Such remarks, intended to persuade his American audience, only confirmed the belief of hostile Europeans that American aid was being given merely to serve selfish American purposes. Yet officials of the Department of State, then and for many years thereafter, would be caught in the middle. Their American critics objected that Europeans were only using the Bolshevik bogeyman to blackmail the United States into giving further, unnecessary help. Europeans were indeed becoming addicted to American support. General George Marshall, now Secretary of State, was therefore compelled to add the weight of his great prestige to his juniors' plans for further aid to Western Europe that would be a "give-away program," precisely what Congress had been refusing.

Having recently visited Western Europe, Marshall was able to declare convincingly in a speech at Harvard University on June 5:

> The truth of the matter is that Europe's requirements for the next 3 or 4 years of
> foreign food and other essential products—principally from America—are so

much greater than her present ability to pay that she must have substantial additional help, or face economic, social and political deterioration of a very grave character.

So began the European Recovery Program, popularly remembered as the "Marshall Plan." President Truman was quite content to let Marshall take full credit for it—or any further blame, as the outcome might determine. An academic supporter wrote:

> Above all, it is essential that the ERP should not be oversold as the Bretton Woods Program was to some extent. Thus government officials are not justified in telling the country that the program is not inflationary or that it may not require the imposition of controls. Miracles should not be expected from expenditures of fifteen or twenty billion dollars over four years; and it is preferable to warn the country now against over-optimism rather than to have the public disillusioned in the next few years.[20]

Republicans led by Senator Vandenberg were responsible for passage of that legislation through Congress. They were assisted by William Yandell Elliott, a portly, often pompous professor of government who had no interest in economics. At Harvard University Elliott had an aggressive, ingratiating pupil named Henry Kissinger, who was still more ignorant of economics. But Kissinger had an unusual claim to Elliott's attention. As a German–Jewish immigrant, he not only spoke German but also had had brief, first-hand experience as an enlisted man in the American military occupation government of West Germany. Both Elliott and his protégé regarded the Marshall Plan as a political tool, whose moneys should be used lavishly. Neither understood how to employ economic aid properly, because they lacked any knowledge of the functioning of monetary systems. When American foreign economic policies fell into the prodigal hands of Elliott, Kissinger and their friends, the gold-exchange system inaugurated at Bretton Woods was doomed to eventual failure. Its planners had assumed that the United States, as manager of that monetary system, would exercise restraint.

On December 17, 1947, the United States Congress authorized $522 million in aid to France, Austria and Italy. Then on April 3, 1948, President Truman signed the Foreign Assistance Act, which formally, legally established the European Recovery Program. On April 16 the Organization for European Economic Cooperation (OEEC) was born. By early 1949 the total of ERP aid granted to Western Europe had reached $5.070 billion, and Truman signed a bill that extended it for another 15 months. Essentially Marshall Plan aid was a series of gifts of dollars to eighteen countries participating in the OEEC that enabled them to buy American goods without

[20] Harris, *The European Recovery Program,* pp. vii–ix.

drawing upon their own tenuous dollar reserves or any other dollars they could obtain by trade. The OEEC administrators allotted those Marshall Program dollars to each country. European importers, merchants and manufacturers in each of the eighteen paid for those Marshall Program goods at market prices but in their own currencies. Thus each European government and central bank approximately balanced its Marshall Program account in terms of dollars while receiving from its own citizens the ultimate payments for those goods in its own currency. Funds so received were used for varied domestic purposes, with the agreement of the American administrators. Known as "counterpart funds," they were spent primarily on domestic social, educational and charitable needs. Gradually West Europeans began to work together once more in the OEEC as the fears and hatreds of the Second World War slowly receded into the past.

By the summer of 1949 it had become possible to implement the oft-revised plans for the Bretton Woods monetary system. As of September of that year the United States held 71 percent of the non-Communist world's monetary gold stocks. Though American gold reserves had reached their peak and would begin to dwindle, that would not be allowed to affect the domestic money supply of the United States. The classical rules no longer applied, gold having become merely one of several forms of money accepted in international settlements. In a letter to Camille Gutt at the International Monetary Fund, Secretary of the Treasury John Snyder committed the United States to maintain the external value of the dollar by buying and selling gold at $35 per fine ounce. Other countries were pledged to maintain the external values of their currencies by buying or selling dollars in their foreign-exchange markets. Having held the pound at $4.03 for a decade, the British government devalued it to $2.80 on September 18. Thirty countries followed suit within the next few weeks by devaluing their own currencies. Together they accounted for two-thirds of all world trade. Those parity changes were approved by the International Monetary Fund, and were accepted by the American Departments of State and the Treasury.

For the next two decades and more, to assist the postwar recovery and to promote the prosperity of Western Europe and Japan, those leading competitors of the United States strove consistently to undervalue their currencies against the dollar. American consumers enjoyed two decades of cheap imports and low domestic interest rates. American exporters and labor unions might soon have begun to protest, if the North Koreans had not invaded South Korea in June 1950. Another war boom began, from which European and Japanese industries also benefited. A week later, on June 30, the European Payments Union was formed to supplement earlier bilateral with multilateral clearing agreements. The dollar shortage began to disappear, and American gifts through the European Recovery Program should have ended at that time. But West Europeans would continue to clamor for more dollars, insisting that they still had too few to cope with their external payments problems. A massive American bureaucracy had been created, and it became self-perpetuating. The Marshall Plan aid therefore continued until 1953.[21]

The total cost to American taxpayers for those first 8 postwar years was approximately $53 billion for all economic aid given away abroad. That substantially exceeded the $41 billion the United States had given its allies during the war years. Though Senator Taft was indeed appalled, he could only feebly protest. In 1952 he had lost the Republican presidential nomination to General Dwight Eisenhower, the choice of New York's spendthrift bankers.

GOLD AND THE DOLLAR BECOME RIVALS

The political events of the first postwar decade must always be studied against that background of world economic reconstruction. Invariably they were directly related to it.

By 1947 the British had begun their withdrawal from India, and the Dutch from the East Indies. Behind them they left chaos and a few apologies. The United States was becoming permanently entrapped in Southeast Asia, in futile attempts to prevent a bad situation from getting worse. In 1948, in alarmed response to Soviet occupation of Czechoslovakia, West Europeans had also signed the Treaty of Brussels, their first postwar effort to cooperate for their common defense. Requests for further American military help had been answered in President Truman's inaugural address of January 20, 1949, in which he had proposed that the United States should provide military aid and equipment to any nations willing to cooperate in the maintenance of peace and collective security. On April 4 a treaty had therefore been signed to found the North Atlantic Treaty Organization. Ratification by Congress had been questionable until Truman announced on September 23 that the Soviet Union had successfully conducted its first test of a nuclear bomb. Suddenly the American people began to take the "cold war" seriously. Three days later the Mutual Defense Assistance Act was passed. Among other provisions it authorized military aid programs that would cost $1.450 billion in the first year alone. Between 1946 and 1958 the United States would give military grants of $16.569 billion to West Europeans and an additional $6.040 billion to other nations. The defense of Western Europe began to be a costly hobby of the United States Department of Defense that permitted European governments to use their own tax revenues to establish the world's most costly social services.

No one has ever doubted the Russians' enjoyment of the game of chequers.

---

[21] See also Kindleberger, *The Dollar Shortage*.

In his old age Joseph Stalin found that somehow he had survived all earlier competitors. Only Harry Truman was available to play on the scale to which Stalin had become accustomed. He had countered formation of the International Monetary Fund by organizing the Comecon monetary system, over which Moscow's bankers would preside, using an inconvertible paper ruble as their trading currency. His riposte to NATO had been the Warsaw Pact, which Moscow's generals and marshals would command, using Russian manufactures as their standardized weapons. The United States became deeply troubled by the unwillingness of its West European allies, not only to defend themselves, but also to help elsewhere. For the first postwar decade that would be attributed to the economic weakness of Europe. The Department of State therefore made strenuous efforts to determine what Western Europe could do for itself and how Americans might help Europeans to help themselves. Novel techniques were proposed, to revive world trade on a multilateral basis. One of them, the International Trade Organization, failed. Another, the General Agreements on Tariffs and Trade, has survived.

Having so long urged West Europeans to cooperate more closely with each other, many Americans were pleasantly surprised on May 9, 1950, to hear that a few of the French had been listening. Robert Schuman, the French Minister of Foreign Affairs, announced "the French government proposes that the entire French–German production of coal and steel be placed under a common High Authority, in an organization open to the participation of the other countries of Europe." He described his proposed coal-steel pool as "the first step in the federation of Europe, which would make it plain that any war between France and Germany becomes, not merely unthinkable, but materially impossible." The Bank for International Settlements in Basle would be used as the agent for loans to be issued by that new Coal–Steel Community. Thus Schuman prepared the way for later formation of the European Economic Community. As a quiet *quid pro quo*, Secretary of State Dean Acheson had promised him that the United States would give substantial cash and materiel support for the French attempts to hold their colonies in Indochina.[22]

The Departments of State and Commerce were also urging American industry to assist European reconstruction by establishing European affiliates and subsidiaries, thus providing American investment capital, technology and management skills to compensate for European deficiencies. At first American businessmen had been reluctant to do so. Before 1939 only American oil companies had held substantial interests abroad, begun during the First World War.[23] Most other American industrial ventures abroad, opti-

[22] See Harris, *Foreign Economic Policy for the United States*; Brown, *The United States and the Restoration of World Trade;* and Diebold, *The Schuman Plan.*
[23] Feis, *Petroleum and American Foreign Policy.*

mistically undertaken during the prosperous 1920s, had collapsed during the depression years that had followed. American entrepreneurs had therefore remained wary. But the program for European economic cooperation announced by Robert Schuman convinced many American bankers that conditions in Western Europe had become sufficiently stable to justify investment. They also anticipated higher profits than they could earn in the United States.

Suddenly it became fashionable for American banks and companies to open offices in London, Paris and Rome, if only to enable wives to enjoy a tour of Europe at the company's expense. The United States and European governments colluded by offering tax incentives. Anything was preferable to repetition of the errors of the 1920s, and the careless American lending and European borrowing that Cordell Hull had deplored. This time joint ventures would be encouraged. With an equity stake in those new European enterprises, American businessmen would work hard to ensure their success. And European investors such as Edmond Giscard could slowly regain their shattered confidence by placing their time, talents and money in ventures guaranteed by American banks and companies. Jointly they would achieve a spectacular economic recovery in the following decade. In 1950, to counter Soviet propaganda against "dollar imperialism," the Department of State adopted the policy that any other country could nationalize American investments within its borders whenever sound social or economic reasons for doing so might exist, and fair compensation would be paid. If, however, American properties should be expropriated without compensation, the government responsible could not reasonably expect to receive any further American official or private assistance.

Thus not only American aid but also defense, financial and industrial ventures began to spread dollars throughout the world, wherever they were welcomed—and sometimes where they were not. Willy-nilly the paper dollar became the world's primary trading currency, used even by the Russians in their own foreign trade. Though gold did not cede its ancient role in international commerce without a struggle, the contest would be unequal, almost unfair. It became a murky, prolonged debate between a small minority of gold producers and investors on one side and on another the billions of the world's peoples who yearned for peace and prosperity after history's most devastating war. The materially improved lives they sought could be achieved only by use of credit and paper currencies.

World gold production had become too small to support economic growth at the rate now expected. It had fallen from a peak of 36.5 million fine ounces in 1940 to a low of 22 million ounces in 1945, owing to wartime dislocation of the markets and increasing production costs. Only in South Africa and the Soviet Union had labor costs remained so low that extensive mining operations had remained profitable. In the United States, Canada and Australia new production of bullion had been sharply reduced during the war years. By 1950 world production was still only 24 million fine ounces. From 1934 to the end of 1951 the United States purchased $14.5 billion in gold, a sum that exceeded the $14.3 billion produced outside the United States and the Soviet Union during those years. There was simply not enough gold available at $35 per ounce to meet the world's rapidly growing needs for money, and the only alternative that commanded universal confidence was the American paper dollar. Moreover, throughout large parts of the world, universal suffrage had become the governing political principle. Wherever the poor have been allowed to vote, the price stability that had been one of the purposes of the 19th century gold standard has invariably been sacrificed in the futile, inflationary pursuit of full employment and rising wages for all industrial and agricultural workers.

As soon as peace had permitted reopening the unofficial markets for gold, South African producers had been the first to agitate for an increase in its official price. In effect that would have required another devaluation of the dollar. But the South Africans had argued their increased production costs and the comparative fall in the real value of gold when measured against the prices of all other metals and commodities. In 1948 the first market had reopened in Paris, and in 1952 the Swiss removed maximum price ceilings on gold traded there. South African producers were able to point to free and black market prices considerably higher than the $35 per ounce the United States Treasury was authorized to pay. When the London market reopened in March 1954, the South African government ordered its producers to begin selling all their bullion to its Chamber of Mines, which became the single controlling agency for the sale of that South African gold to the world's markets. A growing number of interested British, French and Swiss voices also began to cry that "something should be done for the gold miners"—and, quite incidentally, for the value of their gold hoards and mining investments.

Charles Rist spent the last 10 years of his life writing articles and delivering speeches that urged increased gold production, increased monetary use of gold and an increased official price for gold. On the competition between gold and paper he had written in 1949:

> The public's distrust of paper money is too strong, and its increase in every country would only amplify the confusion of the exchange rates and the disorder in international commerce, at the same time as the social crisis . . . the only instrument of international payment which has the confidence of the public is gold.

Allan Sproul of the New York Federal Reserve Bank firmly replied:

> If we raised the price of gold . . . the largest increases would go to the largest holders which are the Soviet Union, Switzerland and the United Kingdom. . . . That would be an indiscriminate way to extend our aid to foreign countries, both as to direction and as to timing.

Nevertheless, after the death of Rist in 1955, pious friends among bankers in New York and London would publish a memorial collection of his written pleadings for their favorite form of money. Printed by the Vision Press, without foresight, it would be unhappily titled *The Triumph of Gold.*

Two decades after the disappearance of gold from their coinage the American people had almost forgotten it. European conservatives had not. In 1949 the aged Hjalmar Schacht had written: "There can be no international finance without gold." And he had urged the new West German government to rebuild its gold reserves. British Conservatives, angered by the inflationary policies of their Labour government, warmly applauded Schacht's argument that "Money, to be internationally stable, must be based upon a commodity which, independent of governmental and economic influence, is in demand and accepted anywhere and at any time." London's bullion traders, and British investors in the South African mining shares popularly called "Kaffirs," agreed wholeheartedly with Schacht's crushing dictum: "Of such commodities, gold is the one that has best stood the test of time."[24]

Once again it was becoming respectable to have German friends, in the cause of reconciliation and unification of Western Europe against the Bolsheviks. In 1953 the aging Edmond Giscard therefore reappeared in public, with a book on *La France et l'unification économique de l'Europe*. Right royally, he proclaimed:

> We are persuaded that gold is the best money in the world. And we are equally persuaded that on the foundation of a gold money the world can build the most effective, even the most audacious credit structures, because banking technique is capable, upon a base that can at times appear narrow, of building an edifice that will respond precisely to the most varied economic needs.

Giscard also supported the idea of a common European currency as by no means "Utopian." Then he blamed the departed "dollar gap" entirely on the economic and monetary policies of the United States. "Consequently it would be vain to try to correct it solely by internal European action." Though that "dollar gap" had already been corrected by prodigal American spending in Europe, once again the United States had become the favorite scapegoat of French conservatives.

Wearily one American spokesman after another repeated the official re-

---

[24] Schacht, *Mehr Geld, Mehr Kapital, Mehr Arbeit,* misleadingly retitled *More Gold for Europe* in the English translation published in London.

frain of the United States. Europeans should not expect Americans to solve all their problems in miraculous ways. And so far as gold was concerned:

> maintenance of the present price appears imperative for the following reasons. First, there is nothing fundamentally "unrealistic" in the present official price of $35 per fine ounce. . . . Second, to argue that a rise in the commodity price level should be followed by an increase in the price of gold is a version of the economics of perpetual inflation. . . . Third, the potential gains for international liquidity and the foreign exchange reserves of other countries that might be derived from a gold price manipulation would be comparatively small, and their distribution uneven and haphazard. . . . Fourth, a world gold price is a deceptive formula, and not a rational way of dealing with the political, economic and social problems that the United States, the British Commonwealth of Nations, Continental Europe, and other parts of the free world are facing today. . . . Fifth, the world needs a fixed point of reference for national currencies, and in view of the weight of the United States in world economy and finance, this point of reference can only be the United States dollar and the dollar price of gold. . . . The stability of this price is, in these uncertain times, of such great value to the United States as well as to the world at large that it must be maintained.[25]

That was becoming increasingly difficult to do. Foreign dollar balances in the United States, which had reached a low of $400 million in 1933 and had still been less than $5 billion in 1947, would soar to $13 billion by 1955. Suddenly bankers and economists, though not the American people and their political leaders, became aware that the "dollar gap" was becoming a "dollar glut." Rigorous retrenchment in American governmental spending abroad should therefore have begun as early as 1953, by withdrawal of all American armed forces stationed in Western Europe. But the gold reserves of the United States still exceeded $21 billion, and there were several compelling political reasons for the initial decision of President Eisenhower and George Humphrey, his new Secretary of the Treasury, not to curtail that American defense spending in Western Europe. The "cold war" continued. West Europeans remained divided and distrustful of one another. Nor had British and French conservatives accepted gracefully their diminished standing in world affairs.

For the British, the death of George VI had marked the end of a splendid era, and the beginning of humiliation and impoverishment. Never again would a British monarch be styled King-Emperor. Their justified pride affronted by the decline and fall of imperial glories, the British people and their leaders were seized by romantic fancies and absurd delusions. The ministers of the new Queen had scrutinized with utmost concern the appropriateness of the titles with which Elizabeth II was to be invested. Was it proper to acclaim

[25] Kriz, *The Price of Gold,* published in 1952.

her Queen of "the British Dominions beyond the Seas" when some were not British and none considered the ambiguous designation "dominion" a happy one? In a Commonwealth of many faiths could the Queen everywhere be fittingly described as "Defender of the Faith"? The prime ministers of those dominions had been consulted and had solemnly pondered whether it would be correct to leave in her title the traditional words "by the Grace of God." As any student of human nature could have foreseen, they had reached quite different conclusions.

Moreover, Britain was losing control over the mines that had produced the gold bullion used to mint royal sovereigns. In the South African Parliament, so frequently insulted by Clement Attlee's Labour followers, the concern had been that the form of the royal titles embodied in South African law should not become a barrier to the declaration of a republic, if the people of that country should ever desire to establish one. Thus the coronation of Queen Elizabeth in 1952 had become:

> an occasion for the expression of unbounded faith in the future of the Common-
> wealth and Empire by writers who had hitherto shown little interest in either
> and who were apparently inspired by a steady resolve to press, beyond the limits
> of sense and endurance, analogies with sixteenth-century Tudor England. . . .
> Yet "know thyself" is a wise maxim for nations as for individuals, and those who
> prefer indulgence in fanciful parallels with other ages are usually those with least
> confidence in their own.[26]

That parade of archaic pageantry, and the torrent of purple prose that had accompanied it, had indeed been "inspired." Since 1949 the British Foreign Office had been ruled by Lord Strang. As Permanent Under Secretary he had persuaded himself that British power could be perpetuated by maintaining appearances long after the realities had departed. Strang and the Foreign Secretaries for whom he served as "eyes and ears" shared the belief that their unique inheritance, centuries of experience with Europe and its colonies overseas, had somehow endowed them with a wisdom the United States would respect. In their schemes for the future, British leaders would provide the tutelage and policy guidance, while Americans would pay the costs in men and money to defend Western Europe and its empires. Persuasively Winston Churchill and Lord Strang had proclaimed that it was the "responsibility" of the United States to provide a "Pax Americana" for the 20th century.

American definition of the duties of the United States differed. The newly appointed American Secretary of State, John Foster Dulles, considered himself a doctrinal heir of Woodrow Wilson, the enemy of empires who had preached "self-determination for all nations and peoples." Moreover, to

[26] Mansergh, *Problems of Wartime Co-operation and Post-War Change*, pp. 420–421.

many Americans, the death of Joseph Stalin in March 1953 appeared to open the way for reconciliation of the costly disputes between the United States and the Soviet Union. In July of that year, deprived of Soviet support, North Korean and Chinese forces agreed to an armistice in the Korean War. Dulles then scheduled for February 1954 his first face-to-face meeting with the new Soviet leaders, in the equally troubled city of Berlin. It would be aborted. Thoroughly frightened that the United States might then withdraw its armed forces from Western Europe and thus compel them to supply the men and money for their own defense, in December 1953 the British and French stymied his proposals for a European Defense Community. The frustrated Dulled promptly, angrily warned them that the United States would have to make an "agonizing reappraisal" of its policies. The European press pilloried him for that insult to their superior judgment.

The strange delusion that the United States could be coaxed into salvaging the British and French empires lasted until the autumn of 1956. Then it was abruptly shattered, in a humbling fiasco—the Anglo–French attempt to re-take the Suez Canal, recently nationalized by the newly independent Egyptians. In Britain a sycophant had just described its new Tory Prime Minister as:

> civilised, urbane and sensitive. . . . One can go through his career and scarcely find an issue of foreign policy on which he has been proved wrong . . . he devotes to national affairs the highest qualities of care and sensibility, an integrity so great it has never been questioned, and a naturally good judgement. . . . History may well reveal him as a Prime Minister of the highest quality.[27]

Instead history quickly revealed the incompetence of British leadership. Anthony Eden had not informed the United States of his plans to retake the Suez Canal, and to punish the presumptuous Egyptians. He had deliberately misled both President Eisenhower and John Foster Dulles. Wrongly he had assumed that, presented with a *fait accompli*, they would be compelled to support those desperate Anglo–French attempts to hold remnants of their colonial empires, rather than risk destruction of the Atlantic Alliance. When that badly coordinated attack of the British, French and Israeli forces began, there was not even a British ambassador available in Washington to answer the questions of an enraged Eisenhower.

On the second morning of that misbegotten military adventure, the British Chancellor of the Exchequer visited his Treasury office before attending a Cabinet meeting. Harold Macmillan was given some ugly facts and figures. A run on the pound, which had begun some weeks earlier, had become so severe that the pound had fallen to its floor rate of $2.78. To support the fixed rate

[27] Rees-Mogg, *Sir Anthony Eden,* pp. 112–113.

of $2.80, the Bank of England was being compelled to buy blocks of a million pounds at a time. In New York sterling was being offered in blocks equivalent to $5 million, and the New York Federal Reserve Bank had begun to sell from its own sterling holdings. Macmillan was advised by British Treasury officials that at least a billion pounds in gold and dollars would be needed to support the rate of the pound, to prevent another devaluation. Yet British reserves had fallen to $2 billion.

In an era of fixed exchange rates, a forced devaluation of the pound would have been an intolerable public humiliation for any Tory minister, especially one who had his eye on Anthony Eden's party leadership. The only recourse was to seek an immediate loan from the International Monetary Fund, and American support was essential. The acting Foreign Secretary of the day was Lord Home, who would later become more widely known as Sir Alexander Douglas-Home. He had a deep-rooted aversion to modern contraptions such as the telephone, and was loathe to call the hot-tempered John Foster Dulles. Macmillan therefore undertook to call Washington himself. Then he informed the Cabinet of the dire straits into which they maneuvered Britain. While that Cabinet meeting was still in session, he received a reply from George Humphrey that the United States would support a British request for a loan of $561.5 million from the Fund and would provide additional financial support, but only if Britain would accept a cease-fire at Suez by midnight. "There seems little doubt that this bleak intelligence, which it was Mr. Macmillan's hard duty to convey to the Cabinet, almost instantaneously convinced everyone that the cease-fire must be accepted."[28]

The British and French had timed that stunt to begin near the end of an American presidential election campaign, hoping that President Eisenhower would be too distracted to interfere. In Washington, John Foster Dulles "cruelly" chastised the French ambassador who had earnestly assured him that France had had no plans for war in the Middle East. Bluntly and bitterly, Dulles informed Hervé Alphand: "I will never again trust the word of a French ambassador." That rupture between the United States and its nominal British and French allies would never be fully repaired. The Federal Republic of Germany became the only reliable ally the United States would have in Europe. The primary, perhaps the only reason for that consistent West German cooperation would be its continuing dependence on the American troops maintained in Berlin and West Germany, not only for defense against the Russians but also for prevention of any further hostilities between Germans and French. The costs of the first two world wars had been so huge that Eisenhower and Dulles would have considered it unthinkable ever again to permit them to cause a third.

[28] Churchill, *The Rise and Fall of Sir Anthony Eden*, p. 289.

7 = The Triumph of Paper
1956–1965

Twice decimated by two world wars, in which the brightest and best of their manhood had been sacrificed in foolhardy attempts to enhance national and imperial glories, the peoples of Europe needed a generation of peace to restore their material prosperity and to recover their political nerve. They required not only new leaders but also new schools to train them and new forms of government that would use them to good purpose. Those transition decades were difficult in many ways. Germany in particular had suffered from the shortage of experienced, responsible leadership. Its bewildered citizens were exceptionally fortunate to find in Konrad Adenauer a confident politician of the finest kind to guide them firmly into the future. He once remarked: "My wish is that sometime in the future, when mankind looks beyond the clouds and dust of our times, it can be said of me that I have done my duty." That time has come.

GERMANS BECOME ALLIES

The first general election in the new Federal Republic of Germany had been held on Sunday, August 14, 1949. Before noon of the next day the intensely interested German people had learned that 7.36 million votes had been cast for Adenauer's Christian Democratic Union and 6.93 million for the Social Democrats. The Free Democratic Party had emerged as the third strongest, with 2.79 million votes. The remaining parties, including the Communists, had been left far behind. For the first time since 1933 it had become possible to form a German government responsible to the German people. On September 17 the former Lord Mayor of Cologne became the new Federal Chancellor. He would remain the cautious master of his country's reconstruction until retirement in 1962 at the age of 87. With dour humor and strict methods, Adenauer would provide the paternal leadership and new traditions his shaken people so badly needed. Before he had even taken office, he had announced in the most determined way his reasons for refusing to include Social Democrats in his new government.

> In the matter of economic structure there exists between ourselves and the Social Democrats an unbridgeable difference. There can only be either a planned economy or a social market economy. There cannot be a mixture of the two. . . . We should never get things moving at all.

To the extent feasible in contemporary circumstances West Germany once again became and remained a proponent of *laissez-faire.* Though Social Democrats eventually achieved power, they had sufficient common sense not to disrupt the thriving economic system firmly established. West Germany has therefore continued to prosper, as Britain has not.

In 1949 Adenauer also commented that he would need 8 years in which "to put the German people on the right road." His efforts to reeducate them in democratic ways, after their disastrous experiences with the Weimar Republic and National Socialism, were extensive and successful. By April 1953 he was able to visit the United States as the respected spokesman of an entirely new Germany. Arriving in New York for a visit described as a "vacation," he made his first statement to the American press while still aboard the new passenger liner *United States.*

> We Germans thank you from the bottom of our hearts for the many acts of help and kindness you have shown to us after our defeat. I think very rarely in past history has a victorious people extended a helping hand towards the vanquished as you have done. . . . This has raised the spirit of the German people and given us new confidence. It has proved to the German people that in the life of nations force and selfishness are not the only motive powers. . . . In the history of our own time, it will be recorded in letters of gold that the United States, faithful to its traditions and on the basis of its strength, has assumed the defense of freedom in the world.

Regardless of his advanced age, he then sought to win the hearts of the American people by making the most strenuous efforts to meet them. The first German Chancellor ever to visit the United States, he traveled nearly 10,000 miles around the American continent during the next 13 days. Astonished statisticians calculated that his speeches totaled 288,000 words. On a single evening he shook some 2500 hands. The American people had heard so few thanks from Europeans that his "vacation" became the most adroit gesture made by any European leader in that decade.

On the morning of April 7 the *Colombine*, President Eisenhower's personal aircraft, transported Adenauer to Washington. There the red carpet had been unrolled, an honor customarily granted only to visiting chiefs of sovereign nations. Vice-President Richard Nixon, Secretary of State Dulles, Secretary of the Treasury Humphrey, and Secretary of Defense Wilson greeted him. The first remarks of Dulles were admiring.

> We are witnessing the birth of a new Europe, and we are encouraged by the fact that the large majority of the German people are ready to unite their fate with the rest of the free nations. American hopes for the realization of unity and strength in Europe are largely due to the contribution which you, Mr. Federal Chancellor, have made in the movement towards these objectives. The whole world can be grateful that you and your country have given the lead to Europe at this critical time.

Then Nixon reminded Adenauer of "the tremendous contribution" millions of German immigrants had made to the progress of the United States in centuries past. Everyone present was well aware of President Eisenhower's ancestry.

Adenauer briefly replied:

> I wish to give you this pledge—the German nation will be a loyal and willing partner of the United States, which is leading the world towards peace and freedom. The German people are on the side of right and justice for all nations. . . . I wish to thank you for the generous manner in which you have paid tribute to the friendship between America and Germany, without mentioning the last few decades. . . .

The next day he walked from Blair House to lay a wreath at the statue of Friedrich Wilhelm von Steuben, the German officer who had volunteered his services to George Washington, to help train the first armies of the United States. After talks with Eisenhower and Dulles, Adenauer received an honorary degree from Georgetown University. Later, when he placed a wreath of red roses at the Tomb of the Unknown Soldier, the Marine Corps Band played the *Deutschland-Lied*. Adenauer commented: "I felt then as though our own dead German soldiers had had their honor restored to them." And upon returning to West Germany, *der Alte* told his countrymen: "We were simply among friends."[1]

The Germans needed friends. In July 1952 a "class war" had been declared in Soviet-occupied East Germany, not only against private enterprise on the land, in trade and in industry, but also against "bourgeois ideologists"—Adenauer's fellow Christian Democrats. By the end of March 1953 the East Germans were failing to meet all the production quotas assigned them by Russian occupation officials. The East German economy as a whole

---

[1] Weymar, *Konrad Adenauer*, pp. 488–496.

was producing only 96 percent of its 1936 output, even though the five-year plan called for doubling it by 1955. There was a shortage of 3 million tons of potatoes and 500,000 tons of grain. With the Communist East German regime's principal efforts concentrated on heavy industry, prices of consumer goods in government shops had risen substantially, but wages had not. Instead the production norms required of each worker had been increased, and all were aware of the massive shipments of their manufactures to the Soviet Union. In exchange, little arrived. They were also aware that they had to work twice or thrice as long as West German workers to achieve the same standard of living. Shoes cost three times more in East Germany, and butter four. Sugar cost approximately two and one-half times the West German price. Only potatoes were the same. Nor had the Russian Communists brought the equality among workers they had promised. Wage differences were much wider in East Germany. Skilled technicians could earn as much as 4000 marks per month, and a few specialists earned as much as 15,000 marks. Yet a transport worker received only 1.10 marks per hour, and a hod carrier 1.40. In the most clumsy way, the East German economy was still being milked to assist the slow reconstruction of the Soviet Union.

On June 12, 1953, a strike began in East Berlin among the élite brigades of construction workers who were building along Stalin Allee the monumental housing project that had been designed to honor Joseph Stalin in his lifetime. Well paid, they had also been considered "activists"—those workers of exceptional efficiency whom the Communist Party had singled out as "politically conscious." But special treatment had not secured their allegiance to the regime of Grotewohl and Ulbricht. The next day, that demonstration swelled and moved toward government buildings on the Leipzigerstrasse, the workers shouting such slogans as: "We don't want a People's Army; we want butter." As news of those events reached towns and villages in the provinces, uprisings also began there. The Russian commander in East Berlin announced a state of emergency, declared all public gatherings illegal, and imposed a curfew from nine in the evening until five the next morning. His orders were ignored. Then Russian troops began to open fire—first over the heads, then into the masses of angry German workers. Their demonstration became a riot. Party buildings, Columbus House, Café Vaterland and police cars were burned. After a day of virtual freedom, Russian tanks and armored cars began to clear the streets systematically, pushing the crowds before them and opening fire whenever they were resisted.

As far away as Poland, Czechoslovakia and Hungary, there were stirrings of protest against Soviet occupation. In Moscow the inexperienced men who had succeeded Stalin began to show signs of irresolution. Ordered to make concessions, Grotewohl and Ulbricht for the first time "admitted error," pledged to do better, actually released 7800 "economic criminals," raised wages and distributed to the shops some consumer goods—100,000 bicycles and 800,000 pairs of shoes.[2] But Westerners who visited East Berlin during the Christmas holidays that year still found empty shops, with long lines of housewives patiently waiting to buy forlorn carp or rabbits for their festive dinners. The *Komische Oper,* maintained in baroque gilt, crimson and white splendor as a showpiece of Communist *Kultur,* served only to emphasize the shabby clothing of the crowds who attended its performances, and the gutted ruins that still surrounded it. At the Café Warschau and Café Budapest on Stalin Allee, Russian officers arriving to dine ostentatiously placed their pistols on the tables beside their plates before glancing at menus handed them by cringing waiters. And the East German police had ceased to travel by subway, for fear of losing their lives between one station and the next. Communist economic measures introduced by force were maintained only by the continuing use of force. Between rulers and ruled, the hostility could not be concealed.

The contrast with West Berlin and the Federal Republic of Germany was harsh, and heartrending to Germans whose families had become divided. A daring French observer, willing to forgive his German neighbors for the past, nevertheless feared that a rearmed Federal Republic might someday attack France or might involve France in a world war for the reunification of the Germanies and the reconquest of territories beyond the Oder and Neisse rivers now occupied by Poland. In 1954 he wrote: "the problem of German rearmament, which has done so much harm in the past, is still with us and is still, alas, a poison for Franco-German relations."[3]

Yet rather than rearm, the new Federal Republic of Konrad Adenauer had decided to concentrate on economic growth, a form of rivalry the French would in time begin to consider equally threatening. Since March 1948, when named to head the bizonal economic council, Ludwig Erhard had directed the economic policies of West Germany. He had sponsored those concepts for a "social market economy" (*Soziale Marktwirtschaft*) that Adenauer had adopted. They derived from the "neo-liberal" teachings of the economist Wilhelm Röpke, who had been teaching in Switzerland. Flattered by use as the model for a new West Germany, relations between the Federal Republic and the Swiss Confederation had become and remained cordial. Erhard had been named Federal Minister of Economics on September 20, 1949, and the success of his programs contributed heavily to the victory of Adenauer's coalition government in the second general election, held in 1953. Not all industries had been benefiting equally from government assistance. Basic industries had been given priority over those that produced consumer

[2] Davidson, *The Death and Life of Germany,* pp. 326–347.
[3] Grosser, *Western Germany, From Defeat to Rearmament,* p. 239.

goods, and the emphasis on exports caused structural distortions in the economy that persisted throughout the 1950s. Though initially encouraged by the
United States, that West German drive to export eventually became a severe
test of the continuing good will of American as well as French and British
exporters.[4]

The economic recovery of the Federal Republic was so vigorous that by
1954 some two million of its citizens were able to take holidays in Italy, in
their traditional search for the sun. Gifts and loans of more than $4 billion
from the United States had achieved remarkable effects, equaled in no other
European country, even though West Germany had received less per capita
than the others. By 1954 those per capita figures totaled only $29 for West
Germany, by comparison with $72 for France, $77 for Britain, $33 for Italy
and $104 for Austria. In West Germany that help had been well timed. It
had arrived precisely at the moment when accumulated pressures for reconstruction had become intense, and the West Germans had no illusions that
anyone owed them anything. Their consequent willingness to work had only
been aggravated by the constant immigration of desperate East Germans, for
whom their cousins felt obliged to find jobs. There were 252,000 of those
immigrants from East Germany in 1955, 279,000 in 1956 and 261,000 in
1957. Though the official exchange rate was one for one, on the black market
in West Berlin the West mark was worth 5 East marks. And the gold reserves
of the new Federal Bank in Frankfurt, which had been zero in 1945 and had
remained zero in 1950, had risen to $1.494 billion in 1956, $2.542 billion in
1957 and $2.639 billion in 1958. To secure independence of judgment for
that new central bank and thus to forestall any further resort to inflationary
excesses by later German governments, the constitutional instruments that
had founded it granted considerable autonomy. Its relations with the Federal
government in Bonn would thus more closely resemble those of the United
States Federal Reserve Board than is the case in any other country.

Regardless of all attempts to resolve the question of West Germany's mili-
tary defense, it would continue to dominate not only the political but also the
economic policies of Western Europe and the United States. In 1954 Premier
Pierre Mendès France, harried by John Foster Dulles and by domestic critics,
had promised to obtain a vote from the French Parliament on the proposed
European Defense Community that had continued to form the keystone of
American policies for the rehabilitation of Western Europe. When at last
Mendès France presented that question, on August 30, it was defeated. Soviet
diplomacy had also been quite active among French politicians. Convinced
that their geographic position was central and indispensable to the defense of
Western Europe, the French believed they could dictate terms. They were

[4] Among others, see Röpke, *The Solution of the German Problem*, pp. 219–278.

dismayed and embittered when their Anglo–American allies proceeded to strengthen NATO without their consent. The Brussels Pact of 1948 was enlarged to include West Germany and Italy. In a "brutal affront" to French vanity, Dulles also informed the French Foreign Ministry that their delays and indecision had at last exhausted American good will. Yet the French were not alone in their doubts. Many West Germans had continued to oppose the formation of a new West German Army, and a poll in December 1954 indicated that only 45 percent favored it. Adenauer did, because he knew that American taxpayers could not be expected to maintain forever a costly American army in the Federal Republic for its defense against neighboring countries that were already well armed. Elaborate efforts began to find pretexts for keeping those American troops on European soil as long as possible.

On April 21, 1955, the American High Commissioner and Chancellor Adenauer exchanged documents granting full sovereignty to the Federal Republic, without giving the French and British Commissioners any chance to invent further delays. On May 9 the Federal Republic was also formally welcomed into NATO as its fifteenth member. While the West German flag was raised to join the other fourteen ranked at the entrance to Supreme Headquarters Allied Powers Europe in Fontainebleau, a military band played *Deutschland, Deutschland über Alles*, then the *Marseillaise*. A senior American officer who witnessed that ceremony laughingly described it as a "shotgun wedding," forgetful that such marriages rarely last.

AMERICAN PAYMENTS DEFICITS BECOME ENDEMIC

The French have always been adept at getting something for nothing. During the futile negotiations for the formation of a European Defense Community, to placate French fears of a rearmed West Germany, the British government of Anthony Eden had guaranteed to keep at least four divisions of British troops and a substantial part of the Royal Air Force on the Continent of Europe. John Foster Dulles had given constitutional reasons for his inability to offer similar commitments, but he had assured Premier Mendès France that he would ask President Eisenhower and the American Congress to continue the policy of maintaining American troops in West Germany. Speaking for the Federal Republic, Chancellor Adenauer had renounced any right to the manufacture of atomic, chemical or biological implements of war, or long-range or guided missiles. Subsequent French governments would never honor the promise of Mendès France to provide a *quid pro quo* by cooperating fully for the defense of Western Europe. Instead they would make every effort to evade those costs.

The last American High Commissioner for Germany, James Bryant Conant, a distinguished chemist and former President of Harvard University, returned to the United States filled with zeal for the cause of defending the new democratic West Germany. In 1954 he had helped to found the Free University in West Berlin, to assist in teaching the Germans peaceful ways. Unaware of the irony, a year later he helped to found the Harvard Defense Studies Program, the first American graduate center for the study of warlike ways. With a grant from the Ford Foundation a handful of American scholars began to urge colleagues in other universities to interest themselves in the defense of the United States and its allies.[5] As happens even within the sacred groves of academe, that Defense Studies Program became an object of political attention and was coveted by several departments. After 3 years of acrid disputes William Yandell Elliott captured it for his Department of Government and awarded that prize to a safely conservative protege—Henry Kissinger.

Though neither Elliott nor Kissinger had any knowledge, experience or reputation in defense studies, both had always had an eye for an opportunity, and the ability quickly to master sufficient facts to appear expert. Drawing on the knowledge of many others, Kissinger promptly compiled a book on *Nuclear Arms and Foreign Policy,* financed by the Rockefeller Foundation. Its President, Dean Rusk, was another of those professors of government heedless of economic costs. A conservative Democrat from Georgia, where military traditions of the romantic kind had always been strong, Rusk was a fervent admirer of General George Marshall and an eager ally of Senator Richard Russell, Chairman of the powerful Armed Services Committee. Lavishly advertised, Kissinger's book appeared in 1957 and became the first American "best-seller" of its kind. That marked the beginning of the only peacetime military mania the United States had ever experienced. The worldwide crusade against Bolshevism became a patriotic duty for both American political parties. Even diehard isolationist Republicans were being persuaded that maintenance of costly armed forces abroad, both in Western Europe and in the Far East, had become essential for the security of the United States itself.

Meanwhile, in Washington, the Treasury headed by George Humphrey was beginning to seek solutions for a problem in which neither Elliott nor Kissinger would ever take the slightest interest. How could those exorbitantly costly defense commitments to the French and the West Germans be financed? By 1955 not only had the world dollar shortage disappeared but also the United States had been incurring deficits in its international payments accounts for every year since 1950. One recourse was to strengthen the International Monetary Fund, not only to divert most of the continuing foreign requests for loans and grants but also to anticipate the day when the United

---

[5] Concurrently a similar Ford grant was used to start the Institute for Strategic Studies in London.

States itself might need the Fund to cope with its excessive spending abroad. Unhappily the Fund was moribund. As recently as May 1951 its Executive Board had adopted a proposal that member nations wishing to draw upon its resources should consult with the Fund's officials to ensure that any use of its moneys would be strictly temporary.

The way had been opened for long-term operations following the appointment in 1952 of a neutral Swede, Ivar Rooth, as the Fund's second Managing Director. Gross drawings by members had fallen to zero in 1950, and had totaled the equivalent of only $35 million in 1951 and $85 million in 1952. As late as 1955 they had been a mere $28 million. Then in 1956 came the Suez crisis, following which both Britain and France sought and obtained large-scale help from the Fund. That year gross drawings totaled $230 million. Suddenly every member became aware of the Fund's potential usefulness, and agitation began for an increase in quotas. Totaling $9.2 billion, those funds consigned to the Fund by its members began to appear small by comparison with the rapid expansion in world trade and the consequent need for a central source of reserves, or "liquidity," upon which members might draw in emergencies. In September 1959 agreement was therefore reached to increase the total of members' quotas by 50 percent, to $14.7 billion. Under the rules of the Bretton Woods system members were required to deposit one-quarter (the so-called gold tranche) of their quotas in gold and the remainder in their own national currencies. The voting strength of each member was determined by the size of its quota, and it was permitted to draw only its gold tranche at will. Successive drawings were subject to increasingly stringent terms.[6]

In December 1956 another Swede, Per Jacobsson, had been selected to succeed Rooth as the third Chairman of the Executive Board and Managing Director of the Fund. A student of the writings of Gustav Cassel, Jacobsson had worked at the Bank for International Settlements in Basle since its beginnings in 1931. He had also been the author of its shrewd *Annual Reports* and had described himself as a "practical economist." He was not interested in conflicting economic doctrines but was concerned to find workable solutions for everyday international economic problems. Widely admired by bankers throughout the world, both for his technical abilities and for his tolerant grasp of their needs, Jacobsson began to infuse new vitality into the International Monetary Fund.

The most conspicuous monetary phenomenon of that decade was the rapidly increasing quantity of American private investment abroad. In American payments accounts, debits for those foreign investments had begun to rival the spending abroad of the Department of Defense. Together they were

[6] Tew, *International Monetary Co-operation 1945-1970*, pp. 107–124.

becoming embarrassing, and many economists had begun to worry about their inflationary effects. When Jacobsson was invited to address American businessmen gathered at the Hotel Commodore in New York on January 17, 1957, it was symbolic of their interests and his worries that he was introduced by an American Secretary of Defense who had formerly been the president of a company with growing subsidiaries abroad. Jacobsson sought to emphasize that the era of postwar recovery in Europe and the Far East had been completed.

> At the end of 1951, the monetary reserves, in gold and United States dollars, of all countries outside the United States were about $15 billion. They are now in excess of $22 billion. This increase of almost 50 percent in five years is very remarkable. . . . One used to say that when America sneezes, Europe gets pneumonia, which means that even a small recession in this country would have a great effect on the other side of the Atlantic. But we found, very much to our own astonishment in Europe, that when there was a minor recession in the United States, in 1953–1954, Europe was not affected but continued an upward line of business.[7]

Jacobsson's words of warning were not heeded. In 1957 the United States was beginning to experience a recession, accompanied by a brief international payments surplus, the first since 1950. A former Chairman of President Eisenhower's Council of Economic Advisers was also arguing for restraint, with a balanced budget at home and diminished government spending abroad, to secure price stability.[8] Unquestionably Per Jacobsson and Arthur Burns were right. Yet the weight of public and professional opinion was against them, both in the United States and abroad. In part that American recession had been caused by the overvalued dollar and the consequent weakening of American export industries. Yet any devaluation of the dollar was becoming one of those "unthinkable" ideas that have so often dogged monetary history. American consumers, benefiting from overvaluation of the dollar, formed a powerful voting interest. New York's bankers were pleased, because the overvalued dollar enabled them to invest abroad cheaply. And Europeans were continuing to encourage the United States in its excessive foreign spending and investing, which supplied additional liquidity for the remarkable expansion in world trade they had begun to enjoy.

No economist has ever developed an accurate method of determining and forecasting the quantity of cash reserves a nation should maintain. Depending on its individual import and export propensities, the quantity each nation may need will differ from its neighbors', and that quantity will vary as economic conditions change. But in the 1950s the belief was prevalent among

[7] Jacobsson, *Some Monetary Problems National and International,* pp. 341–370.
[8] Burns, *Prosperity Without Inflation.*

economists that as "a rule of thumb" each nation should hold reserves approximately equal to the costs of 3 months of imports. To maintain less was risky, because unexpected disasters could occur even in the best managed economies. To maintain more was considered a reversion to the old mercantilist doctrine of hoarding unnecessarily large reserves, to the detriment of domestic consumers and foreign competitors. Under the rules of the Bretton Woods system, as world trade expanded, the increasing need for reserves could be satisfied only by garnering dollars, sterling and gold from the deficits in the international payments accounts of the United States and Britain—or, as gold fanciers continued to urge, by increasing the official price of gold.

The severe postwar depression so widely feared had not occurred. Nor had there been anywhere a devastating deflationary period, deliberately endured, comparable to that of the early 1920s. The American and the British public and the great majority of their economists had therefore become convinced that "Keynesian economics" had succeeded, that deficit spending by governments could ensure continuous economic growth at the cost of a small, painless inflation rate. World population growth, which had begun in the United States with the postwar "baby boom" in 1946, had been adding three million new American citizens each year. That alone had appeared a compelling reason to most of the economists who had been insisting on continuing growth in gross national product. It is one of the simple, basic facts of economics that, if growth in gross national product does not substantially exceed population growth, the consequence will be a painful, socially and politically disruptive decline in the living standards of many. And the 1950s was the decade in which literally billions of debtors had begun for the first time to enjoy the benefits of credit at little cost to themselves. They demanded more. To safeguard savings against the demand inflation caused by that expansion of credit, investment advisers had been urging creditors to place their capital in common stocks. The stock exchanges of New York, London, Paris, Frankfurt and Zürich were booming. As the planners of the Bretton Woods system had foreseen, its regime of fixed exchange rates was encouraging many bankers and traders to venture abroad for the first time.

Nevertheless Per Jacobsson continued to worry about the rapid growth in dollar reserves held abroad. The question in his mind was not doctrinal but eminently practical. How much of a good thing was enough, and how much was too much? A student of monetary history, he was well aware that money is like cake. Too much of any form of money would make any monetary system ill.

> Now when most countries in the Western world are introducing flexible monetary policies, we have to begin to talk about the limitations, for no credit policy is alone sufficient to secure monetary stability.

And in April 1957 he cautioned:

> a stage has now been reached where a return to monetary stability is demanded
> with growing insistence. . . . It seems that the human spirit cannot give of its
> best if it is harassed by all the uncertainties to which rapidly changing money
> values give rise.

Yet the world's billions of debtors did not want to discuss any limitations on
their credit.

Though the United States was becoming one of those debtors, complacent
officials at the New York Federal Reserve Bank were not unduly concerned
about the increase in foreign short-term dollar assets, which had risen to an
historic high of $13.4 billion by the end of 1956. The following May one of
those American officials wrote:

> Foreign dollar gains—to the extent that they accrue to monetary authorities—
> may generally be employed for acquiring gold from the United States Treasury.
> Yet actually they were so used only in the very modest amount of $1.2 billion
> during the 1948–1956 period. Foreign central banks and other monetary author-
> ities as a whole have preferred to add the great bulk of their net dollar acquisi-
> tions to their dollar reserves. The increase in foreign short-term dollar assets thus
> affords clear evidence of the fact that numerous central banks are finding dollar
> assets increasingly attractive relative to gold as an international store of value.[9]

Those dollar assets were interest paying, and gold was not. As late as 1956,
the holdings of the United States and the Soviet Union being excluded, official gold stocks held by central banks had totaled only $14.750 billion.

Nevertheless a rude surprise awaited the New York Federal Reserve Bank.
In 1958, partly to meet anticipated quota increases at the International Monetary Fund, but mostly because the Suez crisis had reminded Europeans of
the political importance of cash in hand, they drained $2.275 billion in gold
from the United States. Though intent on retaining and enhancing all the
trading and monetary advantages they had been enjoying, they became increasingly eager for political independence from the United States. Britain
made the largest increase in its gold reserves, of $1.250 billion. Italy was
second, with an increase of $634 million. Belgium took $357 million and the
Netherlands $306 million.

Later the British biographer of Lord Keynes, implicitly referring to the run
on British reserves before and during the Suez crisis of 1956, would explain
the attitude that was becoming prevalent among European central bankers.

> From a liberal point of view I . . . regard it as a far better thing that liquidity
> should be increased by giving to each country more reserves in the form of more
> gold (or reliable foreign exchange) under its own fist, than by giving it an oppor-

---

[9] Klopstock, *The International Status of the Dollar*, pp. 1–2. See also Appendix.

tunity of constantly having to renegotiate loans, on an ever larger scale, with an international committee. Gold—"that anonymous asset," as Sir Ralph Hawtrey once called it—is the greatest sheet anchor of liberty in the economic world. If you have gold under your fist, you are a free man. If you have to argue with an international committee to get it, you are not.[10]

The lines of battle were emerging for the great debate that would preoccupy monetary experts and vex their political leaders throughout the next decade and more. Gold or credit? Nationalism or internationalism? Though gold had long disappeared from the coinages in circulation and had been relegated to a minor monetary role as an asset never seen by the public, the size of a nation's gold reserves had continued to be a popular if erroneous measure of national power and prestige. Moreover there were many economists like Harrod who had little or no sympathy for speculators and hoarders of gold and yet argued that it continued to provide useful monetary "discipline." Governments would not deliberately inflate their currencies for fear of losing those gold reserves so cherished by their citizens.

By 1959 officials of the New York Federal Reserve Bank, whose primary concern was the stability of the international monetary system, had begun to show signs of anxiety. One of them argued:

Last year's experience points once again to the conclusion that a fundamental underpinning of the working balances and monetary reserves held by other countries in the form of dollars is firm confidence in the ability and determination of the United States to maintain its official price of gold. Any spread of doubt concerning that price can materially lessen the flexibility and reliability of monetary arrangements throughout the world.[11]

In Washington both the United States Treasury and the Federal Reserve Board were more concerned about domestic implications. Quietly and repeatedly they studied the possibility of devaluing the dollar and invariably rejected it. One reason given was that hoary bugbear "prestige." Moreover they agreed that devaluation would have threatened the dollar's further acceptability as an international reserve asset, even if Europeans had been willing to relinquish the export advantages they had gained by undervaluing their currencies. There were no indications that they would have been willing to do so. Another reason given was the need to dampen domestic inflation with cheap, competitive imports. At the International Monetary Fund Per Jacobsson concurred. "So let us leave the gold price alone."[12]

But doubts did begin to spread. In 1958 and 1959 the United States incurred further deficits in its international payments accounts, and they were

[10] Harrod, in *The Dollar in Crisis,* edited by Seymour Harris, p. 62.

[11] Kriz, *Gold in World Monetary Affairs Today,* p. 20.

[12] Jacobsson, *International Monetary Problems 1957–1963,* p. 65.

substantial—$3.5 billion in 1958, $3.8 billion in 1959, and more than $3 billion was forecast for 1960. Because of those continuing American payments deficits, by December 29, 1958, Britain, West Germany, France, the Netherlands, Belgium, Austria, Italy and the Scandinavian countries had been able to rebuild sufficient national reserves to restore the convertibility of their own currencies into dollars for nonresidents. None of them ever contemplated restoring their citizens' right to convert their paper currencies into gold. The European Payments Union having become unnecessary, it was liquidated. To increase their national reserves still further, those West European countries and Japan were continuing to encourage their export industries in every possible way. It was becoming obvious to a few economists that the persistent American payments deficits and consequent loss of gold reserves were simply the "mirror image" of those West European and Japanese payments surpluses and growing national reserves. No one had foreseen that essential flaw in the Bretton Woods system, and Europeans were loath to discuss it.

Members of the United States Congress were not convinced that the problem of American international payments deficits was insoluble. In 1959 their Joint Economic Committee therefore asked a former Assistant to the Secretary of the Treasury and Director of Research at the International Monetary Fund to prepare a study. By January 1960 John Fitzgerald Kennedy, the junior Senator from Massachusetts, was able to read closely Edward Bernstein's conclusion that:

> The large surplus in the U.S. balance of payments, which generated the fear of a persistent dollar shortage, has given way to a U.S. deficit. In the meantime, Western Europe has emerged as a surplus region in its international payments. No doubt, the payments position of the United States will be restored. It is essential, however, that this should be done promptly and without depressing the economy of the United States or inducing a contraction in world trade.

The Eisenhower era was ending. John Foster Dulles had died of cancer, having failed to achieve the European Defense Community he had sought for so many years. His successors would shrink from the onerous task of persuading the French, but Bernstein could not be expected to foresee their errors. Casting a cold eye over the international balance sheet of the United States, he singled out the obvious sector in which major savings could have been made.

> By far the greater part of U.S. government expenditures abroad are in connection with defense—that is, our military expenditures abroad and military grants. In 1951, Europe accounted for about 52 percent of total U.S. expenditures of nearly $2.7 billion for these purposes. In 1958, it accounted for about 57 percent of total expenditures of nearly $6 billion for these purposes. It is not possible to separate the interests of the United States and other countries in the common

defense. What can be said is that the allocation of common defense costs on the basis of economic conditions that prevailed in 1951 is unrealistic in 1960.

As Western Europe had become prosperous, it had become not less dependent on the United States for its defense, but rather more. Because West Europeans had been permitted thus to divert their own tax revenues to domestic improvements and social services, observers had begun to comment on the comparative shabbiness of American cities. Bernstein emphasized the changed financial circumstances.

> Since 1950, the gold reserves of the United States have fallen by about $5 billion and short-term liabilities to foreign banks and official institutions have increased by about $8 billion. . . . The United States cannot permit the continued weakening of its reserve position without losing the freedom it has long had in formulating domestic economic policy. . . . The production, exports and reserves of most European countries have increased enormously. . . . Under these circumstances, it is not unreasonable to discuss with our friends and allies in Europe the desirability of their meeting in larger part some of the costs of their defense now met through our military expenditures and military grants.[13]

In retrospect it seems incredible that as late as 1960 there continued to be any justification for spending so much as an American penny for the defense of Western Europe. The first squadron of Atlas intercontinental ballistic missiles became operational in that year. American outposts on all other continents became obsolete, for the defense of North America. But as President, the Roman Catholic John Kennedy would refuse to contemplate use of that new strategic weapon. Instead he would choose to emphasize conventional armaments to "police" the many small "brushfire wars" that continued to trouble Africa and Asia. Increasing quantities of those weapons would be required, because the "cold war" would resume its virulence during his administration. And West Europeans would consistently refuse to pay the full costs of their own defense, the only measure that could have swiftly ended American payments deficits and restored stability in the Bretton Woods monetary system.

A former British Treasury official candidly expressed the unhelpful attitude of Britain.

> Under present circumstances it seems that some [American] loss of gold is inevitable and must be accepted. . . . At the end of 1959 the United States gold stock alone stood at $19.507 billion—some eighteen years' supply even at the rate of gold loss of 1959. It is true that about $12 billion of this total stands as legal backing for Federal Reserve notes and deposits, in a 1 to 4 ratio, but this ratio is of little significance and, if the legal reserve ratio is ever approached, there is little doubt that the law would be altered to give additional "free reserves". . . .

---

[13] Bernstein, *International Effects of U.S. Economic Policy*, pp. 1, 5 and 71.

> To the United Kingdom, accustomed to looking at the sterling area reserves in terms of a few months' supply, the American reserves appear more than adequate and we may be forgiven if, in the meantime, we regard some redistribution of the world's stock of monetary gold as healthy.(14)

What that spendthrift Britisher carefully neglected to mention was that by 1959 the outstanding short-term dollar claims against the United States had risen to equal that $19.507 billion in gold reserves. Thereafter Europeans would begin to question whether the American dollar was truly "as good as gold." The United States alone, as manager of the Bretton Woods system, was responsible for preserving its smooth functioning. That task was becoming increasingly difficult, and harmful to the domestic economy of the United States. Naturally that was of no concern to the British, who had become parasitic. British economists were urging an end to peacetime conscription and drastic reductions in British defense expenditures.

Nearing the end of a long, unpopular war against Communist guerrilla forces in newly independent Malaya, General Sir Gerald Templer and the British General Staff had therefore been quietly urging their American friends to intervene forcefully in South Vietnam, to defend not only Malaya but also Thailand, Singapore and the new nation of Indonesia against any further Communist expansion. Long after the departure of British, French and Dutch troops and colonial officials, European commercial interests and investments in Southeast Asia would remain extensive. As Prime Minister, Harold Macmillan enticingly invited President Kennedy to protect those European interests. Rashly Kennedy would begin to do so.

THE RETURN OF CHARLES DE GAULLE

Nevertheless no help could be expected from France. In French diplomacy, malice had become the guiding motive. The Fourth Republic had vanished.

> By the beginning of 1958, the regime was so worm-eaten that a strong push would have sufficed to overthrow it. But in fact, it collapsed by itself, slowly, under the weight of its own errors, in the midst of general indifference. Few French were willing to take to the streets to fight against it, but fewer still to defend it, for it no longer commanded either loyalty or respect.(15)

The French Army had become the final arbiter in the political life of France, and there was only one Frenchman who knew how to tame that army. Regardless of prodigious efforts and expenditures, one-third (some $2 billion) of which had been paid by the United States, the war to hold the French colonies in Indochina had been lost. Dien Bien Phu had been a

(14) Scammell, *International Monetary Policy,* p. 349.
(15) Soustelle, *L'espérance trahie,* p. 15.

humiliation not only for the Army but also for the entire French people. The Geneva settlement of 1954 had been regarded by French generals as a betrayal by the politicians. A few months later the insurrection in Algeria had begun. Though French generals had been determined that this time there would not be any failure of political and diplomatic support, they had also been conscious that the Fourth Republic had been disintegrating. Among other signs French gold reserves had been dwindling, from $1.550 billion in 1945 to a low of $575 million in 1957. The appointment of an Anglo–American "good offices team" in February 1958 to investigate French bombings in neighboring Tunisia had confirmed their worst fears and suspicions. Throughout North Africa the French colonists called *pieds-noirs* were affronted suddenly to learn that John Foster Dulles was no longer willing to subsidize French colonial wars. All were deeply offended by Senator John Kennedy's insistent call for an end to the French Empire.

In Paris a constitutional lawyer named Michel Debré had been demanding the return to power of Charles de Gaulle. A bitterly effective pamphleteer, Debré had launched a vitriolic periodical *Le Courrier de la colère* to promote the opinion that only de Gaulle could keep Algeria French. In his office Debré surrounded himself with mementos and engravings of the first French revolution of 1789 and the first Napoleon's subsequent Consulate. In the spring of 1958 de Gaulle himself predicted that "when the wives of the capitalists begin to tremble before the Communists, then yes, they will come to seek me." At the Parisian bank of Guy de Rothschild another of de Gaulle's "barons" named Georges Pompidou had been quietly working since 1954, not only to extend the Rothschild oil investments in North Africa but also to build a widespread network of support for de Gaulle among the bankers and industrialists of France. Though de Gaulle had remained ignorant of public finance, which he scornfully called *l'épicerie,* hard experience had taught him that cash in hand and a reliable source of it were essential for any would-be revolutionary.[16]

At last de Gaulle's opportunity arrived. On May 13, 1958, the generals in Algeria renounced the authority of the Fourth Republic and created a civil and military "Committee of Public Safety" chaired by a general. Paris began to fill with rumors that paratroopers from Algeria would soon descend upon the Élysée Palace, to dictate their terms to the diminutive, calculating President René Coty. On May 15 de Gaulle decided that the time had come to make a public statement.

> Once before the country, in the depths of its being, gave me its trust to lead it, in its entirety, to salvation. Today, before the trials that once again press upon it, it should know that I hold myself ready to take over the powers of the Republic.

[16] Crozier, *De Gaulle,* vol. 2, pp. 453–455; Alexandre, *Le Duel de Gaulle-Pompidou,* pp. 41–74.

Militant Gaullist women began to collect the private telephone numbers of ministers, and to send them anonymous, threatening calls at all hours of the day and night. Others organized the printing and distribution throughout France of tens of thousands of postcards bearing printed demands that the politicians should quit and transfer power to Charles de Gaulle. Soon those postcards were reaching the Élysée Palace by the truckload.

On May 29 Coty decided to submit to that turmoil and agitation. He sent a message to the Senate and the Chamber of Deputies, calling upon:

> the most illustrious of Frenchmen, who, during the darkest years of our history, was our leader for the conquest of liberty and who, having achieved national unanimity around his person, spurned dictatorship to establish the Republic.

His message of surrender was heard in silence by those unrepentant politicians, but de Gaulle immediately agreed to meet Coty. That evening they issued a joint communiqué in which de Gaulle demanded plenary powers and a mandate to be confirmed by referendum that would enable him to make constitutional changes. On June 1, after heated and anguished debate, the Chamber of Deputies approved de Gaulle's return to power by a vote of 329 to 224.

The French economy had already made a remarkable recovery, owing not to skillful management but to its natural advantages. The index of French industrial production, based on 100 in 1952, had reached 160 by the spring of 1958. There had been only a slight increase in manpower, but productivity had been rising at a rate of more than 6 percent each year. However, those gains were being jeopardized by the inflationary policies of French governments, which had led not only to budget deficits but also to considerable deficits in the balance of payments. In 1956 and 1957 the Exchange Stabilization Fund had lost more than a billion dollars each year in costly efforts to support the fixed exchange rate of the franc. In 1957 and 1958 France had therefore been compelled to borrow $1.122 billion from the International Monetary Fund, the European Economic Community and the United States. Restrictive credit policies had been slow to take effect. The exchange rate of the franc, which had remained at 350 to the dollar and 980 to the pound since September 20, 1949, had therefore been devalued once again on August 10, 1957. The new rates had been fixed at 420 to the dollar and 1176 to the pound. August was becoming a month in which the French would anticipate some sudden, painful monetary change by their governments, while they were on holiday and could not organize protests.

Thus gold had remained the form of personal savings widely preferred by the French. Though it did not earn interest, it had remained safe from the fluctuations of paper currencies and securities, and from the requisitions of governments. In 1939 the total of French private gold hoards had been estimated at 1700 metric tons. By 1959 it was estimated that the French owned privately some 3000 metric tons, approximately one-quarter of all the gold privately owned throughout the world. The French owned more gold than all other Europeans combined. Their financial advisers had repeatedly pointed out that 100 francs invested in gold bullion in 1914 would have appreciated to 16,031 paper francs by 1958. Gold bullion had therefore increased in price 160 times, while all other commodities had risen approximately 200 times. But 100 francs placed in 20-franc gold coins in 1914 would have been priced at about 20,000 paper francs in 1958. Meanwhile all other kinds of investments, whether in government bonds, private securities, savings accounts or real property, had been subjected to severe losses. Consequent hoarding of gold had become, and was freely acknowledged by French authorities to be, a national frenzy.

To cure that propensity to hoard gold, and to end that French distrust of paper currencies, only a radical "rehabilitation" of the paper franc would serve. The French people simply did not understand that the market value of their gold was supported only by the United States Treasury. Gold had an "intrinsic" and "immutable" value of at least $35 per ounce only because the United States remained willing to pay that price for any quantity sold to it and had refrained from selling its gold reserves to the private markets. Thus the United States Treasury, which did not permit American citizens to own gold, was subsidizing the hoarding instincts of the French. It was a bizarre relationship, and the constant purpose of conservative French politicians and economists was to perpetuate that form of security for their fellow citizens.[17]

When de Gaulle took office in June 1958, he was preoccupied by the difficulties of suppressing the Army revolt in Algeria and introducing constitutional reforms. Nevertheless, as a student and virtually a prisoner of French history, he was well aware of the political and symbolic use the first and third Napoleons had made of gold in earlier efforts to restore the prestige of France. Moreover he had incurred political debts to the banking friends of Michel Debré, his first Prime Minister, and Georges Pompidou, his acting *chef de cabinet*. As a matter of course he therefore accepted Pompidou's suggestion that Antoine Pinay be named Minister of Finances. The Foreign Ministry was assigned to Maurice Couve de Murville, a former Inspector of Finances and a protégé of Jacques Rueff, who had become the most widely known propagandist for gold since the death of Charles Rist.

By June 1958 the French Exchange Stabilization Fund had dwindled to $19 million. Pinay was able not only to stop further flights from the franc but also to reverse them and to recover almost $200 million for the Exchange Stabilization Fund by floating a loan for repatriated capital with repayment

(17) Sédillot, *Du franc Bonaparte au franc de Gaulle*, pp. 175–233.

guaranteed in terms of gold. That "Pinay Loan" of June 13, 1958, was over-subscribed to a total of 324 billion francs, and 150 metric tons of gold were surrendered to the Bank of France. Then on September 30, with the approval of de Gaulle and Pompidou, Pinay formed a committee of eight experts to recommend further monetary reforms. It was chaired by Jacques Rueff, and twice each week Pompidou visited Pinay's office on the rue de Rivoli to discuss their proposals. They closely resembled the stabilization program undertaken three decades earlier by Premier Poincaré, whom Rueff had served at the beginning of his career as an Inspector of Finances.

Unanimously those eight experts, reared in the same traditional French monetary doctrines, recommended deflation and another devaluation of the franc. They also advised an *alourdissement* of that currency, an exercise in mass psychology intended to restore public confidence in its "heaviness" or soundness. The Treaty of Rome had become effective, inaugurating the European Economic Community. French officials considered it essential for political reasons alone that France should enter with a strong currency. Recent precedents were available for their study. In a similar effort to curb inflation by introducing a new currency, in 1947 the Soviet Union had exchanged 10 old rubles for 1 new. That example had already been followed by Rumania in 1947, Poland in 1950, Bulgaria in 1952 and Czechoslovakia in 1953.

Minister Pinay himself was not easily persuaded. "I shall be called 'Pinay-le-purge,'" he complained. Before taking action of any kind, de Gaulle first sought and obtained plenary powers in the referendum of November. On December 21 he was also elected President of the Republic. Then on December 25, in a secret meeting of the Council of State, his Christmas gift to the French people was decreed. It was a further devaluation of the franc, to 493.705 to the dollar and 1,382.376 to the pound. Those odd rates were chosen because hypothetically they provided an even reference to gold. One franc would equal 2 milligrams .900 pure, or 1.80 milligrams of fine gold. It pleased Charles de Gaulle to believe that the franc could thus become independent of the dollar.

In a covering letter to the final report Jacques Rueff had also written:

> It is essential that the new parity be considered definitive. The Committee considers that the establishment of a heavy franc, by the suppression of two zeros in prices and in all the monetary expressions in francs, would convince public opinion that monetary equilibrium is durably established on its new base.

Moreover devaluation was to be accompanied by restoration of convertibility into other currencies for nonresidents and by lifting many exchange regulations. Unfortunately, however, it was not announced until December 29. During the intervening 4 days Frenchmen who had friends on the Council of State speculated heavily. "Scandalous profits" were gained. Pompidou preferred not to investigate, to find who had leaked such vital information. A few days later he retired from office to resume his private post at the Parisian bank of Guy de Rothschild.

The program to establish a "heavy" New Franc began January 1, 1959, with the denomination of all foreign currencies. The American dollar exchange rate became 4.93 New Francs, and the sterling rate 13.82 New Francs. It was accompanied by the announcement that, no later than January 1, 1960, all prices and wages, all capital investments and revenues, all credits and debts, without exception, were to be divided by one hundred. Public reactions were mixed. Many French bankers were enthusiastic about a new parity that was so close to the 1914 rate of 5 francs to the dollar. However, one Parisian commentator described the program as "a slightly pathological manifestation of monetary fetichism." Among the French people there was consternation, caused not only by misunderstanding but also by fear that some were being impoverished for the enrichment of others.

On January 8, 1959, a month before his 33rd birthday, young Valéry Giscard entered the new Cabinet of Michel Debré as a Secretary of State for Finances, to assist in that monetary reform program. He too was a fervent admirer of Poincaré. For the next year and more, immense efforts were required throughout France, to subtract two zeros from every existing numerical expression of money. They were successful. On the Paris Bourse the gold Napoleon had sold at almost 4000 old francs in May 1958. That had been a premium of 40 percent over its legal parity of 2822 old francs. By May 1959, at 35 New Francs, it commanded a premium barely 8 percent higher than its new parity of 32.22. French monetary authorities had also begun to recover control over the foreign exchanges. In July 1959 the French Mint began to produce and distribute new notes and coins, which would "coexist" with the old until 1965. The first of those new coins was a 5-franc silver piece that was sufficiently heavy to convince most of the French that they once again had real money that could rank with the dollar, the pound, the West German mark and the Swiss franc. The contribution to the personal prestige of President de Gaulle was massive. Foreign critics have severely, correctly faulted Jacques Rueff's knowledge of monetary systems and their history. Unquestionably, however, he understood his own countrymen. Certainly he was not the only monetary expert who has catered to the whims and prejudices of his political masters.

By many perennial apologists for France, those efforts were considered an unqualified success. At the end of 1958 French short-term obligations abroad had exceeded its gold and foreign-exchange reserves by more than $500 million. But by September 1959, when President Eisenhower visited Paris, France was on the road to full recovery. When Charles de Gaulle spoke at the *École de Guerre* in November, to announce his refusal to integrate French armed forces with those of NATO, he was confident that thereafter he would not need any financial help from the United States. By the end of 1959 the French Exchange Stabilization Fund had regained more than $1.5 billion, providing a surplus of more than a billion dollars. Benefiting from undervaluation of the franc, French traders began consistently to earn surpluses in the foreign accounts of France. The domestic price increases that had been feared had not exceeded 6 percent overall. There had been neither social disorders nor increased unemployment. The index of industrial production had risen from 156 in May 1958 to 165 in October 1959, regardless of the rigorous efforts to balance the national budget.[18] In a revival of its old bullionist traditions the Bank of France began assiduously to rebuild its gold reserves. By consolidating all holdings, it was able to report total gold stocks of $1.290 billion at the end of 1959. The first successful French atomic bomb test, on February 13, 1960, provided an additional fillip to French national pride. By the end of that year French gold reserves had increased to $1.641 billion. Then they soared to $2.121 billion at the end of 1961, and to $2.587 billion at the end of 1962.

Neighboring countries were so pleased to see France become orderly and self-sufficient that it seemed churlish to criticize President de Gaulle's obsession with amassing gold reserves, to the detriment of French consumers and the Bretton Woods system. American and British officials watched with tolerant amusement, hopeful that it was only a passing fancy. World gold production, chiefly by South Africa, had been reviving. From 21.7 million fine ounces in 1946, it had increased to 24.1 million in 1953, 33.6 million in 1960, and 34.7 million in 1961, when South Africa declared its political independence of Britain. Almost 75 percent of that new gold was going into industrial uses or private hoards, leaving little to increase the world's monetary stocks. Relations between Charles de Gaulle and the Afrikaners were excellent. They not only shared respect for gold but also were united in their dislike of the "Anglo-Saxons" who had preached for so many years that they must mend their ways. By the end of 1963 the Bank of France held gold reserves of $3.175 billion. And on January 27, 1964, de Gaulle established diplomatic relations with the Chinese Communist government of Mao Tse-tung. The towering President de Gaulle had been deeply offended, not only by decades of American and British condescension, but also by the squat Nikita Khrushchev's mocking refusal to take him seriously. During a private visit to Moscow the aging Paul Reynaud had been asked by Khrushchev whether "his pupil," de Gaulle, could last more than a month or two as President of France.

In the autumn of 1964 President de Gaulle made a ceremonial, 25-day tour of South America aboard the French cruiser *Colbert*, sounding foreign

[18] Aron, *France Steadfast and Changing*, pp. 181–183.

opinion on the United States and the Soviet Union. Upon returning to Paris, he announced to his aides that "Tomorrow there will be a movement of all the states hostile to the hegemony of the superpowers. It is the mission of France to exert its influence in that movement." It was a declaration of diplomatic and economic war. In a repetition of his decision 20 years before, at the time of the Bretton Woods Conference, rather than cooperate with his neighbors for their common good, he would become a wrecker to enhance his own standing and the influence of France in world affairs. By the end of 1964 he had the cash in hand with which to play that role. The gold reserves of the Bank of France totaled $3.729 billion, plus $1.376 billion in foreign exchange, for a total of $5.105 billion. He also had a tidy net position of $619 million in the International Monetary Fund and had deftly gained control of its bureaucracy. Without his consent it could no longer act effectively. He was fully prepared to challenge "Anglo–Saxon supremacy" openly in that dimension they had so long considered their own—money.

THE KENNEDY PLEDGE

Per Jacobsson had given discreet support to that reform of the French currency. During a visit to Paris in the summer of 1958 he had briefly lectured the astonished President de Gaulle on French history. Perhaps with tongue in cheek Jacobsson had admonished him:

> Mon Général, I am sure you will do well to give the French a better constitution, but you never know—the French are awfully politically-minded. But if you could, like Napoleon, give a good currency to the French people, you would certainly have done a permanent service to France.[19]

De Gaulle had promised to remember that lesson. To his subordinates he had also begun quietly to express an interest in that International Monetary Fund.

Regarding the future of the entire Bretton Woods monetary system, Jacobsson could see the writing on the wall. He began to sound opinion in many countries, always reminding his audiences that the 19th century gold standard had become obsolete. When invited to deliver the Stamp Memorial Lecture in London, on November 19, 1959, he chose the significant title "Towards a Modern Monetary Standard." By continuing its excessive expenditures abroad for the defense of Western Europe, the United States would inevitably incur further substantial deficits in its international payments accounts and additional losses from its gold reserves. Sooner or later it would therefore be compelled to declare the dollar inconvertible into gold,

[19] Jacobsson, *op. cit.*, pp. 255–256.

simply to retain a minimal quantity for wartime needs. In the calculations of Jacobsson and many others the questions were how much gold the United States might choose to keep as a war reserve, when the dollar would become inconvertible, and what kind of monetary system should replace the gold-dollar standard. To emphasize to John Kennedy, as a presidential candidate, that Europeans had begun to be wary of the dollar, in the summer and autumn of 1960 there was a flurry of speculation on London's bullion market. For a few days in October the price was driven to more than $40 per fine ounce.

In money matters Kennedy was firmly, instinctively conservative. Nearing the end of a close electoral campaign against Vice-President Richard Nixon, he was also determined not to give that tricky opponent any opportunities to accuse him of abandoning established American policies. On October 31 Kennedy therefore issued a sharp warning that:

> the rise in the price of gold reflected the hope of a small number of speculators in a very thin market that the dollar will one day be devalued. Their hope is that this will be the necessary consequence of a continued shift in the balance of payments against the United States. . . . In 1953, the incoming administration inherited a balance of payments which was the strongest in the world. Almost every nation had a dollar shortage, and our gold reserve was at one of the highest points in our history. But between 1953 and 1960 the flow of gold has been reversed, the balance of payments has gone against us, and our reserves have dwindled. There have been five major reasons for this sharp reversal in our balance-of-payments position. First, we have heavy commitments abroad for military and economic aid, and for the support of our own overseas military forces. . . . What then must we do, what would a new Democratic administration do to reverse the present downward trend in our balance of payments? First, we pledge ourselves to maintain the current value of the dollar. If elected President I shall not devalue the dollar from its present rate. Rather I shall defend the present value and its soundness. Secondly, we will begin immediate and vigorous negotiations to remove artificial barriers to the flow of American goods overseas, as well as restrictions on the flow of capital to this country. We will ask our allies to share the increasing burden of building the military and economic strength of the free world. . . . [20]

In distant California, at The RAND Corporation, studies had already begun on the dim prospects for arms control and disarmament negotiations with the Soviet Union. Secrecy was maintained, largely to prevent frustration by British, French and German conservatives. In November Bonn received a visit from Douglas Dillon, a Francophile banker from New York who had served Eisenhower as Deputy Secretary of State for Economic Affairs and had been designated by President-elect Kennedy as the new Secretary of the

[20] Roosa, *The Dollar and World Liquidity*, pp. 265–268.

Treasury. Dillon's purpose was to impress on Chancellor Adenauer and Lud-wig Erhard the need to make direct, substantial and continuing contributions to the costs of maintaining American troops in West Germany. After long, friendly talks the only tangible result would be meager 4.76 percent revalua-tions of the West German mark and the Dutch guilder in March of 1961. American negotiators have remained remarkably softhearted, and softhead-ed, regarding American expenditures for the defense of Western Europe.[21]

In money as in medicine palliatives do not cure. When President Kennedy and Secretary Dillon impetuously decided not to impose the drastic but over-due cure of devaluing the dollar and withdrawing American troops from Western Europe, the eventual triumph of paper over gold became inevitable. Historically an abundance of any other form of money has always caused the rarer gold to disappear into hoards, both public and private. The continuing American payments deficits were $3.3 billion in 1962, $2.3 billion in 1963 and $1.3 billion in 1964. The gold reserves of the United States were reduced to $16.057 billion by the end of 1962, $15.6 billion by the end of 1963 and $15.5 billion by the end of 1964. Private capital outflows from the United States were also accelerating as Americans sought more profitable invest-ments abroad in a world no longer eager for their dollars. Loudly defended by most American economists in the "liberal" cause of free world trade and capital movements, American banks and companies had begun to believe that their operations overseas were somehow sacrosanct and immune from rational criticism.

The United States was seriously at fault in seeking to postpone essential reforms as long as possible so that it could maintain those commitments to the defense of Western Europe. Europeans themselves were also grievously in error, in their stubborn insistence upon retaining every advantage they had gained since 1945, long after the justifications for American generosity had vanished. Inevitably the consequences of their delays became highly infla-tionary as American payments deficits continued to flood the world with dollars in unnecessarily large quantities. Many a speculative enterprise was launched, and many a suspect, inflationary venture, merely because those dollars became so easy to borrow in the "Eurodollar markets" that began to appear early in the 1960s.

Nor was there any shortage of proposals for international monetary reform. Every economist eager to take his place in the history books alongside Keynes and White suddenly experienced an uncontrollable itch for fame as the au-thor of a new and more daring reform plan. Eminent American economists who should have known better became apologists for the persistent American payments deficits, arguing that expanding world trade required enormous

[21] Erhard, *The Economics of Success,* pp. 347–351.

increases in liquidity that could be satisfied only with dollars. Sharply European critics replied that the United States had become spendthrift, by which they meant that American spending abroad should stop everywhere except in Europe. The plans of White and Keynes were removed from library shelves, dusted, and became required reading in university courses. Few of those students, and still fewer of their instructors, had any accurate knowledge of the provenance. A Bernstein reform plan appeared, one by Reginald Maudling, and another by Sir Roy Harrod, who reminded readers that he had been present while the great Lord Keynes had been drafting his earlier proposals. There was a Triffin Plan, a Stamp Plan, a Machlup Plan and a Lutz Plan. Academic disputes proliferated. Several economists thoughtfully produced variant plans, which enabled them to multiply their arguments endlessly among themselves for more than a decade. It is doubtful that any of them were carefully studied by the finance ministers and central bankers whose attention was so avidly sought. But those well-publicized academic disputes did discredit the dollar and the pound and kept the money markets in a state of constant apprehension, fearing hourly an approaching Doomsday that would end Western civilization forever.

Throughout the 1960s, as countless other currencies were devalued against the dollar and it remained damagingly overvalued, the competitive position of the United States continued to deteriorate. The domestic consequences were unnecessary unemployment and the gradual disappearance of many industries that could no longer compete with cheap imports. Though American consumers benefited, the huge profits were reaped by foreign workers and manufacturers. Slowly the economy of the United States was drained of capital, technology and jobs, for the benefit of Western Europe and Japan. Whenever unemployment in Britain, France or Italy exceeded 2 percent, their trade union leaders began to talk wildly of revolution. In Washington the Department of State became duly alarmed and urged additional American concessions to those prosperous yet unreliable West Europeans and Japanese. Northern Europe was importing more than eleven million "guest workers" from the poor countries of Southern Europe and Africa, to do the manual tasks that had become distasteful to European workers and beneath their dignity. Meanwhile, in the United States, unemployment rarely fell below 5 percent. Feebly attempting to remedy American payments deficits without resort to devaluation, Kennedy's economic advisers recommended a handful of minor palliatives as "long-term correctives," but he did not live long enough to see that they had been wrong.[22]

In November 1963 President Kennedy was unexpectedly succeeded by the

[22] Behold the villains. Harris, *Economics of the Kennedy Years*, pp. 147–175; and Reuss, *The Critical Decade*, pp. 63–103.

ill-educated Lyndon Johnson, and the international payments accounts of the United States began to turn from bad to worse. Johnson had always deferred to the populist traditions and financial leaders of his native Texas, and their incessant demands for an ever-increasing supply of money at low interest rates. His devious efforts to form a national consensus for his proposed "Great Society" by making private deals with Republican leaders secured his own reelection in November 1964 but would wreck his party. Those unchecked Federal spending programs bought votes at home but disillusioned European bankers who had retained some confidence in the ability of the United States to manage the Bretton Woods gold-exchange system. There were no compensating cuts in American expenditures abroad. The Federal budget deficits of the United States began to get out of control. Though devaluation of the dollar and withdrawal of all American armed forces from Western Europe remained the only measures that could have ended the chronic disequilibrium in American payments accounts and might also have stopped the growing political friction between the United States and Western Europe, they had become unmentionable topics that neither would consider.

An unrecognized tragedy of those insensate years had been the premature retirement and death of Per Jacobsson on May 5, 1963. Jacobsson knew how to influence President de Gaulle and how to retain his respect. If he had lived to serve another term at the International Monetary Fund, practical reforms might have been accomplished quickly and quietly, to the lasting benefit of all nations. The incessant, damaging disputes and much of the inflation of the following decade might have been averted. But the "might-have-beens" of history have never been a valid approach to the facts. What did happen was that President Kennedy and Douglas Dillon agreed, as a conciliatory gesture to Charles de Gaulle, that Jacobsson should be succeeded as Managing Director by Pierre-Paul Schweitzer, French Inspector General of Finances.

It has always been an error to make any real concessions to the French. In the case of Schweitzer the reasons given for his nomination were specious. As an Alsatian born in Strasbourg, he was supposedly qualified to mediate in any dispute between France and West Germany. Yet surely the International Monetary Fund should not have been dominated by those archaic squabbles between the French and the Germans. As a nephew of Albert Schweitzer, the famed medical missionary in Zaire, he was also presumed to be acceptable to the new self-governing nations of Africa. At best that was condescending recognition of the end of European empires overseas. For the next decade, whenever a French President sought to stop some measure within the Fund, he could and would apply quiet pressure upon Schweitzer. Yet that appointment had been a precondition for French agreement to discuss any kind of change in the Bretton Woods system. The French had learned how to profit from its existing rules and were loath to consider any changes that might in any way have lessened the advantages they had begun to enjoy. Over the next decade they would demonstrate conclusively that, whenever they refuse to cooperate fully and freely, the only sensible couse for other nations is to proceed without them.

On October 2, 1963, the United States Treasury issued a press release that passed almost unnoticed. On behalf of the Group of Ten,[23] financially the most powerful of the Fund's members, Secretary Dillon announced their agreement that elimination of the payments deficits of the United States and Britain was the most important objective to be sought within the near future. Dillon added that they had also decided to undertake a thorough examination of the outlook for the operation of the international monetary system and of its probable needs for further liquidity. Their studies were to be made "with particular emphasis on the possible magnitude and nature of the future needs for reserves and for supplementary credit facilities which may arise."

By August 10, 1964, Valéry Giscard, now French Finance Minister and acting Chairman of the Ministers of the Group of Ten, was able to report:

> The Ministers and Governors believe that . . . the spirit and practise of coopera-
> tion that have now been achieved warrant confidence that fully adequate, but
> not excessive, resources will be made available to meet the liquidity require-
> ments of the world as a whole. This readiness of their countries to work together
> in meeting unexpected developments or longer range requirements will strength-
> en the capacity of the international monetary system to support and maintain
> the objectives of growth, employment and price stability that are shared among
> all people.[24]

Yet scarcely 6 months later, to the embarrassment of the non-Gaullist Giscard, President de Gaulle would denounce his efforts and would ostentatiously throw a spanner into that new machinery for international monetary cooperation.

At a carefully staged press conference in the gilded ballroom of the Élysée Palace, on February 4, 1965, Charles de Gaulle proclaimed:

> The gold-exchange standard no longer corresponds to present realities and in
> consequence entails heavier and heavier inconveniences. . . . We consider it is
> necessary that international trade should rest, as before the two world wars, on
> an indisputable monetary basis bearing the mark of no particular country. What
> basis? Indeed, there can be no other criterion, no other standard than gold. Yes,
> gold which never changes, which can be shaped into ingots, bars, coins, which

---

[23] Belgium, Britain, Canada, France, West Germany, Italy, Japan, the Netherlands, Sweden and the United States. Switzerland, not a member of the Fund, participated in the Group of Ten's deliberations as an observer.

[24] Roosa, *Monetary Reform for the World Economy,* p. 135.

has no nationality and which is eternally and universally accepted as the inalterable fiduciary value *par excellence*. Indeed the end of the gold-exchange standard without upheavals and the restoration of the gold standard, as well as complementary and provisional measures which are essential, particularly the organization of international credit on this new basis—all this should be examined carefully by the states and particularly by those states which have special responsibilities because of their economic and financial might.

Needless to add, the franc and French gold reserves were now mighty once again.

Throughout the world's money markets there was consternation. Why had Charles de Gaulle decided to disinter the gold standard, a monetary system that had been wrecked beyond repair a half-century before? His long-awaited opportunity to humiliate the United States had arrived at last. Two other events occurred that same day, February 4. The Soviet Prime Minister, Alexei Kosygin, landed in Hanoi, the capital of Communist North Vietnam, for discussions on Soviet aid programs. And McGeorge Bundy, earlier a coauthor of Henry Stimson's diaries and now an Assistant to President Lyndon Johnson, appeared in Saigon, the capital of South Vietnam, for similar though opposed talks. So far as President de Gaulle was concerned, both Vietnams remained areas of continuing French influence in which the "superpowers" had no right to meddle. In league with Mao Tse-tung he had therefore begun his efforts to humble those usurpers. There were opportunities in Eastern Europe to embarrass the Soviet Union, and gold had become a mighty stick to use against the United States. It could only endear him to French voters, so many of whom lived in eager anticipation of the day when the official price of their gold hoards might rise. However, lest anyone accuse Charles de Gaulle of venal motives, he concluded that startling statement to the press by emphasizing that his lofty mission was to achieve "a Europe which exists in agreement and co-operation from the Atlantic to the Urals." French leadership was implicit. It was nothing less than an attempt to revive the 19th century Latin Union, which had been dominated by those gold Napoleons so beloved by the French.

The hapless, overconfident Lyndon Johnson and McGeorge Bundy had not been listening. Three days later, on February 7, American aircraft flew their first bombing missions over North Vietnam. Alexei Kosygin was rudely shaken. The "cold war" would be further prolonged, and the Bretton Woods gold-dollar system would become another of its many victims. The International Monetary Fund itself would narrowly escape destruction.

8 = The Excesses of Paper
1965–

History unfolds in ever-changing combinations and permutations of nations, often defying man's most benevolent efforts. Uncritical American support for Nationalist China throughout the 1930s had so exasperated the Japanese that many had become convinced their nation could survive only by swiftly, decisively crippling the United States Navy at Pearl Harbor in December 1941. And they had. Yet less than 4 years later, on September 2, 1945, a newly launched American battleship named for Harry Truman's *Missouri* had lain at anchor off Yokohama in the same roadstead occupied almost a century before by the flagship of Admiral Perry, who had first opened Japan to Yankee traders. There General Douglas MacArthur had demanded and received the surrender of a Japan that had fully expected to be raped and looted by its conquerors, as the Japanese Army had devastated China. Instead those inscrutable Yankees, in the name of an outlandish ideology called "democracy," began reforms that would radically change the face of Japan, if not its heart. The Constitution of the Emperor Meiji was discarded, and a new Constitution proclaimed that henceforth the babbling Diet would be the highest institution of power, elected by something called "universal suffrage." Yes, that really did mean women too.

THE PROBLEM CALLED JAPAN

The Ninth Article of the new Constitution declared that the Japanese people "forever renounce war as a sovereign right of the nation and the threat or use

206

of force as means of settling disputes." In subsequent efforts to reeducate Japan perhaps the finest object lesson taught by the United States was the summary dismissal of MacArthur on April 11, 1951, for failure to obey the orders of his civilian commander-in-chief President Truman.[1] Yet it remains doubtful that the Japanese understood what had happened and why. The Emperor Hirohito and his people had been only too pleased to disband their own Army and Navy, whose generals and admirals had taken pride in similar disobedience of orders and had always prevailed. For that very reason the Japanese have been delighted ever since to permit American taxpayers to provide costly armed forces for the defense of Japan, so that they could turn to mastering the manufacturing techniques and trading skills of the Yankees. Observers noted that the Japanese excelled because they closely heeded the instructions in training manuals, as Americans never have. Soon those observers would begin to wonder who was teaching whom. And in war-ravaged China, so desperately in need of help, the burgeoning Communist movement of Mao Tse-tung was embittered by the blunt refusal of the United States to permit reparations to be extracted from Japan to assist the reconstruction of traditional allies. Instead those unfathomable Yankees, once again in the name of democracy, began to rebuild, then enrich the ancient enemy, Japan. Orientals could only marvel at such baffling illogic.

Some retribution had been exacted. Several thousand Japanese soldiers and civilians had been tried for war crimes, and almost a quarter-million had been barred from further participation in public affairs. The Soviet Union had occupied southern Sakhalin, the Kurile Islands and several islets near Hokkaido. Korea regained its independence, though divided at the thirty-eight parallel. Manchukuo again became Manchuria and an integral part of China. Formosa also reverted to Chinese rule. The British returned to Hong Kong, and the United States occupied not only Okinawa in the Ryukyus but also the islands throughout the Eastern Pacific that had formerly been mandated to Japan by the League of Nations. Their Empire gone, the Japanese people were confined within the limits of their own archipelago.

At the time of Japan's surrender, its economy was prostrate. Almost all major cities and most factories had been heavily damaged by bombings. The few that had escaped destruction were immobilized by the organizational dislocations that had followed the sudden collapse of Japanese authority. Stocks of raw materials had been almost exhausted, and food supplies were very low. Industrial production, having been reduced to 10 percent of its 1937 levels, was restricted to makeshifts such as converting steel helmets into pots

[1] Sebald and Brines, *With MacArthur in Japan*, pp. 211–241. The irreverent Secretary of the Army Pace, who had been assigned to deliver that dismissal, later denied reports that he "had slipped it under MacArthur's door, then run like hell."

and pans, carving wood scraps into clogs and making wood pulp into ersatz cloth. Unusually bad weather had reduced harvests to abnormally low levels, and fishing had been curtailed by the destruction of boats and the shortage of fuel. Official rations dropped to 1050 calories each day per person, and deliveries were often as much as 2 weeks late. Soon General MacArthur began to cable Washington, requesting emergency shipments of food and medicines. During a brief visit former President Hoover also confirmed the estimates of Japanese officials that at least 2 million tons of grain would be needed during the first year of occupation, to prevent a million deaths from starvation. Slowly Washington was awakening to the heavy costs of victory.

Deficit financing had been a characteristic of Japanese fiscal policies ever since it had abandoned the gold standard in December 1931. From 1932 onward the Finance Minister had been Korekiyo Takahashi, the "Japanese Keynes." He had literally spent Japan out of the depression of that decade, until his assassination in 1936 for resisting further military expenditures. His successors had surrendered. During the war years, 1937 to 1945, they had resorted to rigid controls that had effectively dampened inflation without restricting expansion of the economy. Government budget deficits had risen from 13.4 billion yen in 1941–1942 to 76.6 billion in 1945–1946, while the money supply of currency and demand deposits had soared from 30 billion yen to 140 billion. Disappearance of the wartime controls caused a spending spree and an immediate jump in prices. The note issue of the Bank of Japan totaled 30 billion yen on August 15, 1945, then increased by another 40 billion during the next 6 weeks as Japanese military and civilian disbursing officers paid government debts. As Japanese citizens also withdrew personal bank deposits, fearing confiscation during the Allied occupation, violent inflation began.

Between 1936 and April 1946 the index of wholesale prices rose from 1 to 15, and black market prices even higher. A currency conversion program attempted early in 1946 was only briefly effective. Government deficits continued to increase, from approximately 103 billion yen in 1947–1948 to 166 billion in 1948–1949, as the central government and the banking system infused funds into the economy in futile efforts to reconstruct basic industries at a time when private savings were negligible and raw materials scarce. A Reconstruction Finance Bank, founded in January 1947, obtained funds by selling its debentures to the Bank of Japan. Government debt rose from 150 billion yen in mid-1945 to 531 billion in mid-1949. From the end of 1945 to the beginning of 1949 the money supply rose from 140 billion yen to 787 billion. By March 1949 the index of wholesale prices had therefore soared to 197. But in 1948 industrial production was still no more than 40 percent of 1937 levels, and agricultural output also remained below prewar quantities. There was almost no foreign trade. Wartime destruction of shipping and losses of foreign assets had ended earnings from invisible exports. By 1945 the gold reserves of the Bank of Japan had been reduced to $125 million, and by 1948 to $3 million. As late as 1950 they were only $7 million, and reserves of foreign currencies were negligible.[2]

Slowly it was becoming clear to Allied occupation authorities that the only practical way to provide a livelihood for the Japanese people lay in the expansion of their industrial production and export trade. Their islands were too poor in arable land and raw materials to provide even for their basic needs. But the discovery that neither deficit financing nor official exhortations would cause recovery was tardy. American economic aid had begun in 1946 with grants of $193 million. Part of that sum had been used for short-term Japanese government loans to industry, but most of it had been in the form of grants of food, raw materials, equipment and support for the retraining of technicians. American aid had risen to a peak of $519 million in 1949, and totaled $2.085 billion when those programs and the Allied occupation ended in 1952. American goods received by Japanese authorities had been sold for yen, and the "Aid-Counterpart Funds" thus accumulated had been lent to private businessmen to assist industrial recovery. During the years 1946–1949 that American aid had paid for 68 percent of all imports.

Concurrently, during the years 1945–1952, Japan paid a total of 550 billion yen for occupation costs. Converted into dollars at the various exchange rates that obtained during that period, those payments equaled some $4.8 billion. Therefore American economic aid alone did not account for the eventual recovery of Japan. By subsidies and a multiple exchange rate system Japanese manufacturers had been isolated from world markets since 1937. Their rising, uncompetitive costs had caused ever larger government budget deficits by requiring either higher subsidies or larger deficits in the fund of the Foreign Trade Board. By 1949–1950 price subsidies had surpassed occupation costs as the largest single item of expenditure in the Japanese budget, totaling 202 billion yen. That represented 28.7 percent of the general account of 704 billion yen in 1949–1950.

By the end of 1948, though it was impolitic to say so in public, the United States Departments of State and of the Army had lost confidence in General MacArthur's ability to cope with that economic situation. In December they had therefore issued "A Program to Achieve Economic Stabilization to be Carried Out by the Japanese Government." It was a massive document. In February 1949 Joseph M. Dodge of the Detroit Bank had arrived in Japan with the rank of Minister and the plenary powers needed to bring order out of chaos. Dodge was not a career Foreign Service Officer. He was so undiplomatic that he would later become a successful Director of the Bureau of the

---

[2] Cohen, *Japan's Postwar Economy*, pp. 83–152.

Budget in Washington. His "Nine-Point Stabilization Program" was based on the assumption that Japan would have to become self-supporting and should therefore maximize exports to pay for all essential imports. Production costs had to be reduced until Japanese goods could compete in world markets. That required ending inflation, trimming payrolls and thoroughly rationalizing industry. The trust-busting campaign of American liberals against the *Zaibatsu*, the large industrial combines of prewar Japan, immediately withered.

The Dodge mission ended deficit financing by the Japanese government and caused what one observer described as a "superbalanced budget." Revenues not only covered expenditures in all accounts but also provided enough excess funds to retire one-quarter of the outstanding national debt and to invest additional sums in the rehabilitation of production facilities. By 1950 there was a budget surplus of 125 billion yen. The national debt was reduced from 531 billion yen in mid-1949 to 316 billion at the end of 1950. A single exchange rate was established, at an undervalued 360 yen to the American dollar. During the 1930s the rate had been 3.67 to the dollar, and in September 1945 a military conversion rate of only 15 to 1 had been fixed. But as domestic prices had risen and black markets had begun to flourish, it had been necessary to raise the rate to 50 to the dollar in 1946 and to 270 to the dollar in 1948. When Dodge began to review the situation in 1949, he found that some 80 percent of Japanese exports were taking place at rates less than 360 to the dollar. The remaining 20 percent were manufactured by heavily subsidized industries that were required to reduce their costs to comply with the new exchange rate.

Inflation caused by the excessive issue of paper currencies is not incurable. It can be stopped, quite easily, by anyone who holds sufficient authority and does not fear voters. In Japan, Dodge ended the deficit loans and credit expansion activities of the Reconstruction Finance Bank. New loans were permitted only from the proceeds of loans already outstanding, and all of its debentures were retired. Many government and wholesaling corporations that had been using Reconstruction Finance Bank funds were eliminated, and their functions were returned to private enterprise. Government subsidies in some areas of the economy were terminated immediately, and others were reduced gradually. Thereafter all were openly, explicitly shown in the Japanese government's budget, ending a long tradition of concealment.

Dodge described his program for ending government subsidies as "bringing the Japanese economy down off its stilts." Stock markets were reopened to stimulate the flow of capital into industry, and a Credit Control Board was established to direct bank credit into useful and productive ventures. Dodge informally recommended to the Japanese government that it maximize revenues, and he rejected its inopportune request for an immediate reduction in tax rates. The entire program imposed upon the Japanese people the drastic discipline needed to revive their economy. Strict austerity was required of consumers, because American aid was directed almost entirely into basic production rather than into consumption, and the Japanese people were forced to tax themselves heavily to expand those productive investments. Later a Tokyo newspaper editor would shrewdly comment:

> The Japanese politicians understandably found it expedient publicly to protest against such a severe measure, but privately they recognized its essential soundness and were quite willing to have it imposed upon them so long as it was the Supreme Commander Allied Powers and not themselves who had to bear the onus of imposing it. When it eventually brought about the return of prosperity and the relaxation of austerity, those same politicians ironically were able to turn it to their own credit.[3]

The Dodge program only temporarily stopped inflation in Japan, because of events that no one could have foreseen or forestalled. Nevertheless the success of its monetary stabilization features was displayed in the consumer price index, which rose from 100 in 1948 to a high of 142.5 in May 1949 and then declined to 118.2 in June 1950. The note issue of the Bank of Japan was actually lower in March 1950, at 311.3 billion yen, than it had been in March 1949, at 312.5 billion. Though many Japanese objected to high interest rates, stagnant production levels, rising unemployment and an increase in small business failures, consumers enjoyed substantial benefits from that fall in prices, for the first time in many years. Family expenditures and real consumption were 17 percent higher in the second quarter of 1950 than they had been a year earlier. If there had ever been any serious danger of uprisings against the occupation authority, the Dodge program had ended it.

But the North Korean invasion of South Korea in June of 1950 halted that stabilization program and caused an export boom, raw materials shortages and further inflation in Japan. The United States began its program of "special procurement" for the supplies and equipment needed by the United Nations forces in Korea, and Japanese exports increased 60 percent between June and December of 1950. During that half-year a trade surplus of $9 million was recorded, the first since the 1930s. By June 1951 special procurement purchases in Japan had reached a total of $315 million, and Japanese export prices had risen more than 90 percent. Concurrently domestic wholesale prices had increased, by 52 percent during that first year of the Korean War. They were rising only 17 percent in the United States and 22 percent in Britain. However, the Japanese were delighted to record that in October 1950 their industrial production had begun to exceed 1936 levels for the first

[3] Kawai, *Japan's American Interlude*, p. 178.

time. To compensate for the American troops shipped to Korea, General MacArthur had directed, on July 7, 1950, the formation of a Japanese National Police Reserve of 75,000 and an increase in the Maritime Defense Force to 8000. Yet then and ever since, Japanese leaders have deployed the most ingenious arguments, pleading Japan's poverty and the "psychological inability" of its people to contemplate rearmament. Like the West Europeans, the Japanese have therefore been able to spend almost all their own tax revenues on domestic needs. Has the time come for the United States to begin charging them annual "tribute," to defray the rising costs of their defense and thus balance its own Federal budget?

After April 1951 the Korean War boom began to ebb throughout the world, and international price levels dropped almost everywhere. In Japan they did not, wholesale prices rising still further. The profits from that boom were reinvested by Japanese industry, and the rate of net capital formation rose to a new high. To assist industries (such as textiles) whose exports were overpriced, government investment was increased, and in 1951 the Japanese Export–Import Bank was founded. American markets having been reopened to Japan, it rapidly became one of the largest exporters to the United States, second only to Canada. By the middle of the 1950s, 17 to 22 percent of Japan's exports were going to the United States. Whereas prewar exports had been principally raw silk, tea, fish, pottery and textiles, by the 1950s they included metals and a wide variety of finished manufactures such as electrical apparatus, other light engineering goods, optical and other instruments, and pharmaceuticals. The United States had also become Japan's largest supplier, its share of Japanese imports having risen from one-fourth before 1941 to one-third in postwar years.

A special relationship had begun that would continue to weigh more heavily in Washington's calculations than American trade with Europe. In 1952 Japan joined the International Monetary Fund, though it would be permitted to retain rigorous exchange controls until 1964. Then in 1953 the Japanese began to enjoy their first boom in domestic consumption. The index of industrial production reached a new high of 161, accompanied by a marked expansion of bank credit, primarily to finance imports. Total money supply increased by 174 billion yen, or 14 percent. National income rose 30 percent above its 1936 level, and for the first time per capita income also rose above that prewar level, by 6 percent.

The opposite side of that bright coin was the largest trade deficit Japan had ever experienced. Its 1953 exports totaled only $1.3 billion, while imports soared to $2.6 billion. The result was a balance-of-payments deficit of some $300 million, regardless of American special procurement expenditures of $809 million in Japan. The scarce foreign-exchange reserves of the Bank of Japan dropped sharply, to approximately $700 million. Joseph Dodge enhanced his unpopularity and his reputation for common sense by revisiting

Japan to warn its bankers and business leaders that they could not continue to rely on war booms to provide prosperity. With that encouragement the government of Shigeru Yoshida then resorted to the classic remedy of tight money, not only raising interest rates but also cutting its own budget and reducing public investment 17 percent. By December 1954 the wholesale price index (1936 = 1) had fallen to 343.69, and another inflationary outburst had been checked.

That austerity program aroused less public furor than had been feared, because the Japanese people had recovered not only their prosperity but also their self-confidence. Wartime damage to Tokyo itself had been effaced. Visitors could be entertained at the earthquake-proof Imperial Hotel, whose elegant arcade shops displayed choice brocades, cultured pearls and Russian sables. Once again the service in its impeccable dining room had become the finest in the Far East. On the glittering Ginza, shops were crowded with well-dressed Japanese consumers, who were now able to buy luxuries imported from every corner of the world. Though it was perilous to travel by taxi, and the Yoshiwara District had been declared off limits to United Nations troops, both somehow managed to prosper nonetheless. At the Kabuki Theater the Japanese and their guests indulged themselves in net bags of tangerines, while noisily watching its shrill, traditional drama. Japanese engineers proudly demonstrated the world's fastest train, which reached speeds of more than 100 miles per hour on the run from Tokyo to Osaka. In fierce efforts to bury Japan's prewar reputation for shoddy imitations, they had also begun to produce cameras and watches that rivaled in quality those of West Germany and Switzerland, and they were cheaper.

Premier Yoshida, a former Ambassador to Great Britain, was often favorably compared with Konrad Adenauer, whom he visited in 1954 during a European tour intended to reopen European markets for Japanese exports. They agreed that both Japan and West Germany needed "strong governments." Yoshida also recorded a wry comment on the French government of Pierre Mendès France.

> I had always thought that the bickering and back-biting rampant between contending groups were the curse of the Japanese political world, and I could sympathize with the French Premier when I learned of the equally complicated state of affairs existing in France, with so many small parties contending for power.[4]

In an effort to change another characteristic of Japanese political life, Yoshida was reversing the prewar practice of cloaking all government decisions in excessive secrecy.[5] And he began the cautious policy of husbanding

---

[4] Yoshida, *Memoirs*, p. 106.

[5] Regarding subsequent Japanese governments, a bemused American Assistant Secretary of Defense for International Security Affairs would later comment: "The Japanese ship of state is a most marvelous vessel. It leaks outward, and from the top."

national reserves in foreign exchange, mostly in American dollars, rather than offend the United States by asking for their conversion into gold. In 1954 Japanese exports reached a new postwar high, and those foreign-exchange reserves rose to $950 million. In 1955 they increased to $1.47 billion, almost 60 percent of Japan's imports for that year. By the end of 1956 they had risen to $1.623 billion, of which $128 million was in gold. The "Jimmu Boom" of 1956, so called because it was said to be the biggest since the time of that legendary first Emperor of Japan, was caused partly by a sharp increase in exports after the Suez crisis. Japanese exporters gained a brief, sometimes lasting advantage over their European competitors in many Asian and African markets.

However, faithful to the Japanese pattern, inflation promptly reappeared. As domestic prices and imports rose, payments accounts deteriorated, and by June 1957 currency reserves had fallen to $879 million. Once again deflation was required, and the Bank of Japan tightened its controls over foreign exchange. By the summer of 1958 equilibrium had been restored. And in 1959 industrial production and exports achieved new records, regardless of the recession in the United States. Monetary authorities, eager to prevent that boom from getting out of hand, began to experiment with controls in an effort to achieve a period of "sustainable growth."

By the end of 1960 Japan's gold and foreign-exchange reserves had been rebuilt to $2.166 billion, more than double those of 1958. But by the summer of 1961 inflation and a deterioration in payments accounts had appeared once again. That year national reserves fell to $1.976 billion. The government was unwilling to increase taxation, because all of its own accounts were already in surplus. It therefore relied entirely on monetary restraints that had only limited effect. Private bankers and businessmen remained optimistic about their prospects, and found new sources of credit outside the banking system with which to increase their investments, regardless of high interest rates. It therefore took more than a year to restore equilibrium. By the summer of 1962 the trade balance had improved, and in October government officials began to loosen controls. By the end of that year national reserves had risen to $2.481 billion. And in the early months of 1963 industrial production increased.

Banking conditions were undergoing a radical change. Japanese authorities were no longer operating within a closed system that could be insulated from world monetary conditions. Japan had begun to be more closely linked with international capital and money markets than ever before, and relaxation of monetary and trade controls loosened the effectiveness of the tools available to the Bank of Japan. While Japanese commercial banks were thus becoming more independent of its authority, the Bank of Japan itself was struggling for freedom from political influences and the control over credit policies that had long been exerted by the Ministry of Finance. A Policy Board had been established in 1949, on the recommendation of Joseph Dodge, as the supreme authority for decisions on the policies of the Bank of Japan. It included not only the Governor but also representatives from commercial banks, trade, industry, agriculture, the Ministry of Finance and the Cabinet Offices. Thus the power of the Ministry of Finance had been diluted, yet conflicts had remained, especially where decisions on exchange controls had been involved. And that wide sharing of authority over monetary policies had caused some inconsistencies. By the end of 1964 the national reserves of Japan totaled a gross $1.995 billion. But its commercial banks had begun to borrow so heavily abroad, to a total of $1.185 billion, that net national assets were only $810 million. That seriously worried the cautious officials at the Bank of Japan.[6]

The structure of Japan's export and import trade had completely changed. Before the Second World War, Northeast Asia had been Japan's largest customer and supplier. Korea had been developed for the specific purpose of providing most imported rice, and Formosa had supplied sugar. Together they had furnished one-fourth of Japan's imports, and Manchuria had provided coal and iron ore. China, a constant debtor to Japan, had taken one-third of its exports and had provided 17 percent of its imports. After 1937 a concerted but unsuccessful effort had been made to obtain all imports from Empire or "Yen Bloc" sources. After 1945 the redistribution of Japanese trade had been determined by quite different political and strategic considerations. Deference to American policies and to the United Nations embargo on trade with Communist China imposed in May 1951 had diverted Japanese attention to Southeast Asia, which had been the other major area of Japan's prewar trading enterprise. After 1945 the Indian subcontinent, Ceylon, Burma, Indonesia, Malaya, Borneo, Hong Kong, the Philippines, Thailand and Indochina had appeared to be excellent prospects, both as markets and as suppliers. Trade had grown as rapidly as those nations could recover from their wartime damage by Japan and could forget that grievance. Another inhibiting factor had been the political instability of Southeast Asia, which was a constant source of anxiety to Japanese traders. Disorders in that region throughout the 1950s and 1960s had caused frequent and violent fluctuations in Japanese trade, and efforts to persuade the United States that it should intervene whenever and wherever necessary to support governments friendly to Japan.

Yet the national interests of the United States and Japan have not always marched together, and there have been few American commercial interests in Southeast Asia. It was therefore symptomatic of recent relations—and misun-

[6] Allen, *Japan's Economic Expansion*, pp. 48–77.

derstandings—between those two countries that by 1964 many Japanese traders had convinced themselves that it had become the responsibility of American armed forces to protect their commercial ventures in Vietnam and its neighbors. The Americas and Europe have always been more stable markets and suppliers, as many Japanese were aware. Yet they would never lose their interest in Southeast Asia and in mainland China, and by 1957 Japanese trading companies had also begun to agitate for the renewal of ancient relationships with Northeast Asia. The explosion of Communist China's first thermonuclear device, in October 1964, therefore caused a sensation throughout Japan. Serious reconsideration began of the role Japan could and should play in the future of Asia. That process of adaptation would continue.

THE TRANSFORMATION OF CHINA

In mainland China the revolutionary changes had been thorough and profound. After abandoning its ancient silver standard on November 4, 1935, the Chinese monetary system had been reformed with the help of British experts. A new "foreign-exchange standard" had been established, and the paper notes of the Central Bank of China, the Bank of China and the Communications Bank had been declared the only legal tender. Though no longer redeemable in specie, they could be bought and sold for foreign currencies. At that time the Central Bank of China's official exchange rates had been fixed at 30 U.S. cents, 1s.2½d in sterling or 1.03 Japanese yen for 1 Chinese National Currency (CNC) dollar. Private holdings of gold had been estimated at U.S. $350 million. By June 1937 the various Chinese exchange agencies had collected approximately 1.1 billion silver dollars from the public. The United States had agreed to buy that silver for American dollars, to provide the foreign-exchange reserves needed by the Central Bank. By May 1937 the Chinese Ministry of Finance had exported CNC $830 million in silver and had received U.S. $270 million in payments. In 1936 and 1937 some U.S. $100 million in privately owned gold had also fled to foreign banks, because many Chinese investors had anticipated the approaching hostilities with Japan. The balance remaining in China, of both gold and silver, had been estimated at CNC $950 million. Yet it had been guessed that probably only half that amount would be available to the Chinese authorities, because those holdings were scattered throughout the country, and part had been lost or buried beyond retrieval. Thus China had held limited gold, silver and foreign currency reserves with which to purchase war materiel abroad.

The first open Sino–Japanese hostilities had begun at the Marco Polo Bridge, southwest of Peking, on July 7, 1937. From there they had quickly spread to Peking itself, to Tientsin and to Shanghai. By March 17, 1938, it had become impossible for the Central Bank of China to maintain any official exchange rates. The CNC dollar had dropped sharply to U.S. 21 cents, or 11.875d. By January 1942 the Nationalist government of Chiang Kai-shek had been so weakened that American Secretary of War Stimson had informed Henry Morgenthau: "China must be kept in at any price." A loan of U.S. $500 million had been requested, and the Chinese justification had been that it was: "political above all . . . to demonstrate that China's confidence in the Allied Powers is matched by equal confidence in China of the Allied Powers, in the crucial months of the emergency that lies before us." Though mutual confidence would never exist, an American loan for that amount had been approved by Congress and signed by President Roosevelt on February 7. At the same time the British government had announced a token loan of £50 million to China.

Part of the American loan, U.S. $200 million in gold, had been intended to serve as an exchange stabilization fund. Though it had cemented an alliance, it had then disappeared like sand into the quagmire of wartime China, as Chiang Kai-shek and his officials diverted it for their own purposes. In a futile experiment intended to curb domestic inflation, approximately 1 million ounces of that gold had been subsequently sold by the Farmers' Bank, beginning in November 1943. Buyers had been required to purchase Village Public Welfare Certificates for first 10 percent, and later 20 percent, of their gold purchases. Yet those gold sales had had no noticeable effect on the progressive inflation that had begun years earlier. Though the reason given in China for termination of those sales in November 1944 had been delays in the shipment of gold from the United States, in fact American Treasury officials had remained quite doubtful about the ways in which American loans were being used.

By August 1945 the exchange rate had fallen to CNC $3200 for 1 American dollar. Peace brought a temporary rally, to CNC $680 for U.S. $1. But China was prostrate, and its people watched passively as the Japanese armies were disarmed and withdrawn. Most Chinese had been near exhaustion, all of their savings and marketable possessions having been used in the long struggle to survive. The depredations of marauding Chinese troops and tax collectors had disheartened and embittered the peasants, and some fifty million refugees awaited return to their former homes. Millions of acres of farmland lay deserted and unproductive. Communications had been disrupted, and in many areas of the South the railroads had been severely damaged.

The capital resources required for reconstruction were huge, and the Nationalist government faced two additional obstacles. Its inability to reach agreement with the Communists led by Mao Tse-tung required it to maintain large, costly armies, and the demand for consumer goods repressed through 8 years of war became a major source of instability. Speculators, dealers, landlords, corrupt officials and others having acquired large holdings of cash, they bid up the prices of the limited quantities of consumer goods available. Chiang Kai-shek had greatly overestimated the stabilizing effects of victory. He had assumed that the return of Formosa and Manchuria, the revival of foreign trade, and his accumulation of large amounts of gold and foreign exchange would increase commodity supplies sufficiently to absorb the public's grossly excessive spending power. Prolongation of wartime controls was therefore considered unnecessary, and all controls on prices and the distribution of goods were abandoned.

In the last week of August 1945 there appeared to be sound reasons for that optimism. Suddenly commodity prices fell. Consumer goods hoarded over the years flooded the markets, in many instances being sold at half their earlier prices. In Shanghai, long China's largest commercial center, the price of gold dropped 90 percent. In Chungking it fell 60 percent as the *fapi* or CNC dollar appreciated 100 percent against the American dollar. The wholesale price index fell from 179,500 in August to 122,600 in September, and to 118,418 in October. Victory tasted sweet to Chiang and his followers, who soon demonstrated that they knew no more about the quantity theory of money than their many reckless predecessors since the 7th century, when paper currency had first been tried in China.

In November the wholesale price index began to rise once again. And the CNC dollar fell, until it began to fluctuate between CNC $1800 and 2500 to the American dollar. Those were ominous signals, which the Nationalists ignored. They did not repudiate the currencies that had been issued by Japanese-sponsored governments in North and Central China, because they were intent on reconciling and reuniting all factions of the long-divided Chinese people against the Communists. Therefore the money supply swelled, and capital from the interior began to flow into Shanghai, in the expectation that it would soon regain its position as China's leading money market. That trend intensified as relations between Chiang and Mao worsened, and in Shanghai most of those funds were dissipated in speculation, often in gold. Yet Chiang's budget deficits and the consequent increase in the quantity of money in circulation remained the primary cause of inflation.

In 1946 the Nationalist government's expenditures increased to 3.2 times those of 1945, while revenues covered only 37 percent of expenditures. The administrative machinery for collecting agricultural taxes, always the largest source of Chinese national income, had begun to collapse. And the business community, which had learned through long years of war experience to watch those indicators of future price trends, began to lose confidence in Chiang's ability to revive China. His own civil servants became discontented, and demanded monthly raises in salaries and wages adjusted to increases in the cost-of-living index. In 1947 the Nationalist government's expenditures would therefore rise to 5.7 times those of 1946, while its revenues dropped to

32 percent of expenditures because nontax income declined as receipts from sales of government assets and enemy property were reduced.

Not until February 25, 1946, when the Central Bank of China had begun its struggle to reestablish the foreign-exchange market in Shanghai, had there been any effort to stabilize foreign-exchange rates. Then the American dollar had been fixed at CNC $2020. On August 19 that rate had been raised to CNC $3350. But by January 1947 the black market rate was CNC $6767. Therefore the official rate was increased to 7639 in February 1947 and to 12,000 in March. There it would remain for some months, even though the black market rate would soar to 43,640 by July. On March 8, 1946, the Central Bank of China had resumed sales to the public of gold borrowed from the United States, in its frantic efforts somehow to neutralize the increasing purchasing power produced by Chiang's continuing budget deficits. By January 1946 speculative activity in Shanghai had increased the price of gold to CNC $185,000 per "tael," the ancient Chinese ounce. The Central Bank therefore resumed sales at CNC $165,000 per tael, which appeared to have some influence on commodity prices until June. Then the outbreak of civil war in the North forced the price up to CNC $200,000 per tael. During the next 7 months the price in Shanghai continued to rise sharply as the result of depreciation in the official exchange rate of the CNC dollar and the continuing influx of refugee capital from the interior. As the demand for gold increased, the Central Bank of China found that it simply could not check further rises in the market price by increasing the quantities it sold.

By February 1, 1947, the price of gold in Shanghai reached CNC $407,000 per tael, and a mere 10 days later it was CNC $960,000 per tael. In 11 months the Central Bank of China had sold 3.3 million ounces, some 60 percent of its gold reserves, without any lasting effect on commodity prices. On February 17 it therefore ceased those operations. During the preceding year it had lost U.S. $115,919,823 in gold, U.S. $9,660,000 in silver and U.S. $347,470,675 in paper American dollars. Total national reserves had fallen from U.S. $833,587,211 to U.S. $346,587,121. Yet the Chinese currency withdrawn from circulation had equaled only one-third of the Nationalist fiscal deficit for that period. When printing presses are being worked overtime for deficit financing on the scale in which Chiang Kai-shek indulged, nothing can stop progressive inflation from soaring beyond the limits of human imagination.

In February 1947 the Nationalist government had at last attempted to reintroduce wage and price controls, but they had been effective for no more than a month. The black market in American dollars, operated in successful defiance of the regulations, led to rapid growth in black markets for all commodities. Price controls were therefore abandoned in April and wage controls in May. Regardless of all the stopgap measures subsequently tried, progressive inflation continued, simply because the deficit-financed expenditures of Chiang Kai-shek continued to swamp the markets with new money. Central Bank advances to the Finance Ministry were 5 times higher in 1947 than in 1946. In 1947 the notes issued increased 10 times, whereas they had only tripled in 1946. By December 1947, Shanghai's wholesale prices were nearly 15 times the level of the previous December, and Chiang had lost the confidence not only of Chinese merchants and landowners but also of the foreign banking houses that had traded in China for three centuries. From the colorful, teeming Bund of Shanghai, they began to transfer their assets and operations to Hong Kong.[7]

For many years thereafter the American friends of Chiang Kai-shek would continue fatuously to ask who had "lost" China to the Communists, and when and why. The only and obvious answer is that Chiang lost China to the Communists, within 2 years after victory against the Japanese, largely because he was incompetent to administer its reconstruction. By the end of 1947 the political and economic disintegration of Nationalist China had become so dire that the American Department of State was fully alarmed. An "Economic Aid Program for China" was therefore hastily prepared and presented to Congress, and was passed in January 1948. It authorized grants of U.S. $275 million for the purchase of cotton, petroleum, foodstuffs, construction goods and other commodities. It also provided U.S. $125 million in military aid for the next 12 months. Chiang Kai-shek was angered, disappointed that he was being given so little. Yet his Nationalist government had already received a total of U.S. $3.5 billion, including grants of U.S. $2.422 billion and credits of U.S. $1.101 billion that would never be repaid.

Neither President Truman nor Congress had been persuaded that those funds had been well spent. Chiang was therefore cautioned that further American help could not be expected unless he adopted a comprehensive economic stabilization plan, similar to the one Joseph Dodge would soon carry to Japan. Then at last Chiang's Nationalist government announced a ten-point reform plan based on Washington's recommendations. Its most essential features called for reductions in government expenditures and improvements in the tax system. However, that plan was never implemented. Chiang's own Finance Minister denounced it as impracticable, and he himself feared that he would lose personal popularity by undertaking retrenchments in the spending of his army and bureaucracy at a time when his prestige had already begun to ebb. To the last he would struggle to preserve the appearances of power, while fast losing the realities.

By the end of April 1948 the American dollar balances of the Central Bank of China had been exhausted, and the only remaining reserves of the Nation-

[7] Chang, *The Inflationary Spiral,* pp. 67–85, 259–261, 281–285, 306–321.

alists were gold and silver stocks valued at U.S. $126 million. In June and July wholesale prices in Shanghai increased by 260 and 45 percent, and the market rates of foreign exchange rose by 98 and 181 percent against the CNC dollar. In each of those months the black market price of gold tripled, and the quantity of currency in circulation doubled. Such fearful warnings of impending financial collapse finally forced Chiang's government to undertake an apparently draconian yet actually senseless reform. Introduced on August 19, the new Chinese monetary unit of account was officially defined as 0.2217 centigram of fine gold, to be represented by a paper note called the "gold yuan," in a forlorn effort to lend it credibility. The new notes were to be exchanged for old at the rate of 1 gold yuan (GY) for CNC $3,000,000. A 40 percent reserve of gold, silver and foreign currencies was to be maintained against that new currency, which was limited by law to GY 200 million. Prices of all commodities were frozen at their gold yuan equivalents on August 19. Private possession of gold, silver and foreign currencies was prohibited, and all private holdings were to be surrendered in exchange for gold yuan notes.

For the next 6 weeks Chiang's secret police dragooned Shanghai into price stability. Commodity prices remained at their ceiling levels, and the black markets in gold and foreign exchange disappeared. Specie and foreign exchange valued at U.S. $170 million were surrendered, and the Nationalist government loudly boasted of the success of that reform. In the interior, however, prices continued to rise. And Chiang himself did not stop his deficit spending. He had merely replaced one discredited currency with a new variety, without having changed his fiscal practices in any way. His budget deficits were GY 138 million in September, GY 220 million in October and GY 503 million in November. That represented 50 percent of government expenditures in October and 75 percent in November. Not surprisingly, in the middle of October a wave of panic buying in Shanghai forced commodity prices above their legal ceilings, and price regulations were then abandoned. By the end of that month the circulation of gold yuan had reached 8 times its authorized limitation. To finance military and bureaucratic expenditures, Chiang had brazenly broken his own rules, and those who had surrendered gold and foreign currencies in exchange for his so-called gold yuan never forgave him for doing so.

The last decisive battles between Nationalist armies and those of Mao Tse-tung took place in North Kiangsu during that critical month of November 1948. From the beginning of November through March 1949, when the Nationalists withdrew from the Shanghai area, Chinese imports dwindled drastically. Consequently there was no further drain on Nationalist reserves for nongovernmental purposes, yet government spending in foreign currencies and gold operations of the Central Bank reduced those reserves to U.S.

$96.6 million. Because the public had begun to reject gold yuan notes, Chiang's government was compelled to use specie and even Hong Kong dollars for its domestic payments.

Peking and Tientsin fell at the end of January 1949, and by February the Central Bank's gold stocks had been reduced to 3.955 million ounces, of which 2.556 million had already been transferred to Taiwan (Formosa) for safekeeping. By May most of the 586,000 ounces retained in Shanghai and New York had been used in operations on the Shanghai market. Another 783,000 ounces had been kept at Amoy and Canton, and almost all was used for urgent government needs when Chiang retreated to Canton. After Nanking and Shanghai were lost in April and May, the gold yuan became worthless. In July the U.S. $24.3 million in silver bullion that remained in the Central Bank was coined and issued as silver yuan for use in military payments. When the Nationalists retreated to Taiwan, their only remaining monetary reserves were the 2.556 million ounces of gold that Chiang had prudently stored on that island. Behind him on the mainland, scattered amid the debris of war, he left a balance of something less than 100,000 ounces of American gold, to be scavenged by looters and Communist troops.[8]

During 1949, as the control of Mao Tse-tung spread across the mainland of China, the twin purposes of the Communists' monetary measures were to abolish the many forms of money that had been in circulation and to establish a single Communist currency. The easiest part of that program was the abolition of the various Nationalist currencies, which had been thoroughly discredited by the withdrawal of Chiang's armies. The first "people's currency," or *jen-min pi (¥)*, had been issued in December 1948. And on January 15, 1949, the Communists' Military Control Commission at Tientsin had proclaimed it the only legal tender throughout China. The public were told that the Nationalist gold yuan could be used until February 4, though they were free to refuse it in payment. Only in cases of special hardship, and then only in small quantities, were holders of gold yuan permitted to convert them into *jen-min pi* at the rate of GY 6 to ¥ 1. That policy of driving out the Nationalist currencies by repudiating most of them was continued as additional areas were conquered by the Communists, and further inflation of the gold yuan led to its drastic depreciation. Thus the exchange rate of the *jen-min pi* rose to GY 10 at Peking in February, to GY 2500 at Nanking in May, and to GY 100,000 at Shanghai in June.

Unification of the currencies the Chinese Communists themselves had issued was more difficult, because their practice had always been to finance operations in any area they had occupied by issuing a new local currency. More than thirty had appeared during the Sino–Japanese War, and the need

[8] Chou, *The Chinese Inflation 1937–1949*, pp. 168–172.

for currency unification became pressing as Communist victories began to link together areas that had formerly been isolated. Preparations for that unification had been made at a "Financial and Economic Conference of the North China Liberated Areas" in 1947, and toward the end of 1948 the People's Bank of China had been formed by merging the North China Bank, the North Sea Bank and the Northwest Farmers' Bank. By the end of that year, outside Sinkiang, Manchuria and Inner Mongolia, the number of Communist currencies had been reduced to three.

By the end of 1949 only the *jen-min pi* remained, all local currencies having been fully redeemed, except in those outlying provinces. The new administrators of Mao Tse-tung regarded that effort as a successful exercise in public psychology, essential to establish the good faith of their new regime. They found it much harder, however, to suppress the continuing circulation of gold, silver dollars and foreign currencies. That was partially achieved by prohibiting their use as units of account and media of payments, and was reinforced by police raids on black market centers, especially the shops of goldsmiths and silversmiths. There were wholesale arrests of the street peddlers who sold silver dollars and foreign exchange, supplemented by random search of pedestrians. Yet oddly enough, though gold and silver could no longer be used as money and export was forbidden, possession was permitted and the official rates at which those metals could be voluntarily converted into *jen-min pi* were so low that they discouraged it. Apparently Chinese Communist monetary authorities were disciples of the 1917 Lenin, rather than the 1921 Lenin. Perhaps Mao and his followers were also unwilling to incur too much unpopularity too soon and therefore sought to accustom the Chinese gradually to exclusive use of their new "people's currency" as money.

Formal proclamation on October 1, 1949, that the Communists had assumed control over all of mainland China had not ended two decades of severe inflation. Deficit financing continued to be a characteristic of Chinese governments, partly because Mao Tse-tung had absorbed millions of defectors from the armies and bureaucracy of Chiang Kai-shek. They had to be paid. By 1949 wheat production had fallen to 71 percent, rice to 75 percent, tobacco to 65 percent and raw cotton to 52 percent of their 1936 levels. Light industry and heavy industry were producing at only one-third and two-thirds of their 1936 levels. Persistent shortages therefore caused further price rises. In Northwest China, however, a start had been made toward reconstructing coal mines, and the iron and steel industry. From 1948 to 1949 coal production had risen from 13.8 to 30 million tons. Output of pig iron, steel ingots and finished steel had increased by factors of eight, two and three.

During the second half of 1949, to combat inflation, a novel scheme of "real goods savings deposits" was announced. For that purpose, in October, state trading companies were formed in all major cities. That was followed in

December by the issue of "People's Victory Real Unit Bonds." Both deposit certificates and bonds were denominated in units each of which consisted of 3 kilograms of rice, 0.75 kilogram of wheat flour, 1⅓ meters of white cotton muslin and 8 kilograms of coal. Every 10 days the conversion rate between that unit and the *jen-min pi* was recalculated on the basis of the weighted average of the combined wholesale prices of those commodities in Shanghai, Tientsin, Hankow, Sian, Kwangchow and Chungking. The first hundred million units of certificates and bonds were quickly oversubscribed, some coercion having been used. Payments for them caused such a contraction of the quantity of currency in circulation that by March 1950 inflation had been stopped, at least temporarily. By December of that year commodity prices were said to have fallen 14.5 percent from their March levels. That price stabilization program gave the Communist monetary officials a major propaganda victory over the Nationalists now encamped on Taiwan, and it was loudly advertised. Mao Tse-tung was also given a breathing space in which to reconstruct the fiscal machinery of China. In March 1950 central-ized management and control of national finances had been introduced, and by the end of that year Mao was able to announce proudly that the national budget had been balanced.

From October 1950 onward the Korean War imposed severe strains on the Chinese economy. New construction expenditures were cut, and new taxes were imposed. There was a drive to find substitutes for scarce commodities, and subsidies to municipal governments were reduced. Nevertheless those efforts to mobilize resources for war and for the industrialization of China did not stop the efforts toward monetary rehabilitation. The last phase of curren-cy unification was reached in 1951, with the recall on March 20 of the separate Manchurian and Inner Mongolian currencies, and the abolition on October 1 of the silver dollar notes of the Sinkiang People's Bank. The People's Bank of China became the only bank of issue. Later some supply and marketing cooperatives would begin to issue promissory notes, which would have limited, local circulation as subsidiary currencies. But they could never challenge the People's Bank, which had been granted wide powers as the sole depository of funds for all government and cooperative enterprises. It had also become their only source of credit, and the single clearing center and supervisory authority for all transactions.

In April 1950 government funds deposited in private banks had been with-drawn. By June of that year 233 private banks had been closed. Thus 52 percent of all private banks simply disappeared. By December 1952 the re-maining 213 had been merged to form the Amalgamated Bank, jointly oper-ated by the government and by those private interests that had somehow survived. Even in Communist China "arrangements" would continue that would appear odd and often sinister to Western eyes. By September 23, 1954, at the first session of the first National People's Congress, Chou En-lai was able to claim that the first 3 years of the new regime had witnessed the reunification of the Chinese mainland, the reform of its agrarian system and the rehabilitation of the national economy.[9] However, on March 1, 1955, another conversion program was announced in which new *jen-min pi* notes were exchanged for old at the rate of 1 new for 10,000 old. That implied the persistence of considerable inflation since December 1948. Throughout the country, during March and April 1955, everything expressed in terms of the old currency was converted in the belief that price stability could be encouraged by eliminating so many naughts.

In 1950 the reserves of the People's Bank of China had been negligible. By 1957 it had accumulated foreign-currency balances of $610 million and gold stocks of $35 million. Probably half of those sums had been gathered by calling in private funds and by absorbing the small amounts of gold produced in China. The remainder represented net earnings on transactions with other countries, primarily the Soviet Union and Eastern Europe. Without the help of Joseph Stalin, Mao Tse-tung would have been in dire straits. Short-term Soviet credits equivalent to $300 million and long-term credits of $1.4 billion had made possible not only the reconstruction of mainland China but also its new program of industrialization. Those credits had equaled 15 percent of China's total imports and 30 percent of its imports from the Soviet Union during the critical years 1950–1957.

The Soviet share of China's foreign trade had risen dramatically, from 5 percent before 1946 to approximately 50 percent in 1959. By 1959 China was also supplying 20 percent of the Soviet Union's total imports, equaling East Germany as its most important supplier. The increase in China's exports, from $625 million in 1950 to approximately $1.6 billion in 1957, had indicated the rapid recovery of its foreign trade. Then adoption in 1958 of the "Leap Forward," the pursuit of maximum growth in every sector of the economy, stimulated new demand for imports. Gross national reserves fell to $530 million in 1959, $415 million in 1960, $355 million in 1961 and $320 million in 1962.

An interesting feature of Chinese Communist fiscal policies during those years was the stubborn refusal of the People's Bank to use any part of its small gold reserves. Instead it gradually, painstakingly increased those gold stocks to $80 million in 1959, $115 million in 1960, $140 million in 1961 and $165 million in 1962. While Chairman Mao and Premier Chou were so loudly, fiercely denouncing every kind of capitalism throughout the world, they somehow neglected to inform their many millions of followers that they were hoarding its archetypal monetary form, gold. That golden Chinese treasury increased to $190 million in 1963, and to $215 million in 1964.

The People's Bank of China had been saving for a rainy day. Comradely

(9) Wu, *An Economic Survey of Communist China*, pp. 64–112, 395–423.

relations between China and the Soviet Union had chilled. As early as 1953 Communist China had also begun to extend credits and grants to nations it had sought to influence. During the mid-1950s Soviet bankers awoke slowly to the incredible fact that their Chinese protégés had begun to steal their ideological thunder. While the Soviet Union had been continuing to pour grants and credits into China, the latter had been extending its own grants and credits to the new nations of Southern Asia and Africa, where Chinese representatives heaped scorn on Joseph Stalin and his successors as impure heirs of Marxist–Leninist ideals. By 1965 those Chinese Communist grants and credits would reach an estimated total of $2.038 billion, truly an extraordinary sum for a nation so poor.

The Soviet Union had thus been soundly outsmarted by its Chinese pupils, and the "agonizing reappraisal" in Moscow's Kremlin must have been a wondrous sight for anyone privileged to observe it. Doubtless Soviet leaders had never had any desire to see their Chinese neighbors become strong and independent, and had not foreseen that possibility. In 1959 they had therefore cancelled a "defense technology agreement" and had refused to supply any further information on Soviet thermonuclear research programs. In 1960 Soviet technicians had been abruptly withdrawn from China, and economic planner Po I-po had protested that the sudden end of Soviet support had resembled "taking away all the dishes when you have only eaten half a meal." The Soviet Union had also begun to insist on rapid repayment of earlier loans, and the Chinese "Leap Forward" had promptly collapsed. As Chinese officials had begun to lessen their dependence on the Soviet Union, anticipating the possibility of a complete rupture in relations, the People's Bank had been forced to sell abroad $22 million of silver in 1960, more than $50 million in 1961 and $41 million in 1962, to meet debt repayments that had fallen due.

Nevertheless, with strict foreign trade and exchange controls, Communist Chinese administrators were able to accomplish a remarkable reorientation during those years. As late as 1959 Japan and other non-Communist countries had accounted for only $1.3 billion, or approximately one-third of China's total foreign trade. By 1964 that would increase to $2.12 billion, or two-thirds. But Chinese Communist officials had been slow to recognize that their ideal program for achieving complete national self-sufficiency had miscalculated the food requirements of their growing population. By 1961 they had begun to need imports of some 6 million tons of grain each year, at an average annual cost of some $400 million. Only a substantial increase in exports or large foreign credits could have provided such sums. Though both Australia and Canada demonstrated that the world trade in grain paid little heed to ideologies, neither could afford to extend large credits. Nor could they provide adequate markets for Chinese manufactures, which tended to be shoddy in quality. Too proud to seek large capitalist loans openly, Communist China began to search for additional markets, especially among the overseas Chinese in Southeast Asia.

By 1965 those efforts had been sufficiently successful to enable the People's Bank of China to increase its gold stocks by making its first purchases on the London bullion market, where it converted part of its sterling reserves for the equivalent of $150 million in gold. In 1966 it would buy another $75 million. Taking their cue from Charles de Gaulle, leaders of the revolutionary new China sought in that most ancient way to enhance their own independence and China's prestige in world finance.[10]

MISADVENTURE IN VIETNAM

Since August 1964 the attention of the obstinate Lyndon Baines Johnson and his incompetent generals had also been riveted on Southeast Asia. All were afflicted with a peculiar kind of myopia, the belief that somehow the economy of the United States had become immune from the savage, destructive excesses that have always accompanied mismanagement of every form of money. For a decade and more thereafter, world monetary history would serve as a cautionary tale of the effects of the chronic, growing deficits in the Federal budget and international payments accounts of the United States.

The relations between Japan and China had always been profoundly disturbing to the American officials and diplomats who now considered themselves responsible for maintaining peace in Asia. Japan and China had formally recognized each other's existence for less than a century, and their diplomatic exchanges had been acrimonious from the very beginning. Arguments over Taiwan, Okinawa, Korea and Manchuria had caused war in 1894, near-war in 1917 and the long bloodbath that had begun in 1937. Japan had borne the brunt of China's new nationalism, and China in turn had suffered from Japan's imperial search for overseas markets, raw materials and foodstuffs. The peace that had existed since 1945 had been one of the longest known, and the United States had not gained any popularity with anyone for preserving it. Though trade between Japan and mainland China had been resumed, it was impossible to foresee the restoration of relations that might have been described as normal and amicable. Until 1945 Japan had justified its dominance by citing the need to protect East Asia from the West. Since 1945 the Chinese Communists had begun to claim that they were now responsible for that task. Moreover China had always been a disturbing factor in Japanese domestic politics. Before 1945 it had angered the Japanese

---

[10] Joint Economic Committee, United States Congress, *An Economic Profile of Mainland China*, pp. 325–339, 580–608, 622–637.

Right. Since 1945 it had agitated the Japanese Left, who were one-third of the electorate.

By 1964 Communist China had also become a major military power that refused to enter into nuclear test agreements with anyone, and it had been manipulating for political purposes its expanding export trade with Southeast Asia. In Indonesia the overseas Chinese had become a powerful subversive force, and the ultimate purpose of Chinese Communist support for revolutionary movements throughout that region appeared to be nothing less than seizure of control over the vital maritime trade routes that passed by Singapore. Not only Japanese leaders but also those of the Philippines, Malaysia, Singapore and Thailand had therefore been urging the United States to do something to prevent the collapse of the independent, anti-Communist government of South Vietnam. Though Japanese trade with mainland China once again surpassed its commerce with Chiang Kai-shek's Taiwan, Japanese diplomats pleaded that they were helpless and stymied by Chinese Communist intransigence on political matters. In 1964 a Japanese liberal wrote: "The problem, frankly, is too great for Japan to deal with by itself."

Vietnam had always been irrelevant to the security of the United States. Moreover American private investments in the southern half of that divided country would never exceed $30 million, by comparison with the $255 million French citizens had invested there. As an additional irony, in November 1964, President Johnson ran for reelection as a "peace candidate," opposed by the far more bellicose Republican Senator Barry Goldwater. Yet for that very reason Johnson rightly feared that his Congressional adversaries would accuse him of "losing" South Vietnam in the same "treasonable" way that mainland China had been lost to the Communists during an earlier Democratic administration. He was therefore determined to persevere in policies that had been formed and upheld by Presidents Truman, Eisenhower and Kennedy.

The Department of State had not developed any credible, publicly accepted revision of the policy of "containment" first enunciated in 1947. Though the United States had not been a signatory to the Geneva agreement of 1954, Johnson's predecessors had supplemented it by repeatedly pledging American support for the continuing independence of South Vietnam. Nevertheless the North Vietnamese regime of Ho Chi-minh, encouraged by Communist China and the Soviet Union, had consistently violated the intent of that Geneva agreement by supporting in South Vietnam the guerrilla forces that called themselves Viet Cong. North Vietnamese patrol vessels had begun to provoke units of the United States Seventh Fleet in the China Sea, and its senior officers were eager to answer those baiting tactics with suitable force. Viet Cong attacks against American Army advisers in South Vietnam had also become an embarrassing nuisance. Johnson's aides had informed him that Ho Chi-minh would not agree to participate in any further negotiations until all of those American military advisers had been withdrawn. By the beginning of 1965 they included thirteen generals, who were unanimous in advising Johnson that their withdrawal would cause the immediate collapse of South Vietnam's armies. The situation there had reached an impasse. Any and every decision Johnson might have taken would have been wrong, in one way or another.

On February 25, 1965, a spokesman for the exasperated Dean Rusk, Secretary of State since 1960 and therefore the official guardian of that American policy of containing Communist power, explained succinctly the perplexity of President Johnson.

> Our policy towards Communist China is inextricably connected with our policies towards China's neighbors, some of whom are directly threatened by Communist expansionism. We have responsibilities towards those nations and, having had a role of leadership thrust upon us, we must give clear and unwavering evidence as to our intentions, for those who seek our support. An effort to show flexibility and to better relations with Communist China would be disastrous if not accompanied by clear willingness to stand by our friendships, our principles, and our commitments in the Far East. . . . Peking's policy towards the United States is very simple. It is one of avowed hostility. It does not allow even for the working out of lesser problems in our relations, to say nothing of an exploration of fundamental solutions of issues between us. As a Chinese Communist document puts it: "We do not wish to settle our disputes with the United States on a piecemeal basis; else we will undermine the revolutionary fervor of our own people. When the time comes for a settlement, it will be done all at once." This is not a climate in which one may look for quick or easy solutions. . . . It takes two to tango.[11]

Long the favorite target for abusive Soviet and Communist Chinese propaganda designed to divert attention from domestic failures, Americans would soon find their efforts derided by Europeans who were only too eager to forget their own historic responsibilities for those disorders in Southeast Asia.

Since 1945, American presidents had made grossly excessive commitments abroad for the defense of European and Asian countries. Very few Americans were conscious of that when President Johnson decided to seek a "military solution" for the problems of South Vietnam, initially by ordering two battalions of United States Marines to land at Da Nang on March 8, 1965, to defend its airfield against further Viet Cong attacks. In Washington the fallacious argument had prevailed that all American commitments abroad must be kept at all times and in all circumstances, or the prestige and influence of

[11] Marshall Green, Deputy Assistant Secretary of State for Far Eastern Affairs, at Princeton University.

the United States would have been damaged and its many allies would have become distrustful. No one thought to ask whether those allies would be needed, and could be trusted. Nor was there any recognition of the many changes in circumstances since 1945, that now enabled most of those allies to fend for themselves without any further American subsidies.

At first Johnson had been assured by the Joint Chiefs of Staff that only small numbers of American troops would be required in South Vietnam, to "stiffen" its forces. Everyone was confident that the thriving American economy could now afford "both guns and butter." Johnson decided not to ask Congress to declare war against North Vietnam, because debate would have been lengthy and the outcome doubtful. Nor had he any desire to bring Communist China openly, fully to the aid of North Vietnam and the Viet Cong. Consequently he would not be able to ask Congress to pay the sharply increasing costs of American intervention by increased taxation. He was repeatedly warned by the Chairman of the House Ways and Means Committee that, if he had asked, he would have been refused. Outside Washington anti-Communism was no longer a vital issue among the American people. Yet throughout the corridors and conference rooms of the many Federal departments and agencies involved, overconfidence prevailed. The United States had never lost a war abroad, and its countless generals and admirals had become habituated to solving any and every foreign crisis by lavish outlays of men and money. Two decades had passed since the end of the Second World War, and a new generation of officers were keen to win promotions and decorations. Many commented that Vietnam would be useful "to blood the troops." A few could have defined the term *deficit financing*, but not one in a thousand understood the balance-of-payments situation of the United States.

Through a failure of judgment and diplomacy, this war would not become a repetition of the United Nations defense of South Korea. Though many West European conservatives had been urging the United States to intervene in Vietnam, their governments were not disposed to help. Harold Wilson, a trimmer who had become the new Labour Prime Minister of Britain and was indebted to Johnson for hefty American support of the pound's weakening fixed rate of $2.80, had cheered Washington's decision to intervene and had promised his support. He soon found, however, that only Tories were willing to defend South Vietnam, to protect British investments in Malaysia and Singapore. When rabid pacifists among Wilson's own Labour flock began loudly to parrot Communist propaganda against "imperialist war-mongering," he quickly backed away.

The Soviet Union had been competing with Communist China for the allegiance of North Vietnam. For the first time since 1945 Russian leaders had also been courting Charles de Gaulle. On February 23, 1965, he agreed to act in concert with Moscow by calling yet another international conference "to redefine and guarantee a policy of nonintervention" in Vietnam. Nothing was said, however, about guaranteeing the independence of South Vietnam. Not surprisingly, when his Foreign Minister began that day to discuss the situation with Johnson and Rusk in Washington, he found them chilly. He could not reassure them that the "political solution" favored by Paris and Moscow would prevent North Vietnam from conquering the South by force. De Gaulle was serving his own cause. Another presidential election was approaching in France. By aligning himself with Moscow and pursuing a "balanced policy" toward divided Vietnam, he sought to neutralize his French Communist critics.

After the first 7 years of a Gaullist France, its Foreign Minister complained that the normally garrulous President Johnson had become "as secretive and enigmatic as his predecessor had been open and willing to discuss." Years later M Couve de Murville would recall that:

> Between Lyndon Johnson and de Gaulle, contact was never really established. They met [at the funeral of President Kennedy] and saw each other again only once in 1967 at the funeral of Adenauer. . . . Protocol difficulties—who should make the first visit?—were at first the official explanation. But at bottom, and increasingly thereafter, there was another reason. . . . Vietnam became Johnson's almost exclusive preoccupation. What he sought from Europe was that he be spared its worries so that he could concentrate upon what represented, for him, increasingly the essential problem.[12]

In reality, however, those costly, useless European allies had no worries. There was no longer any serious threat of a Soviet invasion, because the missile-rattling Nikita Khrushchev had been deposed. West Europeans were enjoying the most prosperous, untroubled decade they had known for a half-century. What they could not stomach was to be ignored by American presidents. Yet that was the brusque treatment they would receive for many years to come. And the French earned Johnson's scorn. By no coincidence, in February 1965, while he was discussing the problems of Vietnam with M Couve de Murville, the Bank of France publicly announced not only that it would continue its new policy of converting dollars into American gold at the United States Treasury, taking $150 million in American gold each month, but also that thereafter it would take in gold the entire surplus in its international payments accounts. While thus rejecting the American dollar, was Couve truly surprised to find President Johnson "secretive and enigmatic," or was he merely trying to conceal French malice? With such a greedy, importunate friend, the United States could no longer afford any enemies. Yet that had not deterred Johnson and Rusk from deciding to help Saigon defend itself against the attacks of Hanoi.

(12) Couve de Murville, *Une politique étrangère 1958–1969*, pp. 121–122.

That last week in February demand for gold on the London bullion market became more intense than at any time since its reopening in March 1954. Despite the usual denials by the United States Treasury, French-inspired rumors had begun to circulate in European capitals that an increase in the official price of gold was imminent. What did follow in March was Congressional action to abolish the statutory gold cover for the Federal Reserve System's deposit liabilities. That did nothing at all to calm the world's money markets. It was well known that, by the end of 1964, the gold reserves of the United States had fallen to $15.471 billion, while short-term dollar obligations held abroad had risen to double that sum.

In March 1965 the "fixing price" of gold sold on the London market was held at a peak of $35.17 per ounce only because it was being amply supplied by the Bank of England, acting on behalf of an official gold pool. Those official sales on the London market had begun in October 1960, when the Bank of England had bought $350 million in gold from the United States for a "bridging operation." Some $225 million of it had then been sold over the next 4 months, until private speculators had been dissuaded by President Kennedy's emphatic refusals to devalue the dollar, and the market price had again been stabilized near $35 per fine ounce. After that disturbance the central banks of the United States, Britain, France, West Germany, Italy, Switzerland, the Netherlands and Belgium had agreed in November 1961 that they would refrain from buying gold in the private markets whenever prices were at or above the gold export point from New York, which was $35.0875. Forming a consortium that became known as the "London Gold Pool," those eight central banks had also agreed to buy when the price fell and to sell when it rose, sharing both gains and losses according to fixed percentages.

Thus the United States had sought to ease the increasing burdens of managing the Bretton Woods gold-exchange system, by taking only a 50 percent share in that London Gold Pool. The shares of Britain, France and Italy had been slightly more than 9 percent each. West Germany's share had been approximately 11 percent, while the Netherlands, Belgium and Switzerland had each taken 3.5 percent. For the next 4 years their operations on the London market had functioned satisfactorily, in the sense that they had been able to buy and divide among themselves more gold at $35 per ounce than they had been obliged to sell. Collectively, with the Bank of England serving as their agent, they had been able to prevent the markets from raising or lowering that price.

During the early 1960s a steady, increasing supply of new gold had been reaching those markets. New production had risen from an estimated 33.6 million ounces in 1960 to 40.1 million in 1964, excluding the output of the Soviet Union, which had been a regular seller of varying amounts from $200 million to $550 million each year. Private demand had remained almost constant, at slightly more than a billion dollars per annum. The eight central banks of the London Gold Pool had therefore been able to take the remainder for addition to their national reserves, and total monetary stocks owned by non-Communist countries had increased from $40.523 billion at the end of 1960 to $41.112 billion at the end of 1961. Though flurries of uneasiness caused by political crises had increased private demand, during the disputes over Berlin in 1961 and Cuba in 1962, the determined, coordinated intervention of those eight central banks had prevented disturbance of the London price. Public knowledge that they were active and effective had served as a stabilizing factor by discouraging speculators. Non-Communist monetary stocks had risen to $41.44 billion at the end of 1962, $42.3 billion at the end of 1963 and $43 billion at the end of 1964.[13]

Though unheralded at the time, early in 1965 a decisive sea change had begun to appear in relations between the United States and Western Europe. American intervention in Vietnam was not the cause. It merely provided another excuse for Europeans to criticize the United States. That widening rift was symbolized by the death of Winston Churchill on January 24 and the lavish state funeral that followed. For many decades he had served as a persuasive negotiator between the disparate interests on opposite sides of the Atlantic, and there was no other European of comparable stature who could have replaced him in the esteem of the American people.

Throughout Western Europe it was now taken for granted that the United States would forever provide the men and money for its defense. Few Europeans had understood the direct connection between those American defense commitments and the persistent deficits in American payments accounts. Many had persuaded themselves that more than 300,000 American troops had been retained in Western Europe only to use it as a "buffer" against the Soviet Union and to defend American private investments, as Europeans themselves had formerly stationed troops in their vanished colonial empires. Sir Anthony Eden, now retired to the House of Lords as Earl of Avon, fatuously commented: "It would be naive to believe that American troops are in Europe for any reason except to protect American interests." Conscious only of their own traditions and imperial pasts, complacent West Europeans had therefore begun resentfully to talk of themselves as Greeks tutoring an arrogant new Rome. With Europe's postwar reconstruction fully completed and its prospering economies now firmly established, the deficit spending of American administrations was no longer regarded as an incredible blessing but rather as the crucial curse.

Inflation had remained the bane of the European *bourgeoisie*, partly because their own governments were engaged in headlong, competitive pursuit of

[13] *Annual Reports* of the Bank for International Settlements, 1961–1965.

economic growth and full employment. Yet it was so much easier to blame the United States. The glaring incongruities in the Europeans' demands that the United States should balance its payments accounts were their blind refusals to pay the full costs of their own defenses and to revalue their currencies against the dollar. Instead they insisted that the United States should adopt precisely those domestic deflationary measures their own electorates refused. American payments deficits continued as logically as night followed day.

Deficit spending by governments was supplying so much new money that speculation had become easy, and gold began to appear more attractive as confidence in the dollar and sterling ebbed. The price on the London market began to rise, and throughout 1965 it remained above the New York export point. Twice it exceeded $35.15 per ounce, regardless of persistent, heavy intervention by the Bank of England. Though the total supply of new gold that year was 52.6 million ounces, including 11.4 million sold by the Soviet Union, all but $250 million was taken by private buyers. Many observers noted that only those Russian sales were enabling the eight central banks of the London Gold Pool to avoid the obligation to sell from their own national reserves.

The French were especially attentive, because Georges Pompidou had returned to public office as Premier of France. President de Gaulle transferred the faithful Michel Debré to the Finance Ministry, and dismissed Valéry Giscard "like a servant" because his loyalty to Gaullism had become suspect. Hervé Alphand was withdrawn from the French Embassy in Washington and became Secretary General at the Foreign Ministry. Having found that he could now defy the United States at will, without incurring any retaliation, de Gaulle became both bolder and more erratic. Because it had become impossible for American officials to argue that the Bretton Woods gold-exchange system was functioning satisfactorily, they countered his emotional championship of gold by announcing more quietly yet with equal determination that the United States intended to demonetize that metal.

President Johnson's decision to send American troops into South Vietnam caused a full-scale review by the United States Treasury of the many minor measures undertaken during the Kennedy administration to correct American payments deficits. In 1959 only 40 percent of American development assistance grants to other countries had been spent in the United States. Therefore "Buy American" requirements had been stiffened. By 1964 some 80 percent of the commitments of the Agency for International Development had been tied to procurement within the United States. In 1965 that was increased to 85 percent, regardless of endless excuses by foreign recipients to justify spending those dollars elsewhere. In 1961 duty-free allowances for American travelers abroad had been reduced from $500 to $100 per person, but Congress had rejected a proposal to restrict American tourists still further. Strenuous efforts had been made to curtail spending abroad by government agencies, again with only limited success. Though continuing efforts to persuade West Germany to pay for the maintenance of American troops stationed there had been shipwrecked on the shoals of propaganda, when the Federal Republic's Defense Ministry had ingeniously protested that East German Communists might describe such payments as "occupation costs," in 1962 the Federal Bank had agreed to buy interest-free "Roosa Bonds" with part of its growing hoard of American dollars.

Other special transactions had occurred: sales of special notes and bonds to foreign monetary authorities to absorb their liquid dollar balances, negotiated prepayment of many foreign debts and advance payments by other countries for military purchases in the United States. In 1962, under Regulation Q, the Federal Reserve Board had raised from 3 to 4 percent the interest-rate ceiling American banks could charge. In July 1963 an "interest equalization tax" of 15 percent had been imposed on American private investment in foreign stock issues, as well as a graduated tax on the purchase of foreign bonds. Yet those measures had only provided new incentives for Americans to hold dollars and dollar earnings abroad, where higher interest rates could be earned. By 1964 the "Eurodollar markets" centered on London had been estimated at $4 to $5 billion. British bankers were delighted by those increasing restrictions on the furious bankers of the United States. Yet the American payments deficits were continuing, regardless of all those palliatives.[14]

Foreseeing that operations in Vietnam would certainly cause still larger deficits, in February 1965 President Johnson recommended to Congress additional measures intended to affect not only the current but also the capital account. Unlike the centralized banking systems of Europe, banking in the United States had always been heterogeneous and decentralized. Soon a favorite saying among bankers was that all attempts to impose controls on American capital exports were "as vain as Prohibition." Well aware that he was dealing with confirmed alcoholics, Johnson asked Congress for voluntary controls, and accompanied them with patriotic appeals to American banks and companies to restrict their direct investments abroad. By the second quarter of 1965 a small, anomalous payments surplus did appear. Cheerfully Secretary Dillon chose April 1 as an appropriate date for his retirement from office. He did so just in time to escape the troubles reaped by his successor, a loyal Democratic lawyer from Virginia named Henry Fowler, who had served an apprenticeship as Under Secretary of the Treasury.

Both Dillon and Fowler had high hopes that world trade negotiations initiated by President Kennedy through GATT would reduce foreign tariffs

(14) Aubrey, *The Dollar in World Affairs*, pp. 28–107.

and other obstacles to American exports sufficiently to correct the disequilibrium in American payments accounts. With considerable fanfare those negotiations were completed in May 1967. However, in a period of rising domestic inflation, when the dollar was becoming so overvalued that many exports were no longer competitively priced, the net effects of that prodigious "Kennedy Round" of tariff cuts would be questionable. At best it did no harm. On current account American payments deficits rose to $1.814 billion for 1965, $1.614 billion for 1966 and an unprecedented $3.196 billion for 1967. Yet Secretary Fowler was simply adjured by President Johnson to keep the Bretton Woods monetary system patched together, until military operations in Vietnam could be successfully concluded. The honor of American arms had been wagered in a full-scale test of American and Communist Chinese intentions in Southeast Asia. By comparison Johnson regarded the survival of the gold-dollar standard as unimportant. The gold stocks of the United States therefore fell by a net $1.47 billion in 1965, $690 million in 1966 and $150 million in 1967, regardless of Fowler's best efforts. When 1968 began, the remaining gold reserves of the United States had dwindled to $12.065 billion. By comparison those of Western Europe had risen to $22.350 billion, more than half of the non-Communist world's total monetary stocks of $41.580 billion. Highly satisfied with that symbol of their own prudence, West Europeans had become scathing in their denunciations of American improvidence.

In 1966 the Soviet Union had begun to abstain from selling any of its gold on world markets, and South African production had increased by a mere 329,000 ounces. Total output by the non-Communist world had therefore remained almost constant at 41.2 million ounces, no more than the year before. Yet private demand had been increasing, and for the first time the eight central banks of the London Gold Pool had been compelled to sell from their national reserves. Though their sales had totaled only $95 million in 1966, they had alerted the Bank of France to that new Anglo–Saxon vulnerability. The price of gold coins had risen considerably on the Paris market, from $48.25 per fine ounce at the end of May 1966 to a 14-year high of $53.75 at the end of December. On January 31, 1967, French authorities had lifted the long-standing ban on private gold imports and exports, to enable Paris to compete with London as a bullion market. Rumors of supply shortages to come, initiated by the Afrikaners, had raised the price of coins to $54 per fine ounce in May. Then in July the Bank of France abruptly withdrew from the London Gold Pool upon receiving factual reports that world gold production had begun to decline for the first time since 1945. The French willingness to participate had been based on the assumption that the Bank of France would gain reserves, not lose them. The United States assumed the French share of 9 percent in the London Gold Pool, increasing its own liability to 59 percent, because no one else would take it.

By the end of 1967 total world production of gold had fallen to 40.170 million ounces for that year, and a sellers' market had appeared that was vulnerable to manipulation by the only large producer, South Africa. The Afrikaners had begun to mint a new type of coin called the Krugerrand that was intended to compete with the world's now dominant but suspect paper currencies. Each Krugerrand weighed precisely 1 ounce of fine gold, and its market price in terms of those currencies would fluctuate, plus a small premium. Private demand for gold had again increased, and the London market price had risen from a low of $35.15 in March 1967 to close at almost $35.20 in December. Though the difference was only a few pennies, it was regarded as a momentous change in world monetary conditions. Central bankers were losing the control they had maintained so strictly since 1939.

That rise in the market price of gold had accompanied first another Middle Eastern crisis in June 1967, then a run on sterling that had been openly encouraged by French authorities. Having shed imperial responsibilities, the British had become frivolous. No one had perceived that more quickly than the French, and Premier Pompidou had been urging Prime Minister Wilson to devalue the pound. The British economy had been suffering from a series of reverses, capped by a crippling dock strike that had begun in September. Payments deficits of £200 million in the third quarter and £300 million in the fourth quarter of 1967 had been further aggravated by a fall of £225 million in total net sterling balances held by the countries that had remained in the sterling area. Bowing to those pressures and to the inspired speculation, in November Wilson devalued the pound by 14.3 percent, from $2.80 to $2.40.

Then and there the American dollar should also have been devalued, to restore the competitive position of the United States. But neither Lyndon Johnson nor the combative Henry Fowler was inclined to let Charles de Gaulle claim a double victory against both reserve currencies of the Bretton Woods system. By the end of 1967 the seven central banks that had remained in the London Gold Pool were disturbed to find that they had been compelled to sell $1.6 billion from their gold reserves to keep the price on the London market from exceeding $35.20 per ounce. The principal losers had been the United States and Britain. The latter alone had lost $1.17 billion from its gold reserves, and it is doubtful that Harold Wilson has ever forgiven the French. Private buyers had absorbed $900 million of that official loss, and by the end of 1967 the gold reserves of Britain had been reduced to $1.290 billion. On the Paris Bourse the premium of the Napoleon over its gold content had risen from 48½ percent in March to 61½ percent in December. Speculators were jubilant, confident that they could now control the markets. Secretly the central bankers of the United States, Britain and West Germany had been devising a "contingency plan" to restrain them, but this time the Bank of France had not been invited to participate. Though still idolized at home, Charles de Gaulle had become a pariah among his neighbors.

It is characteristic of the United States that it must win any minor war abroad within 2 years, deploying first regular troops, then volunteers. If such a war should last any longer without receiving the full support of the American people, the only advice that can be given to any American president is to quit forthwith. Thereafter the armed forces of the United States must resort to the draft to fill their depleted ranks, and American draftees are useless. Federal budget deficits had grown inexorably, from a mere $1.6 billion in fiscal year (FY) 1965 to $3.8 billion in FY 1966, and to $8.7 billion in FY 1967.

By the end of December 1967 the American forces available in South Vietnam for operations planned by the inept General William Westmoreland totaled 500,000 men, yet there had been no tangible accomplishments. As an explanation he demanded more men and money. War costs estimated at $10 billion for fiscal year 1967 had soared to $21 billion in that year, and the Department of Defense had been demanding at least $30 billion for the Vietnam war in fiscal year 1968, when the Federal budget deficit would become an astounding $25.2 billion. The national debt had begun to soar, and Treasury borrowing operations had become difficult. Finally, much too late, a timid, irresponsible Congress began to worry. In the absence of wage and price controls, those budget deficits had inevitably become inflationary. Wartime demand inflation was also becoming noticeable, as supply shortages appeared throughout the economy. On July 14, 1967, the Treasury had therefore ceased its efforts to stabilize the price of silver by selling from its stocks to all comers at the official price of $1.29 per ounce, maintained for three decades. The coinage of silver had been stopped, and dozens of other governments had promptly followed suit. By January 1968, pushed by extensive speculation, the market price had almost doubled, to $2.40 per ounce.

A century earlier, Abraham Lincoln had summarily retired one general after another until at last he found a winner. The ineffectual Lyndon Johnson turned that precedent inside out, by promoting his losers. On January 29, 1968, the armies of North Vietnam launched their surprise "Tet" offensive and shattered the myth of infallibility that had long protected the Department of Defense from serious criticism. Westmoreland was retired from South Vietnam, to the post of Army Chief of Staff. After weeks of heated rumors, and an increasing flight from dollars and sterling not only into gold and silver but also into platinum and palladium, the largest gold run in history reached the front pages of newspapers throughout the world on Friday, March 8. That day the London market sold 100 tons, and in Paris the Bourse sold a record 4 tons of 1 kilogram gold ingots alone. Arriving in Basle for a monthly meeting at the Bank for International Settlements, Chairman William McChesney Martin of the Federal Reserve Board reassured anxious reporters that "One of my colleagues was coming to Basle anyway, so I thought it very desirable that I come along too. My visit has no special significance whatever." No one believed him.

A bland official communiqué emerged from that meeting in Basle. Though it did not mention that the central banks of Switzerland, Belgium and Italy were now fully alarmed and had asked to withdraw from the London Gold Pool, the Bank of France was well informed. On Monday, March 11, the gold-buying spree in Paris therefore reached 8 tons, and the demand for gold mining shares rose both in London and in New York. In Washington the Chairman of the House Ways and Means Committee denounced as "unthinkable" the press suggestions that the dollar might be allowed to float, by severing its tie to gold, or that the world could ever revert to the pre-1914 gold standard so vehemently advocated by President de Gaulle. Privately, however, members of Congress had become quite disturbed by the continuing sale of American gold reserves to European speculators and were determined to stop it. By March 13, when Senator Robert Kennedy committed *lèse-majesté*, announcing that he would be a candidate for the presidency in open defiance of his party's leader, the worldwide scramble for gold had become intense. London dealers described as "phenomenal" their Tuesday sales of 200 tons. Zürich had sold 80 tons that day, and Paris 16 tons. Everywhere speculation was fed by the candid hope that the United States would be forced to abandon its policy of holding the official price of gold at $35 per ounce, as it had renounced any further official price for silver. And the French had another reason for fomenting international speculation precisely at that time.

Finance ministers and central bankers of the Group of Ten had been developing plans for a radical reform of the Bretton Woods monetary system. An entirely new form of international reserve asset had been invented, to supplement and possibly to replace not only dollars and sterling but also gold. The deadline for agreement among the Group of Ten had been scheduled for March 31, 1968, at a meeting to be held in Stockholm. The best, though certainly not the last, opportunity for the French to spoil that reform plan was at hand. Finally aroused, President Johnson asked Congress to approve "an urgent and concerted effort" to maintain the official price of gold at $35 per ounce by continuing sales of monetary gold on the London market. He found them quite reluctant to oblige, because they had lost confidence in his judgment and leadership.

In London the prices of almost all commodities soared. Spot silver rose to a record 237 pence per ounce. Market uneasiness caused even cocoa, coffee, wool, sugar and wheat to rise. Only rubber somehow eluded the fever for speculation. A disheartened idealist writing for the London *Times* had begun fervently to dislike both gold and the French. Deploring the entire greedy spectacle, he reported: "There is an increasingly ugly quality, not only of malicious mischief, but also of Gadarene hysteria about this week's gold rush." In London alone 175 tons had been sold on Wednesday and 225 tons on Thursday. That earnest Londoner added:

> Some future Gibbon will no doubt one day describe the extraordinary psychological flaw in twentieth century man which can induce almost the whole civilized world simultaneously to risk and perhaps to destroy the whole basis of its prosperity in a fit of self-immolation.

This Gibbon will comment only that London's financial journalists, in their extravagant excitement, have at times exaggerated the significance of gold.

At seven that Thursday evening, March 14, Prime Minister Wilson received a telephone call from President Johnson. Wilson immediately requested an audience of the Queen. At one the next morning a proclamation was issued declaring a bank holiday in London. In the late-sitting House of Commons, near riot followed. The orotund spokesman for the Tory Opposition, Edward Heath, demanded reassurance that the gold interests of London would be fully protected. In New York the discount rate was raised from 4½ percent to 5, the highest since 1929. And in Washington the Treasury announced that closing of the London gold market would not affect the commitment of the United States to buy and sell gold "in transactions with monetary authorities." As finance ministers and central bankers began to assemble in Washington for an emergency meeting to which the French had not been invited, the outlines of their contingency planning for a "two-tier gold market" began to appear. French desires had again been thwarted. The dollar would not be devalued, nor would the official price of gold be affected. Angrily Charles de Gaulle ordered the Paris Bourse to remain open, to permit speculators to push the market price of gold as high as they could.

On March 17 the London Gold Pool was dissolved, and agreement was reached among the remaining members of the Group of Ten that thereafter monetary gold would be used only for official settlements within a "closed system" of central banks. The United States further stipulated that it would sell to other central banks from its own gold reserves only where necessary to enable them to settle their obligations to the International Monetary Fund. Private buyers would be allowed to obtain gold only from the "free markets," as they were designated when the London bank holiday ended April 1. By then speculation had calmed. In Zürich, the price rose to a high of $43 per ounce, then gradually fell to $36.50. Nevertheless, during those last 6 months of the London Gold Pool's operations, sales by its seven central banks had caused their gold reserves to fall an astonishing $2.72 billion. New production during that period had been an estimated $700 million. Monetary purchases had been only $300 million. The balance of $3.1 billion had been sold for nonmonetary purposes, and only an estimated $650 million had been absorbed by current industrial uses and traditional saving. The remaining $2.5 billion had been taken by speculators.

The biggest of those buyers in the London market had been the Swiss, who had been forming a competitive Gold Pool of their own in Zürich. They had therefore been taking large quantities of gold from London while it could still be bought at little more than the official price, and they had been closely followed by the French and the Belgians. By the end of 1968 private French gold hoards alone would rise to an estimated 7000 metric tons. The scale of speculative operations had surpassed anything previously witnessed, and the vulnerability of the Bretton Woods regime of fixed exchange rates had been clearly revealed. Another period of frantic speculation in currencies and commodities had begun.

Few Americans had noted those disorders on the distant, inaccessible gold markets of Europe. American attention was focused on domestic troubles—growing opposition to the war in Vietnam, urban riots by blacks who demanded more and bigger Federal giveaway programs, and violence in the approaching national elections. Yet the gold speculators of Europe had helped to shake the determination of Lyndon Johnson. On March 31 he halted American bombing sorties against North Vietnam and announced that he would not be a candidate for reelection. Thus basic decisions on the war in Vietnam and the future of the dollar were postponed for yet another year. Both in the United States and abroad, inflation caused primarily by the deficit spending of governments would continue unabated.

9 = Invention of an Abstract Standard
1963–1974

A digression is needed, to describe more fully the intensive negotiations for an unprecedented international monetary change that had just culminated in the Group of Ten's meeting at Stockholm on March 31, 1968.

Among central bankers, who are subject to their governments' whims and decrees, only the tried is trusted. Changes are resisted until they can no longer be avoided, even by the most clever subterfuge. Consequently the international monetary system has evolved piecemeal, as crises in the money markets have forced governments to agree that innovations must be tested. To the surprised public the sudden appearance of any change then appears casual, often uncertain to the point of folly. Growing familiarity with it may or may not bring widespread acceptance. Little factual publicity is given to the many months and years of tedious, sometimes heated international discussions that have preceded change, as experts and their governments have weighed the advantages to be gained or lost and have awaited opportunities to secure the agreement of other nations. That process is always arduous and wasteful, because each crisis exacts a price in money and in good will. Yet no other way has been found to obtain the consent of sovereign nations that are unwilling to concede anything unless they must. Moreover, since 1945 the control those governments can in fact exert, not in law but in the money markets, has been steadily eroded. Once again the markets have become more powerful than their masters and pay little heed to their guidance. Today the typical central banker resembles the unhappy rider of a tiger, who is fearful of the unruly beast yet dares not dismount. Pretense is therefore pervasive whenever finance ministers and central bankers discuss change. They claim more power than they have.

FORMATION OF THE GROUP OF TEN

Throughout the 1960s, one of the most controversial problems had been the proposals for the creation of new international money to be used as national reserve assets. Before the First World War, a handful of experts had foreseen that gold alone could not forever continue to provide the expanding supply of international liquidity needed to finance growing world trade. The available sources had favored some nations to the exclusion of others, and new supplies had been assumed to be finite. Yet by the end of 1938, gold had still constituted 93 percent of the total reserves held by all countries outside the Soviet Union. No international agreement had been reached on any of the suggested "gold-economizing measures" needed to supplement it, and President Franklin Roosevelt's increase in its official price had obviated any immediate requirement for such an agreement. Though sterling had been readily accepted by many of Great Britain's trading partners, that privileged relationship had been resented by its competitors. And sterling had been tried and then rejected after its devaluation in 1931 by the Netherlands, Belgium and Switzerland. Their legislatures had become intent on preserving to the penny the book value of their citizens' national reserves. So long as the United States would guarantee a floor price of $35 per ounce, gold had therefore remained the asset those European countries had preferred, and they had written laws to prevent their central bankers from holding anything more than "working balances" in foreign currencies. Other nations had imitated that example, because it was considered the most prudent.

Yet by the end of 1949, gold had fallen to 74 percent of total reserves—gold, foreign exchange and gold tranche positions in the International Monetary Fund. First necessity, then general usage, had secured widespread acceptance of dollars and sterling not only as trading currencies but also as the primary component of the reserves held by the new nations of Asia and Africa. By the end of 1957, gold had therefore constituted only 66 percent of total non-Communist reserves. And by the end of 1964, it had fallen to 59 percent. That increase in foreign-exchange reserves relative to gold had been unplanned and haphazard, but it had not been excessive. Between 1958 and 1964, the gross reserves of all countries had increased at an average annual rate of only 2.8 percent. However, the reserves of the half-dozen countries of the European Community had risen at an average annual rate of 13 percent, larger than their real needs. Those national reserves had become a popular symbol of Europe's revived prominence in world affairs, and the insistence on monetary reform first arose among Europeans who no longer considered themselves dependent on the United States and Britain. They demanded a voice in the creation of new international assets.

An extraordinary dilemma had also appeared, whose novel resolution would provide a landmark in monetary history. Approximately 75 percent of the new supplies of gold were being produced by South Africa, and another 15 percent by the Soviet Union. Both were considered unreliable and potentially hostile sources by many Americans. If only for that political reason, the United States had been consistently refusing to consider any substantial increase in the official price of gold. Though that would have increased the monetary value of existing stocks, there was no credible evidence that it would have caused new sources to appear. Most producers would simply have reopened old mines that had become unprofitable. The United States would therefore have preferred to expand the use of reserve currencies, and within many parts of the former French empire the franc had continued to serve that purpose. But France had not been alone in rejecting all national currencies as basic reserve assets, and it was widely believed that another devaluation of the dollar or the pound would have drastically curtailed the extensive acceptance they had gained. Moreover, within the United States and Britain there were powerful domestic interests that had not been appreciative of the advantages the private bankers of New York and London had been enjoying. By 1964 the taxpayers of the United States were paying $750 million per annum in interest charges on the Federal securities held by foreigners. That seemed a high price for the prestige and profits presumably reaped by the bankers of New York from international use of the dollar.

Where there were so many firm objections to both gold and national currencies as the monetary forms for further increases in international liquidity, it seemed desirable to many economists that an entirely new kind of international money should be created. But that did not imply widespread understanding of, or agreement on, the precise form it should take. Describing the first, tentative steps toward that radical innovation in the Bretton Woods system, the American Treasury official most closely involved would later write:

> We were convinced that the dollar should continue to have a key role . . . but we also knew that the world was becoming too large for the United States to carry so large a proportion of the international currency task alone. And we were looking for evidence, in the mechanics of our operations and in the attitudes of other countries, that would suggest promising paths for further cautious exploration in the future.[1]

_____

[1] Roosa, *The Dollar and World Liquidity*, p. 24.

As recently as September 1960, when delegates from the member nations of the International Monetary Fund had assembled in Washington for its annual meeting, there had not been any widespread recognition that anything might be wrong. Within weeks the speculation in gold that began in October changed many minds. As the United States had slowly become a debtor nation, confidence in the dollar had begun to wither. By September 1961, when the Fund met again in Vienna, the finance ministers and central bankers who attended had become willing to say that all was not well. Secretary Dillon and Chairman Martin had agreed between themselves that they should try to persuade the others to make large supplies of their currencies available to the Fund on some kind of contingent, bilateral basis so that jointly they could cope with sudden shifts of private capital from one currency into another. At Vienna, however, they had found their colleagues unwilling to go further than assent to a proposal for "new borrowing arrangements . . . designed to provide the Fund with additional resources" needed to handle any unusually large movements of short-term capital.

Extensive discussions had followed. And in December 1961, at a meeting held in Paris, the ten largest countries (Belgium, Britain, Canada, France, West Germany, Italy, Japan, the Netherlands, Sweden and the United States) had agreed on "General Arrangements to Borrow," a formal understanding with the Fund that they would provide their currencies under certain conditions and on the basis of voting formulae that were carefully specified. That had been the beginning of the supplementary organization later dubbed the "Group of Ten," and it had offered to the Fund potential resources that had initially totaled the equivalent of $6 billion, to be used only by the Ten. Switzerland, though not a member of the Fund, had been asked to participate in those new "swap arrangements" and had offered the equivalent in Swiss francs of another $200 million. Thus the French had also gained Swiss support within that new "club" for their arguments that the monetary role of gold should be preserved and enhanced.

Consequently the first step toward increasing the supply and diversifying the kinds of international liquidity available had not been creation of new money but rather provision for additional lines of credit on a multilateral basis. It had been undertaken "to share the burden" of defending the dollar and sterling parities against speculative attacks and on the understanding that the payments deficits of the United States and Britain would soon end. In 1962 a new British Chancellor of the Exchequer, Reginald Maudling, had blithely proposed another scheme that would have enabled official holders of sterling or dollars to deposit them in a special account at the Fund, with their full gold value and transfer rights guaranteed. The British, having begun to tire of the varied costs of maintaining sterling as a reserve currency, proposed to ease their own burdens by making it easy for foreign official holders "to run into the Fund." Unhappily, though the idea was sound, they found not only the American Treasury but also all the other members of the Group of Ten alarmed by their apparent rashness. Though premature, that British initiative did arouse sufficient interest to secure agreement that more searching studies would be needed to ensure the adequacy of international liquidity in years ahead.

At that point Pierre-Paul Schweitzer was instaled as Managing Director of the Fund, just in time for its annual meeting in September 1963. There two studies on "the outlook for the functioning of the international monetary system" were authorized. One was to be made by the staff of the Fund itself, and the other by deputies of the finance ministers and central bankers of the Group of Ten. Meeting separately at Washington's Alibi Club, they had agreed among themselves that they should retain control over any changes in the Fund's rules, because they provided most of its money. Habitually many of them thought as international creditors, whereas too many of the international civil servants on the staff of the Fund considered themselves obliged to sympathize with the world's far larger number of debtors. And in the reform negotiations that lay ahead, the United States, the largest member of the Fund, would appear in the garb of a debtor and would reject the disciplinary rules it had demanded as a creditor when the Bretton Woods agreements had been drafted two decades earlier.

The first session of the Group of Ten's deputies was held informally in Paris on November 5, 1963. It was chaired by Robert Roosa of the United States Treasury, and observers from the Fund, the Bank for International Settlements and the Organization for Economic Cooperation and Development participated in the monthly discussions held thereafter. From the beginning two subjects—gold and floating exchange rates—were rejected as topics for discussion. Therefore no one would later raise any question about whether there might be some connection between fixed exchange rates and the use of gold as the basis of the system. No one would ask whether a system of fixed exchange rates could be based on anything except gold. It would simply be assumed that one could do so.

Wary of the many "wild ideas" for international monetary reform that had already been hatched in academic nests, Roosa voiced Secretary Dillon's conviction that there could and should be no serious consideration of any basic changes in the system so long as American and British payments deficits continued to expand the supply of world liquidity. Both were sympathetic toward the interests of New York's banking community and were using delaying tactics in hopes that the "long-term corrective measures" President Kennedy had approved to correct American payments deficits would soon become effective. However, as discussions progressed, a diplomatic, magical term appeared—"contingency planning." Roosa was disconcerted to find that the Europeans present were quite prepared to discuss immediate, radical changes in the media of international payments authorized by the Bretton Woods agreements. In their view the essential problem in the system was "the adjustment process." In other words the system was not functioning properly because the United States and Britain had large payments deficits that they were not really attempting to correct.

Shrewdly those Europeans had already seized upon a concept for a new form of money to be called a Composite Reserve Unit (CRU). It had originally been suggested by Edward Bernstein, an American whose credentials and access to President Kennedy Roosa could not deny. Bernstein had described his CRUs as units that might have been instantly created by the deposit of a specified amount of each of the Group of Ten's national currencies. Distributed to each in proportion to its deposits, CRUs might have joined gold, dollars, sterling and gold tranche positions in the Fund as officially accepted reserve assets. However, at that meeting in Paris, the French and the Dutch representatives modified Bernstein's proposal. While continuing to use his term *CRU*, they urged that units be distributed to each of the Group of Ten in proportion to its gold reserves. That would have been a somewhat devious way of increasing the official price of gold. By the end of 1963, French national gold reserves had risen to their highest level since 1935, and all French debts abroad had been repaid. Moreover, they recommended that any further accumulations of dollars and sterling by central banks should be prohibited.

Thus the French threat to deplete further the dwindling gold reserves of the United States and Britain became explicit for the first time, behind closed doors, a few days before the assassination of President Kennedy. Roosa was frankly offended by that challenge to the continuing use of the dollar as a reserve asset and countered by arguing that the French proposal would have contracted rather than expanded reserve holdings. As that debate developed, both the German and the Italian representatives found it expedient to remain on the sidelines. The meeting had ceased to be the pleasant "tea party" most had anticipated. And Roosa fell back on the argument that there should be a further expansion of the General Arrangements to Borrow already established to meet short-term liquidity problems.

In June 1964, when the finance ministers and central bankers of the Group of Ten met to review the progress of their deputies, they found that none had been made. Wide divergences of opinion had been revealed on the essential nature of the reforms needed. The deputies were therefore assigned a deadline for the preparation of a report that would summarize their discussions, so that something might appear to coincide with the Fund's own study on liquidity, scheduled for publication in its *Annual Report* for 1963–1964. Not surprisingly those deputies of the Ten found it politic to permit their five-man secretariat to prepare their meaningless report. When it appeared on August 10, it disappointed academic critics by failing to recommend any innovations.

Yet no effort had been made to conceal the basic differences between the United States and France that continued to dominate negotiations for the next decade. Initially the Americans favored simple extension of claims on the Fund that "could be enlarged to meet an open need." By contrast the French first wanted an entirely new and wholly owned reserve asset, to be created "according to appraised over-all need for reserves," that would be tied to gold, would not enable any country to incur payments deficits and might be used freely by any holder. Thus the United States was willing to strengthen the Fund's ability to influence the domestic policies of its members, whereas France was intent on enhancing national independence. Somewhat discomfited, the West Germans and the Italians sought to find a middle way by suggesting a "harmonization ratio" for the gold and foreign-exchange components of national reserves, to prevent holders of dollars and sterling from exceeding agreed limitations. And the British fell silent, for fear of offending any of the contending interests. Though there was general agreement that the quantity of liquidity already in existence was adequate, Europeans were adamant that there should be further study of the possibilities of creating a new international reserve asset.[2]

MONEY OR CREDIT?

Though conducted behind closed doors, those discussions among the Group of Ten's finance ministers, central bankers and their deputies had not entirely escaped public attention. By September 1964, when the International Monetary Fund met in Tokyo, private interests were in full cry. The two interim reports, by the Group of Ten's deputies and the Fund's staff, were belittled by the press as "meager and inadequate"—and a third report appeared, uninvited. Thirty-two academic economists, of widely different backgrounds and beliefs, had met at Princeton and Bellagio to prepare a protest against the Group of Ten's refusal to grant them formal hearings. Styling themselves the "Group of Thirty-Two," they did their utmost to stampede the United States Treasury into action, without noticeable effect. Robert Roosa was preparing to retire from office at the end of 1964, to be succeeded as Under Secretary for Monetary Affairs by Frederick Deming. And as chairman of the deputies of the Group of Ten, he was replaced by the candid Otmar Emminger of the German Federal Bank.

Nevertheless in Tokyo the Ten did approve the formation of a related "Study Group on the Creation of Reserve Assets," chaired by Rinaldo Ossola of the Bank of Italy. Its twenty-five members and eight observers began their

[2] Cohen, *International Monetary Reform, 1964–1969,* pp. 15–35.

discussions in October, with strict instructions that they were neither to pre-judge any aspect of the question nor to commit any participating country. Acting as individual experts rather than as representatives of their govern-ments, they were directed, not to study all the academic proposals for increas-ing international liquidity that had already appeared, but rather to concen-trate on those types of proposals the deputies had already considered and had decided were practical possibilities for the further evolution of the interna-tional monetary system. The Study Group was also instructed "to assemble the elements necessary for an evaluation by the Deputies of the various pro-posals," without expressing any preferences or passing any judgments.

The situation was sensitive. Producers of gold and their European support-ers had been calling loudly for a "once and for all increase" in its official price.[3] Yet that possibility had already been excluded from the proposals to be considered by the Study Group. Karl Blessing of the West German Feder-al Bank had dismissed it as "unrealistic." Aside from political considerations, his compelling and purely monetary arguments had been that the immediate effect would have been inflationary and that in time the expansion of world trade would have required another increase. Instead the international mone-tary system needed an asset that could be expanded (or contracted) gradu-ally, to meet current needs as they might develop.[4] The Study Group there-fore ignored Charles de Gaulle's dramatic call for revival of the classical gold standard and reviewed other proposals classified into three categories. First was the Collective (or Composite) Reserve Unit scheme originally favored by the French and the Dutch, together with plans that might have been imple-mented by the Group of Ten acting on their own. The second involved proposals for varied kinds of extensions of drawing rights or special operations by the International Monetary Fund. The third consisted of plans that might have provided discontented holders of reserve currencies with an alternative asset.

Within the Study Group itself there was no disagreement on the place of gold as the basic reserve asset, but considerable differences emerged on its role in relation to any new reserve assets that might be introduced. Several experts wanted any new assets to be "as good as gold" and therefore closely linked to that metal, whereas others objected that countries whose policies called for maintaining a low ratio of gold to total reserves should not be penalized for doing so.[5] When the Study Group presented its formal report to the Group of Ten on May 31, 1965, it therefore concluded that:

---

[3] For French official views at that time, see Rueff, *Le péché monétaire de l'Occident*, pp. 77–195.
[4] For the arguments, see Hinshaw, *Monetary Reform and the Price of Gold.*
[5] For a description of the link between gold and the varied concepts for a CRU, see National Industrial Conference Board, *Gold and World Monetary Problems,* pp. 55–73.

the differences which confront us ultimately reflect a range of views on four fundamental issues . . . (i) the question of a link between gold and a new reserve asset, the closeness of that link, and its effects on the existing system; (ii) the width of membership for purposes of management and distribution of the assets; (iii) the role of the International Monetary Fund as regards deliberate reserve creation; (iv) the rules for decision-making concerning the creation of reserve assets.[6]

As a permanent record of expert thinking at that time the report of Ossola's Study Group would continue to be a useful document. Yet before it could be printed, political events had rendered it obsolete. President de Gaulle's sweeping refusal to consider any possibility except reversion to the pre-1914 gold standard had repudiated his own Finance Ministry's advocacy of the CRU. As Premier Georges Pompidou sought full control over French economic policies, Valéry Giscard was being slowly eased from prominence and office. The indignant Giscard was accused of prolonging unnecessarily the austerity program that had restored the reputation of the franc and had enabled the Bank of France to amass its huge gold reserves. Though Charles de Gaulle did not yet understand cause and effect, he would soon be taught. And throughout the membership of the International Monetary Fund, cries had arisen that even the smallest nation should be allowed to participate in the creation and distribution of any new reserve assets.

At the United States Treasury the promotion of Henry Fowler to Secretary on April 1, 1965, ended the complacent era in which its policies had been guided by men content with the existing international role of the dollar. On July 11 Fowler astonished everyone except President Johnson by abandoning the previous American position that the international monetary system needed nothing more than an expansion of existing credit facilities. Partly to counter the campaign for gold being waged by Charles de Gaulle, but also to gain support from poor countries, and without proposing any specific plan that might have been attacked in detail, Fowler announced simply that the United States was now "prepared to attend and participate in a multilateral conference that would consider what steps could jointly be taken to secure substantial improvements in international monetary arrangements."

American officials had been encouraged by the fact that most of the members of Ossola's Study Group had preferred some kind of supplement to gold and the reserve currencies rather than a substitute for the latter. Moreover American academic and Congressional support for the creation of a new reserve asset had been growing. Gold's fervent partisans in Congress had departed. To Fowler there appeared to be more danger in standing still than in doing something, no matter how novel and untried. In an expansive speech

[6] Group of Ten, *Report of the Study Group on the Creation of Reserve Assets,* p. 95.

at the annual meeting of the International Monetary Fund, in September 1965, expounding his most optimistic beliefs, President Johnson therefore conceded that it was no longer "appropriate or possible" for one country alone to provide, through its deficits, the major source of new world reserves. International wisdom and cooperation should and would devise the new assets needed to secure infinite growth in world trade, and prosperity for all mankind. Among Americans the belief prevailed that the only limitations were those imposed by defects in human vision and imagination. Thereafter Americans would argue that the real hazard to prosperity was the potential shortage of reserves.

Karl Blessing also spoke at that 1965 meeting of the Fund. Expressing not only West German official opinion but also the views of many other Europeans, he quietly rebuked both France and the United States. Cautiously he argued that if all leading countries would strive for equilibrium in their balance of payments, their real need for national reserves would be small. Temporary deficits could be financed either from owned reserves or from conditional reserves such as those provided by the Fund and by other credit institutions.

> I cannot help thinking that too perfect a machinery for financing balance-of-payments deficits weakens monetary discipline and contributes to creeping inflation.

Those Europeans saw no urgent need for additional liquidity, especially since Fund quotas were being substantially increased. They considered price stability more important than further growth and full employment, which their undervalued currencies had already secured for them. Moreover, unlike Johnson and Fowler, they were not concerned to finance a war in Vietnam.

When the deputies of the Group of Ten resumed discussions, in January 1966, their chairman therefore introduced a German plan intended to satisfy both European and American demands. Dubbed the "Emminger Compromise," it stipulated that the new reserve asset should be created within the Group of Ten and should be limited to them, with the possibility of extension to others whose currencies were convertible and were usable in world trade. Emminger also believed that the new asset should be handled in a separate account at the Fund. Where voting procedures were concerned, a compromise was proposed. Though unanimity would be required for such "basic issues" as the establishment of the new asset, operational decisions could be made by a weighted majority. Emminger rejected the French insistence that distribution should be linked to existing gold reserves. France's proposed ban on holdings of foreign currencies was also discarded, though Emminger did agree that there might be a one-for-one link between gold and the new reserve asset in the actual financing of external payments deficits. Where price stability was concerned, the West Germans were far more prudent than the French, but they did not suffer from the delusion that gold was essential to it. Furthermore, quite unlike the French, they refused to agree to any measure that might have enhanced the market value and political influence of the Soviet Union's gold reserves.

With the advantage of hindsight, it is now obvious that by the middle of the 1960s gold could no longer be relied on to provide any substantial increase in total reserves, at $35 per ounce. In those circumstances, further growth in world reserves simply meant increasing dollar reserves. In turn, because of the impending shortage of gold at that official price, the United States was being forced into payments deficits. Yet very few participants in those reform negotiations grasped that sequential change in events. Fowler and Deming did. For the first time, at that meeting of the Group of Ten's deputies in January 1966, the United States presented a plan of its own. Deming tried the ancient political ploy of offering something to everyone. In an effort to satisfy European insistence on creating any new asset within a limited group, while accommodating the interests of all other members of the Fund, two different devices were proposed. First a special drawing right was suggested that would have expanded automatic drawing rights in the Fund. Though repayable, it would have become usable merely on a country's declaration that a need for it existed. Second a new international reserve asset was proposed that would have been guaranteed against depreciation in terms of gold but would not have been linked to it in any other way. Distributed to a limited number of countries, that new asset would have been a composite obligation of those nations that had deposited their currencies in a common pool. Each would then have received units that it could have declared part of its fully owned reserves.

There was nothing novel in that concept, which resembled the CRU Giscard had favored, but the French delegation maintained "a stony silence." Michel Debré had just been named French Finance Minister, and President de Gaulle's most recent wishes were not yet known. On February 25 he instructed Debré that there would be no changes in French policies. Gold remained the only valid basis for the international monetary system. All schemes for creating any new reserve asset were "inane" and were to be dismissed. The French delegation would continue to participate in the meetings of the Group of Ten but only to prevent agreement on the creation of such an asset. Both de Gaulle and Jacques Rueff, whose role as court sage was now well established, were convinced that eventually only a substantial increase in the official price of gold would prove to be a satisfactory way to provide the additional liquidity that would someday be needed. And in 1966 French gold reserves rose to a new high of $5.240 billion. The bargaining position of France appeared to be stronger than ever before.

Though French intransigence hindered further discussions within the Group of Ten on the technical issues involved in the creation of a new reserve asset, the practical possibilities had already been identified. Most other members were willing to bide their time while further refining their own proposals. After another meeting of the Group of Ten in April 1966, Emminger explained quite frankly why they would not be able to reach agreement on a compromise plan by June 1966, when their third report was scheduled for completion and delivery to ministers. "Though an insufficiency of reserves will have disadvantageous effects and will produce unsatisfactory national policies," there was no urgency. So long as American payments deficits continued, there would be enough reserves for the rest of the world. Emminger added: "On some points we won't get an entirely agreed report." That was a masterly understatement. One of the major issues still unresolved was the choice between money and credit—a new reserve unit or further Fund drawing rights. Nor had there been agreement on the new unit's link to gold or on the wider forum in which further discussions should take place. France had even prevented unanimity on the question of the need to consider and prepare a contingency plan. Emminger concluded that the differences of opinion among the experts:

> must finally be resolved on the political levels, that is to say, by ministers and primarily by governments themselves, but the governments cannot really form themselves an opinion on any possible disagreements without having a very good, well reasoned report on when we agree, where there are still disagreements, and what are the reasons for the disagreements.

The time had come for public, political maneuvering to begin. Well coached by their deputies, the leading actors took their positions on the world stage.

THE STRUGGLE BETWEEN JOHNSON AND DE GAULLE

Unfortunately the public were then confronted with a gross oversimplification, the supposed need to choose between paper and gold. In and of itself, neither form of money had ever been able to prevent inflation or deflation. Neither national currencies nor nature's commodities, whose supply was also unregulated, should have been expected to do so. If the French had been truly intent on securing price stability, they would not only have demanded the end of American and British payments deficits, and would have revalued their franc for that purpose, but would also have been willing to accept any new form of international money whose creation could have been rigorously controlled. If they had done so, they would probably have prevailed, because the power and the popularity of the United States and Britain had begun to ebb. Instead the French insistence on an increase in the official price of gold not only estranged most economists but also offended everyone who would not have benefited from such an increase. Because that included the vast majority of the human race, the French succeeded only in severely weakening the conservative influence of the European Economic Community in the decisions and operations of the International Monetary Fund. Though a respectable case could have been made for increasing the official price of gold, and many quite respectable Europeans were in favor of doing so, they were silenced by the blatant way in which the French were using it as a weapon against the United States.

When the finance ministers and central bankers of the Group of Ten met at The Hague, on July 25, 1966, relations between the United States and France became rancorous. Secretary Fowler's patience had worn threadbare. Rather than serve as a useful organization for consultation and decision, the Group of Ten had become a pulpit from which the French could and did denounce American policies to the financial journalists assembled from every corner of the globe. There was no semblance of diplomacy in Minister De-bré's vehement refusals to admit any need for contingency planning. Fowler therefore made his own appeal to a wider audience by urging that the discussions of the Ten be expanded immediately to include the entire membership of the Fund, so that the Ten would not appear to be "dictating the nature and terms of monetary reform to the rest of the world." He got his way. The ministers agreed that "deliberately created reserve assets, as and when needed, should be distributed to all members of the Fund on the basis of IMF quotas or of similar criteria." They also "thought it appropriate to look now for a wider framework in which to consider the questions that affect the world economy as a whole." For that purpose, the ministers and governors of the Ten recommended "a series of joint meetings in which the deputies would take part together with the executive directors of the Fund." Three years of study had not been entirely wasted. The deputies of the Ten had reached agreement among themselves that certain basic principles should be included in any contingency plan. The deadlock intended by France was broken.

At the time, the European press had been filled with dire predictions that the creation of any new reserve asset would become a massive giveaway program to support overconsumption by the United States and Britain, and to assist the economic development of poor countries. But the philosophy the Ten's deputies had developed among themselves could not have been described as imprudent. On the fundamental purposes of deliberate reserve creation, they had agreed that it should not be directed to financing the balance-of-payments deficits of individual countries but should instead be based on "a collective judgment of the reserve needs of the entire world." Unhappily no one could say precisely how that altruistic wisdom could be achieved. The deputies also recorded their opinion that:

reserves should be created (1) on a long-term basis to meet probable needs over a three-to-five year period with provision for adjustment to changing circumstances, and (2) in amounts sufficient to assure the growth in reserves needed to avoid worldwide deflationary pressures, disruptive policies, or excessive strain on the monetary system, but not so large as to create inflationary pressure or to undermine payments discipline and the general stability of the system.

Thus price stability was to be an objective, even though no one knew precisely how to accomplish it.

On the basic characteristics of the schemes that had been considered, the deputies agreed that the new assets should be "unconditional in principle" but that "there must be arrangements to prevent misuse and to prevent them from being used simply to change the composition of a country's reserves." They added "the new reserve units should be directly transferable between monetary authorities and/or through special reserve drawing rights in the Fund." A new term had appeared—"special drawing rights"—that seemed to reconcile the proponents of money with those who preferred credit. Both kinds of assets considered would have originated in an automatic giving and receiving of credit. Either would have conferred the right to obtain other participants' currencies. The deputies were further agreed that:

decisions on creation and management of deliberately created reserve assets should consider the legitimate interests of all countries in the adequacy of international reserves, but should be made by the Group of Ten.

Finally the deputies urged that any contingency plan be implemented only when there was "a consensus that a clear need for reserves would arise in the near future." Only the end of American and British payments deficits could provide that signal.

A skilled, experienced agitator, Michel Debré repeatedly tried but failed to stop further planning for a new reserve asset by arguing within the European Economic Community that all six of its member nations should present a common front. But the others would not agree to an increase in the official price of gold, and France would not accede to the desires of the Community's majority. Therefore the Community could not take joint positions in the Group of Ten and in the Fund itself. That caused much soul-searching among Europeans devoted to the cause of unifying Europe, and many efforts to conciliate France. It also disturbed many American supporters of European unification, who had begun to consider President Johnson a bully—which indeed he was. Harvard's Henry Kissinger was only one of the many Americans who protested Washington's policies, without understanding the necessity for them. Only time could demonstrate that a newly insolent Europe would defer only to force.

On November 28, 1966, when the deputies of the Group of Ten and the executive directors of the Fund assembled in Washington for their first joint

meeting, both groups were therefore on their best behavior, eager for "a very
full and frank exchange of views." Their embarrassment was heightened by
the widely publicized insistence of Debré's representative that creation of a
new reserve asset to provide further liquidity could not be justified unless "it
did not seem possible to meet it in any other way," such as an increase in the
official price of gold. He demanded that the question be placed on the agenda. When reminded that it was not even within the terms of reference granted by the finance ministers of the Group of Ten, he bitterly criticized the
United States for imposing a ban on the study of gold and insisted that the
American "taboo" be lifted. His tactics were so divisive that little progress
could be made. Crucial questions remained undecided, such as the conditions
and circumstances in which a contingency plan should be activated, the rules
for decision making, and the question whether there should be any transfer
ratio between gold and the new asset.

Having found themselves a small minority, fanciers of gold as money had
been peculiarly prone to the belief that they had been skillfully opposed by
a sinister conspiracy whose anonymous planners sat in Washington. Alas,
American diplomacy has never been sufficiently competent to arrange such a
coup. As 1967 began, French representatives did withdraw from the lonely
position they had taken on gold, but their reasons for doing so were domestic.
The expansionary policies adopted by de Gaulle, Pompidou and Debré, in
their efforts to match the rapid economic growth of West Germany, had
begun to affect the French balance of payments. They were also facing parliamentary elections in March, and when Georges Pompidou sought campaign
funds from the bankers and industrialists of France, he found them alarmed
by the increasing isolation of their country. De Gaulle therefore decided on a
change of tactics, *reculer pour mieux sauter.*

At The Hague, on January 16, 1967, the finance ministers and central
bankers of the European Economic Community were surprised to find that
Debré was discarding his antagonistic demand for an increase in the official
price of gold. In an ironic *volte-face,* France became the advocate of studying
improved methods of providing international credit, precisely the position
Secretary Fowler had abandoned in July 1965. Anxious to accommodate de
Gaulle, the remaining members of the European Community promptly shifted their support from reserve unit schemes to conventional credit expansion,
which offered better opportunities to influence the policies of those "Anglo-
Saxons." The French also sought and gained European Community approval
for a proposal to give the European six the power to veto whenever they voted
as a bloc. If gold was not an acceptable stick with which to beat the United
States and Britain, de Gaulle would find others. Because the European Community had also agreed at The Hague that its Monetary Committee should
have the responsibility for providing the technical data and advice on which

to construct common Community positions, de Gaulle took particular care to ensure that it would be dominated by French officials. The European Economic Community became and would remain an instrument of French diplomacy, not American.

By March 1967 both the United States and Britain were experiencing serious difficulties in financing their international payments deficits. They not only needed fresh credits abroad but also were forced to contemplate the disorderly consequences if one of both of the Fund's reserve currencies should be devalued. In a speech delivered to the American Bankers Association, Secretary Fowler openly threatened unilateral action by the United States if the European Community could not or would not cooperate in changing the rules of the Fund. That was the opening shot, followed by the appearance of a variety of articles in the American press, in which the merits of monetary reform were debated. Many had been inspired, and the dollar's convertibility into gold ceased to be described as "immutable." Leading private bankers urged that the United States unilaterally terminate its commitment to automatic sales of gold to foreign monetary authorities if the drain of American gold reserves should continue. Hastily the West German Federal Bank renewed its pledge that it would refrain from conversions of its dollar balances into American gold, and bilateral talks began between Minister Debré and the West German Economics and Finance Ministers, Karl Schiller and Franz Josef Strauss. Once again, American officials had begun to talk ominously of "agonizing reappraisals," and their worries were hammered home when President Johnson met Chancellor Kurt Kiesinger in August.

Defense matters were the primary item on the agenda for those talks between Johnson and Kiesinger. Inevitably the balance-of-payments costs of the American commitment to maintain troops in West Germany led to discussion of the prospects for international monetary reform. Impatiently Johnson repeated the demands his Treasury had been making. First the United States argued that if the Fund should be unprepared for an eventual shortage of international liquidity, countries intent on safeguarding increasingly scarce reserves would be forced into restrictive, deflationary domestic policies. Second the United States wanted a new and "first-class asset," a unit as good as gold and the dollar, rather than an extension of conventional credit facilities. Johnson did not enjoy going into debt abroad to pay for the defense commitments in Western Europe and the Far East he had inherited. Third the United States refused to grant a formal veto on monetary reform planning to the European Economic Community whenever it voted as a bloc, because that would simply have enabled France to stymie the rest of the world. The United States was, however, intent on retaining its own power to veto.

After consulting his advisers, Johnson also confided to his German visitor that if American gold reserves should ever fall to $10 billion, one-quarter of world monetary stocks, he would call "a screeching halt" to any further foreign conversions of dollars into American gold. With many a sigh the West Germans then cast themselves as mediators between the United States and France. That role could have been refused. The Dutch would have been more acceptable and perhaps more effective. But German officials had been sufficiently shrewd to see that skillful go-betweens could often get what they themselves wanted, and what the West Germans wanted was to be in a position to influence the policies of both the United States and France.

The negotiations seemed interminable. Four joint meetings of the Group of Ten's deputies and the Fund's executive directors had been held, without reaching any conclusions. Though the press mockingly described them as mere "teach-ins for the lesser nations," in fact the small members of the Fund had been exercising considerable influence on the Group of Ten. Once the principle of "universality" had been accepted, it had become essential to let every nation voice its opinions. In that process the concept of a "transfer ratio" between gold and the new reserve asset had been quickly swept aside, because it was simply impossible to apply if the many small countries with negligible gold reserves were to be included in the plan. By the fourth joint meeting a single draft document had been produced by the Fund's staff, and it contained an outline for the creation of a new system of drawing rights on the Fund. Yet by the end of that meeting, the French had riddled the outline with objections, reservations and alternative proposals. Two meetings of the finance ministers and central bankers of the Group of Ten had then been called, beginning in London on July 18, 1967. Of the many questions to be resolved, two were of critical importance. The first was the problem of voting rules. The European Economic Community insisted that only a majority of 85 percent should be able to activate the drawing rights plan and decide on the amounts to be issued. The United States countered with a proposal that 80 percent should suffice, so that the European Community with its 16.5 percent of the total votes would not be able to veto when voting as a bloc.

More significant was the question of "reconstitution," a euphemism for repayment. The higher the percentage of the new drawing rights that would have to be reconstituted, the more like credit and the less like money they would be. After consulting the West Germans, Michel Debré proposed 50 percent. Any member nation that might use more than 50 percent of its allocation over a 4-year period would have to reconstitute that excess. It was an apparent compromise between the supporters of money and those of credit. Debré basked in the applause for that new French moderation. Secretary Fowler vehemently opposed it, arguing that no agreement at all would have been better than an inadequate or unworkable plan. However, he was eventually overruled by the "horse traders." Near midnight on August 26 the

West Germans, Italians and Canadians devised a reconstitution formula that both the United States and France were willing to accept. The level beyond which reconstitution would be required was set at 70 percent, and the United States agreed to give the European Economic Community a veto in the activation and allocation of the new Special Drawing Rights (SDRs). Attempting to describe that novel form of money-credit to the press, Otmar Emminger likened it to a zebra, "so that one can say they are a black animal with white stripes and another can say they are a white animal with black stripes." The public were thoroughly confused. And President Johnson had been overheard grumbling that, on the first try, half a horse was better than none at all.

On September 9 the twenty executive directors of the International Monetary Fund approved the outline agreement adopted in London by the Group of Ten, and 2 days later the full text was published.[7] Carefully the new facility was described as "intended to meet the need, as and when it arises, for a supplement to existing reserve assets." Though not convertible into gold, the Special Drawing Right was defined as a unit of value equal to 0.888671 gram of fine gold. By a convenient coincidence, that was also the gold parity of the American dollar at the time. In its beginnings, 1 SDR would therefore equal $1. Calculations were eased. Absolute maintenance of the gold value of SDRs was written into the agreement, so that the Fund would assume some responsibility for helping to preserve the floor price of $35 per fine ounce.

The agreement also called for the provision of "a moderate rate of interest" payable in SDRs, the cost of that interest to be assessed against all participants in proportion to their net cumulative allocations. Participation in the Special Drawing Account was opened to any member of the Fund willing to undertake the corresponding obligations. The mechanics of that Account were then explained in nine sections written in terminology so ambiguous that Michel Debré was able to say: "they do not and cannot establish a new currency designed to replace gold. If such were the purport of the agreement, it is quite clear that France would not sign it." Therefore Special Drawing Rights would not take any tangible form but would exist only as abstract bookkeeping entries in the Fund's Special Drawing Account. With no ceremony, that agreement was submitted as Resolution No. 22-8 on September 29, the last day of the Fund's annual meeting for 1967. After a report by the Procedures Committee, and without any objections from the 107 nations represented at that meeting in Rio de Janeiro, Eric Brofors of Norway declared the resolution adopted.

The executive directors of the Fund immediately began their thankless task of drafting the formal, legal text for the amendments to the Articles and

[7] IMF press release of September 11, 1967.

bylaws needed to establish the Special Drawing Account. Their assigned deadline was March 31, 1968. But they quickly found they could not resolve a half-dozen technical issues, of which the most important was the question of "opting out." Nor could they ignore the growing clamor beyond their doors in the money markets of the world. The speculation against the pound that would force its devaluation within weeks, and the beginnings of the run on the gold reserves of the London Gold Pool's remaining seven central banks, once again emboldened the French. Seizing that new opportunity to force an increase in the official price of gold, the French representative insisted that members of the Fund be allowed to withdraw from their obligation to participate in the Special Drawing Account after its establishment. No one now knew whether France would renege on the compromise agreement that had at last been reached after more than 4 years of tedious negotiations. Nor could anyone foresee whether, if France should reject that reform plan, it could also persuade other members of the European Economic Community to do so.

When the finance ministers and central bankers of the Group of Ten arrived in Stockholm, on March 29, 1968, they therefore found the drafting incomplete. They also found themselves in a melodramatic showdown with Michel Debré. Angered by their recent formation of the two-tier gold markets without French consent and convinced that they could not withstand further opposition and speculation, he revived the French demands for broad changes in the international monetary system that would include "a realistic price for gold." Politely they ignored him. France was granted the right to withdraw at will from the Special Drawing Account, and the final communiqué of the Stockholm conference coldly stated that: "One delegation did not associate itself with these decisions . . . because the problems which it considers fundamental have not been examined." No matter how important the unity of the European Economic Community might be, the remaining five members were no longer willing to tolerate the vagaries of Charles de Gaulle and his ministers. After a decade of power, his Napoleonic efforts to impose French leadership on Europe had exhausted even their infinite patience. At Stockholm, Gaullist France was therefore fully exposed—alone and friendless.

By April 16, only 2 weeks behind schedule, the executive directors of the Fund were able to complete the final details of the agreement. Submitted to the Board of Governors on May 31, their "Report . . . Proposing Amendment of the Articles of Agreement" was quickly approved. There were no negative votes. Instead France and its former colonies chose to abstain. They had begun to experience an intriguing reversal in the fortunes of Charles de Gaulle.

THE GAULLISTS ECLIPSED

The year 1968 was *annus mirabilis*. An entirely new generation of French youth had begun to mature. Born in peace and reared in prosperity, they considered themselves European. The historic animosities of the aged President de Gaulle held no meaning for them, even though they too had been watching the war in Vietnam with hostile eyes. It had been a good excuse for the springtime *bagarres* between student groups of the extreme Left and Right that had led to closing of the Sorbonne on Friday, May 3. Nevertheless the announcement that Paris had been chosen as the site for peace talks had done nothing whatever to subdue the demonstrations that had rapidly spread along the Boulevard Saint-Michel and throughout the University quarter. Nor had the rioters been impressed by the heavy-handed methods of the paternalistic Gaullist police, because they had gained "spontaneous" support from French industrial workers.[8]

A general strike, begun on May 15, had paralyzed the banks and the gold market of Paris. Pompidou's offers of increased wages and social benefits had had no immediate effects. By May 24 the New York Federal Reserve Bank had been obliged to begin support operations to help defend the parity of the franc. And on May 30 Michel Debré had reintroduced rigorous exchange controls. Yet the panicky flight from the franc only gained momentum as French investors sought safe havens abroad for their funds. The press reported that French francs were being smuggled into Switzerland by the carload, and the next day Debré was replaced at the Finance Ministry by the less volatile Maurice Couve de Murville. A diplomat was needed there.

Though the strikes would soon begin to evaporate, confidence in President de Gaulle had been shattered forever. Commentators began to anticipate another devaluation of the franc, regardless of his scornful refusal to accept a measure he considered so damaging to the prestige of France. Its payments accounts had already slipped into a deficit of $75 million during the first quarter of 1968, and that deficit swelled to $685 million in the second quarter. Striving to keep its gold reserves intact, the Bank of France resorted to the International Monetary Fund and to the General Arrangements to Borrow facilities for $885 million, yet the flight from the franc continued. During the last half of 1968, the French payments deficit became a massive $2.390 billion. Throughout that year, even though the Bank of France recalled funds held abroad, it incurred a net loss of $2.793 billion from its reserves, $1.355 billion of that loss being cherished gold. It became not merely expedient but also essential to the welfare of France that Charles de Gaulle begin to cooper-

---

[8] While West Europeans were thus distracted and divided, stubborn Czech leaders were being abducted and transported to Moscow under armed guard.

ate with the remaining nine member-nations of the Group of Ten. In his last few months of power, he no longer sought to obstruct their creation of new reserve assets.

Early in June 1968 that monetary reform plan had been submitted to the members of the International Monetary Fund for their governments' approval. To become effective, the proposed Amendment to the Articles of Agreement required ratification by 65 countries holding at least 80 percent of the total votes. Moreover members with at least 75 percent of the voting power had to deposit with the Fund written instruments acknowledging acceptance of all the obligations of participation in the Special Drawing Account. By the end of June those notices of ratification and instruments of acceptance had begun to arrive, rapid action by the United States Congress enabling it to be among the first. The ratification of Belgium, always so sympathetic to Charles de Gaulle, provided the votes needed to enable that reform plan to take effect on July 28, 1969, 3 months after his abrupt retirement from the Presidency of France. By September, when the Fund held its annual meeting, 74 of its 111 members had formally accepted the obligations of participation in the Special Drawing Account.

As yet, however, no decisions had been made on the timing of that Account's activation or the amount of Special Drawing Rights to be allocated. The United States approached the Europeans to obtain agreement on those questions, and it was in a hurry. By the end of 1968 the gold reserves of the United States had dwindled to $10.890 billion. American officials found the French in a more amiable mood, because their payments deficits had also continued into 1969. During the first three quarters of 1969, the payments deficit of France totaled an additional $1.9 billion, and its new President, Georges Pompidou, hastened to devalue the franc by 12.5 percent on August 8. He did so without consulting the International Monetary Fund and thus defied the rule that required members to obtain its permission for any devaluation in excess of 10 percent. Somewhat chastened by experience, Pompidou had also resolved his differences with Valéry Giscard, who again became Finance Minister when Pinay refused that office. The payments accounts of France began to show a surplus in the final quarter of 1969, as they rebuilt confidence in the stability of its government. Nevertheless the annual deficit for 1969 was $1.680 billion, and the Bank of France had lost another $330 million in gold. By the end of the year those French gold reserves were reduced to $3.545 billion, and the tenor of French diplomacy remained subdued.

There had appeared to be few basic changes in the policies of the United States. When asked to indicate which of the many candidates would be the most effective as President of the United States, the embittered Lyndon Johnson had spurned his own party by naming the Republican Richard Nixon, who had given him flattering reassurances that he would continue American support for an independent South Vietnam. And Nixon had led the American people to believe that he had a secret plan with which he could quickly obtain an honorable retreat from the mainland of Asia, as Dwight Eisenhower had found an armistice in the Korean War. To gain the backing of New York's bankers, Nixon had pledged to maintain the parity of the dollar. He had also sought West European support by promising to keep all American commitments to NATO, including those costly troop contingents in West Germany. Though purposes so contradictory could not be pursued much longer, to capture office Nixon had been willing to promise anything to anyone. Ignorant of economics, he had never taken any serious interest in the Federal budget. The only sound economic advice he had been hearing had been privately given by Arthur Burns, the eclectic head of the National Bureau for Economic Research. Repaying political debts, Nixon had chosen as Secretary of the Treasury a private banker from Chicago, David Kennedy, whose most noticeable trait was an ingratiating desire to be nice to bankers at home and abroad. Kennedy would become another example of the rule that private bankers cannot effectively fill that office, because they are so unable to be nasty to their fellow bankers.

Quietly Secretary Kennedy had begun to urge West Europeans to revalue their currencies against the dollar, only to find that most of them had become deaf to polite Americans. Eventually West Germany did revalue its mark by 9.29 percent on October 24, 1969, but only when compelled to do so by prolonged speculation. However, in the wake of those speculative surges that engulfed the franc and the mark, Kennedy did coax $500 million in gold from West Germany, another $325 million in gold from France and $200 million in gold from the Bank for International Settlements. By the end of 1969 the United States Treasury was able to announce somewhat disingenuously that its gold reserves had risen to $11.890 billion. Though that was merely "window dressing," many Americans believed that confidence in the dollar had been restored, and it served Nixon's purposes to claim that it had. South African gold sales were exceeding its production, and by the middle of January 1970 the price on the London free market fell to a low of $34.75 per ounce. That was only a lull in the storm. Like hawks, speculators had begun to watch closely the monthly statistical reports on the trade and payments accounts of the United States. Nixon and Kennedy had not initiated any determined efforts to remove the basic causes of the American budget and payments deficits. Throughout 1969 their efforts to deflate the wartime boom had been relying entirely on monetary tools. Nixon had been unwilling to ask the Democratic majority in Congress for the essential tax increases and spending cuts, and he rightly distrusted wage and price controls, having learned during the Second World War how easily they could be evaded regardless of an extensive bureaucracy. By the beginning of 1970, as the rate of domestic inflation increased, the dollar was widely recognized as a dangerously overvalued currency.

Initially the only appointee of the Nixon Administration who had had any grasp of international economics had been an obscure and junior official, Paul Volcker, who had become Under Secretary of the Treasury for Monetary Affairs. Though unknown to the public, he will be remembered by historians as the New Yorker who reluctantly presided over the demise of the gold-exchange standard. Every man is a prisoner of his friends, and Volcker had been recommended to Nixon by the Rockefellers and the Chase Manhattan Bank. They were wholeheartedly devoted to preservation of the central role the dollar had gained in world finance. In their view gold had become an anomaly, useless in a world whose trade had become entirely dependent on credit. Because the gross national product of the United States had been growing by inflated leaps and bounds, it seemed obvious to them that the credit rating of its dollar should be higher than ever before.

Though Europeans no longer shared that opinion, Volcker did find them obliging during his first few meetings with the deputies of the Group of Ten. They had become seriously alarmed by the scale and intensity of the private capital movements that had been shifting from one currency into another, anticipating changes in interest and exchange rates. If only for that reason, they had become willing to agree that central banks should have much larger resources at their disposal with which to defend parities. It had proved impossible to measure objectively the optimal rate of growth in liquidity. Several methods had been tried, without any agreement that one or another was truly accurate. But estimates of the growth desired could be correlated with forecast increases in world trade.

Later the International Monetary Fund reported that the various estimates of the annual worldwide increase in liquidity needed ranged from $3.5 billion to $6 billion. Most estimates, including those prepared by the Fund's own staff and the United States, were $4 billion to $5 billion per annum. Moreover it was mistakenly assumed that American and British payments deficits would provide no more than an increase of $1 billion to 1.5 billion each year. In July 1969 the European Economic Community therefore proposed that the first allocation of Special Drawing Rights be SDR 2 billion each year, whereas Volcker urged SDR 4 billion to SDR 5 billion. Both agreed, however, that the first allocation should be disproportionately large, and a compromise was reached on the distribution period. Allocations were projected for 3 years rather than 5. The first was fixed at SDR 3.5 billion, and the second and third at SDR 3 billion each, for a total of SDR 9.5 billion. The French quietly participated in those meetings of the Ten's deputies, and their Parliament ratified the reform plan soon after. On September 23 Pierre-Paul

Schweitzer formally proposed to the member nations of the International Monetary Fund that the first allocation of SDRs should be made on January 1, 1970. By October the necessary majority of 73 nations had approved. All were pleased to get something for nothing. South Africa chose to abstain.

When the advocates of Special Drawing Rights witnessed the initial allocation on the first day of 1970, they were confident that the cornerstone of a "rational" world monetary system had at last been firmly laid. SDR 3.41 billion were divided among 104 participants, in proportion (17 percent) to their regular quotas in the Fund. The Group of Ten therefore received 65 percent, and as the largest among them, the share of the United States was SDR 867 million. Britain received SDR 410 million, France SDR 165 million, Japan SDR 122 million and Brazil SDR 59 million. The smallest, the African states of Lesotho and Botswana, each gained SDR 500,000. At the last moment Nationalist China (Taiwan) had decided to opt out of its first allocation of SDR 90 million and the corresponding obligations. Another 10 nations had not deposited their instruments of acceptance and were therefore ineligible. However, most of them (Kuwait, Saudi Arabia, Libya, Lebanon, Singapore and Portugal) had ample reserves of gold and dollars, and would probably have been recipients rather than users of SDRs in 1970. South Africa had decided to participate, even though its leading bankers would never cease to denounce "paper gold" SDRs as a contradiction in terms. The second allocation of SDR 3 billion duly followed on January 1, 1971, and the third of SDR 3 billion on January 1, 1972, regardless of belated objections.

Nevertheless, Special Drawing Rights were not formally recognized as a new international monetary standard until March 1973. And that new standard was redefined in June 1974. Many doubts persisted. Therein lies another tale of the ways in which unforeseen events impose their own logic and coerce even the most reluctant central bankers.

10 = The Disappearance of Gold
August–December 1971

Often to their destruction, men have always been lured by legendary riches that lie beyond their horizons. While Russians endured their "Time of Troubles" in the 17th century, it was only natural that they should plan to recover lost territories and extend them. Kiev, the door to Moscow's trade with the South, had been frequently threatened and sometimes held by Tatars. In the North Novgorod had been the center for trade by rivers and portages, and the dynasty of Rurik had been ambitious colonizers. But the armies of the usurper Boris Godunov had melted before the conquering Swedes, who had extended their frontiers to the very gates of Novgorod by 1617. Gustavus Adolphus of Sweden had demanded seventy barrels of Russian gold as his price for peace, and had dismissed as "intolerable" the Russian offer of a mere forty barrels.

THE ORIGINS OF RUSSO–AMERICAN DÉTENTE

Not until the time of Peter the Great were the Russians able to achieve their goals. After forming the Northern Coalition, Peter Alexeïevitch embarked on the task of regaining territorial access to the Baltic Sea. The ill-fated Swedish king, Charles XII, was enticed into lasting disaster at the Battle of Poltava. While sending Russian armies into Poland and Livonia, Peter himself then went to Arkhangelsk, where he planned and implemented the construction of a new fleet of Russian transports and warships. They were brought down by rivers and lakes, and by new roads over portages, and then through Lake Onego and the River Svir', until they reached Lake Ladoga, the River Neva

266

and the Baltic Sea. Angered by the Polish king's taunt that the Russians had only "sat quietly at home while Poland was being devasted by the Swedes," Peter launched an attack in April 1703 on Nienshants near the mouth of the Neva, where it empties into the Gulf of Finland. That Swedish fortress fell on May 1, and Narva and Dorpat were taken in the following year. In 1710 Vyborg and Kexholm fell to Peter, and he had the good sense to stop there. The frontier agreed at Nystadt in 1721 was close to that arranged in 1940 between the Soviet Union and Finland. Vyborg, Kexholm and all of Lake Ladoga became Russian, a boundary determined by the location of the rivers and portages. To the extent that Russians have desired trade with the West, their northern water route had been reopened. The log cabin by the River Neva from which Tsar Peter directed those remarkable operations has been enshrined. Though the city that later grew around it no longer bears his name, his tomb in the Fortress of Peter and Paul is eternally guarded by fresh flowers.[1]

For more than two centuries after the death of Peter I, Russian navies remained small, defensive in purpose and confined to coastal waters for the support of those mass armies that have traditionally represented the essence of Russian power. Having been forced repeatedly to guard their kremlins against the invasions of Tatars, Turks, Poles, Swedes, French and Germans, the Russians became deeply defensive in their attitudes. Today their civic symbols and national monuments are cannon and tanks facing westward, to commemorate victories in their battles with the armies of Napoleon and Hitler. Navies were almost useless in those wars. More than 30 years after the most recent fall of Berlin the defensive, national fear of Germany is still expressed not only by citizens in Moscow's streets but also by Russian leaders in the Council of Ministers. But Soviet policies, strategic thinking and armaments programs now reflect diverse, often competing and sometimes conflicting interests and ambitions.

Moscow is also the seat of a quite different type of governmental institution. Where the concerns of the Council of Ministers are national, the complementary and often overbearing Central Committee of the Communist Party of the USSR is the heir of the Comintern. Its purpose is to propagate Communism abroad. Among the new and still primitive nations of this world, it seeks converts. It busies itself to foster and protect those recruits, and to maintain its own hegemony as the oldest and largest of the proliferating Communist bureaucracies now scattered around the world. Consequently its policies are aggressive. Its planning calls for penetration by all available means, for aid programs wherever foreign friends and allies are to be found, and for their defense by Soviet weapons, preferably manned by Soviet per-

[1] Kerner, *The Urge to the Sea*, pp. 35–88.

sonnel. The corollary of those policies is planning for the harassment and interdiction of support required by present or potential adversaries.

In 1937 the ruble had been pegged at 4 to 1 American dollar. Later wartime inflation had been severe. In 1947, when the currency had again been reformed to punish speculative hoarders, outstanding notes had been exchanged for new at the rate of 10 old rubles to 1 new. With the "cold war" developing, Soviet leaders had also taken that opportunity to declare their independence of the dollar. The new parity had been fixed at 32 rubles per ounce of gold. That was and would remain meaningless, because the new ruble was not convertible into gold. Nor has the official or the market price of gold ever determined the quantity the Soviet Union has decided to produce, the purpose of that production or the timing of its gold sales abroad. However with the ruble defined in that way, the exchange rate became 1 to $1.10. Many Russians were pleased to hear and were willing to believe that their ruble was now "worth more than the dollar." In terms of purchasing power, that rate so overvalued the ruble that by 1970 the black markets would be quoting it at 6 to the dollar. Yet for decades that overvaluation would serve as a serious deterrent to trade with the West and would help Soviet officials obtain many advantages in the East–West barter deals they could arrange. Soviet products would never be considered bargains by the few Western tourists able to visit Moscow.

Meanwhile all East European currencies had also been substantially overvalued against the dollar. By 1970 the official rates for the Polish złoty, the Czech crown, the Hungarian forint and the Rumanian len were 4, 7.20, 11.73 and 6 to the dollar. The black market rates were 145, 68, 54 and 36 to the dollar. At the same time those currencies were greatly undervalued against the ruble, to reduce the foreign-exchange costs incurred by the Soviet Union in maintaining 38 divisions of Soviet troops in Eastern Europe. For example the rate of the Polish złoty in 1970 was 13.8 to the ruble. Thus the Soviet Union applied the ancient mercantile precept "buy cheap and sell dear" in its exchange rate policies.

In the last years of Joseph Stalin, the new strategic weapons of the thermonuclear age had remained so unreliable that no effort had been made to find a place for them in Soviet foreign policies. Among Stalin's immediate successors, however, Nikita Khrushchev had had almost unlimited confidence in them. Khrushchev had continued the policies of increasing risks, of vigorous diplomatic campaigns coupled with nuclear threats, that had culminated in that ultimate adventure, the attempt to base Soviet strategic missiles in Cuba. Yet Soviet leaders had not been willing to sacrifice their domestic development programs to obtain the resources needed for a race with the United States to determine which could produce most rapidly the largest number of intercontinental ballistic missiles. By June 1963 they had decided to sign the first of a succession of agreements to control and stabilize the development, production and deployment of those weapons.

Rivalry between the Soviet Union and the United States had then shifted to another dimension. The Soviet reversal in Cuba, linked with increasing involvement in the Middle East, Asia and Africa, had emphasized the usefulness of long-range naval forces, surface as well as submarine. Admiral Sergei Gorshkov had written in 1963:

> Formerly our warships and naval aviation were a junior service. . . . Now . . . we must be prepared through broad offensive operations to deliver crushing strikes against sea and ground targets of the imperialists on any point of the world oceans and adjacent territories.

However, the construction costs of a strike carrier exceed a billion rubles when its armaments and aircraft are included, and the continuing costs of manning and maintenance are high. Those sums had appalled the utilitarian consciences of Soviet planners, many of whom had not been impressed by the prestige that newest and largest of naval ornaments might gain for their country. Gorshkov had been forced to compromise, and in September 1968 a smaller helicopter carrier called the *Moskva* had joined the Mediterranean Squadron of the Soviet Union.

Though it is not rich, the Soviet Union is centralized to an extent no democracy would want to emulate. Moscow, its *Zentrum* in the most literal way, can therefore exercise selectivity in its choice of programs with the expectation that those given the highest priority will be implemented with zeal. By June 1968, worried that the new Soviet leader, Leonid Brezhnev, might become another "adventurer" like Khrushchev, NATO defense ministers assembled in Reykjavik had concluded that ways should be found to accommodate the Soviet Union's urge for maritime importance. Though increasingly dependent on imports of raw materials, Western Europe no longer had any navies that could compete. Nor were West Europeans willing to spend any of their new riches on their navies.

It was a Russian who had first observed that the European Economic Community had been "born in a cage," though most West Europeans have been too nearsighted to see the bars. Many Russians and Americans had also begun to recognize that they had certain interests in common. There were limits to the amounts of trouble and expense that client nations could be permitted to cause. It was one thing to grant aid to a helpful ally. It was something quite different to be forced to pay extortion money to a malicious "friend." Among others Charles de Gaulle had been compelling both doctrinaire Russian Communists and dogmatic American capitalists to see a light he had not intended. The third Arab–Israeli war in June 1967 had also aroused heated, lengthy debate in Moscow's Central Committee and had caused a radical reappraisal of its policies in the Middle East and elsewhere. Though the combat performance of the Egyptian and Syrian armies had shamed their Russian advisers, there had appeared to be no alternative to rearming them, regardless of the high costs. Concurrently the decision had been made that it should not be allowed to happen again. Arab leaders were warned that the next time they would be required to pay cash on delivery, and desultory Russo–American discussions began on a wide range of problems.

Though the naval monopoly of the United States Sixth Fleet in the Mediterranean had ended, the closing of the Suez Canal provided several years for careful thought. Throughout 1967 and 1968, Soviet naval visits to Egypt had a reassuring effect there. Growing Soviet anxiety regarding Communist Chinese intentions in Southeast Asia was expressed by its Pacific Squadron based in Vladivostok, in repeated visits to Singapore. And Soviet cruisers with their escorts showed the flag in the Indian Ocean and the Persian Gulf, calling at Mogadishu, Madras, Bombay and Karachi. Impressively modern ships flying the hammer and sickle alarmed Asian and African diplomats, who had never before seen Soviet gunnery, a science in which Russians had always excelled.

With the pound devalued, the British government of Harold Wilson felt compelled still further to reduce its defense spending abroad. Its Continental creditors had become demanding, while British voters took for granted that Britain's social services would continue forever to improve, regardless of their incessantly rising costs. Complacently all assumed that, if any difficulties abroad should ever again arise, the United States would be pleased to attend to them. Bland diplomacy could serve all British purposes, and there would be no further need to support it with armed force. West Europeans generally shared those fatuous beliefs and happily concentrated their attentions on the satisfaction of consumer wants. The highways of Western Europe were crowded with new cars, and the night clubs of London, Paris and Rome sparkled as never before. Yet Arab rulers and their planners had not been reassured by Wilson's decision. What could those Arabs do for themselves, from 1971 onward, after the British withdrew their armed forces from East of Suez?[2]

CANADA DECIDES TO FLOAT

While West Europeans marched proudly toward a still distant debacle, Americans had been enduring many losses and humiliations. Time had exposed the harsh fact that President Nixon's only idea for ending the war in Vietnam had been to return the task of fighting it to the South Vietnamese

[2] Laqueur, *The Struggle for the Middle East*, pp. 173–191.

themselves. Not surprisingly, Saigon had been loath to accept that bloody burden, and Hanoi had been encouraged to persist. As the Congressional elections of 1970 approached, the United States was still deeply involved in Southeast Asia. The number of Americans killed in action there exceeded 50,000, and the costs had passed the $100 billion mark.

Nor had Nixon's "monetarist" economic advisers, led by the Chicago conservative Milton Friedman, provided appropriate cures for the worsening ailments of the American economy. Their simple-minded remedies—high interest rates and slow growth of the money supply, unaided by fiscal measures— had delighted American bankers, who had promptly defeated them by borrowing some $15 billion in the Eurodollar markets to relend at still higher interest rates in the United States. Real growth in gross national product had almost stopped, and nearly 25 percent of the productive capacity of American industry remained unused in the third quarter of 1970. Though 5½ percent of the labor force was unemployed, and that percentage was rising, the annual rate of inflation had not fallen below 4.2 percent in any quarter of 1970, and it would exceed 5 percent for the year as a whole. Nixon was quite willing to renounce his conservative forebears and to proclaim himself a "Keynesian," if that would gain votes for the Republican minority in Congress. Most other major industrial nations were also beset by rising rates of inflation and slowing growth, because they too had been relying on monetary policies alone to solve their domestic problems. Heatedly they had been blaming each other for their failures to do so, yet their arguments had produced little light, because they could not agree on anything except the folly of American support for South Vietnam.

Highly sensitive to changes in interest and inflation rates, many international investors had become speculators in currencies. Almost unnoticed, they had been joined by the treasurers of the largest multinational companies, who were anxious to hedge against losses by banking their cash balances wherever high interest rates were paid and currency revaluations were predictable. In a monetary system of fixed exchange rates, losses were impossible and profits could be handsome whenever that thundering herd moved together. Cautiously they eyed each other and the monthly statistical reports of the central banks. The Canadian dollar had become a conspicuous opportunity, because it had remained at its effective ceiling of U.S. $0.9324 since December 1969. Though the Bank of Canada had lowered its discount rate from 8 to 7½ percent on May 11, 1970, short-term funds had continued to enter Canada. On May 31 central bankers around the world were startled to hear that the Canadian Finance Ministry was no longer willing to defend the upper limit of the permitted fluctuations around the parity of the Canadian dollar. Though that broke the basic rules of the Bretton Woods system and the International Monetary Fund, the Canadians had sensibly decided to commit heresy by permitting their dollar to float for an indefinite period. Canadian national reserves had risen some U.S. $1.2 billion since the beginning of 1970, $622 million in May alone, and they had no possible use for additional reserves of that magnitude. By September the defiantly floating Canadian dollar appreciated to U.S. $0.98. And on the opposite side of the Atlantic, the Eurodollar markets now held an estimated U.S. $50 billion, much of which was available to speculators.

The annual meeting of the International Monetary Fund was held at Copenhagen in September 1970. An uneventful occasion had been forecast, but there were many signs of trouble ahead. As disgruntled finance ministers and central bankers assembled in the Danish capital, they found a new face among them. The United States Congress had consented to Nixon's nomination of the phlegmatic Arthur Burns as the new Chairman of the Board of Governors of the Federal Reserve System. Concealing his own thoughts behind a pipe, Burns listened as his colleagues aired their grievances against the United States. The Fund's *Annual Report* had singled out the American payments deficits as "the most urgent remaining task in the field of international payments." In strong language the United States was called upon to "rectify" a payments deficit expected to exceed $5 billion that year. As an authority on the American defense budget Burns was reasonably sure that a payments deficit of at least $5 billion was quite possible.

American gold reserves had fallen to $11.5 billion, and the official dollar balances held by foreign monetary authorities had risen to $18 billion. Yet in his opening address Pierre-Paul Schweitzer declared:

> Until the payments position of the United States is brought into balance, it is important that the deficit should be financed by use of U.S. reserve assets to the extent necessary to avoid an extensive expansion of official holdings of dollars by other countries.

Later Schweitzer emphasized his firm conviction that "gold is the basic standard of the international monetary system," not the dollar. Anticipating further demands on American gold reserves, another European present commented: "The United States needs a good wallop—it would be good discipline for them." Many Europeans had been pleased to see the United States bleeding into the mud of Vietnam. And outside that conference hall the streets were littered with the mendicant youth of Europe, who had descended on Copenhagen to demonstrate against the Vietnam War. They only echoed the protests that had reached a crescendo in the United States. With some asperity, Treasury Secretary Kennedy informed the other finance ministers present that the United States was willing to convert their official dollar holdings into gold.

Seizing an obvious political opportunity, French Finance Minister Valéry

Giscard had emerged as the most outspoken European critic of American monetary policies. He expressed uncertainty about the issues of Special Drawing Rights scheduled for 1971 and 1972 by reminding the members of the International Monetary Fund that:

> When we had to decide upon the scheme for SDRs, the indication was that there would be a need for additional liquidity on the order of $5 billion a year. . . . But now we know that . . . for 1970 . . . the American deficit alone will be about that much.

Quietly information was leaked to the press that the European Economic Community had agreed on a plan to form a single European economic and monetary authority by the end of the 1970s. At the time, the market rates for their currencies were allowed to fluctuate by 1 percent on either side of the dollar's parity in gold. Therefore fluctuations in the market cross-rate between any two of the European Community's currencies could be as much as 4 percent. By narrowing those margins step by step, beginning in January 1971, they hoped eventually to reduce fluctuations to zero and thereby to create a single European monetary unit.

Many Europeans had considered it humiliating that the American dollar should continue to serve as the European unit of account and had believed that a common European currency could be devised to help unify their Economic Community. Caustically Giscard compared reliance on the American dollar to setting a watch "by a clock that is out of order." European chauvinists were entranced by the idea of establishing a European currency that might rival the dollar, much as small boys enjoy waving flags at a bull. Yet it remains doubtful that the authors of that Werner Plan were serious about it. Though they would spend another 5 years and more experimenting, they were unwilling to cede any of their national sovereignty to the European Community. And a common currency is possible only where states are governed by identical monetary policies, and experience the same rates of inflation or deflation, as the Latin Union had demonstrated a century before. Though most Europeans had not grasped that basic flaw in the Werner Plan, the French did foresee that if such a common currency could be linked to gold, it would continue to preserve a floor price for their private holdings of that metal if the United States should ever abandon its official price.

Consistently unwilling to discuss any changes in the American financing of Western Europe's defense, the French had another reason for concentrating European attention on that plan for monetary unification of the European Economic Community. Aside from a customs union, and a bureaucracy seated in Brussels, after 15 years it was still little more than the Common Agricultural policy that had been providing high price supports and subsidies for European farmers. Each year French farmers in particular had been drawing from that Common Agricultural Policy 1.5 billion francs more than France had been contributing. And the votes of those increasingly prosperous French farmers had been essential in the elections of President Pompidou and Minister Giscard. They had therefore become quite alarmed by the public discussion of floating that had originated in May with the floating of the Canadian dollar. At Copenhagen there was also considerable talk about introducing more flexibility into the Fund's rules on fixed exchange rates. Because the European Common Agricultural Policy was tied together by those fixed rates, the French demanded preservation of that system and regarded floating as anathema. Yet in September 1970 the money markets were alerted by those discussions in Copenhagen that the American, West German and Italian governments had become interested in more flexibility as a way to cope with massive short-term capital movements.

Upon returning to Washington, Secretary Kennedy and Chairman Burns compared notes on their dismal prospects. Central bankers had begun to talk publicly about the possibility of devaluing the dollar, and international confidence in it had been fading rapidly. Pompidou and Giscard had been refusing to consider any revaluation of the French franc, for fear of risking not only their national reserves but also the competitive advantages enjoyed by French exporters and their workers. French economic policies simply assumed an undervalued franc. In French thinking there was an additional objection to revaluation. It would have depreciated gold's purchasing power in paper francs, which would have been unthinkable, entirely contrary to all of their historical experience with money. Unfortunately, if the French could not be persuaded to revalue their franc, lesser European neighbors would also refuse. The Swiss were unwilling "to rock the boat" by being the only nation to revalue. Kennedy and Burns therefore reported to President Nixon that a devaluation of the dollar might become the only possible course of action, but there were serious doubts about it. The rules of the International Monetary Fund required that it be consulted on any devaluation of more than 10 percent, and a dollar devaluation of perhaps 20 percent might be required to restore substantial surpluses in American payments accounts. The accumulation of American controls had become so extensive that no one could estimate with any accuracy the precise effects they had had. If those controls were to be discarded, as many American bankers and economists had been demanding, a devaluation of at least 20 percent might be needed.

Unhappily there was no reason to believe that the French, the Japanese and others would agree to so large a devaluation by their largest trading competitor. Profiting from the war in Vietnam, Japan had also been amassing large dollar reserves and had been as adamant as France that the fixed, undervalued exchange rate of its currency must be preserved. As the only major ally of the United States in the Far East, the Japanese had convinced themselves that they deserved trade and monetary concessions from the United States as the reward for their political cooperation. There was a very definite possibility that the French, the Japanese and others might try to compete with any American devaluation of the dollar and might defeat its purpose by devaluing their own currencies in a race to retain their national reserves and export advantages.

To Nixon, in the midst of a war, with an election at hand, the thought of asking a Democratic Congress for a devaluation of the dollar therefore fell into the category of political impossibilities. He preferred to wait, until events might force Congressional hands and his own. The public were informed that the policy of the United States toward its payments deficits would continue to be "benign neglect," a term European bankers considered extraordinarily offensive, if only because it appeared to class them with American blacks. And on October 8 the money markets became sharply aware that the Federal Reserve Board had abandoned its efforts to curb domestic inflation by monetary restraints. In an attempt to stimulate the economy just before those Congressional elections, American interest rates began to fall. The European outcry was immediate, and became shrill when the White House announced that Nixon would give highest priority to the needs of the American economy. He also decided to look for a new Secretary of the Treasury, one who could bluster with the best of them. Is anyone surprised that he turned for advice to Lyndon Johnson, who had had some experience dealing with Europeans?

As interest rates in the United States began to fall, capital fled. London had become the favorite Eurodollar market, because the Bank of England had consistently refused to consider any international agreements to control capital movements. Moreover interest rates in London were always kept a percentage point or two higher than those in New York. Britain's payments accounts had at last returned to surplus. In October 1970 the Bank of England's reserves gained $72 million, the largest increase since the sterling devaluation of 1967. In November those British reserves rose another $270 million. The unpopularity of the United States became quite profitable to the Bank of England. It began to repay British debts abroad, using $114 million of those newly garnered dollars to pay the Bank for International Settlements and the United States the sixth of eight quarterly installments still due on loans contracted in 1966.

Scenting further gains ahead, the new Tory government led by Edward Heath selected a British ambassador to the United States who was unusually well qualified for that purpose. Lord Cromer had been not only a managing director of the merchant bankers Baring Brothers but also a Governor of the Bank of England. He could be relied on to guess accurately the significance of every move Arthur Burns might make. And the longer a devaluation of the dollar could be postponed, the longer the flight from the dollar could be sustained, the fatter British national reserves would grow. Heath himself vis-

ited the United States in December 1970, then went to the presidential retreat at Camp David in the hills of Maryland for talks with President Nixon.
Describing their meeting to the press, one of Heath's aides archly told the
self-appointed *doyen* of the British journalists in Washington that "It was just
short of love-making." It had indeed been far short. Heath and Nixon had
distrusted one another on sight.

Three decades in which Britain had enjoyed a "special relationship" with
the United States had ended. Heath and his Tory Cabinet, advised by a
Rothschild, were determined to take Britain into the European Economic
Community. They had quite extravagant notions on the benefits Britain
might derive from access to that market for its exports, and they were willing
to pay any price France might charge. On his part, Nixon had hired the
devious, opportunistic Henry Kissinger as his adviser on foreign policies,
largely because he had been recommended by the Rockefellers. Where
Rothschilds viewed the world in terms of gold, Rockefellers thought of oil.
One of Kissinger's first assignments had been to open discussions with the
Russians and the Chinese, without informing those British Conservatives who
had obstructed them for so many years. Perhaps someday Heath will forgive
Nixon for having informed him at Camp David that Russo–American relations had "deteriorated," at the precise moment Nixon's representatives were
exchanging cordial holiday greetings with Soviet leaders in Moscow.

On October 30 the first Soviet foreign minister ever to visit the Federal
Republic of Germany had begun talks on the problem of Berlin with Chancellor Willy Brandt at the Castle Hotel in Kronberg. And in January 1971
the Soviet Bank for Foreign Trade resumed sales of gold in the West, coincid-
ing with a visit to Moscow by former American Ambassador Averell Harri-
man. With bipartisan support, Kissinger at last began to make some progress.
The five-year plan that had guided the Soviet economy from 1966 to 1970
had not achieved its objectives. Both Americans and Russians had practical
reasons to expand their areas of cooperation. While the attention of West
Europeans was focused on American payments deficits, Russo–American *dé-
tente* began to take substantial form. On both sides there was recognition that
neither the Soviet Union nor the United States could afford any longer to
subsidize its allies on the scale to which they had become accustomed. Both
underestimated the ferocity with which those dependents would resist any
changes in the status quo. For Western Europe and Japan, the "cold war"
had been quite profitable.

FLIGHT FROM THE DOLLAR

In a disorderly world, a Western Europe now rich in gold reserves appeared
to have become the only apostle of monetary stability. For obvious reasons,

West Europeans were eager to foster that belief. By January 1, 1971, after repaying an additional $264 million on debts abroad, Britain's gold and dollar reserves had risen to $2.827 billion. Then it received the second allocation of SDR 300 million, and the bankers of London recovered their aplomb. Confidence in sterling was being restored as trust in the dollar rapidly vanished. However, in their careful calculations, the nearsighted officials of the British Treasury and the Bank of England had been neglecting to consider the possibility that less clever nations might become envious.

On February 1, 1971, when the American payments deficit for the previous year was announced, it proved to be not the $5 billion that had been forecast but rather a record-breaking $9.5 billion, when calculated on the official settlements basis. That day in Washington the agile Rinaldo Ossola of the Bank of Italy warned that the United States was inviting "calamity." He reported "the conviction is spreading" among European central bankers that the International Monetary Fund should suspend or limit to token amounts the next issue of SDRs, scheduled to begin in 1973. Events had commenced that would slowly thwart the aspirations of the advocates of a monetary system based on Special Drawing Rights. Ossola also raised the specter of new European exchange controls that might introduce "a long period of monetary disorder" similar to the 1930s. And in Frankfurt, the Federal Bank reported that West Germany had achieved a payments surplus of DM 21.91 billion ($5.98 billion) in 1970. Because of those consistent surpluses and the consequent increases in West German national reserves, the mark had become the favorite refuge for anyone wary of holding any other currency.

One of the most widely known "secrets" in monetary history was the intention of the United States to retain a minimum of $10 billion in gold reserves. In February those American gold stocks fell to $11.039 billion, and the central bankers of Western Europe were preparing to take another $76 million. They were not merely startled but frightened and angered by the prospect that the growing flood of dollars might compel them eventually to revalue their undervalued currencies. During the last week in February the West German Federal Bank alone absorbed $800 million, and additional dollars moved into Britain, the Netherlands, Belgium, France and Switzerland. The anxieties of European exporters had become so acute that on March 10 President Georges Pompidou voiced his opinions through Raymond Barre, Commissioner for Monetary Affairs of the European Economic Community. Never a friend of the United States, Barre bluntly warned:

> To the eminent American experts who advocate a policy of "benign neglect" for the problem of the U.S. balance-of-payments deficits, it should be recalled that the countries of the Community have strong reasons to feel bitterly concerned on this same subject. . . . The situation has never been as disquieting as it is now.

There were strong feelings on both sides of the Atlantic. After more than a half-century of American generosity to Europe many Americans had become deeply resentful of the stubborn European refusal to concede any of the advantages granted them at Bretton Woods in 1944 for a postwar recovery completed long ago.

Though most Americans remained heedless of that growing fuss in Western Europe, President Nixon could not. And at last he had found a new Secretary of the Treasury. John Connally was a conservative Democrat from Texas, a protégé of Lyndon Johnson and a former Secretary of the Navy. Those were significant qualifications. With bipartisan support in Congress, Connally was also a lawyer skilled in both political and commercial negotiations. Oil had interested him for many years. His comparative ignorance of international monetary affairs became an advantage. He had neither personal interests at stake, nor doctrinaire biases to unlearn, nor time to waste on trivial details. When asked by a condescending journalist whether he could cope with experienced finance ministers, his reply was simply: "I know how to add. That's enough." Impelled by high ambitions, Connally had learned how to use expert advisers. Yet it would take months for Paul Volcker and Arthur Burns to brief him for the arduous tasks ahead. Connally's first and lasting impression was that they had been too gentle in their handling of West Europeans and Japanese. Though many American historians will agree with him, European historians most certainly will not.

The efforts of Volcker and Burns to obtain some kind of coordinated control of the Eurodollar markets had proved futile, largely because the Bank of England had refused to cooperate. Burns had been more successful in persuading European central bankers to lower their own discount rates, but too late. On March 24 the Belgian rate was reduced to 6 percent. The West German Federal Bank followed suit a week later. The Bank of England appropriately chose to reduce its rate on April 1, and both the Netherlands National Bank and the Bank of Italy did so the next day. But the opposition of the French and the Swiss had been strong, and all of those reductions in discount rates proved ineffective. Central bankers who had been accustomed for a generation to obedient money markets had been overconfident of their own authority, and their awakening was tardy. As late as April 28 Pierre-Paul Schweitzer was proclaiming that there was no crisis.

During the preceding year, the official reserves of West Germany had almost doubled, from $7.129 billion to $13.610 billion. By mid-April, the European press was reporting with only slight exaggeration that those West German reserves were rising by a billion dollars per day. The speculative stampede had begun. Most West Germans believed those massive increases were well-deserved recognition for their decades of hard work. In Bonn jubilant members of the Bundestag therefore urged that $400 million in West German gold reserves be minted into a new and triumphant issue of golden

marks, the first since 1914. And West German exporters, who wielded considerable influence in that Bundestag, were adamantly opposed to any further
revaluation of the mark. John Connally deflated their joy. In one of his first
public statements as Secretary of the Treasury, Connally announced that he
was advising President Nixon to decide upon "a radical change in our basic
trade position. . . . We can't continue to hold a military, economic and
political umbrella over the free world by ourselves as we have been doing."
He had just read a report that, for the first quarter of 1971 alone, the American payments deficit had been $5 billion, of which $3.5 billion had been
short-term capital flows to Western Europe. American trade was being affected, as importers and exporters adjusted their orders and payments to anticipate a devaluation of the dollar.

Chancellor Willy Brandt and his Economics Minister, the didactic Karl
Schiller, were doing their feeble best to help Nixon and Connally by arguing
within the European Economic Community that its members should undertake a joint float of their currencies against the dollar. But Pompidou and
Giscard, convinced that arrogant Americans could at last be humbled by a
conventional devaluation of "the almighty dollar" against gold, were determined to force it. The possible effects on the defense of Western Europe
did not concern them. At a long afterdinner meeting in Hamburg on April 26
Giscard therefore defeated the proposed joint European float by reasserting
the old French arguments for an increase in the official price of gold. Though
Schiller was the better economist, demonstrably Giscard has been the better
politician. Neither Pompidou nor Giscard was disposed to forgive and
forget those efforts Brandt and Schiller had been making to help the United
States. When information on their disputes was leaked to the press, the free
market price of gold rose to a new high for 1971. On April 29 the afternoon
fixing in London was $39.45 per ounce. In Paris the price of a 12.5-kilogram
bar climbed to $39.79 per ounce. And in Zürich the closing prices were
$39.40 bid, $39.55 asked. The free-market price of gold began to rise steadily.

After a quarter-century of increasingly free world trade and capital movements, there was a resurgence of economic nationalism. In 7 months the flight
from the dollar had brought Britain more than $3.5 billion. Avarice out-
weighed all other considerations in the calculations of the British Treasury.
In April Britain's national reserves swelled to $3.446 billion, the highest level
ever recorded. It was able to repay £8 million to West Germany, the final
installment on a debt that dated back to liquidation of the European Payments Union in 1958. The vaults of the Bank of England now held more than
enough cash to repay the $2 billion in British short- and medium-term debts
still outstanding, principally to the International Monetary Fund. Yet that
windfall had not been enough to satisfy Edward Heath and Anthony Barber,
his pallid Chancellor of the Exchequer.

Happily the West Germans had better judgment. On Monday, May 3,

four of the West German economic institutes issued an annual report in
which they recommended that the mark be allowed to float for an indefinite
period, not only to curb the influx of dollars but also to brake the rising rate
of domestic inflation. Grateful for their "useful" advice, Karl Schiller informed Chancellor Brandt that prompt action had become essential. On
Tuesday the Federal Bank was forced to buy a billion to support the dollar at
its floor price of DM 3.6300. And during the first half-hour of trading on
Wednesday it was compelled to buy another billion. Swiftly the West German money markets were closed. The Swiss National Bank, after taking in
$600 million by 10 that morning, closed the Swiss foreign exchanges as soon
as it heard of the West German decision. Sellers of dollars then turned to the
Netherlands, whose central bank absorbed $400 million before closing at
11:15 a.m. The Belgian and Austrian central banks adopted similar measures
at noon, after taking in $75 million each. Portugal and Finland also closed
their foreign exchanges, but those in London, Paris, Rome and Tokyo remained open. Eager for more unearned dollars, those four central banks became the most stubborn in their refusal to revalue their currencies. The Bank
of Japan alone gained $350 million that day. With its competitive eye on the
West German national reserves, those of Japan soared beyond $6 billion.

On the morning of May 6, banner headlines proclaimed throughout the
world that the Bretton Woods gold-exchange system had entered its final
agonies. Immediately Georges Pompidou summoned the British to Paris, to
dictate his terms for their entry into the European Economic Community.
There Edward Heath would deliver into the grasping hands of Pompidou
those 9 percent of the votes in the International Monetary Fund held by
Britain. Subsequently the British would consistently vote with France against
their former allies, the United States. Parvenus have a deserved reputation
for biting the hand that feeds them. While Pompidou was angrily denouncing
the dollar, thanks to that capital flight the reserves of the Bank of France had
risen to $5.2 billion.

Nor had Pompidou been pleased by the scanty information his Foreign
Ministry had been able to glean on the impending rapprochement between
Americans and Russians. As the heir of General de Gaulle, he had fancied
himself in the glorious role of neutral arbiter between West and East. Americans would pay dearly for Pompidou's displeasure, as the French encouraged
the North Vietnamese representatives in Paris to prolong the negotiations for
peace in Southeast Asia. Soon President Nixon would announce his now
scheduled trips to Peking and Moscow in search of that peace. Conservative
West Europeans and Japanese, who preferred to see the world rigidly divided
into hostile capitalist and communist blocs, would protest that American
diplomacy was rank betrayal. The United States and Western Europe had
ceased to be a natural alliance that shared common interests and purposes.

Attempting to preserve the integrity of the European Economic Community, on May 8, at an emergency meeting in Brussels that lasted 20 hours, Brandt and Schiller made one last effort to find a "European solution" for its monetary difficulties. It was no longer possible, however, to reason calmly with the suspicious French. Absolute in their refusal either to revalue the franc or to participate in a joint European float, they alleged that the United States had deliberately initiated the crisis to "torpedo" the Common Agricultural Policy, simply because French farmers profited most from it. With Belgium, France had decided to resort to the rigorous exchange controls and increased discount rates approved by the Community's Monetary Commission but opposed by Bonn. Suddenly millions of American residents and tourists abroad awoke to the end of an era. Hotels in Amsterdam, railroad ticket offices in Zürich and restaurants in Paris either would not accept their dollars or would exchange them only in limited quantities, at discounts as much as 10 percent less than official parities.

When Europe's money markets reopened on Monday, May 10, the West German mark began to float, with the Dutch guilder bobbing along in its wake. Slowly floating began to gain some respectability and widening recognition that it is the natural order in a world whose national currencies experience different rates of inflation. Yet the orthodox Swiss National Bank, anxious to protect Swiss exporters, had rejected as "unthinkable" the suggestion that the Swiss franc should also be allowed to float. When the exchanges reopened May 10, it was therefore revalued by 7.07 percent, and the Austrians revalued their schilling by 5.05 percent. Privately both the Swiss and the Austrians wondered if that would be enough. A nervous, confused quiet returned to the foreign exchanges, but not for long.

With appetites whetted by such easy gains, speculators had begun to look for other currencies that might appreciate and were buying Japanese yen. In Washington officials boasted that the gross national product of the United States now exceeded a trillion dollars per annum, but that did not interest speculators. They were far more intrigued by a rumor that France, the Netherlands and Belgium had taken another $422 million from American gold reserves during the first 2 weeks of May. On May 13 the free-market price in London therefore closed at a new high of $41.30 per fine ounce. And in Paris, Jacques Rueff received an American journalist in his paneled study at the Institut de France. Ornately furnished in the style of Louis XV, its walls were covered with books lavishly gilt. With an apologetic smile, Rueff confided that the monetary crisis had made a best-seller of his most recent book, *Le péché monétaire de l'Occident*. Then he revealed the official French decision for which speculators in gold had waited so long.

I fear that the problem has got out of hand and that the American balance of payments will be restored only by a forced consolidation—that is, bankruptcy—as in 1931.

John Connally had never before dealt with that kind of veiled, allusive European mind and now found an opportunity to test European reactions for himself. On the eve of the 18th annual International Banking Conference in Munich, devaluation of the dollar had become the most prominent topic for discussion among West European bankers, even though it was not on the agenda. When the American delegation led by Connally, Volcker and Burns arrived at the rococo Linderhof Palace, built a century earlier by the mad Ludwig II of Bavaria, they found even their German hosts in an ugly mood. Otmar Emminger quoted the Canadians, saying that: "It is always uncomfortable to share a bed with an elephant, even if he is good-natured." Volcker protested: "The United States is on the way to regaining its rightful position as an island of stability." But from Brussels, President Pompidou thundered: "We cannot keep a monetary standard that constantly loses its value as a result of American internal policy." And one of Minister Schiller's assistants recommended eliminating the dollar as the world's monetary standard by replacing it with the SDR. The chairman of the largest Swiss commercial bank replied: "SDRs have not worked. In Europe, gold is the only real basis for a reserve. We Europeans are not ready to accept anything else. The people won't stand for it." Schiller himself had discreetly failed to appear. He was in Switzerland on honeymoon with his third wife. And for the first time the press reported that American trade accounts had begun to slip into deficits.

At last Connally retorted on May 28, in the final session of the conference, that:

> We are not going to devalue . . . or change the price of gold. . . . We fully recognize that other nations are not willing to live with a system dictated by the United States. But, as you share in the system, we have the right to expect you to accept the responsibility to share more fully in the cost of defending the free world.

Emphasizing that the underlying American payments deficit of $2 billion to $3 billion each year was substantially exceeded by the $5 billion in overseas costs alone of defending Western Europe and Japan, he added: "I find that an impressive and a depressing fact." Noting that his European and Japanese audience had remained quite cold and unimpressed by that appeal, upon returning to Washington he advised the dithering President Nixon to "kick them in the balls." Presumably Connally no longer believed the game was billiards. His trip had been an instructive experience. For the first time, he had been exposed to the full force of the venomous hostilities with which West Europeans regarded the United States. Mere words could not move or impress them in any way.

The times were out of joint, and Richard Milhouse Nixon was not qualified to set them right. Americans were learning the hard way that if Uncle

Sam did not take care of himself, no one else would. On May 22 the Swiss National Bank had confirmed rumors that it had asked for another $50 million in American gold and had thus increased its conversions to $125 million since January 1. In concert with the central banks of France, Belgium and the Netherlands, it had reduced those official American gold stocks to $10.568 billion by June 3, when the Democrat Henry Reuss of Wisconsin introduced a "sense of Congress" resolution in the House of Representatives. As Chairman of its Joint Economic Subcommittee on International Exchange and Payments, Reuss proposed to end formally the commitment to sell American gold to foreign central banks at $35 per ounce and to float the dollar, "to remove present disequilibrium" in exchange rates.

> Only by closing the gold window and letting the dollar find a newer and sounder relationship with the yen and other undervalued currencies can we avoid the deterioration of our trading position and a return to trade autarchy.

But President Nixon still could not make up his mind. Paul Volcker therefore informed Congressman Reuss and his Subcommittee that: "We prefer to make every effort to preserve the present system." In their cloakrooms and committee rooms, hundreds of Senators and Congressmen began to discuss Nixon's habit of doing too little too late.

On June 8 in Paris Secretary of State William Rogers utterly failed to obtain formal agreement from the twenty-two member nations of the Organization for Economic Cooperation and Development that they should "share the burden of America's worldwide responsibilities." From Brussels the Republican Senator Charles Percy of Illinois reported that he had found the other member nations of NATO hostile to his proposal that they increase their contributions to its costs, so that the United States could reduce its own. And in Bonn related discussions with Helmut Schmidt, the Social Democratic Defense Minister, simply broke down. Chancellor Brandt's Finance Minister had already resigned rather than approve Schmidt's earlier defense budget.

In Tokyo, though Japan's trade surplus with the United States alone had been exceeding a billion dollars per year, Assistant Secretary of State Philip Trezise infuriated the government of Prime Minister Eisaku Sato by urging revaluation of the yen. Struggling to prevent domestic recession, Sato complained to a Japanese television audience that: "There could not have been a more outrageous case of interference in domestic matters." Finance Minister Takeo Fukuda added that so experienced a diplomat as Trezise should not have committed such a fault. "In no corner of my brain is there any thought of revaluing the yen." Japan's gross national product had been growing at the extraordinary rate of 10 percent per annum because of the war in Vietnam and that undervalued yen. Tenaciously the Japanese were determined to

prolong their "economic miracle" as long as possible. During the preceding
year Japan's reserves had doubled, from $3.5 billion to $7 billion. Sato had
decreed that revaluation of the yen should be considered only if those vener-
ated reserves should reach an exorbitant $16 billion to $17 billion. The United States was being not merely milked but bilked by most of its supposed
friends and allies abroad, as they took full advantage of that opportunity to
repay earlier debts and to build massive national reserves for a future in
which it might not be so easy to obtain dollars.

That fiasco had only begun. By July "hot dollars" were entering France at
a rate of $300 million per week, regardless of its exchange controls. French
national reserves rose to $5.8 billion, and those of Britain to $3.87 billion. The
gold reserves of the United States had fallen to $10.507 billion, and only
cognoscenti were aware that $548 million of that gold had been borrowed from
the International Monetary Fund. The "great, unwashed public" remained
blissfully ignorant that net American gold reserves had been reduced to $9.96
billion. The bullion dealers of London and Zürich were not only better informed but more percipient. In anticipation of a devaluation of the dollar,
the free-market price of gold had risen to a precise 20 percent premium over
its official price. And on July 28 the United States Treasury announced that
the Federal budget deficit for the preceding fiscal year had been an awesome
$23.2 billion. Though domestic inflation had risen to an annual rate of 7
percent, the American economy had not been responding to the stimuli Nixon had chosen. Economists had been discussing a new phenomenon they
unhappily described as "stagflation." For more than a year Arthur Burns had
been risking Nixon's wrath by calling for wage and price controls. The Federal Reserve Board and the White House were barely on speaking terms. And
on Wall Street, the Dow Jones average dropped 30 points during the last
week of July. That fall would continue, and Richard Nixon was not the only
one who had been watching it closely. The French were well aware that it
was an important factor in his calculations.

In the Salon Murat of the Élysée Palace, during a weekly meeting of his
Council of Ministers on Wednesday, August 4, President Georges Pompidou
decided that the time had come to repay a grudge, by repaying 2 years early
the $608.7 million France still owed to the International Monetary Fund.
Thus France's short- and medium-term debts abroad, incurred in 1968 and
1969, would be settled in full. Pompidou also issued orders that introduced
the most rigorous exchange controls, to prevent the sale of francs for dollars.
That circular from the Bank of France caused bewildered consternation
among Parisian bankers and exchange dealers, until they learned
Pompidou's purpose. Then speculation in gold and dollars was excited, not
calmed. Rather than use French gold for repaying the debts of France to the
International Monetary Fund, he demanded another $191 million in Ameri-

can gold from the United States Treasury. *Dies irae!* Later Minister Giscard would try, with conspicuous lack of success, to persuade the public that: "It would have been absurd deliberately to have precipitated a world monetary crisis." Throughout the world, thousands of bankers had been closely watching the United States Treasury. They burst into nervous laughter when they heard Giscard's plea of innocence.

In Washington, on August 6, the White House announced presidential approval of the first export licenses for the shipment of American equipment that was to be used in the Soviet Union's Kama River truck factory. Suddenly reversing an earlier position, that day the House of Representatives approved and sent to the White House for signature a bill authorizing the Export–Import Bank to extend export credits to the Soviet Union and China. One explanation given was that unemployment in the United States had risen to 5.8 percent. The next morning, Congressman Reuss and his Joint Economic Subcommittee issued a report calling for "action now" on the parity of the dollar and gave Nixon that final push for which he had waited so long. He was also studying a report that recommended the imposition of import surcharges. As a roving ambassador, David Kennedy had utterly failed to persuade Japan, Taiwan, Hong Kong and South Korea that they should voluntarily curb their exports to the United States. Cheap textiles from the Far East had been overwhelming American manufacturers, and the domestic cry for protection against cheap imports of all kinds had become too strong to ignore any further.

With speculation against the dollar renewed, the British Treasury asked for a gold guarantee on its dollar holdings and was refused. On August 9 it also announced early repayment of the $620 million Britain still owed to the International Monetary Fund on a loan contracted in 1968. No longer required to listen to the Fund's strictures on their mismanagement of Britain's inflation-ridden economy, Edward Heath and Anthony Barber were freed to inflate still more in frantic efforts to force economic growth regardless of the declining productivity of British industry. Britain's workers had become accustomed to being paid more for working less. Japan's national reserves were approaching $9.5 billion, and those of Switzerland were rising at the rate of a billion dollars per week. In Zürich the free-market price of gold jumped to a record $44.10 per ounce, and across the Continent gold fanciers were eagerly discussing a rumor that the United States would soon be forced to double its official price. The foreign-trade surplus of France had reached a record high, the value of its exports having exceeded its imports by more than 10 percent in July. President Pompidou was confident of the renewed strength of his bargaining position.

On Friday, August 13, President Nixon gathered his own economic advisers at Camp David in Maryland for a 2-day conference. After the foreign exchanges had closed for the weekend, American television networks were informed that 20 minutes of their time would be required on Sunday evening, August 15. Bankers and officials who sought to escape the heat of summer by spending that Sunday sailing on Long Island Sound or the Potomac River, with radios fixed on the navigation band to catch weather reports and Coast Guard bulletins, also heard Nixon's speech announcing his "New Economic Policy." Neatly he stole the growing thunder of his Democratic critics by adopting precisely those changes they had been urging. There was a 90-day freeze on prices and wages, and a 10 percent surcharge on all imports, in that "package" of economic measures. Later, and casually, almost as an afterthought, he "suspended" the dollar's convertibility into gold.

No one could have forecast what would happen next. Then and there, all American support for the defense of Western Europe should also have been withdrawn, to correct not only balance-of-payments but also Federal budget deficits. Unhappily, however, Nixon had surrounded himself with advisers guided by the outworn concepts of New York's banking community. They were determined to maintain American armed forces abroad, long after that necessity had disappeared. And Nixon lacked the courage, the abilities and the overwhelming Congressional support President Franklin Roosevelt had enjoyed three decades before. The price Americans would pay for Nixon's feckless delays would therefore become staggering. From January 1 to mid-August, the United States had already paid out $3.1 billion in reserve assets, including $865.2 million in gold, $394 million in foreign exchange, $480 million in SDRs and $1.362 billion from its position in the Fund. $456.6 million of that gold had been paid out in the second quarter and another $299.6 million in the third. France had been the largest taker, having demanded $282 million in gold during the second quarter and $191 million in the third. Final American gold conversions in the third quarter included $50 million for Switzerland, $30 million for Singapore and $20 million for Finland. Though that had been the largest official "bear raid" ever known, the flight from the dollar would continue.

The following morning, nature wrote its own epitaph for the gold-exchange standard. In Hong Kong, the gold market was closed by a typhoon called Rose.

GRESHAM'S LAW SILENTLY TAKES EFFECT

Long inured to more sensational news, the American people received Nixon's announcement quite calmly. Unlike New York's bankers, most Americans were not disturbed to hear that their dollar had begun to float. Everyday experience in American shops and supermarkets had already taught them that it had lost value.

In Western Europe, however, there was an immediate roar of rage and disappointment. Gold hoarders and speculators had been anticipating a repetition of Roosevelt's gold-buying program of 1933–1934. They had persuaded themselves that the United States should at least double, perhaps triple, possibly even quadruple the official price of its gold reserves, to settle its debts abroad. For several generations, they had been assuming that they had a certain proprietary interest in the United States Treasury. Without their consent, its policies should not have been changed. Many had been prepared to watch with equanimity while their own governments drained American gold reserves to the last ounce. Heatedly they reminded Americans that their paper dollars represented legal commitments that they could do so if they pleased. Bizarre incidents occurred. In Paris taxi drivers spurned dollars as worthless and would not accept them. In London American tourists waiting in a long line outside the American Express Office to cash travelers' checks listened patiently but without curiosity as a little old Englishwoman in tennis shoes, waving her umbrella, denounced their "national decadence." For many people the certainties of a generation simply vanished. International postal rate agreements, airline fare structures, oil payments contracts, the Common Agricultural Policy, all collapsed as the dollar began to float. In fact, though not in law, the non-Communist world was now on an inconvertible paper dollar standard. Valéry Giscard quickly reminded Frenchmen of the similarity to the situation in Eastern Europe, whose unhappy peoples had been subjected to an inconvertible paper ruble. And in Washington, at the United States Treasury, workmen began to repaint its traditionally golden pillars white.

After a decade of angry complaints against the inflationary effects of American payments deficits, the governments of Western Europe and Japan changed their tune. Swiftly they moved "to protect the dollar", by devising ways to prevent it from depreciating against their own currencies. With such helpful "friends", the United States really did need the protection of China and the Soviet Union. European money markets had been closed for a week, and one last opportunity had appeared to revive the gold-exchange system. It was short-lived and was quickly demolished by the French. A devaluation of the dollar on the order of 20 percent or a revaluation of that magnitude by the other major trading currencies would have rapidly reversed the American trade and payments deficits. With those accounts restored to lasting surpluses of some $5 billion each year, the "dollar glut" abroad could have been absorbed by the United States within the next decade. As that supply of international money contracted, it could have been replaced by new issues of Special Drawing Rights.

On August 20 a "high government official" in Washington named Paul Volcker therefore announced that the "major preconditions" for restoring the

dollar's convertibility into gold were "a substantial readjustment" or realignment of major exchange rates around the world; "progress" in reducing the
burden of American defense costs abroad; and an easing of trade rules the
United States considered unfair "in an open world." American experts were
publicly discussing a modest devaluation of the dollar or revaluation of other
major currencies on the order of 15 percent. That was wishful thinking. Most
of those "trading partners" of the United States had already decided that
they would not relinquish any of the advantages they had gained since 1944.
And as competitors of the United States, their purposes were served by continuing to evade the defense costs it had been bearing for their benefit.

On August 18 President Pompidou had simply preempted all negotiations
by announcing that the gold parity of the franc would be maintained and a
complicated two-tier exchange control system was introduced to defend it.
For French commercial transactions, the exchange rate of the franc would
continue to be fixed at its old rate. For speculative and long-term capital
movements, the franc would be allowed to float but its rate would be controlled by the intervention of the Bank of France. The Bank of Japan, equally opposed to any revaluation of the yen, was continuing to buy several
hundred million dollars each day. When representatives of the European
Economic Community met at the Charlemagne Building in Brussels on August 19, the clash between Giscard and Schiller became open and was prolonged into the following morning. Then all went their separate ways. Britain
chose to follow the Italian example by deciding to maintain its old parity
against the dollar but with fluctuations permitted within wider bands.

Thus Americans quickly learned that West Europeans and Japanese
would permit only "dirty" floating, as their central banks intervened in the
foreign exchanges to prevent depreciation of the dollar. With blatant hypo-
crisy, the newspapers of Western Europe and Japan began to descry the
"brutality" of Nixon's "shocks," which they had been anticipating for almost
a year. In London, *The Sunday Times* protested that Nixon's new policies
represented "a stick without a carrot." West European chauvinists became
highly emotional. The American emergency measure most resented was that
10 percent surcharge on imports, which threatened West European exporters
and their workers with a small loss of sales in American markets. During the
preceding decade, seven other nations had adopted similar import surcharges
when in comparable balance-of-payments difficulties. However, as champion
of the free-trade rules of the General Agreement on Tariffs and Trade, it was
unforgivable for the United States to do so. American relations with Western
Europe and Japan became a "dialogue of the deaf."

The Managing Director of the International Monetary Fund is obligated
to intervene in crises and can be effective if he does so in private. Having
intervened, he has the further, overriding obligation to be right and thus seen

to be unbiased. On August 23 Pierre-Paul Schweitzer publicly called for an 8 percent devaluation of the dollar against gold and received widespread attention. That was a *fait du prince,* in which Schweitzer simply made known the terms on which President Pompidou would eventually be willing to "compromise." The blunder was appalling, because subsequent events would prove Schweitzer wrong, and the United States Treasury would never forgive him for that public opposition to its justified demands. Later he compounded his errors by appearing on television to present his case directly to the American people. That merely strengthened American distrust of the International Monetary Fund.

This was another situation in which a so-called compromise would prove to be the worst of all possible choices, and the world's foremost central bankers began to demonstrate the truth of that adage when the money markets reopened August 23. A London journalist described it as "the week money went funny." Secretary Connally commented: "We have awakened forces that nobody is at all familiar with." American consumers began to experience a double jolt of inflation. The 10 percent surcharge on imports not only raised their prices but also tempted the domestic producers of substitutes to do so. Though Nixon's 90-day freeze on prices and wages would briefly dampen those increases, it also discouraged domestic production at the time when foreign demand for American exports began to revive. Shortages and higher prices inevitably followed.

In Western Europe alarmist propaganda began. A newspaper in London bore the headline: "Nixon Risking Trade War." In Paris the French were informed that: "The Monetary Crisis Threatens to Wreck Europe." And in Hamburg West Germans were warned of the "Alarm for Many Jobs." West European journalists rewrote the monetary history of the preceding quarter-century, to depict Nixon and the United States as the most brazen of villains. At last, on August 28, when Japanese national reserves exceeded $12 billion, the yen was allowed to float. British reserves had risen to $4.807 billion, and French reserves to $6.888 billion, yet both the British and the French governments continued to oppose any revaluation of their currencies.

When the deputies of the Group of Ten assembled, on September 3, at the International Monetary Fund's new, modernistic European headquarters on the Avénue d'Iéna in Paris, Paul Volcker found them solidly arrayed against the United States. They described as "stunning" his insistence on a $13 billion "turnaround" in American payments accounts, to be accomplished within a year. That represented an average 15 percent revaluation of their own currencies, which they simply refused to consider. Instead they demanded a devaluation of the dollar against gold that would discredit it as a reserve currency and would reinstate gold as the primary reserve asset. They were not impressed by Volcker's plea that political reasons prevented Nixon from asking Congress for the authority to devalue the dollar. In public Giscard began to forecast a catastrophic depression in world trade, unless the French got their way. That deadlock would continue, as each side awaited events that might compel one or the other to concede.

Once again the international monetary system had become an object for political bargaining at the highest levels. On September 13 the six finance ministers of the European Community, with Britain as a guest, agreed on an outline for a reorganization of the system that called for a selective realignment of parities among the major Western currencies and for wider margins of fluctuation around those parities. Giscard conceded that France might slightly revalue the franc, in return for Schiller's acceptance of a clause that read:

> The standard of international currencies should continue to be expressed in gold, but gradually expanded to include Special Drawing Rights to the International Monetary Fund while the roles of the dollar and pound sterling were reduced.

Pierre-Paul Schweitzer and Britain's Anthony Barber, present in Brussels as observers, concurred. All agreed to continue their demand that the United States devalue its dollar against gold. The British, who were making every effort to reduce their own defense commitments abroad, were simply heedless of the consequences if the United States should be compelled to do so. In Washington the Department of Commerce announced that the American payments deficit for the second quarter of 1971 alone had been $5.7 billion on the official settlements account. On current and long-term capital account, the deficit for the first half of that year had been $4.447 billion. Though the West European finance ministers assembled in Brussels were unwilling to face those facts, the need for a decisive "turnaround" in American payments accounts was only too obvious.

Two days later, on September 15, the finance ministers and central bankers of the Group of Ten met in London, in the ornate music room of Lancaster House, where Frederic Chopin had played for Queen Victoria. In his own way, John Connally became an equally flamboyant performer. Accompanied by Paul Volcker and Arthur Burns, he sought but failed to shock the remaining nine finance ministers into recognition of the magnitude of the changes needed. Candidly Connally explained: "We have a problem and we're sharing it with the world, just like we shared our prosperity. That's what friends are for." But the Italian Finance Minister, Mario Ferrari-Aggradi, protested that a turnaround of $13 billion would be "too ambitious" and might disrupt others' economies. He asked the United States not to go too far, too fast in ending its payments deficits. The plea for "gradualness" appeared that would have such damaging effects on the world's economy in the years ahead.

It was an extraordinary situation. West Europeans argued that every other country should have full control over its own exchange rate, but not the United States. The staff of the International Monetary Fund, and the Monetary Commission of the European Economic Community, had already presumed to decide on an 8 percent devaluation of the dollar against gold. And the staff of the Organization for Economic Cooperation and Development were recommending that the devaluation be no more than 10 percent. For the first time, a serious doubt arose. Was it in the best interests of the United States to retain its memberships in those organizations, or should it have gone its own way? Were the costs of "cooperation" with Western Europe and Japan too high? When Connally insisted on a revaluation of the other nine currencies rather than a devaluation of the dollar, Valéry Giscard stalked from the room muttering "Intransigence!" Though intransigence was admirable in the French, it was repugnant in Americans.

John Connally was learning for himself what Lyndon Johnson already knew—that whenever the United States needed help, it could not rely on those West European and Japanese "allies." During that London conference, they simply refused to consider either a sharing of American defense costs or trade concessions to the United States. By the second afternoon, Connally had become quite angry, when he found that the others would concede nothing yet attempted to push him into commitments on an increase in the official price of gold and removal of the American imports surcharge. The conference dissolved in utter disagreement, the West Europeans protesting to the public that it was unfair to expect them to negotiate with "American bullyboys."

The only proposal that would later become significant had passed almost unnoticed. Ferrari-Aggradi had suggested a return to parities fixed not in terms of gold but rather the politically neutral Special Drawing Right, whose tenuous link to gold should be severed. Though that suggestion had immediately aroused the hostility of the French, Rinaldo Ossola had been reelected chairman of the Group of Ten's deputies. After their ministers had dispersed, they began to study the technical problems that had arisen. At least there had been a tacit assumption that there could not be a return to a gold-dollar system. All the ministers present had also assumed that there would be a "realignment" of parities and eventually an end to the floating of the dollar. Nevertheless, many private economists would continue ever more cogently to argue the merits of floating. Among them, Milton Friedman would become the most widely known, perhaps because he had the ear of Arthur Burns. Thirty years before, while the Bretton Woods system was being designed, they had worked together at the National Bureau for Economic Research.

The 27th annual meeting of the International Monetary Fund began in Washington on Monday, September 27, so soon after the London conference that West European finance ministers and central bankers could do nothing more than stubbornly repeat the positions they had already taken. Again President Pompidou had foreclosed negotiations by announcing:

> I do not believe that the United States is disposed to negotiate in a useful manner at the IMF meeting. The import surcharge is a big stick that could eventually be transformed into a carrot—if only one were willing to play the role of the donkey. That is not our intention.

The money markets had not fallen into the chaos so many had confidently predicted. West European and Japanese exchange controls had prevented the dollar from depreciating more than an average 3 or 4 percent against their currencies, far less than the 15 percent American experts had hopefully forecast. After Pierre-Paul Schweitzer opened the meeting with his now ritual call for an immediate devaluation of the dollar against gold, most of the formal speeches were noncommittal and meaningless. In the corridors, however, the discussions were acrimonious, as the members of the Group of Ten fired charges and countercharges. And all the smaller members of the Fund were furious, with good reason. Their dollar reserves had been depreciating in value, and they too were being affected by the American imports surcharge, even though they had done little to cause the American payments deficits.

Britain had always been extraordinarily sensitive and vulnerable to those overseas suppliers of its raw materials and markets for its manufactures. Moreover the traditions of Lord Keynes had remained very much alive at the British Treasury. Karl Schiller had therefore been urging Anthony Barber to take the lead in proposing to the Fund that it adopt the Special Drawing Right as its new international monetary standard. That appeared to Barber and his advisers a viable alternative. The French would no longer recognize the dollar, and Americans had become equally adamant in their demand for the demonetization of gold. With quiet support from the West Germans and the Italians, Barber therefore formally proposed on September 28 a vague plan for a reform of the international monetary system in which SDRs would replace both the dollar and gold as the primary reserve asset. Naturally the British press applauded his "historic" speech. The Japanese Finance Minister, Mikio Mizuta, concurred. None of them made any effort to explain how the United States could end its commitments to South Vietnam or finance its continuing defense commitments to Western Europe and Japan within the constraints such a system would impose. And in the gloomiest speech of the meeting, Valéry Giscard forecast:

> a worldwide economic recession within a few months, during which problems of activity and of employment will raise universal concern. This probability increases the urgency of restoring order to the trade and payments system.

The French have always been prone to predict disaster if the rest of the world does not conform to their wishes.

After a quarter-century of uninhibited, unprecedented growth, the multi-national banks and companies with headquarters in the United States had become an extraordinarily subversive force. While their treasurers continued to convert dollars into appreciating currencies wherever possible, their spokesmen began to demand that: "Connally should quit while he is ahead." From Paris Ambassador Arthur Watson was reporting the French threats of retaliation, trade warfare and the probable division of the world into conflicting monetary and trading blocs, as had happened after "Roosevelt torpedoed the London Conference of 1933." That "scare talk" was becoming ferocious. American bankers and businessmen, fearful for their investments abroad, became the most effective propagandists that Western Europe and Japan had ever had in the United States.

For the first time in his life, Henry Kissinger was compelled to recognize the existence of economics. He had no knowledge of monetary history and not the foggiest understanding of what had been happening. Unaware that Western Europe and Japan were far more vulnerable to monetary and trade warfare, Kissinger believed that propaganda. Though he was quite aware that Western Europe and Japan were dependent on the United States for their defense, he nevertheless feared for the survival of NATO. Time alone could demonstrate that it was a sham, in which American taxpayers were being fleeced of some $15 billion each year, without receiving anything in return. Nor were Secretary William Rogers and his staff any better prepared to resist that French propaganda. For decades, careerists at the Department of State had considered themselves responsible for representing in Washington the hungry West Europeans and Japanese. Once again, those clients were clamoring for soft words and rich gifts. At the Federal Reserve Board, Arthur Burns had a better reason for urging President Nixon to seek a quick compromise. Burns feared that cooperation among central bankers would collapse and vanish, as it had in 1931. He would not retain much longer his high regard for their judgment and fairness.

During that meeting of the International Monetary Fund the Group of Ten instructed their deputies to meet again in Paris on October 18 to explore four basic issues: (1) the magnitude and method of obtaining a realignment of currencies; (2) the temporary adoption of wider margins around parities; (3) the abolition of the American imports surcharge; and (4) additional measures, outside the scope of exchange rates, that would improve the American payments accounts. Primarily because the French insisted, those "nonmonetary measures," which included sharing defense costs and granting trade concessions to the United States, were being slowly shunted aside. Moreover, so far as President Pompidou and Minister Giscard were concerned, a real concession from the United States on the official price of gold had become a political necessity. Ever alert to the effects of monetary change on the value of their gold holdings, the French people were incensed by the diminishing prospect that the United States ever would or could restore the dollar's convertibility into gold. In the French press, that had become the foremost issue. False reports that Pompidou and Giscard were lending tacit support to the Anglo–German–Italian proposal for the acceptance of an SDR standard aroused widespread apprehension among conservative Frenchmen who had always regarded gold as the essential foundation of their personal and national security. And Giscard was running for reelection to the presidency of his own party.

When the annual congress of the French Independent Republicans met at Toulouse on October 10, Giscard reassured his loyal followers that: "There are no professionals among us, no old foxes, but men who exercise their responsibilities in professional life." In Bonn the caustic Karl Schiller was ridiculing Giscard as "an industrial Colbert," but the two thousand solid Frenchmen gathered in Toulouse were delighted by Giscard's promise that: "Our movement imposes upon itself the absolute rule of putting the interests of France before all other interests." To celebrate his reelection, they drank and feasted far into the night, entertained by folk singing, dancing and by Giscard himself. He received warm applause for his bonhomie when he went on stage to display his skill with the accordion and obliged the delegates by singing a popular song that was said to be his favorite. Appropriately it began: "I am trying to make a fortune." And the crowd took up the refrain. What they could not foresee did not trouble them.

As a national reserve asset, gold's monetary role had ended August 15. While the free-market price gradually rose and enriched those private French owners of gold, central banks had been gaining ample supplies of dollars and had ceased to use their gold for official settlements. It had become undervalued at the official price of $35 per ounce, and for all practical purposes it simply disappeared from circulation among central banks. In fact, though not in law, national gold reserves had been frozen at their August 15th levels, because central bankers were no longer willing to pay in that officially undervalued medium.[3] Yet not all refrains were as joyful as those heard in Toulouse. In Vienna the 11 nations that formed the Organization of Petroleum Exporting Countries (OPEC), and controlled 90 percent of world oil exports, were enraged. They were demanding not only "compensation for the dollar devaluation" but also "immediate steps towards the implementation of effective participation in the existing oil concessions." As an "interim increase" in the price of their oil exports, they required prompt payment of $500 million by the oil companies. That was an increase of 5 to 7.5 percent in the "posted

[3] See Appendix.

price" of their oil, retroactive to August 15. Georges Pompidou and Valéry Giscard had opened Pandora's proverbial box.

In the calculations of President Nixon, the planning for his trips to Peking and Moscow overrode all other considerations. There appeared to be no other road that might reach his long-promised peace in Vietnam before the presidential elections of 1972. Secluded from the harsh realities beyond the doors of his Oval Office in the White House, he daydreamed of presenting himself to the divided East as the confident leader of a united West. For that purpose, some kind of a monetary deal with Pompidou had become essential. Because Nixon neither understood monetary details nor wanted to learn, he delegated to others the task of arranging that deal. Yet he grasped as well as Pompidou that the propaganda of the French had already affected the confidence of Wall Street, from which he had always drawn so much political support. Throughout October, while the deputies of the Group of Ten continued their tortuous discussions, the Dow Jones average drifted lower and lower, opening at 894 on October 1 and closing at 839 on October 29. Though Pompidou could afford to wait, Nixon could not.

To the bitter end and beyond, Connally and Volcker would continue to insist on the large, decisive change in the dollar's parity that provided the only possible way to restore order and stability in the international monetary system. Among Nixon's advisers, however, they were outvoted by Kissinger, Rogers, Burns and many lesser men. In the wider world the United States Treasury became a very lonely voice, the only advocate of rational measures that would have served concurrently the long-term best interests of the United States and the world at large.

A WRETCHED "COMPROMISE"

Sticks and carrots.

By the end of October, supported by those rigorous French exchange controls, the dollar had not depreciated against the French "commercial" franc by so much as 1 centime. Instead it had actually appreciated 0.4 percent. Thus President Pompidou had gained a 10 percent depreciation of the French franc against the West German mark, which had appreciated 9 percent against the dollar. Though Pompidou and Giscard hotly resented all West German efforts to help the United States, Brandt and Schiller had been permitting the mark to float freely. That was the only example of "clean" floating to be seen anywhere. On October 19 Schiller had also made another forlorn appeal to the European Community, asking its members to join West Germany in a "fair and balanced offer to help the United States solve the balance-of-payments crisis." It was a waste of breath. Britain's Prime Minister Heath had immediately replied:

The United States is acting drastically to protect its own balance of payments and trading position. . . . The countries of Western Europe must secure their own prosperity.

Though surprised multinational companies were learning how to live with the floating exchange rates so many had believed would be disastrous, and London's banks were flourishing, any loss of export advantages aroused the fury of the Confederation of British Industry. Tories had therefore become virulent in their denunciations of Nixon's new economic policies, even though their pound had appreciated only 3.4 percent against the dollar. Perhaps the supreme irony in that situation was the growing anxiety of the French *Patronat,* who were disturbed by their own government's bellicose propaganda against the United States. They were not comforted by Valéry Giscard's confident prediction that the world was on the road to ruin. Several practical voices began to make themselves heard. The aged Jean Monnet, now respectfully regarded as "the father of Europe," warned the French people that:

> The process started by Nixon in August is part of a great international change. The world is getting a new face. . . . A monetary agreement is imperative and, to achieve this, it is necessary to have an accord between Paris and Bonn by the end of 1971.

Encouraged by those few realistic European voices, Secretary Connally called for a meeting in Rome of the Group of Ten, with the expectation that some kind of an end to the crisis was in sight. To emphasize American distaste for the behavior of so many of its "friends" and "allies" abroad, Senate majority Leader Mike Mansfield arranged a suitable penalty. The annual foreign aid bill was defeated, by a decisive vote of 41 to 27 in the United States Senate. To strengthen Connally's bargaining hand further, on November 4 the Senate Finance Committee granted President Nixon the authority to increase the imports surcharge from 10 to 15 percent. Promptly President Pompidou conceded "in principle" that some revaluation of the franc might be considered, in a realignment of the parities of all major currencies. And the next morning, Washington announced that $136 million in American feed grains would be sold to the Soviet Union.

Throughout November the world's leading moneymen crisscrossed its skies in a dazzling display of aerobatics as they visited a dozen capitals seeking some kind of an international monetary deal. By November 27 President Nixon was able to announce from his hideaway at San Clemente that, before proceeding to Peking and Moscow, he would confer with all worried allies—with Pompidou in the Azores on December 13, with Heath in Bermuda on December 20, with Brandt in Florida on December 28, and with Sato in California on January 6. Washington had sound reasons to feel neglected, and Congressional distrust of Nixon grew as they watched his spectacular mishandling of that monetary crisis.

The following day, November 28, the finance ministers and central bankers of the Group of Ten assembled in Rome, at the 18th-century Palazzo Corsini. The galaxy of American officials headed by Connally, Volcker and Burns, surrounded by bodyguards, received some applause when they proposed a compromise in which the American demand for an average 15 percent revaluation of the other nine currencies was reduced to a meager 11 percent and was accompanied by an offer to withdraw the 10 percent imports surcharge immediately. But that was still far more than the West Europeans and Japanese were willing to concede without a formal devaluation of the dollar against gold. At last Connally therefore drew that "gold card" from his sleeve and asked his colleagues what they would do if the United States should devalue the dollar by 10 percent. It was indeed the long-awaited moment of truth. After prolonged silence, lasting almost an hour, they admitted that they would permit a 5 or even a 7 percent devaluation of the dollar. But if the United States should devalue against gold by so much as 10 percent, they too would devalue their own currencies. Tension increased, and Valéry Giscard interrupted to announce that President Pompidou intended to stall still further, until he could negotiate with President Nixon face to face. Resolution of the crisis would then appear to the public as a *coup de théâtre*, the personal handiwork of Georges Pompidou.

Quietly, in Paris, Ambassador Watson had already negotiated the essential elements of such an agreement with Michel Jobert, the inconspicuous Secretary General at the Élysée Palace. Chancellor Brandt, Prime Minister Heath and all the other West Europeans were compelled to defer to that French leadership, because Pompidou was a chief of state and they were not. In a conciliatory visit to Paris on December 3 Brandt was also forced to disown Minister Schiller by formally promising to end the floating of the mark. Unquestionably Schiller had been right. An era of fixed exchange rates was nearing its troubled end, simply because central bankers could not control their money markets much longer. Yet Pompidou had been dogmatic in his determination to preserve the monetary regime that had enabled him to maintain large trade and payments surpluses, high employment at home, profits for French exporters and that very profitable Common Agricultural Policy, at the expense of French consumers and other nations. Though foreigners might deplore his calculating pedantry, it gained the French votes he needed.

To symbolize his leadership of a European Economic Community that now claimed to be fully equal to the United States, Pompidou had agreed "to meet Nixon halfway," on the windswept island of Terceira in the Portuguese Azores. To demonstrate not only the new financial prestige but also the technological superiority of the European Community, he flew to Terceira from Orly Airport in 105 minutes aboard Prototype 001 of the supersonic *Concorde,* for which French and British taxpayers were spending more than a billion pounds sterling without any hope of recovering those costs. His staff dutifully recorded that the distance was 1870 miles and that Pompidou reached a maximum speed of 1440 miles per hour. After a rainy arrival, he stayed on one end of the island and Nixon at the other. Then they met in the middle, on the morning of December 13, at the stucco-covered town hall in Angra do Heroismo.

While those chieftains discussed the grand issues of the globe, in a lofty *tour d'horizon,* their senior aides began separate discussions on the prosaic details of an agreement, following an agenda prepared by Michel Jobert and Henry Kissinger. In one room Foreign Minister Maurice Schumann and Secretary of State William Rogers held talks on defense costs and trade concessions. The West European members of NATO had at last agreed to increase their own defense budgets by $1 billion each year. West Germany had also promised to pay toward American costs an additional DM 600 million per annum, which represented a ludicrous 1 percent of the sum American taxpayers were donating to the defense of Western Europe. In return for American commitments to devalue the dollar against gold, and to remove the 10 percent imports surcharge, Schumann and Pompidou further promised that France would subsequently participate in negotiations for "reciprocal" reduction of barriers to trade. Months later, when the time arrived for the French to honor that provision in the agreement, they would renege.

Meanwhile, in a second room, Valéry Giscard grudgingly conceded to John Connally that the dollar could be devalued against gold by as much as 8 percent without any devaluation of the franc. However, he insisted that the United States must then defend that new dollar parity in the money markets and must return to convertibility as rapidly as possible, even though those stipulations were patently absurd. So small a devaluation would not restore surpluses in American payments accounts, and it was well understood at the time that at best an 8 percent devaluation might enable the United States to reach bare equilibrium in 2 or 3 years. Nixon therefore exacted a promise from Pompidou that West Europeans would maintain order in their own money markets for another year, through the American presidential elections of November 1972. In public every effort was then made to convince the world that the Franco–American agreement reached in the Azores was a sparkling success. In reality, however, many observers immediately recognized that it had been a resounding defeat for the United States at the hands of its supposed allies. The prospects for restoring long-term order and stability in the international monetary system simply vanished. Pompidou, Giscard and Schumann had sacrificed them, to gain short-term advantages for French farmers, exporters and their workers.

As an anticlimax, on Thursday, December 16, the finance ministers and central bankers of the Group of Ten began in Washington to negotiate the details of a grand realignment of their currencies' parities. The venue chosen was the Smithsonian Institution, and the agreement formally concluded in that museum of the Industrial Age would soon become infamous. The pressures to reach agreement had become intense. On Saturday afternoon Secretary Connally shut the ministers of the Group of Ten into a room with all doors closed, to complete their discussions. Bluntly he informed them that he had "given them lunch, but would be damned if he would give them dinner, until they finished those negotiations." By Saturday evening the futile President Nixon was able to make a brief appearance among them. To the waiting television cameras, he announced "the most significant monetary agreement in the history of the world." Attendant journalists, to whom his penchant for hyperbole was well known, roared with laughter. Discreetly Connally would comment only that: "Everyone's pleased it's settled. We will return to a degree of stability."

Nixon had agreed to propose to Congress a 7.89 percent devaluation of the dollar against gold that would increase its official price to $38 per ounce. For all practical purposes, however, that new official price would become operational only for the small, restricted gold transactions of the International Monetary Fund. Though the Canadian dollar would continue to float, the remaining eight currencies of the Group of Ten returned to fixed parities against the American dollar that would perpetuate the inability of the United States to determine its own exchange rate. There were no changes in the gold parities of the French franc and the pound sterling. The Swedish crown and the Italian lira were actually devalued 1 percent each. But the Belgian franc and the Dutch guilder were revalued by 2.76 percent, the West German mark and the Swiss franc by 4.89 percent, and the Japanese yen by 7.66 percent. Against those revalued currencies, the effective devaluation of the dollar was approximately 9.7 percent. However, against all the currencies of the world, including those that had seized the opportunity to devalue against the American dollar (Israel, Ghana, South Africa and Jugoslavia), it was only 7.5 percent. The massive labors of the Group of Ten had produced a mouse. As an experiment, they also agreed that the permitted fluctuations around the new parities should be widened to 4.5 percent, to determine whether wider bands would ease the increasing difficulties of maintaining fixed parities. The most realistic observation on that new exchange rate structure was made by Karl Schiller, who described it as "a fragile building, a fragile work of art." However, he took quiet pride in the success of his efforts to overcome French objections to the third allocation of Special Drawing Rights, the SDR 3 billion scheduled for issue on January 1, 1972. It would occur as planned.

Lest anyone forget those traumatic last 5 months of 1971, on December 21 Valéry Giscard reassured the French people that:

Gold must keep a central role in the renewed international monetary system. The effort instantly to demonetize gold that accompanied the American decisions in August has failed. The critical phase of the monetary crisis was resolved in the way that conformed to our wishes.

And the following evening, December 22, President Georges Pompidou addressed his nation on television. With sardonic humor, he warned the United States that the Smithsonian Agreement was only "a first step" and that no new international monetary system could be built until the United States had kept its "moral engagements" to end its balance-of-payments deficits "through its own efforts, and not simply by the mechanical effects of devaluation." His self-righteous taunts were skillfully calculated to anger Americans and to delight French Gaullists. Pompidou emphasized that:

> No national currency, in my eyes, can have a sort of general privilege. . . . Europe has proved its strength, in America's realization that it could not act alone indefinitely and that it is necessary to act with Europe. . . . So far as I am concerned, I find a certain number of satisfactions in the Washington agreements. In a world where everyone was talking only about the merits of floating currencies, we have returned to fixed parities, which is the French theory. Moreover, those parities have been fixed in terms of gold, and you know that there too we have always defended the role of gold and in particular its role as the monetary standard.

The next day a triumphant *Le Monde* proclaimed him "A President Without Worries."

Pompidou was incurably ill, of the rare Kahler's disease. Though he certainly could not confide that fear to his own ministers, at last he was confident that he had become the worthy successor of Charles de Gaulle. Could the rest of the world afford that kind of French leadership? Clearly the United States could not.

11 = Hiatus December 1971–March 1973

Only in history books can one end an era and begin the next with the crisp precision used to turn a page. In any time of transition, reality is so untidy that few can see its dominant trends. As the year 1972 opened, the non-Communist world remained on an inconvertible paper dollar standard, regardless of the loud, sustained protests against it. Dollars held abroad could be used only to buy goods and services in the United States. At the British Treasury and the International Monetary Fund, experts toiled to draft plans for a Special Drawing Rights system in which they alone professed confidence. And in Western Europe's free gold markets, speculators were pushing the price beyond $45 per ounce in the belief that gold would prevail if the Franco–American dispute on convertibility should continue. The prospects for peaceful coexistence among dollars, SDRs and gold appeared dim.

AFTERMATH

Accepting *le défi français*, Secretary John Connally won widespread popularity throughout the United States by repeated speeches urging the formation of a "dollar bloc," to include Canada, Australia, New Zealand, South America and possibly Spain, that could compete forcefully with the preferential trading area the European Economic Community had been forming. He did so with the tacit approval of President Nixon. In private Connally made no effort to conceal his bitterness about the unified positions the European Economic Community had taken in the negotiations of the Group of Ten, and

301

his determination never again to have to face that situation. Loyally echoing his Secretary, whose scorn for New York's banking community was resented there, Paul Volcker announced that he had attended his last meeting of the Group of Ten. Mexico and Indonesia were asked if they would be interested in joining a new and expanded monetary "club."

Connally and Volcker voiced the growing anger against West European and Japanese greed that had become prevalent among American businessmen, labor leaders and farmers, whose traditional generosity and tolerance were badly frayed. President Nixon, Secretary Rogers, Henry Kissinger and Arthur Burns found it expedient to use more conciliatory words, but their meaning was plain. In Nixon's annual foreign policy message to Congress, presented February 9, he declared that: "There is only one constructive solution—to face up to the political necessity of accommodating conflicting economic interests." That day he therefore proposed to Congress a formal revaluation of gold, to $38 per ounce, and the responsible committees in the Senate and the House began their deliberations. However, Nixon pointedly omitted any reference to resumption of the dollar's convertibility into gold, and he made it quite clear that he was asking for an increase in the official price only because President Pompidou had been insistent upon it.

> The failure of one nation to participate [in the Smithsonian Agreement] would have made it difficult for others to agree to significant revaluation vis-à-vis the dollar. The participation of France, in particular, was important because of the significance certain other countries attached to the exchange rate between their currencies and the franc. We recognized France's strong interest in its competitive position in Europe and in maintaining the gold parity of the franc at the level established in 1969.

The American payments deficit for 1971 had established a new record, of a doubtful kind. On the official settlements account it had tripled, to $29.75 billion. Foreign official dollar holdings had risen from $23.77 billion at the end of 1970 to $50.64 billion at the end of 1971. By contrast the national reserves of the United States had been reduced to $13.19 billion at the end of 1971, including the $1.15 billion net gain anticipated from the revaluation of its gold stocks. American trade accounts, which had shown a still healthy surplus of $2.176 billion in 1970, had fallen into a net deficit of $2.698 billion in 1971, for the first time since 1888.

Experts of the Group of Ten, the European Economic Community, the International Monetary Fund and the Organization for Economic Cooperation and Development had mistakenly assumed that most of the estimated $25 billion to $30 billion converted into other currencies during the crisis of 1971 would return to dollars and the United States after the Smithsonian Agreement, as speculators realized their estimated profits of $2.5 billion to $3 billion. That did not happen. No more than $2 billion returned. In the principal money markets of the world, private bankers and exchange dealers had lost confidence in the collective judgment of the Group of Ten's finance ministers and central bankers. The small devaluation of the dollar and the realignment of other currencies' parities, which had been agreed at the Smithsonian Institution after so many months of bitter haggling, were immediately adjudged inadequate to correct the deficits in American payments accounts.[1] Speculators therefore retained and even increased their positions in West German marks, Swiss francs and Japanese yen, in the expectation that they would soon be revalued again. Throughout January and early February, the money markets remained disturbed, troubled by conflicting rumors. Almost everywhere, the dollar fell to its new floor rates.

Unhappy to be caught in their own self-serving miscalculations, Western Europe's central bankers again sought to blame the United States, insisting not only that it resume limited convertibility but also that it raise domestic interest rates and tighten credit policies to halt the continuing flight from the dollar. Ignoring the warnings of Karl Schiller, the West German Federal Bank allied itself with the victorious Bank of France. On February 9 Otmar Emminger protested against the American "refusal to co-operate." He charged that the United States was "unjustifiably" and "unwarrantedly" hampering the operations of the International Monetary Fund. "We do not see that it is always three or four other countries that have to do something in order to keep the Fund going, and the United States just keeps aloof and does nothing."

Perhaps Emminger had not grasped that at that time many Americans would have been happy to see the Fund go to blazes. Generations of historians yet unborn will argue the merits of an American resignation from the Fund, and continued floating of the dollar, as preferable to the Smithsonian Agreement of December 18, 1971. The West Germans were fully committed to preservation of the Fund, because it served their purposes. It no longer served those of the United States. Emminger added: "This is something which I find unjustifiably negative. It would really do a lot of good if the United States would now find a way towards its proper contribution." The word *contribution* had become a euphemism for the French demand for more American gold. West European central bankers were distressed by the necessity to absorb still more American dollars, even though Arthur Burns had quietly informed them that they must do so and that the United States was ready to float the dollar again if they did not restore order in their money markets.

A week later, on February 16, Secretary Connally replied in public that

---

[1] For example, see Paul Einzig's *The Destiny of the Dollar,* published in February 1972.

the domestic needs of the American economy would continue to receive the highest priority in the policies of the Nixon administration. Western Europe had no unemployment problems, and the United States did. Therefore "our main problem is to bring down interest rates. There is more to think about than what the international bankers and central bankers of Europe are concerned about." Connally was also worried by the Nixon administration's failure to regain control over the Federal budget.

> We recognize that we live in a family of nations and we are mindful that the outflow of dollars creates problems for other governments. But I told other governments at the time of the Smithsonian Agreement in December that we are not going to make the dollar convertible, and if they were asking for convertibility, we would have to ask for three times the realignment we got. As it is, it will take two years or more for the parity changes to work through. It would be sheer folly to restore convertibility before the United States has achieved a turnaround in its balance-of-payments position. We would be back in the same trap. But we will make a start on restructuring the international monetary system.

In Frankfurt, Zürich, Brussels, Amsterdam and London, the dollar promptly slumped and their embarrassed central bankers were required to support its new rates by buying more. Against the French franc and the Japanese yen, the dollar fell to the lowest levels ever known. President Pompidou immediately made known his determination to maintain the new franc exchange rate established by the Smithsonian Agreement. But in Britain, with the quiet approval of its Tory government, economists began to discuss cheating on that agreement by another devaluation of the pound.

The United States had become the butt of the international monetary system, and every other nation remained intent upon profiting at its expense.

BRITAIN BREAKS THE SMITHSONIAN AGREEMENT

President Nixon was content to let Connally, Volcker and Burns devise an escape from those snares. As before, the war in Southeast Asia fully preoccupied him and excluded all other vital matters both foreign and domestic.

Since 1966 there had been a thorough reversal in Chinese policies. The Cultural Revolution had run its course. The universal revolution against the cities of the world preached by Lin Piao 6 years before had vanished with Lin Piao himself. The Red Guards had purged the Party, then the Army had purged the Red Guards, then the senior generals of the Army had been purged, and finally the old Party cadres had returned to the positions for which they had been found indispensable. Premier Chou En-lai had proved as adept at survival as Chairman Mao himself. When Nixon left China on February 28, he took with him as a souvenir a photo of Premier Chou demonstrating the proper way to use chopsticks. A quarter-century of Sino–American hostility had ended, and only a Republican president could have accomplished that task without facing charges in Congress that he was "soft on Communism." Nixon had assured his Chinese hosts that:

> In the absence of a negotiated settlement [in Vietnam] the United States envisages the ultimate withdrawal of all United States forces from the region consistent with the aim of self-determination for each country of Indo-China.

That signaled the beginning of the end for the discredited though still independent government of South Vietnam. With the Soviet Union in mind the Chinese had emphasized that

> All nations, big or small, should be equal; big nations should not bully the small and strong nations should not bully the weak. China will never be a superpower and it opposes hegemony and power politics of any kind.

In Moscow American diplomats were immediately asked by suspicious Russians for reassurance that Mao Tse-tung and Richard Nixon had not formed some secret, diabolical plot against the Soviet Union. *Komsomolskaya Pravda* sourly commented that: "The attempts at a deal with Washington were a predictable product of Chinese anti-Sovietism."

Meanwhile, in Paris, President Pompidou was being embarrassed by a seemingly endless succession of financial scandals among Gaullists. They reached into his own offices. One senior aide, Jacques Chirac, had bought a château that had then been classified an historic monument, so that he could deduct the costs of restoration from his taxable income. The Prime Minister himself, Jacques Chaban-Delmas, had not been paying any taxes at all. His deductions had been quite legal, but their exposure jeopardized his political future. Only Valéry Giscard, whose Finance Ministry housed the prying tax inspectors, remained aloof from those scandals. To their chagrin, the large Gaullist majority in the National Assembly suddenly became aware that they needed the support of Giscard's Independent Republicans. In London, Prime Minister Heath had just survived the first round of another kind of trouble. British coal miners were beginning to demonstrate the power of their trade union to break any government, and their scorn for the bluster of politicians. As usual the soft, futile center of modern Britain had urged abject surrender to the pay demands of the miners. British wage inflation entered a phase of critical excess.

Regardless of those domestic disorders, Pompidou and Heath were determined to forge an enlarged European Economic Community that could challenge the economic strength of the United States, even though it would remain dependent on American protection against the Soviet Union. That contradiction did not disturb them. In return for their support in the American presidential election campaign of 1972, Nixon had again guaranteed that all American forces stationed in Europe would remain there. When Pompidou and Heath met at Chequers on March 18, both assumed that monetary policy would therefore be the most promising area for an advance in West European unification, even though Pompidou insisted on a monetary system based on gold and Heath was toying with schemes for an extension of Special Drawing Rights. Pompidou could no longer ignore them, and Heath conceded that: "Gold must also play an important role in any future international system." With the concurrence of Chancellor Brandt, they agreed to hold a "summit" conference of the European Community in October. Yet that new Franco–British amity was not flawless. When the French unveiled their designs for the formation of a European political secretariat, whose capital would be Paris rather than Brussels, the British began to feel somewhat queasy. Once again, French ambitions had become only too clear.

Nor had the staff of the International Monetary Fund been idle. Later Congressman Reuss would comment: "Nothing concentrates a monetary expert's mind better than the knowledge that he is expected to produce something." Smarting from the criticism by Secretary Connally, on January 24 Pierre-Paul Schweitzer had proposed in some detail a plan for the formation of a ministerial group of twenty who would represent all 120 members of the Fund. It simply involved replacing the existing Executive Directors of the Fund with the finance ministers to whom they were responsible in their respective capitals. Five of those Executive Directors represented one major country each—the United States, Canada, Britain, France and West Germany. Others represented a group of countries, such as the Netherlands–Austria–Jugoslavia–Israel grouping. Still others represented a large number of small countries, such as the Executive Director responsible for eighteen of the former French colonies in Africa.

Dozens of staff papers had culminated in the appearance on March 7 of a basic document entitled "Reform of the International Monetary System—A Sketch of Its Scope and Content." The basic questions of monetary reform had been defined as: (1) how to bring about prompter changes in exchange rates; (2) how to consolidate outstanding dollar and sterling balances into Special Drawing Rights; (3) how to finance balance-of-payments deficits and surpluses of reserve countries; (4) how to attain "symmetrical" multicurrency intervention; (5) how to make Special Drawing Rights rather than gold the standard in which par values were to be expressed; (6) how to provide an attractive rate of interest for Special Drawing Rights; and (7) how to make the international monetary system better serve the needs of developing countries. Discussions had begun among the Executive Directors, even though the essential obstacle to the "symmetrical" monetary system many experts envisioned was not widely understood. It would have required the withdrawal of

American armed forces not only from Vietnam but also from South Korea, Japan and Western Europe. Otherwise the United States could not have agreed to the implied constraints on its defense spending abroad. Nevertheless Congressman Reuss commented on March 22 that:

> Negotiations must start somewhere, and the "Sketch" is a good place to start. . . . If the broader questions of international monetary reform are pursued with the same zeal that attended the pursuit of the realignment last December, there should be no difficulty in accomplishing what is needed in the six months between now and the September meeting of the Fund.

Nixon and Kissinger were on the run, trying to get ahead of Reuss and other domestic critics. A new North Vietnamese invasion of South Vietnam that began March 30 demonstrated conclusively that Hanoi was still more interested in a military solution. It also threatened to disrupt President Nixon's plans to visit the Soviet Union. Henry Kissinger therefore flew to Moscow and informed Leonid Brezhnev on April 20 that the United States would accept a ceasefire *in situ*. That major concession enabled North Vietnam to occupy South Vietnamese territory and to maintain troops there by right, which the government in Saigon had refused since 1954 to permit. The delighted Brezhnev immediately told the North Vietnamese that, so far as the United States was concerned, they had virtually won the war. American forces in South Vietnam had been gradually reduced to 69,000 men, and at last there were hopes for the stability of the neighboring governments in Thailand, Malaysia, Singapore and Indonesia.

The long, costly efforts of the United States to reconstruct Southeast Asia after the devastation of the Second World War were nearing a bitter and violent end. The direct, immediate costs to the United States of the preceding decade of futile involvement in those internecine Vietnamese squabbles would total 56,000 dead and $140.6 billion. Nixon felt obliged to retaliate against North Vietnam's renewal of hostilities, and on May 8 the bombing and mining of its harbors were resumed. Soviet reactions were mild, and he arrived in Moscow on May 20, to be greeted by the scheduled fanfare. The first visit to Moscow by an American president was regarded as an extraordinary event, and the Russians welcomed him with suitable acclaim. Nine days later, during a farewell gala in the white marble splendor of the Kremlin's St. George's Hall, more than a thousand guests listened to an orchestra play "The Star-Spangled Banner" as Nixon and Brezhnev entered discussing proposed joint ventures in space.

That first meeting of Nixon and Brezhnev had produced formal signatures for a declaration of principles to guide Russo–American relations, and six specific agreements. In addition to the space program planned for 1975, they included: pacts to limit strategic thermo-nuclear weapons; cooperation on health, environmental protection, science and technology; and rules for the safe conduct of navies at sea, to prevent incidents. There was also a new, mutual interest in improving economic relations, because the trade deficit of the United States had been a staggering $2.2 billion for the first 4 months of 1972. Diehard Republican bankers from New York promptly forgot their anti-Bolshevik traditions and followed Nixon to Moscow.

In the free markets of Western Europe, the price of gold was pushed beyond $58 per ounce by speculators eager to believe a rumor that Nixon and Brezhnev had concluded some kind of a secret deal for the marketing of Russian gold. In Paris, Paul Volcker did not discourage that rising price by his loud remark that a second devaluation of the dollar might be needed. The first had not even dented the continuing growth of world trade, and European prophets of doom had been exposed as the fools and charlatans they were. From 1971 to 1972, world trade rose 19 percent. In terms of constant exchange rates, it rose 12 percent to an annual $414.7 billion in 1972. The predictable effect of the sudden doubling and tripling of West European and Japanese national reserves had been to release a wave of speculation and consumer buying that was pushing world commodity prices to new extremes. Buoyed by that false prosperity, not only West Europeans and Japanese but also commodity-producing countries everywhere were enjoying a brief spell of euphoria and overconfidence.

In London, the Labour Party's "shadow" Chancellor of the Exchequer seems to have had unusually good sources of information. By May 28 Denis Healey had perceived that:

> if as is likely the Moscow summit opens a period in which the East–West conflict ceases to dominate world affairs and military problems assume less importance, the real priority for the European and the Western world as a whole must be the construction of a more efficient system for their trade and payments. No one now believes the Smithsonian Agreement was more than a stop-gap. The trend towards protectionism in the major trading groups is scarcely halted. Partly because of the American election, partly because of the European Community's difficulty in reaching a collective position except by surrender to France, there is now little hope of real movement before 1973. A year will have been wasted.

In Ottawa, at a banking conference the week before, Arthur Burns had outlined the first American proposals for a new international monetary system, amid high hopes that substantial progress could soon be made. His principal points had been that: as part of a complete reform, the dollar's convertibility into gold could be restored, as the French continued to demand; the role of gold should diminish, and it should gradually be replaced by Special Drawing Rights; both debtor and creditor nations should be compelled to reduce their deficits and surpluses; and parallel negotiations should lower foreign barriers to American exports. Yet the French had quickly disclosed their unwillingness to concede anything further.

An annual meeting of the Organization for Economic Cooperation and Development, held at the Château la Muette in Paris while President Nixon was still in Moscow, had concluded May 26 without any agreement whatever on linking monetary and trade negotiations. Valéry Giscard had announced that there had been "no progress on the principles" of monetary and trade reforms, and France had even had reservations on the procedures the International Monetary Fund had proposed to begin those discussions. Giscard had commented: "France will make amendments. I am opposed to too formal or. paralyzing a forum for negotiations."

In an unbroken succession since 1914, ten American presidents had lost angry battles with the French about money. That tradition would continue. John Connally therefore announced his resignation as Secretary of the Treasury, confident that he had played his part and could do no more. Most of his income was drawn from a ranch, and his wife had explained: "Every so often we have to go home to refill the well." His brief, dramatic career "as a bullyboy on the manicured playing fields of international finance" was heartily applauded by many Americans, including some who had never before had any use for Texans. The Republican Minority Leader in the House of Representatives, Gerald Ford, congratulated him on "a fine job." Congress had completed and approved the legislation devaluing the dollar to $38 per ounce of gold on March 21 without a murmur of opposition. In Europe, however, the sighs of relief were audible. At the Royal Institute of International Affairs in London, the mere mention of Connally's name aroused instantaneous hostility in a ladylike economist whose strange complaint was: "He leads with his chin."

Connally was succeeded at the Treasury by the deceptively mild-mannered George Shultz, whose talents were better suited to the genteel sparring ahead. A protégé of Milton Friedman at the University of Chicago, Shultz had been a conservative, academic economist who had specialized in labor relations. Though he had had no previous experience in international monetary affairs, he had a sure grasp of the theories that had disguised French interests. He had also had hard experience with American fiscal difficulties, as Director of the Office of Management and Budget. Upon taking office, with a sincerity rare in Washington, Shultz commented: "Big John Connally has put on an extraordinary performance. . . . There will be a changing of the guard but no change of the rules here." Western Europe had been alive with rumors that the appointment of Shultz meant a doubling or tripling of the official price of gold. Shultz added: "In the world monetary system, I am quite sure hard bargaining will be necessary." Democratic Congressmen were not reassured. The Chairman of the Senate Finance Committee grumbled: "We would prefer Secretary Connally to anyone, including Mr. Shultz."

Thereafter, so far as the Democratic majority in Congress were concerned, the Nixon administration could no longer do anything right. His trips to Peking and Moscow completed, Nixon had served their purpose and was living on borrowed time. Nonetheless the appointment of the patient Shultz, who had never been active in partisan politics and had always shunned the limelight, signaled to those with eyes to see the determination of the United States to recover the freedom of action France had so long and so triumphantly denied it. Shultz was known to be an advocate of floating exchange rates, who worked closely with Arthur Burns. And Burns had gained the support of both parties and both Houses of Congress.

West Europeans were heedless of such incomprehensible American folkways. The European Economic Community had taken its first, stumbling step toward the formation of a single monetary bloc in a meeting of its finance ministers at Brussels on March 21 with the decision to narrow to 2.25 percent the margin of fluctuations permitted around the fixed exchange rates of their currencies. A "hot line" had been set up among their central banks to coordinate their defenses against the dollar. That forlorn effort was widely heralded as the grand beginning of Europe's glorious future. Olivier Wormser, then Governor of the Bank of France, described it as "a closing of ranks against the United States." The French had also sought acceptance throughout the European Community of their elaborate exchange controls and two-tier currency market, and had found the West German Federal Bank receptive. But Karl Schiller, now in control of both the Economics and the Finance Ministries in Bonn, had remained determined to preserve freedom of capital movements. He had therefore countered by proposing once again that the six nations of the European Community and its new members be prepared for a joint float against the dollar, if that need should ever arise. This time he found the French more sympathetic, because the survival of the Common Agricultural Policy had become an obsession for Pompidou.

Schiller and Giscard publicly "buried the hatchet," but the British were not so enthusiastic. In his Spring Budget, presented that same March 21, Chancellor Barber had alerted speculators to Prime Minister Heath's unwillingness to defend the pound's Smithsonian parity of $2.60.

> I am sure all Members will agree that the lesson of the past few years is that it is not necessary or indeed desirable to distort domestic economies to an unacceptable extent in order to maintain unrealistic exchange rates, whether they are too high or too low.

Barber had been immediately warned by angry Americans that another de-

valuation of the pound against the dollar would have been considered an
unfriendly act, and by the French that Britain's policies must conform to
those of the European Community if it sincerely desired admittance. During
a 2-day conference of the Community's finance ministers in Rome, Barber
therefore agreed on April 24, the day their new monetary scheme became
effective, that Britain would join May 1. And it did, though not for long.

There is one point, and perhaps only one, on which Americans and French
have always been able to reach accord. It is almost impossible to hold *perfide
Albion* to its most solemn engagements. The British are masters of the art of
evading their international responsibilities and invariably leave the table before the waiter presents the bill. On June 9, during a luncheon at the Élysée
Palace, President Pompidou therefore warned them that he expected their
obedience in the preparations for the European Community's summit meeting in October.

> I will not, so far as I am concerned, take the responsibility of inviting nine heads
> of government, if their meeting should lead only to vague declarations of intent,
> to agreement on minor issues, or worse still to ill-camouflaged divergences.

Yet they promptly ignored him. The Bank of England's reserves had risen to
the highest level ever recorded, having exceeded $7 billion on April 1.
Thanks to the continuing flight from the dollar, Britain's payments accounts
were continuing to record fat surpluses. But so many of the British (of whom
Denis Healey was only one) had become intent on "talking down the pound"
to gain export advantages that a flurry of speculation against it began on
June 15. Rather than risk losing that unearned $7 billion, by June 23 the
tricky Edward Heath had decided to float the pound "temporarily." European monetary unity was broken permanently, and French protests were shrill.

In Bonn, Karl Schiller purred satisfaction.

> The Federal Government understands the temporary floating of the pound. It
> regards the course taken by the British currency authorities in the face of the
> latest movements of the pound as appropriate. The Federal Government wel-
> comes the fact that Great Britain has reacted speedily to the changed circum-
> stances in the currency market.

True-blue Tories had committed the heresy of floating, and they devised the
most elaborate justifications for that decision. Floating began to become the
new orthodoxy.

STALEMATE

On June 17 there had been "a third-rate burglary attempt" at the Democratic National Headquarters in Washington's Watergate Office Building.
For the next 2 years and more, it would serve as the focal point for the

constitutional struggle between President Nixon and the Democratic majority in Congress that would gradually paralyze the diplomacy of the United States. It would also insert another cause of strain in relations between the United States and a self-righteous Western Europe. However, a few Europeans had begun to recognize that in President Pompidou they too had a problem.

Pompidou had been threatening to cancel the European Community's scheduled summit conference in October if the other heads of government would not accept his precondition that the Community's proposed political secretariat be located in Paris, under his personal thumb. That was the last straw, so far as they were concerned. They were not willing to endure another Napoleonic president of France. But all feared to dispute openly with Pompidou, because he was a chief of state jealous of his prerogatives, and they were mere premiers, prime ministers and chancellors. The doughty Queen Juliana of the Netherlands had no qualms of that kind. She reassured her own prime minister that she was quite willing and able to cope with Georges Pompidou.

During a state visit to Paris, Queen Juliana's rebuffs were public and forceful. At the embassy of the Netherlands, during her reception for French ministers, the Dutch foreign minister bluntly told Maurice Schumann that: "It would not be a disaster if the summit were postponed." And at the Palace of Versailles, exchanging toasts after a state dinner on the evening of June 19, Queen Juliana simply repudiated Pompidou's assertion of Europe's independence by calling for an extension of democratic control over the Community's executive bodies and improved cooperation with the United States. The following day, addressing students at the University of Strasbourg, she repeated that:

> The strategy of conflicts has given way in the greater part of our Continent to the strategy of co-operation. . . . European co-operation was born in suffering— and without the help of the United States, Europe would perhaps never have risen from the ashes. . . . It is neither possible nor desirable to build European unity except in the context of a larger co-operation with the United States. . . . Let us not forget that we must move forward—that co-operation and unity are not ends in themselves. They are means which must enable us to assume our responsibilities both towards our nations and towards the world community.

Behind her in Paris, she left a baffled Georges Pompidou spluttering to his Council of Ministers "Europe must be European!" The other nations of the European Community did not dispute that sentiment. They simply refused French leadership, and the French definition of European purpose.

Unlike the French, Queen Juliana could not believe that the dollar represented any real threat to Europe. Nor had she been impressed by the elaborate French schemes for a European monetary fund to combat the dollar.

Her visit to Paris had immediate, practical effects. On June 20, at the International Monetary Fund in Washington, the French Executive Director announced that he would abstain from voting on the mandate for the formation of a Committee of Twenty, the new forum that would replace the Group of Ten for the negotiation of reforms in the international monetary system. That ended one deadlock between France and the United States, in which the French had insisted that the Committee of Twenty should be restricted to consideration of monetary problems. The resolution acceptable to the remaining nineteen Executive Directors, including the United States, had included a passage that instructed the Committee of Twenty to give full attention to the interrelationships among monetary, trade and investment issues. The French had foreseen quite clearly that in the Committee of Twenty not only their own weight but also the power of the European Community would be drastically weakened. Moreover, Switzerland would not be represented at all. The gold interests of Western Europe and South Africa could be decisively outvoted.

The resolution proposed that the Committee of Twenty meet at three levels: (1) at the top, Governors' meetings would consist of one minister and two assistants in each delegation; (2) at the level of deputies each delegation would have two representatives, one from the finance ministry and one from the central bank; (3) at the third level, the Executive Directors of the Fund would be in permanent session in Washington. With France abstaining, the Fund then sent that resolution to member nations for their postal votes. Two days later, testifying before the House Banking and Finance Committee, Paul Volcker announced that the United States was ready to move ahead on monetary reform "as rapidly as other nations will move . . . but it would be criminal to accept an unsatisfactory agreement for the sake of a prompt agreement." He cautioned Congressmen, and the many anxious spectators unnerved by the incessant monetary crises since 1967, that: "The broad outline of international monetary reforms could be worked out within two years, but it might take longer than that to reach agreement on all details." The United States no longer dominated world affairs as it had at Bretton Woods in July of 1944.

With John Connally gone, Georges Pompidou briefly squelched and the pound floating, the summer of 1972 became placid for everyone not involved in the vicious American presidential election campaign. Senator George McGovern's call for massive cuts in American forces stationed abroad caused widespread anxiety among West Europeans, who were fearful that they might have to begin paying the full costs of their own defense. In Bonn an official of the West German Defense Ministry complained: "McGovern would be a catastrophe for NATO." Even the Russians wanted Nixon. A Soviet official explained: "We know him and have just dealt with him successfully." An Israeli added: "The simple fact is that we trust Nixon and we do not trust any of the others." Nixon had pledged to continue American economic and military subsidies to Israel.

When President Pompidou and Chancellor Brandt met in Bonn on July 3, they also had domestic issues to consider. The proposal to establish a European political secretariat was shelved, because there had not been agreement on its site. And Pompidou remained adamant that the European summit in October could take place only if it concentrated on questions of monetary and economic union. "We must first be united on the monetary issue," he told Brandt. Not until the European Community had created a common currency would he consider granting it increased powers and initiating common political efforts among its members. Nor could Brandt persuade him that the monetary policies of the European Community should be formed in cooperation with the United States, rather than in opposition to it. Pompidou continued to insist that the dollar's convertibility into gold be restored, and that national reserves consist primarily of gold, in any reformed monetary system. He was opposed to any expansion in the use of SDRs, and the efforts of the West Germans, British and Italians to obtain agreement for at least a token issue of SDRs in 1973 failed then and there.

West Germany had already made another major concession to France by adopting exchange controls. Forced by the continuing flight from the dollar to choose between the floating recommended by Karl Schiller and the controls advocated both by France and by the Federal Bank's Karl Klasen, Brandt's cabinet had decided to support Klasen. West German exporters were so strongly opposed to any further revaluation of the mark that the exhausted, exasperated Schiller found himself a minority of one. He promptly resigned in the most spectacular manner, and was succeeded at the Economics and Finance Ministries by Helmut Schmidt, who had completed his apprenticeship at the Defense Ministry. Though the French were overjoyed to see Schiller depart, the change was more apparent than real. Years before, Schmidt had been one of Schiller's students at the University of Hamburg. Like many another before and since, he had always enjoyed baiting the professor.

Encouraged by President Pompidou's consistent defense of gold's monetary role, speculators pushed the free-market price to $68 per ounce in July. As that price rose, industrial use of gold began to decline, but the South African Reserve Bank was skillfully regulating the quantities it released to the free markets to support that rising price. There were no signs of recovery in the Federal budget of the United States, or in its foreign trade and payments accounts. The Federal budget deficit for Fiscal Year 1972 had been $23 billion, and a deficit of at least $27 billion was forecast for Fiscal Year 1973. For the first half of calendar year 1972, the American trade deficit had been

$3.34 billion, and the payments deficit had been $4.5 billion on the official settlements account.

Whenever officials publicly discussed the possibility of a second devaluation of the dollar, rumors swept through Western Europe's gold markets that the official price would be doubled or tripled. And in private talks with President Giovanni Leone and Premier Giulio Andreotti of Italy, at the Villa Torrigiani near Lucca, Georges Pompidou sought Italian support for "a realistic revaluation" of monetary gold at the free-market price, so that the central banks of the European Community could resume using it for settlements among themselves. But the Italians were debtors. They did not intend to relinquish any of their gold reserves. Instead they maneuvered until at last they gained agreement that they could settle their obligations in inconvertible dollars. The West Germans also rejected that French scheme for an official revaluation of gold within the European Community. West German reserves had risen to an extraordinary, embarrassing DM 75.4 billion ($24 billion), and its leaders were slowly awakening to their new role—that of Europe's rich uncle, whom Americans would expect to pay all of its bills.

In 2 days of talks at Lancaster House in London, beginning July 17, the finance ministers of the European Community had begun to seek a common position on monetary reform. Nine different voices with historically divergent attitudes on so many of the key issues could not be expected to prepare a detailed agreement. Nor had they any desire for another pitched battle with the Nixon administration during an American election campaign. What they therefore achieved was a public statement of eight general objectives that appeared to express a new willingness to compromise in negotiations with the United States. Later Valéry Giscard would comment:

> There has been a fundamental conflict starting ten years ago over our respective interpretations of the U.S. argument that the dollar was as good as gold. That conflict has been resolved since August 1971. . . . We could have dug our heels in during July's London conference on monetary reform. We did not, and French moderation was recognized by all concerned. . . . Under a new system, central banks should only accumulate gold and Special Drawing Rights and keep working balances in different national currencies. The international community will then agree to settle debts only by selling internationally accepted assets and not by accumulating unwanted dollars as it is presently doing. The key question then is what happens to present dollar balances. We could consolidate them under one roof, and then gradually reduce them as new SDRs are issued.

Though Giscard spoke in a newly moderate tone of voice, the future monetary system in his mind's eye remained one that would have put an end to American spending abroad for the defense of Western Europe, and it assumed precisely those large, consistent surpluses in American payments accounts that France had so stubbornly refused to permit. Yet Giscard and his officials remained oddly untroubled by the inconsistencies in their arguments. They preferred to ponder not the real world around them but rather an "intellectually pure" and rational world of their own invention that would dignify the enrichment of French owners of gold. Moreover they had persuaded themselves that France had become invulnerable to the economic difficulties they had so long foisted on others by maintaining an undervalued franc. Someday there would be an awakening, and it would be painful.

Meanwhile their European partners schemed to bypass the French without any public disputes. There had been general agreement at their London conference that Special Drawing Rights should play a more important role in future, both as the primary, "neutral" reserve asset and as the standard or *numéraire* for the expression of parities. Yet fundamental differences of opinion had continued on the valuation of SDRs. Many participants no longer believed that the original definition of an SDR as equal to 0.888671 gram of fine gold had any reality, when the free-market price of gold was in a state of flux. There had been increasing discussion of redefining SDRs, so that each would represent a "cocktail" of the national currencies most used in world trade. The riposte by European advocates of gold had been: "Who wants to drink a paper cocktail?"

Though gold had ceased to serve as a national reserve asset, and it was unreal to use as a monetary standard a commodity whose official price was $38 per ounce while its free-market price was soaring beyond $70, gold remained at the heart of the official disputes between the European Community and the United States on reform of the international monetary system. Moreover central bankers had become reluctant to settle their debts with Special Drawing Rights, whose value was no longer certain. Regardless of the French designs for an international monetary system cleansed of unwanted dollars, and their scorn for a currency that even Americans no longer claimed was "as good as gold," throughout the world everyone continued to use the dollar. There was no practical alternative, and world trade continued to grow, ignoring the dogmas of the French and the niceties of central bankers. Arthur Burns, George Shultz and Paul Volcker were in despair, wondering how to call home all those dollars that had gone abroad. Like bad pennies, they turned up everywhere. They could even be found in the pockets of violently anti-American Viet Cong guerrillas in the jungles of South Vietnam.

Unnoticed by central bankers, an historic revolution had occurred. Many of the world's more primitive peoples had become accustomed to the paper dollar. They had learned to prefer it to the other forms of money readily available to them, because it still bore some prestige and was easily transferable.

STALEMATE PROLONGED

In Washington, on September 25, President Nixon addressed the finance ministers and central bankers assembled for the annual meeting of the International Monetary Fund. His speech was an emotional, conciliatory appeal for complete reform of the monetary system.

> Very little of what is done in these negotiations will be widely understood or generally appreciated. But history will record the vital nature of the challenge before us. . . . We must come to grips with the paradoxes of peace. As the danger of armed conflict between major powers is reduced, the potential for economic conflict is increased. As the possibility of peace grows stronger, some of the original ties that first bound our postwar alliance grow weaker. As nations around the world gain new economic strength, the points of commercial contact multiply along with the possibilities of disagreement. . . . We cannot afford a system that almost every year presents a new invitation to a monetary crisis. That is why we must face the need to develop procedures for prompt and orderly adjustment.

Nixon's audience politely applauded that plea for united action, then proceeded to demonstrate that they were more disunited than ever before. Though the European Community had not been able to agree on a detailed reform plan, the *Annual Report* of the Fund had contained both an historical analysis of the Bretton Woods system and detailed proposals for exchange rate realignments, convertibility, consolidation of dollar and sterling balances, the handling of disruptive capital movements and the needs of poor countries. It had emphasized that the role of the dollar should decrease, because world reserves had grown to $125 billion, of which $75 billion were dollars and sterling. That was excessive. For the first time, the Fund had begun to use the Special Drawing Right rather than the dollar for its numerical statements. At French and Italian insistence, the *Annual Report* had also contained a section that discussed the "option" of increasing the official price of gold, compared with the options of continuing the two-tier markets or selling gold from monetary reserves to force down free-market prices. The French had not been alone in their dissatisfaction. The United States Treasury had also been displeased because the Fund's staff had been emphasizing the resumption of convertibility for the dollar and the consolidation of dollar balances held abroad without suggesting any way to restore large, lasting surpluses in American payments accounts.

During that meeting of the Fund, American resentment against its anti-American biases reached boiling point. George Shultz personally informed Pierre-Paul Schweitzer that the United States would oppose his reelection to a third 5-year term as Managing Director. That angered the French, who promptly informed the press that Schweitzer had been deeply offended. Valéry Giscard countered by opposing the American candidate, Rinaldo Ossola of the Bank of Italy, for the chairmanship of the deputies of the new Committee of Twenty. Instead West Europeans solidly supported Jeremy Morse of the Bank of England. By a narrow margin, they won that one.

After some coaxing, the United States Treasury had prepared a reform plan of its own, with every expectation that it would immediately be attacked in detail. It was. Presented by Shultz on September 26, it conceded dollar convertibility as part of a complete reform of the monetary system, but not convertibility into gold. And Shultz demanded that the United States be granted full control over its own exchange rate. He called for strong disciplinary measures against countries such as France that had chronic payments surpluses yet persistently refused to take any corrective action. Shultz agreed that the Special Drawing Right should increase in importance and that it should become the formal standard of the new monetary system, "freed from the encumbrances of reconstitution obligations, designation procedures, and holding limits which would be unnecessary in a reformed system." However, he added that official holdings of national currencies should be "neither banned nor encouraged," and he reminded the French that "orderly procedures are available to facilitate a diminishing role of gold in international monetary affairs in the future." He meant sales of monetary gold on the free markets.

Shultz did not have to wait long for the French reply. On September 28 Valéry Giscard simply repeated his ritual insistence on an absolute ban against the dollar. He emphasized that neither the dollar nor any other national currency should be used as a reserve asset. Though he agreed that the Special Drawing Right might become the primary asset of the new system, he insisted that it must continue to be valued in terms of gold—"a common value which will not be submitted to national or even group influences." And he refused to consider any measures that might restrict French payments surpluses or restore American payments surpluses. French officials were convinced that in time they could thoroughly discredit the dollar.

Though Shultz and Giscard were now smiling and talking softly, the discord between the United States and France remained profound. It would continue to be the principal division within the Fund. As so often before, only events could compel one or the other to concede. Piecemeal reform, achieved through patience and perseverance, was therefore the best that could be foreseen. Nevertheless, in their anxiety to restore the badly shaken confidence of the public, not only governments but also the Fund's staff were encouraging the belief that a thorough reform of the monetary system could be achieved within the following year.

That was straining public credulity too far. It was becoming apparent to private bankers and foreign-exchange dealers that those official reform efforts had been too ambitious, and they began to lose confidence in the ability of governments to control events. Speculators had been anticipating another revaluation of the yen, because month after month there had been no diminution in Japan's massive trade and payments surpluses. Early in October, dollars began to enter that country at a rate of $50 million per day, more than $1 billion per month. On October 20, the Japanese Finance Ministry at last announced that the "true level" of Japan's dollar reserves now exceeded the astonishing sum of $21 billion. Coyly they admitted that all of their earlier statements had "neglected to mention" some $5 billion they must have been hiding for a rainy day. In London, on October 20, a British Treasury spokesman denounced as "rubbish" French reports that the pound would return to a fixed parity by the end of the European Community's summit meeting, convened in Paris by President Pompidou the day before. Though no longer able to guide monetary events, many finance ministers and central bankers had been relearning the opportunistic art of riding them.

In the melancholy splendor of a Parisian autumn, Georges Pompidou was enjoying his last hour of glory, before the European Community began to enter a long, lasting winter of discontent. Assembled around a huge, 60-foot table in the conference room of the Hotel Majestic, nine West European heads of government formally agreed to his proposals for the creation of a European monetary fund, whose operations should begin in April 1973 with 1.4 billion units of account jointly subscribed. The central banks of its nine members were also called upon to pool their reserves, regardless of the noticeable reluctance of West Germany to share its new wealth with its newly affectionate partners. Pompidou's satisfaction would have been complete, if only those obstinate Dutch had not struck a discordant note. French *dirigisme* was anathema to the cautious burghers of the Netherlands.

Prime Minister Biesheuvel threatened to block any further progress toward monetary union unless decisions were submitted to effective parliamentary control. He added:

> Life is not lived at the summit, but at the level of daily cares. If the impulse is not understood at the base, if we do not succeed in making the idea of Europe alive for our peoples and inspire younger generations, then we shall head for failure despite our apparent successes.

With distaste, Pompidou was obliged to concede that there might possibly be something more in the European Community than money for French farmers. He replied that efforts could also be made to achieve political union by the end of the 1970s, even though: "It is not natural to try to unite men and states whose entire past and interests often diverged. But there is no other way for our countries." There is another way, though the retrogressive Pompidou did not mention it. That is the road to disintegration he himself was following.

In times of transition, pretense too often becomes the dominant preoccupa-

tion of governments. Appearances seem more important than inglorious realities to those who occupy the seats of power yet lack the wisdom and the skills
to use it well. On November 7, President Nixon was reelected by an overwhelming majority. He chose to interpret that victory as a mandate to do
anything he pleased and to defy Congress, even though American voters had
decisively rejected his party by reelecting Democratic majorities in both
Houses. The Dow Jones average would soar to a high of 1061 in January, as
his Wall Street supporters celebrated that ephemeral triumph. Both Nixon
and Kissinger had prematurely promised "peace with honor" in Vietnam,
ignoring the experts who had warned that lasting peace was improbable
unless one side could conquer the other. Casually Kissinger announced that
1973 would be "the year of Europe." In the third quarter of 1972, the payments accounts of the United States had mocked Nixon's Smithsonian Agreement by recording a massive deficit of $4.7 billion.

Inflation had become a worldwide scourge. Yet in Britain, whose annual
inflation rate of 7.5 percent was now Europe's worst, Prime Minister Heath
had done nothing until November. Though London's property and commodities speculators had become a national scandal, they voted Tory. When at
last a 90-day freeze on wages and prices was tried, it merely encouraged the
British to invent "adjustments" to evade those controls. Newly rich British
trade union members had more money in their pockets than ever before, and
they spent it like water. Other Europeans regarded Britain as a fine market
for their own exports but refused to invest in its obsolescing, unprofitable and
strike-ridden industries.

In Washington, on November 12, the deferential Jeremy Morse convened
the first meeting of the deputies of the new Committee of Twenty, only to
find that the world's poorest nations had also devised a scheme "to get rich
quick." Lured by many British proponents of Special Drawing Rights, who
had become paid, professional spokesmen for the poor, they believed that
new form of international money could and should be used for their immediate industrialization, so that every one of their workers could enjoy benefits
equal to those Europeans and Americans had gained after several centuries of
toil. No one could have been more self-righteous than the representatives
from some of the most deservedly impoverished countries this world has ever
known. They threatened to stall—and would stall—further reform of the
international monetary system unless richer nations would concede a "link"
between creation of Special Drawing Rights and development aid for them.
To be precise, of the proposed next issue of SDR 6 billion, they demanded
half. There have been no further issues of SDRs.

History does not wait upon the whims of weak, indecisive leaders. By the
end of 1972, the money markets had concluded that the Committee of Twenty would fail. Preliminary estimates of the American trade and payments

deficits for that year indicated that they would exceed the most pessimistic forecasts made a year earlier. When the deputies of the Committee of Twenty reassembled in Paris, on January 23, 1973, their agenda called for discussion of the dollar's convertibility and the constitution of national reserves, the standard or *numéraire* of the new world monetary system, the role of gold and the consolidation of dollar balances held abroad. As so often before, the French presented a paper demanding that the new system be based on gold, at a much higher official price. Paul Volcker denounced it as "ridiculous." With cautious support from Belgium, West Germany and Italy, the British proposed for the first time that the link between Special Drawing Rights and gold be severed, and that the SDR be redefined in terms of currencies alone. But that evening a laughing Paul Volcker announced: "The international monetary system was not revolutionized here today."

It was being revolutionized elsewhere. Official announcement earlier in the day that the American trade deficit for 1972 had tripled, to $6.912 billion, had renewed the flight from the dollar. Signature of the Vietnam peace treaty in Paris that afternoon had had no effect. Swiftly and without hesitation, the Swiss National Bank had done the unthinkable. It had permitted the sacrosanct Swiss franc to float, even though it refused to use that nasty, forbidden word *floating*. Steadfastly the Swiss government insisted that it was only "a temporary measure." Its dollar reserves had risen to $2.870 billion. Its ancient policy of maintaining national reserves in gold alone had been disintegrating, as it began to adapt to a world in which gold could no longer be used as money, and the Swiss franc would not have a fixed, certain value. Not a member of the International Monetary Fund, Switzerland had not been a recipient of Special Drawing Rights. Dollars were the only possible resort, because the Swiss had consistently refused to permit their franc to be used as a reserve currency.

Thus one citadel of golden orthodoxy fell. That was indeed a revolution.

COLLAPSE

By February 1, 1973, the dollar had fallen to its floor rates against most major currencies except the French franc and the Italian lira. The central banks of Western Europe and Japan were buying dollars at the rate of a billion per day to defend their Smithsonian parities. Exchange controls had become ineffectual. That day the West German Federal Bank alone bought $350 million. During the week that followed, it was forced to buy $6 billion.

On February 9 Helmut Schmidt and Anthony Barber hastily flew into Paris to discuss with Valéry Giscard "a joint European solution" to the renewed crisis in the Smithsonian regime of fixed exchange rates. Stubbornly both the West Germans and the French had refused either to revalue or to float their currencies, regardless of American warnings that the United States would take unilateral action if they could not agree. In Washington, spokesmen began to threaten the imposition of another imports surcharge. In Paris, the French press accused the United States of deliberately inciting that renewed flight from the dollar, to destroy the European Community's new monetary solidarity. Revaluation or floating of the French franc were denounced by *Le Monde* as "capitulation to the United States."

The situation was so painfully reminiscent of the acrid disputes in the autumn of 1971 that this time cooler heads prevailed. Pompidou was no longer willing to challenge a bellicose American president who had just been reelected and was not distracted by a war in Southeast Asia. Nor were Nixon and Shultz willing to waste months on futile slanging matches. On February 6 they had therefore quietly dispatched Paul Volcker on a circumnavigation of the globe. First Volcker had flown to Tokyo for a midnight talk with Kiichi Aichi, the surprised Japanese Finance Minister. Then he went to Bonn, by way of the North Pole. After brief flights to London and Rome, Volcker joined Schmidt, Barber and Italy's Giovanni Malagodi in Paris, at Valéry Giscard's town house in the fashionable 16th *arrondissement*. By early Tuesday morning (Monday evening in Washington), February 13, a new agreement had been reached.

This time the chastened President Nixon did not announce that it represented a remarkable event in the history of human achievement. Instead George Shultz briefly emerged from a dinner party, just long enough to tell the press that the dollar would be devalued a second time—by a full 10 percent, to a new gold parity of $42.22 per ounce. To fulfill one of Nixon's campaign pledges, he also announced that all controls on American capital exports would be removed as soon as possible. Japan and Italy had agreed to float the yen and the lira. Premier Kakuei Tanaka informed the Japanese Diet that Nixon alone should be blamed for the loss of Japan's export advantage. "The United States itself decided upon the ten percent devaluation, and other nations had to take appropriate measures." In Paris, however, the French claimed that they had single-handedly forced devaluation upon the United States. Describing that specious victory, Valéry Giscard explained:

> The United States offered Europeans two choices, between a joint float of Common Market currencies or a unilateral devaluation of the dollar. It was impossible to accept the former. The crisis was of America's own making.

Giscard's memory and perception have often been faulty.

Fixed exchange rates had become the cause of chronic monetary instability and bitter political disputes. The benefits they conferred simply did not justify those heavy costs. Though French hearts had been gladdened by double devaluation of "the almighty dollar" within 14 months, the excessive effort and confusion had convinced disinterested observers that the Bretton Woods system of fixed exchange rates had been fatally flawed from the very beginning. It had established an overvalued dollar, with no provision for swift, timely devaluation. Two devaluations had only depreciated the dollar approximately 15.5 percent against the currencies of all members of the Organization for Economic Cooperation and Development, 23 percent if Canada was excluded. European money markets remained turbulent. The Eurodollar markets alone had risen to $80 billion, and immense sums were available for speculation against fixed parities. The free-market price of gold, reflecting those disorders, soared to a new high of $90 per ounce on February 22, before closing at $87.

That day there had been serious debate in the British House of Commons, and Chancellor Barber had announced that the European Community would begin "a substantial study" on the collective float of its currencies. In reply Denis Healey had criticized the "complacency" of Heath and Barber, and the profits speculators had gained in that most recent crisis. They had been estimated at $600 million on the West German mark alone. Healey had added: "The advantages of floating prove to be very real." Across the water, in Washington, Paul Volcker could be heard cheering on those European studies of the joint float that Giscard had so recently described as "impossible."

The gold interests still had a few, last-ditch defenders. Jacques Rueff had just visited London, to make another forlorn plea for a return to the classical gold standard. In the House of Lords, the Tory Lord Boothby spurned both the dollar and the Special Drawing Right and insisted that they were "no substitutes for gold." Like so many others, he had failed to grasp that the cause of those recurrent crises had never been the forms of money now in use but rather the exchange rates among currencies and the competitive advantages to be gained or lost whenever those rates were changed. With the dollar and all other paper currencies no longer convertible into gold, gold parities had become merely the traditional bookkeeping device for recording the exchange rate relationships among them.

Nominally gold therefore remained a monetary standard. Quite incidentally, it provided a floor price for the holdings of private investors in gold, and that security was most highly prized by the French. But the exchange rates among national currencies would not have been affected in any way whatever if the official price of gold had been increased by a factor of 2, 20 or 2000, to enrich the small minority who owned gold. And such an increase would indeed have destroyed the dwindling confidence the public still placed in paper currencies, after 6 years of incessant monetary crises. Chaos would have been the consequence, from which only wreckers could have profited.

Lord Boothby's nostalgic yearnings for the Victorian era, when the golden sovereign had ruled world trade, were therefore highly impertinent to the real difficulties of the year 1973.

What that rising free-market price of gold had reflected was investors' loss of confidence in the inflation-ridden dollar, in paper currencies in general, and in securities denominated in them. Nonetheless, for the first time, there were reports that Arab countries of the Middle East, long regarded as traditional hoarders of gold and middlemen in the transport of gold to India, had lost interest in it. Instead Saudi Arabia, Kuwait and Libya had begun to use their billions in oil revenues for speculation in currencies. By Thursday, March 1, the flight from the dollar had resumed. That day the West German Federal Bank was compelled to buy $2.7 billion before it ceased support operations. Its experiment with exchange controls had failed. Throughout Western Europe, the dollar fell through its new floor rates as other central bankers followed the West German example. Their currencies also began to float, and that evening President Pompidou called an emergency meeting of his advisers.

The vaunted French two-tier exchange market was collapsing. On the morning of March 2 the Bank of France closed Parisian foreign exchanges after they had absorbed almost $400 million during the first 90 minutes of trading. In Washington, President Nixon immediately announced that there would not be a third, formal devaluation of the dollar. American patience had been exhausted. Left to devise their own remedies, West European central banks closed most of their foreign exchanges "for an indefinite period." The hectic, tediously familiar round of European conferences began again. Prime Minister Heath conferred with Chancellor Brandt in Bonn. And in Rome, Guido Carli of the Bank of Italy told the press: "If the situation should deteriorate into a permanent crisis, there would be no other possibility than a joint float." Munich's popular *Abendzeitung* protested: "The dollar ruins our economies." And in Washington, the Democratic Chairman of the House Ways and Means Committee suggested that the Soviet Union, the United States and the European Community sell $700 million in monetary gold "to break the speculators." The Russians were not attracted by that idea. In far-off Chicago, however, a jubilant Milton Friedman was heard rejoicing in "the crisis that refreshes." He described it as "another nail in the coffin of fixed exchange rates."

The dénouement of that most recent European muddle was simple, though not easily arranged. The distraught Valéry Giscard insisted: "The United States must also assume its responsibilities in the current crisis." But it was obvious to all observers that there was no longer anything the United States could have done. On his way to Moscow, George Shultz visited a massive assembly of European finance ministers, central bankers and their aides in

Paris, on March 9. He listened politely to the many absurd schemes they proposed, before rejecting all of them. Chancellor Brandt and Helmut Schmidt had already provided the solution by coldly informing President Pompidou and Valéry Giscard on March 4 that the mark would be allowed to float alone if they refused to join a joint float of the European Community's currencies.

By March 11 the Monetary Committee of the European Community had devised a formula for that joint float, from which the British pound and the Italian lira were excluded. It was described to the public as "a temporary expedient," an "interim solution" pending complete reform of the international monetary system. *C'est le provisoire qui dure.* Helmut Schmidt cheerfully announced upon returning to Bonn: "It marks the end of the Bretton Woods currency arrangements of nearly three decades ago. . . . The dollar does not threaten us at all any more." With domestic elections past, Valéry Giscard also became candid. He complained:

> I cannot be accused both of being a dogmatist in economic and monetary policies and of changing my doctrine to suit circumstances. The objective of French policy has been to maintain growth and a high level of employment. That is the fundamental principle of French economic policy, and not the gold standard, fixed parities, or the dollar standard, since we shall no longer support it.

Schmidt had offered, and Giscard had accepted, a small sweetener—a 3 percent revaluation of the mark against the French franc. And on March 14 Schmidt reported to the Bundestag that thereafter Chancellor Brandt's Cabinet had decided to use the moribund Special Drawing Right rather than the dollar or gold as the standard in which to express the parity of the mark. The West Germans were still trying to stay in the middle, on politically neutral ground. Valéry Giscard would continue to demand that every possible effort must be made to minimize the appreciation of West European currencies against the dollar, and the rapacious Olivier Wormser of the Bank of France remained adamantly opposed to floating. Reality did not interest Wormser. Dogma, and the advantages that accrued to France from French dogma, obsessed him. He declared: "The development of the world's economy stands to gain nothing from the general instability that would follow from internal slackness," permitted by floating. He added:

> Whatever the views of the United States, other nations want to maintain the discipline that only a gold-based system can imply, and that paper money cannot guarantee. . . . It is largely American intransigence on this that has caused only limited progress in the monetary reform discussions of the IMF's Committee of Twenty.

Ignoring that defiant flight of fancy, when West European foreign exchanges reopened on Monday, March 19, calm quickly returned. They began to enjoy a political peace and stability they had not known since the advent of Charles de Gaulle 15 years before. Sweden and Norway had joined West Germany, Denmark, the three Benelux countries and France in their collective and "controlled" (the new euphemism for *dirty*) float against the dollar. A decade of unending, increasingly angry international disputes on the composition of national reserves suddenly became almost meaningless. With most major currencies floating, national reserves were no longer needed either to defend fixed parities or to settle international debts. Within reason, closely watched by other central banks, any country that needed foreign currencies could simply buy them in the money markets with its own. Unquestionably that would become an inflationary practice, unless the French and others would agree on rigorous rules to govern floating. Valéry Giscard was overheard saying quite softly that he could foresee the day when gold would be demonetized.

12 = Gold Demonetized
March 1973

At last the United States had regained its freedom of action, though the ransom extorted by Western Europe and Japan had been huge. On the official settlements account, the unnecessary American payments deficit for the year 1972 had been $10.3 billion. For the first quarter of 1973, the payments deficit was another $10.5 billion. The efforts of President Nixon, Henry Kissinger and Arthur Burns to "accommodate conflicting economic interests" had been an egregious blunder they could no longer conceal. Like so many of Kissinger's specious ideas, in theory "accommodation" had appeared a fair and reasonable policy that would persuade other nations to cooperate fully. In practice, it had simply granted a license to all other nations to invent exorbitant demands on the United States, with confidence that they could obtain rich booty in an eventual "compromise."

THE SPECIAL DRAWING RIGHT AS A STANDARD

Within little more than 2 years, the central banks of Western Europe and Japan had extracted more than $50 billion from the United States. As of March 1973, the reserves of the fourteen largest industrial competitors of the United States had increased sharply, to $117 billion. The Eurodollar markets had also swollen, to an estimated $120 billion. They laughed at a Congressional resolution urging President Nixon to demand repayment of the $46 billion in outstanding debts to the United States, one-third of which had been owing since the First World War. Those foreign holdings of dollars, official

327

and private, enabled the complacent West Europeans and Japanese to continue their speculation and spending for imports and domestic consumption on a scale they had never before known. Their political leaders encouraged them to expect further, infinite economic growth. Their governments' budgets were predicated upon continuation of that growth.

One certain consequence was endemic inflation that would exceed all recent records, because their political and financial leaders lacked both the desire and the authority to stop it. Though inflation in Britain had already become severe, having risen to an annual rate of 12 percent, its overweening "neo-Keynesian" economists vastly outnumbered the few killjoys who still had the courage to argue the merits of price stability. Forecasters at the British Treasury simply assumed that any kind of deflationary measure would be "a political impossibility." Nations whose currencies were becoming overvalued, such as West Germany and Switzerland, only postponed their own hour of reckoning. Yet the incessant French efforts to discredit the United States had been so successful that the flight from the dollar would continue. The plundering of the United States had only begun.

Having demonstrated its ineptitude in such squalid ways, the International Monetary Fund had ceased to serve as a useful institution for fostering world monetary stability. In his last few months as Managing Director, the now pathetic figures of Pierre-Paul Schweitzer and his henchmen had become targets for the ridicule of those who had "shot the policeman." The sight saddened economists who had long urged the creation of a powerful world central bank. That had indeed become a political impossibility, because its self-important bureaucrats had demonstrated so conclusively that they could not be trusted. Thereafter the prospect of dissolving the Fund would no longer be unthinkable but rather a constant possibility in the considerations of American political leaders. Both in the United States and in Western Europe, there was an unspoken understanding that the Fund had degenerated into an academic forum for technical discussions increasingly remote from the realities of world finance and trade. Decisions of any importance would be made elsewhere, in quiet, bilateral negotiations.

When the finance ministers of the new Committee of Twenty assembled in Washington on March 25 for their first formal meeting chaired by Ali Wardhana of Indonesia, they therefore dutifully pretended that nothing whatever had changed. But their solemn, overriding concern was to debate the choice of a successor for Schweitzer. They did so amid the clatter of knives and forks at a dinner given by the Belgian Ambassador to the United States. Hastily their leading candidate, the frightened Jelle Zijlstra of the Netherlands Central Bank, made known his unwillingness to let them use their cutlery on him. They spent the remainder of their 2-day meeting reading to each other elegant, beautifully typed, set speeches that had been prepared in advance.

There were no serious negotiations of any kind. Tacitly they accepted floating as a fact of life. But they instructed Jeremy Morse and his fellow deputies
to prepare reports on reform issues and an outline for a hypothetical monetary system. In their customary, fatal deference to the French, the European
ministers had agreed among themselves that it should be based on "stable but
adjustable par values," with floating permitted only in exceptional circumstances. George Shultz, a realist, did not waste any breath arguing with them.
Outside in the streets, American journalists were already applauding the
widespread recognition that central banks could no longer preserve the fixed
exchange rates that finance ministers would so tediously postulate in every
subsequent meeting of the Committee of Twenty. An editorialist of the *New
York Times* concluded:

> The best thing that can be said about the Washington meeting of the finance
> ministers is that it really did nothing—that is, nothing to reverse the progress
> already made toward developing a more flexible monetary order.

Anyone who seeks to please everyone satisfies no one. Again at French
insistence, the finance ministers of the Committee of Twenty had directed the
inexperienced Jeremy Morse to prepare a paper on the role of gold in the
proposed new system. Morse would spend his next year on futile efforts to
satisfy the French. Jacques Rueff had been demanding another opportunity
to restate his arguments for gold and would be permitted to do so *en titre
personnel*. Georges Pompidou was determined that the world must continue to
provide security for French owners of gold, even though they had already
shattered the integrity of the Fund on that submerged rock. There had been
general agreement among the ministers of the Committee of Twenty that
"the role of reserve currencies should be reduced and that Special Drawing
Rights should become the principal reserve asset of the reform system." As
the primary reserve asset, SDRs would also serve as the international monetary standard. Yet Otmar Emminger hastened to reassure the French and the
Swiss that there had not been any real change.

> Gold, making up almost 30 percent of total world monetary reserves, will contin-
> ue to play a role in the monetary system. As long as Special Drawing Rights are
> defined in terms of gold, it makes only a formal difference if new parities are
> fixed in terms of SDRs rather than gold.

Elsewhere there were different ambiguities. British economists were cele-
brating apparent American acceptance of the Special Drawing Right as the
standard for a new world monetary system. They had been assuming as by
right that former British colonies would use any SDRs issued them to "Buy
British", and would thereby contribute to British exports and employment.
Few had noted that American acceptance of the Special Drawing Right as

the new standard had been based on several preconditions that had been stated quite explicitly. On March 25 the Joint Economic Committee of the United States Congress had approved negotiation of:

> monetary reforms that provide for prompt adjustment of currency values to eliminate balance-of-payments crises. This would make Special Drawing Rights . . . the chief international reserve asset. But there must be an understanding that trade negotiations would lead to elimination of tariffs on manufactured goods in 10 to 20 years, to reduction of non-tariff trade barriers and to reform of agricultural support mechanisms. There must also be a firm agreement to compensate the United States fully, immediately and in cash for our net overseas expenditures which contribute to the mutual defense of the free world.

When President Nixon and Henry Kissinger began to seek compliance with those Congressional terms, West Europeans would feign outrage.

The status of the Special Drawing Right as a monetary standard would remain shadowy, confined mostly to the operations of the International Monetary Fund.

THE "YEAR OF EUROPE"

With Britain now a formal though fickle member of the European Economic Community, President Nixon and Henry Kissinger had decided quite tardily that the time had come to call for a redefinition of all the troubled relationships between the United States and Western Europe—in defense, in trade and in monetary affairs. For American taxpayers, the costs of defending the European Community had risen to some $17 billion per annum, and had begun to soar because of rising inflation and the depreciating dollar. They had tired of paying those bills to enable West Europeans to enjoy the luxury of their petty courts, their endless squabbling among themselves, and their calculated contempt for Uncle Sam. It is never easy to cope with a harem, and Arabs are said to prefer the whip. Kissinger decided to try charm, and failed utterly.

Nixon himself had become a recluse. On April 23 Kissinger therefore presented the presidential address to the annual meeting of the Associated Press in New York.

> The Atlantic nations must join in a fresh act of creation, equal to that undertaken by the postwar generation of leaders of Europe and America. The era that was shaped by decisions of a generation ago is ending. . . . The historic opportunity for this generation is to build a new structure of international relations for the decades ahead. A revitalized Atlantic partnership is indispensable for it. . . . We owe to our peoples a rational defense posture, at the safest minimum size and cost, with burdens equitably shared.

Rather than demand the full $17 billion per annum, Nixon and Kissinger mentioned only the derisory sum of $3 billion and aped the grandiloquence affected by Heath and Pompidou in their own public addresses.

> The United States proposes to its Atlantic partners that, by the time the President travels to Europe toward the end of the year, we will have worked out a new Atlantic Charter setting the goals for the future.

For the defense of North America, there were no longer any reasons to maintain American forces in Western Europe. The 300,000 American troops in West Germany, the Netherlands, Belgium, Britain and Italy served only the purposes of those countries and enabled them bit by bit to cut their own defense budgets.

Nixon and Kissinger had wider worries. They also proposed that the United States and the European Community, which together consumed approximately 60 percent of the world's annual production of oil, should collaborate in a common energy program. The response of the Arabs was immediate. The next day in Vienna, prodded by Libya's revolutionary colonels, the Organization of Petroleum Exporting Countries (OPEC) gave the oil companies of the West a 10-day ultimatum—either to produce a "positive" new price offer or to risk unspecified counter measures. Western Europe and Japan had been so blatantly getting rich quick at the expense of the United States that OPEC governments believed they were fully entitled to a price increase of 10 to 15 percent. The oil companies had been offering no more than 9 percent. Officially OPEC stated that its demands would "only compensate for the billions of dollars we are losing because of the dollar devaluations." Its spokesmen were adamant and resolutely self-righteous. Arab grudges against Europe were ancient.

Whenever confronted with another American demand that they pay for their own defenses, the governments of the European Community have made it a practice to equivocate. Correctly they had assumed that, if they remained divided, exasperated American presidents could forever be taunted into compensating for any European failures. Though their anti-Bolshevik crusade had waned, European conservatives had perceived quite clearly that the Arabs now threatened them from another direction. Western Europe had become heavily dependent on Arab oil. European foreign ministries had therefore been assiduously courting Arab princes, confident that they could foist onto the United States the full responsibility and costs of defending Israel if there should ever be a renewal of hostilities in the Middle East. President Nixon's proposal for a new Atlantic Charter was a direct challenge to those ambiguities, and to the European Community's covert diplomacy.

The British chose to stall. They had joined the Community to gain its support, not to provide any. Officially Prime Minister Heath was said to "give genuine and warm welcome" to Nixon's initiative and to:

describe it as important and constructive, welcoming particularly the concept of a United Europe working co-operatively with the United States. . . . The Government does not underestimate, however, the difficulties of achieving a political will by the partners in so wide a framework in order to give the alliance an overriding sense of purpose.

Heath's Foreign Secretary was that same Sir Alexander Douglas-Home who had been so terrified of John Foster Dulles during the Suez crisis of 1956. He had never forgotten the severe dressing down Anthony Eden had then received. On April 29 his crony, the Editor of London's *Observer*, sneered:

At a time when the Watergate affair threatens to engulf the White House in Washington's scandal of the century, President Nixon might seem to have chosen an odd moment to appeal to his European allies . . . to put broad principles above short-term economic interests in their future dealings with the United States. . . .

French hostility was more forthright. That day a conservative British journalist in Paris reported:

Not that M Pompidou's Government is going to leap forward with outright opposition. A chilly formality, rather than a flood of counter-proposals, is the official line. . . . It is a cardinal tenet of French thinking (and of most aggressive Europeans) that the Americans have no right to mix defense with trade. If they defend us, it is because they want to. . . . It does not mean that we must buy their cheap wheat or their expensive computers. . . .

President Pompidou had been reshuffling his ministers. To everyone's surprise, he had elevated to Foreign Minister that obscure clerk Michel Jobert. Another of those embittered North African *pieds noirs,* Jobert typified their engrained hostility toward the Americans who had opposed French imperialism, and his personal loyalty to his own faltering President was absolute. With the gall that became so characteristic during Pompidou's final illness, he had also tried to assign Olivier Wormser as French Ambassador to Washington. Brusquely President Nixon refused him. For the next year, Pompidou and Jobert would gleefully foil the intensive efforts of Nixon and Kissinger to form a new "Atlantic Charter" of substance.

Attempts to form a coordinated program on oil broke down in June, when American negotiators found that none of NATO's members was willing to consider sharing oil supplies in any emergency. And American taxpayers have been burdened ever since with the excessive, rising costs of defending the European Community, historically the basic cause of American budget and balance-of-payments deficits, even though the North Atlantic Treaty Organization had ceased to serve any American needs. West Europeans would continue to insist stubbornly that it was only an alliance for their defense against armed attack by the Soviet Union and for no other purpose. Whenever asked to consider allied planning for another Middle Eastern war, the consistent reply of the European Community would be *"Ohne mich!"* Each of its nine members was confident that, so far as the Arabs were concerned, its privy arrangements were already quite satisfactory.

The seemingly interminable flight from the dollar ended at last in the summer of 1973. Events had fully vindicated those who had forecast 2 years earlier that it could have been stopped only by a large devaluation that would have rapidly restored substantial surpluses in American trade accounts. It should never be forgotten that the consequences of a single large devaluation are less harmful than the prolonged agony caused by a series of small ones. An entire monetary system had been wrecked, and it is doubtful that this generation will ever again see in operation another as intellectually coherent as the Bretton Woods gold-exchange system. The circumstances in which it had flourished, with rules intended to benefit Western Europe and Japan during their postwar recovery, are unlikely ever again to be duplicated. By the summer of 1973, the American people were fully aware of the heavy costs they had incurred while maintaining it. Neither the United States nor the European Community could afford to establish another like it. Lacking ample supplies of new gold from mines within their own frontiers, Europeans would have been foolish to have been entrapped by the French schemes to try. And it had become demonstrable that it would never again be in the national interest of the United States to accept any kind of formal link between the French franc and the floating dollar. Inevitably any franc–dollar parity would become distorted by selfish French efforts to secure export advantages and to influence the political policies of the United States.

The improvement in American trade accounts had begun to appear in March, when the deficit of $52.6 million had been the smallest since September 1971. Approximately half of the increase in American exports during the first quarter of 1973 had been in agricultural products. The excessive world commodity prices, now nearing historic highs, were contributing not only to the rising rate of inflation in the United States but also to the increase in the dollar value of its exports. Shipments to the Soviet Union had continued at high levels. The floating of the dollar and the yen had eased political tensions between the United States and Japan, whose huge, consistent trade surpluses began to shrink as American consumers adapted themselves to a future in which West German and Japanese products would no longer be the cheapest and best to be found in American shops. Congress was considering a trade bill that would have given President Nixon broad authority to negotiate tariff levels and elimination of nontariff barriers to American exports, but it would soon be forgotten in the furor of the investigations into illegal Executive practices aroused by the Watergate burglary.

By June of 1973, the dollar had depreciated 11 percent from its Smithsonian parity against the currencies of the fourteen largest trading competitors of the United States. It had depreciated 20.8 percent since May 1970 against the currencies of the twenty-four member nations of the Organization for Economic Cooperation and Development. That was enough to convince bankers, exchange dealers and traders abroad that American exports had once again become good buys. In the free markets of Western Europe, speculators had pushed gold past $100 per ounce. Briefly it had risen to $110 in London and to $124 in Paris. Those flurries of speculation had been caused partly by concern about the effects of the Watergate scandals on American economic policies, and West Europeans were scathing in their denunciations of the depreciated "Watergate dollar" that was so helpfully restoring healthy American trade surpluses.

With so many currencies floating, finance ministers and central bankers were able to watch those "crises" with equanimity. Speculators were quite disappointed to discover that there was no longer any need for the hasty, melodramatic assemblies of world leaders that had been so characteristic and so troublesome since 1967. Increased supplies of South African and Russian gold also helped to calm the feverish hopes of the gold speculators in London, Paris and Zürich. One of President Nixon's advisers commented: "As for the price of gold, I find it much less interesting than the price of hamburger— and we are very optimistic about the price of hamburger." Though the price of gold had been rising, the price of hamburger had been falling—and the constant purpose of American governments had always been to benefit the many, not the few.

Though the annual meeting of the International Monetary Fund was no longer a significant event in world affairs, preparations began quite early. After more than twenty candidates had been discussed, early in July the European Community authorized Valéry Giscard to ask Dr. Hendrikus Witteveen to serve as the next Managing Director. A Liberal Party member of the Upper Chamber in the Netherlands, Witteveen had been its Finance Minister from 1963 to 1965, and again from 1965 to 1971. The role of gold remained a hotly disputed issue, and the Dutch had begun to serve as neutral negotiators between France and the United States.

On July 13 Jeremy Morse announced general agreement among the deputies of the Committee of Twenty that central banks should be allowed to sell monetary gold on the free markets as soon as complete reform of the monetary system had been accomplished. That meant modification of the rules that had established the two-tier markets in March 1968, and Morse emphasized that the ban on purchases of gold by monetary authorities would be retained. No central bank would be allowed to support a rising free-market price by buying. The Bank of France and others that held a high percentage of their reserves in gold had been complaining bitterly that the rising free-market price had "frozen" and "sterilized" those stocks, because the official price was only $42.22 per ounce. Any of them could have continued to use their gold for official settlements at that lower price, but their instincts had rebelled at the thought. Legal permission to sell official stocks on the free markets should have ended their complaints. Quite incidentally, however, official sales on the free markets would force down prices and would gradually demonetize gold.

As of July 1973, world monetary stocks represented more than a 30-year supply at the current rate of private demand on the free markets. The price would have dropped like a stone, and gold could have become cheaper than copper, if large quantities had suddenly been dumped on them. It would therefore be interesting to observe, whenever official sales might begin, whether the Bank of France would do so. Would French hoarders of gold then rise in righteous wrath, to storm *La Monnaie* and to besiege President Pompidou in his Elysian Palace? Meanwhile the French would continue their incessant, now absurd demands that the United States restore the dollar's convertibility into gold. There was no longer the most remote possibility that the United States could have agreed to do so. *Nécessité fait loi.* Necessity France had caused.

On July 26 Valéry Giscard informed the sympathetic London *Times* that he had somewhat revised his opinions on monetary reform. He now agreed that new rules should be devised to curb substantial payments surpluses. As American payments accounts began to register surpluses for the first time in more than two decades, there was a risk that French surpluses might diminish. Giscard added:

> The objectives of reform can be summed up as follows: to substitute for the present disorder [the French epithet for floating] an organized world trade system which will promote the development of international trade, and which is applied by all countries in a spirit of strict equality under the control of an international authority.

Giscard was confident that Witteveen, an advocate of fixed exchange rates, would defend French interests at the International Monetary Fund. He therefore emphasized that: "The achievement of these objectives rests upon three simple principles: first, it is necessary to return to a system of fixed parities." With so many currencies floating, he could not maintain an undervalued franc by periodic devaluations, and without an undervalued franc, he did not know how to secure consistent payments surpluses and high employment for France.

> The second fundamental principle consists in submitting the creation of international liquidities to an effective international control, and in banning from the system the possibility for some countries to issue their currency themselves in settlement of their deficits.

Never again would the United States be permitted to assist a beleaguered nation such as South Vietnam, in Asia, in Europe or elsewhere.

> The third principle of reform involves the choice of a *numéraire*—a unit of reference and instrument of payments and of reserve. . . . Gold and SDRs are the two components of international liquidity that are called upon to play that key role.

President Pompidou and Valéry Giscard were certain they now held the European Community so firmly by the throat that the rules of the International Monetary Fund could be changed only on French terms. There would be no agreement on rules to govern floating.

Later that day, in Washington, American officials celebrated with (American) champagne the first good news they had received for more than 2 years. The Department of Commerce announced that American trade accounts had at last recorded a minute surplus of $22 million during the second quarter of 1973, the first trade surplus since the beginning quarter of 1971. At the Treasury, Secretary Shultz proudly reported that the Federal budget deficit for Fiscal Year 1973 had been reduced to $14.4 billion. He praised Congress for its efforts to check Federal spending and estimated that $2.2 billion of the Federal debt could be retired. At the White House, President Nixon added that every effort would be made to balance the Federal budget in Fiscal Year 1974. But Congressional Democrats had utterly lost confidence in him, and were completing the War Powers Act of 1973 that would soon hobble him hand and foot.

Nor did it serve French purposes to concede any advantages to the United States. In Brussels the impudent Michel Jobert was insisting that the foreign ministers of the European Community should require the United States to "push the undervalued dollar back to its level of March" before agreeing to start the trade negotiations the United States Congress had stipulated before accepting any monetary reforms that would include an SDR standard. To appreciate the dollar, Jobert demanded that the United States use its remaining gold reserves for intervention in the foreign-exchange markets. He was thoroughly confounding relations between the European Community and the United States.

West Europeans had reached the apogee of a quarter-century of peace, security and prosperity quite unparalleled throughout their history. Though they had always been dependent on the continuing generosity and tolerance of the American people, European leaders had been quite successful in concealing that embarrassing fact from their own voters. The nations of Western Europe had become entirely dependent on diplomacy, unsupported by armed force, to protect their interests abroad. Neither France nor Britain had retained any major naval, air or troop units in the Mediterranean or the Middle East. Once again, they had committed the classic error of inviting rape. And the material expectations of the peoples of Western Europe had risen to ridiculous extremes. In Britain every bankrupt lordling and butcher's apprentice believed that his birthrights included a winter vacation in the Balearic Isles. Prime Minister Heath sacked his chief adviser, Lord Rothschild, for presuming to doubt in public that the inflated Smithsonian boom could last forever.

But as the bankers of more than 120 nations assembled in Nairobi on September 21 for the annual meeting of the International Monetary Fund, many were aware that serious trouble was in the air. The Fund's annual report had indicated that since the beginning of 1970 the official reserves held by member nations had almost doubled, to SDR 144.6 billion. At last they had fully awakened to Schweitzer's betrayal. There was now too much liquidity, and those excessive reserves were concentrated in a few countries. Tolerantly "excess" had been defined as any quantity exceeding 6 months of imports, and the Fund's staff had estimated that excessive reserves totaled SDR 30 billion. More than half of that excess could be ascribed to four industrialized countries—Australia, West Germany, Switzerland and Japan. Another quarter was in the hands of five oil producers—Iraq, Kuwait, Libya, Saudi Arabia and Venezuela. Israeli intelligence may have been blind, but no one else was. George Shultz complained that he was tired of seeing Arab princes swaggering through the United States Treasury.

The Kenyans had hopefully lavished £4 million on the Kenyatta Conference Center and the adjacent KANU party headquarters, whose circular tower dominated the skyline of Nairobi. Every effort had been made to complete them on time, before the arrival of the two thousand delegates and the additional three thousand observers. It had been an ambitious undertaking, and a Kenyan official had proudly explained: "These will be high-powered people, and when they return home they will talk about Kenya. We cannot afford anything except a success." Sadly he then witnessed a shambles. The Committee of Twenty had failed to agree on any reform plan to be presented for formal approval. And every delegate present voiced the rising, increasingly impossible material expectations of his own people.

The Smithsonian boom was nearing its natural end. No matter how rapidly world economic growth might have continued, it would not have been possible to provide a "fair share" of that cake to everyone who was clamoring for it. In terms of real production of goods and services, growth had been fast dwindling. Only the world's money supply had been rising by leaps and bounds. And the attempts to grab much larger shares of that money supply, either by increasing the official price of gold or by linking creation of Special Drawing Rights to development aid, were so heatedly disputed in Nairobi that the Committee of Twenty wisely decided to withdraw those questions from public debate. The Executive Directors of the Fund were instructed to continue in private sessions their studies on the future role of gold and the definition of Special Drawing Rights.

Delegates had scarcely returned to their capitals when the impatient Arabs struck. It was in the month of Ramadan, and on the day of Yom Kippur, that the coordinated tank armies of Syria and Iraq attacked the Golan Heights and the frogmen of Egypt recrossed the Suez Canal to assault the fortified but sleeping positions of Israel. In the weeks that followed, the disunity of the West so apparent at Nairobi would be turned to stunning advantage by the Arabs. Quickly it became obvious that West Europeans had been ready to let Israel fall. Though there were French and British conservatives eager to fight to the last American in defense of European interests in the Middle East, neither President Pompidou nor Prime Minister Heath was willing to commit French and British forces for that purpose.

On October 17 the Arabs therefore cracked their whip. The Soviet Union had been demanding cash for resupplying weapons to Syria and Egypt, and would realize $2 billion from that sale. Unilaterally the six nations of the Persian Gulf met in Kuwait and announced that a 17 percent increase in the market price of crude oil would be their first demand. They also specified that in future the "posted price" should be fixed some 40 percent higher than the market price, to ensure that the oil companies of the West would in fact have to pay at least two-thirds more in royalties and taxes than they ever had before. The 600 million oil consumers in Western Europe, the United States and Japan would be compelled to pay for the Arabs' war against Israel.

Further to divide the West and to reinforce their demands for more money, an embargo was placed on Arab oil shipments to the Netherlands and the United States. The other nations of the European Community were bluntly warned that they too would be added to the embargo list if they did not prove themselves "friendly." It was the most brazen example of extortion seen since the Second World War. Saudi production costs were a mere 12 cents per barrel. Liberal American and European economists, who had proclaimed for so many decades the concept of a "fair and reasonable profit," had simply been ignored by Arabs trained not only at Harvard and Cambridge but also in Oriental bazaars. The European Community dissolved into its constituent parts, disowning the Netherlands. *Sauve qui peut* became the motto of West Europeans, whose arch pride had been so suddenly, brutally shattered. Their boasts of European grandeur had become a mockery, and the North Atlantic Treaty Organization was exposed as an empty, useless shell. Members of its Council bitterly criticized American support for Israel and did everything they could to obstruct it. Only the stolid Dutch and the Portuguese had remained reliable.

Where Nixon and Kissinger had been genteel in their negotiations with West Europeans, the Arabs' analysis had been more realistic. Upon hearing those Arab demands, the central bankers of Western Europe and Japan fell to their knees, begging for mercy from this new, implacable foe. European attention was riveted on tiny principalities such as Kuwait. How could the Arabs be so cruel to their affectionate old tutors at the Bank of England and the Bank of France? Would they demand gold in payment for their oil, as they often had during the 1930s and 1940s? The mere thought aroused terror. Valéry Giscard wailed: "Penury!" It was indeed Arab *revanchisme*. France had become reliant on oil imports for 75 percent of its production of power from all sources. Most of its coal mines had been exhausted and abandoned, after decades of troubling strikes by French miners. More dependent on Arab oil than most of its European neighbors, France was the primary target of the Arabs, for reasons unrelated to Israel. The Syrians and Algerians had never forgotten their experience as French colonies.

Abruptly there appeared a real possibility that within the next 2 or 3 years the Arabs might strip from Western Europe and Japan that massive hoard of gold and dollar reserves they had gained from the United States since 1945, with so much effort and deceit.

THE COSTS OF THE YOM KIPPUR WAR

In that climactic month of October 1973, understanding quickly spread among the American people that their alliances with Western Europe and Japan had always been costly liabilities. But as the Watergate scandals slowly weakened President Nixon's authority at home, he became more intent on buying support abroad. Henry Kissinger had been named Secretary of State on the eve of that Yom Kippur War, simply because Nixon could no longer find anyone of standing who was willing to obey his orders unquestioningly. Nixon and Kissinger were determined to arrange an Arab–Israeli peace that would not only end the oil embargo but also reassert the prestige of his presidency. To do so, they needed the cooperation of Western Europe. Kissinger and Defense Secretary James Schlesinger so vigorously criticized the supine position of Britain that they stung Sir Alexander Douglas-Home into the public retort: "Kissinger is just another German bullyboy!" Is there another way to deal with the Foreign Office? Firmly the British remained tied to the French policy of appeasing the Arabs. Only months later, when European appeasement became a blatant failure and Prime Minister Heath was bought by an offer to share American domestic oil supplies, did Britain begin grudgingly to support American policies in the Middle East. Privately but bluntly, Nixon also told Chancellor Brandt that West Germany would have to choose between the United States and France.

The sudden doubling in the price of OPEC's oil exports, to a posted price of $5.11 per barrel, had radically disrupted economic planning in all consuming countries. At first no one believed that OPEC would and could maintain it. In September, the trade accounts of the United States had registered a surplus of $873 million, the largest for more than 8 years. Two devaluations and further depreciation of the dollar had at last accomplished a decisive turnaround. The competitive position of the United States had been restored, more than a decade too late. That meant new jobs for American workers and increased profits for American exporters. There had been sound prospects that the trade accounts of the United States would record a surplus of several hundred million dollars for 1973, and forecasts had confidently indicated that American payments accounts for 1974 would also be in surplus. But by November a cautious official at the U.S. Department of Commerce was warning: "We are going to see a testing of the Europeans' willingness to let American payments return to balance. . . ." And once again, Europeans did indeed change their tune. Discussions on the "consolidation" of official dollar balances held by West European governments abruptly ended. They began to seek more dollars. All could have deflated their own economies to divert from consumer and public spending the funds needed to pay the higher costs of oil imports. Deflationary measures would also have dampened the soaring inflation that everyone could now foresee. Without exception, however, West European governments of both Left and Right remained committed to policies of growth and full employment. All feared the wrath of voters, if they had taken the sensible course of deliberate deflation.

Once again, national reserves had therefore become a primary worry of governments. On Tuesday, November 13, at a monthly meeting of the Bank for International Settlements in Basle, the seven signatories to the Washington agreement of March 1968 accepted the suggestion of Arthur Burns that the hour had come to permit central banks to sell their gold stocks on the free markets for any price they could get. The prohibition on buying was retained, and the option to sell was described as "discretionary." Few central banks would avail themselves of that new right, and only small quantities would be sold in the months ahead. As so often before, the French had insisted on an increase in the official price and had been overruled. The next morning, the free market price in London fell $9 to $88 per ounce, before closing at $90.

On Saturday, November 24, the finance ministers of Britain, France, West Germany, Japan and the United States met privately at the Château d'Artigny in the Loire Valley near Tours, to discuss monetary reform and the rapidly deteriorating international situation. Disregarding further, weakening protests by Valéry Giscard, they decided to instruct their Executive Directors at the International Monetary Fund to sever the link between SDRs and gold and to redefine the Special Drawing Right in a way that would exclude all commodities, by using a "basket" of national currencies. They might soon need to use their SDRs. Following a doubtful precedent devised by the Bank of Italy, they also agreed that central banks could resort to borrowing from the Eurodollar markets through public institutions and nationalized industries. Rather than forego present consumption or use national reserves for the purpose for which they had always been intended, the British, French and Italians would subsequently mortgage the future of their children and grandchildren. Finally they agreed that industrial countries should not react to the oil crisis by cutting domestic demand in any way that might hasten the recession that had so clearly appeared on the horizon. Then George Shultz and Arthur Burns made a major concession that would become quite damaging to the United States. They agreed to let the dollar appreciate, to give West Europeans export advantages. Though the unemployment rate in the United States would therefore continue to be almost twice the highest rate found anywhere in Western Europe, Heath and Pompidou were angrily insisting that they would suffer most from the structural changes in world finance caused by the rising price of oil.

Nine centuries ago, while European Christians and the Saracens were struggling for possession of the Holy City of Jerusalem, the Franks were notorious renegades. So it was in 1973. Near desperation and resentful that he was being ignored as a "nonperson" by the Soviet Union and the United States while they sought a peace settlement in the Middle East, President Pompidou had called for a summit meeting of the European Community, to be held in Copenhagen. Europe would decide on a common energy policy of its own and thus would make its "declaration of independence." Pompidou had become a bloated, querulous hulk, sustained only by constant medication that could not arrest terminal disease but eased its increasing pain. Yet none of his ministers had sufficient courage to request his resignation for the welfare of France. Faithfully Michel Jobert announced that Pompidou's last summit would begin December 14 and would be "without constraints, without procedure, and with an open heart." French policy had been clearly revealed. Pompidou would let the United States make all the efforts to "roll back" the OPEC price increase. If Nixon and Kissinger should succeed, France too would quietly benefit. If Nixon should fail, Georges Pompidou could continue to proclaim to the Arabs that France alone had always been their only true friend in the West. It was a textbook example of French skill in duplicity, and they sought full support from their European partners— except, of course, from those black sheep the Dutch. But popular support for Israel had been rising throughout Western Europe. Even in France, millions had been shamed by the behavior of their government. The Dutch had become the folk heroes of the hour.

The French themselves turned their Copenhagen summit into a spotlit farce by unilaterally inviting the foreign ministers of Algeria, Tunisia, the

Sudan and the United Arab Emirates to appear and to participate in discussions that had been advertised as "intimate, secret and informal." The European Community's first effort to make common political decisions became a silly failure. European disunity and futility were so vividly exposed in Copenhagen that the members of OPEC seized the opportunity to make Georges Pompidou's last Christmas on earth the most miserable he had ever known.

Mohammed Reza Pahlavi, the calculating playboy who had become the most domineering Shahinshah Iran had known for several centuries, was "inspired" to wrest leadership of OPEC from the radical regimes of Algeria and Libya. He did so quite adroitly. On the morning of December 23, at a hastily convened press conference in Teheran's Niavaran Palace, while the oil ministers of OPEC were still haggling among themselves, he announced that he alone had decided to redouble the posted price of oil, to $11.651 per barrel. The political leaders of Western Europe collapsed into deep shock. Arab members of OPEC were also alarmed by the economic repercussions they could immediately foresee, and they resented the Shah's preemption of their decision. But he got away with it. In doing so, he solved his urgent domestic problems. The Shah, unhappily, could not command his loyal subjects to pay their taxes. Iranian tax collections therefore represented only 3.5 percent of its gross national product. His Imperial Majesty had become entirely dependent on oil revenues to satisfy the rapidly rising material expectations of his people. Rather than risk their wrath and his throne, he preferred to bleed Western Europe, the United States and Japan. His soldierly father, whom the British had deposed in 1941 for his pro-German sympathies, would have been proud of him.

Hasty calculations made Christmas Eve, on the backs of envelopes, indicated that in 1974 the oil-exporting countries could have payments surpluses of $50 billion. George Shultz immediately protested that such a distortion in the world monetary system would be "unmanageable." Oil-consuming nations would be plunged into a financial "bath." Official planning for a "symmetrical" world monetary system became patently absurd. The governments of Western Europe, the United States and Japan scurried to increase their exports to the OPEC nations, and many sought to borrow cash from them. "Recycling" became the fashionable euphemism for going deeply into debt, to sustain high levels of production and consumer spending in the West. In the confusion, some European economists devised specious arguments to justify the oil price increases, while others made vain efforts to devise painless escapes from the trap into which they had fallen. Imitating the Arabs, Britain's coal miners struck for drastic wage increases and would soon break the Conservative Government of the feckless Edward Heath. It became a dreary winter of chill pubs, half-lit shops and grim forebodings, the first real trouble Europeans under the age of 30 had ever experienced. They did not enjoy it.

Higher oil prices directly or indirectly affected the price of every item consumed, and in every industrial country the rate of inflation soared. Regardless of their governments' policies, that had deflationary effects on domestic demand, comparable to a sudden, sharp increase in indirect taxation. Panicky European investors, fearing complete collapse, converted so much of their money into dollars that by mid-January the pound had depreciated to $2.15. Yet the extreme fluctuations in exchange rates, caused by capital flights, did not seriously trouble central banks. Exchange rates, rather than national reserves, took the punishment. Floating proved its worth to everyone except the French, and the speculators in currencies. To their frequent distress, the latter began to learn that speculation could be unprofitable when currencies were floating. As the dollar appreciated, its "prestige" returned, and that pleased Americans who had been more disturbed by inflation than by unemployment. At last the United States was able to discard all of its ineffective controls on capital movements. By January 12 London's *Economist* wryly observed:

> The almighty dollar, top beast of the economic jungle, has returned to suzerain ty. It has happened not a moment too soon. Open warfare threatens among the other animals.

Rather than cooperate for their common good, the nations of the European Community were competing fiercely for the favors of OPEC. Valéry Giscard announced that France alone would have to increase its exports by 18 billion francs to prevent a trade deficit in 1974.

Scant months before, the United States Treasury had forecast a payments surplus of $8.7 billion for 1974. Now it was anticipating an American payments deficit of at least $500 million. But when the finance ministers and deputies of the Committee of Twenty met in Rome on January 14, Paul Volcker noted: "There has been a complete change of mood." Exposed to new perils the governments of most oil-consuming nations had become willing to consider changes in their previously entrenched positions on many issues. Most of the first day was devoted to an inconclusive discussion on a new method for defining the Special Drawing Right that had been devised by the Executive Directors of the Fund. Many ministers present hoped the members of OPEC would be willing to hold large parts of their payments surpluses in the new medium of payments, rather than in short-term deposits in the largest commercial banks of the United States and Western Europe. The private banking world was awash with money, and many of its bankers had become careless.

During that discussion on a new definition for the Special Drawing Right, the French were noticeably less doctrinaire than ever before. But the West Germans remained committed to their position that the SDR should be "hard," stable enough to be preferred to any other form of reserve asset.

Several delegates questioned whether valuing the SDR in terms of a "basket" of currencies would be realistic when the currencies themselves were unstable. If all were inflating, and presumably all would do so in terms of their domestic purchasing power, there would be an inflationary bias in the valuation of the SDR. Proponents of the "basket" could only reply that, in an unsafe, uncertain world, every search for the investor's ideal of absolute stability had always found it an illusion. At least an SDR valued as a "basket" of currencies could not be subjected to the speculative attacks in the money markets that had so heavily damaged the credibility of the dollar, sterling and gold as world standards. SDRs would continue to circulate only among central banks and the Fund, a circuit closed and invulnerable to attack by private speculators.

On January 16 Helmut Schmidt therefore announced the joint position taken by the nine members of the European Community. They had agreed to support redefinition of the SDR as a "standard basket" of currencies and proposed that it should contain the currencies of seven countries, each of which accounted for more than 3 percent of world trade. Those were the American dollar, the Japanese yen, the West German mark, the British pound, the Italian lira, and the French and Belgian francs. Schmidt also proposed an interest rate of 2 percent for SDRs, though that question would continue to be debated within the European Community. Others preferred 5 or 6 percent. Valéry Giscard had appeared in Rome only long enough to attend a dinner the evening before, at which the French desire for a large increase in the official price of gold had again been denied. In Paris, President Pompidou's immediate problem was speculation against the franc's fixed parity within the European joint float. Defense of that fixed exchange rate was rapidly draining the dollar reserves of France. Rather than borrow dollars from West Germany or sell French gold reserves on the free markets, Pompidou and Giscard decided to commit the heresy of floating the franc. *Nécessité fait loi.*

By January 18 the finance ministers assembled in Rome had concluded that the disequilibria anticipated in world trade and payments accounts would become so extreme that it would be impossible to design a comprehensive new monetary plan. Reflecting their uncertainties and the anxieties of billions of people throughout the world, the free-market price of gold had risen to a new high of $130 per ounce. That day the gold market in Paris had had its largest turnover since 1968. Oil rather than monetary reform had dominated the thinking of everyone in Rome, and the ministers of the Twenty agreed that subsequent efforts should approach reform piece by piece, each to be implemented as soon as it had been fully approved. The centerpiece needed was a new world monetary standard that would enable central bankers to express the value of their reserves in terms more reliable than the fluctuating price of gold or floating currencies could provide. The Executive Directors of the Fund were therefore instructed to prepare the new definition of the Special Drawing Right for approval by the ministers at their next meeting in June. Helmut Schmidt proposed that the Committee of Twenty should then disband, to be succeeded by a similar group that would meet three or four times each year to supervise the functioning of international monetary rules.

For purposes of negotiation the Committee of Twenty, with its several hundred aides and retainers, had simply been too large and unwieldy. But George Shultz and Paul Volcker, who intended to retire from the United States Treasury in June, urged that "interim" rules on floating should also be prepared by the deputies of the Twenty, to complete the tentative outline of a new international monetary system.

REDEFINITION OF THE SPECIAL DRAWING RIGHT

Private owners of gold, whose belief in gold as money bore all the hallmarks of a religion, had remained convinced that growth in world trade built on credit and paper currencies would someday collapse. Then gold might again emerge as the only national asset and private store of value with timeless, "immutable" worth. They could not be expected to abstain from attempts to stop official installation of a new international monetary standard entirely divorced from gold, an absolute denial not only of their most cherished beliefs but also of their right to a security guaranteed by governments. World commodity prices had continued to rise, and the free-market price of gold reached an extraordinary $180 per ounce, before that artificially inflated boom broke in March of 1974. Then a long, sharp decline in commodity prices began.

West European and South African producers, speculators and hoarders of gold had therefore been agitating vigorously for establishment of the new floor price a new official price at that higher level would have given them. By March 1974, monetary gold stocks had fallen to a quarter of world reserves, at the official price of $42.22 per ounce. However, if monetary gold had been officially revalued at the high free-market price of $180 per ounce, it would have constituted more than half of world monetary reserves. Hypothetically it might then have been reinstated as the primary reserve asset and international monetary standard. The huge profits made by private owners of gold would have been permanently secured. Georges Pompidou, their leading champion for the preceding decade and more, lay on his deathbed. They therefore sought commitments from Valéry Giscard, widely regarded as the leading candidate to succeed him as President of France. On March 5 the new monthly *Europa* asked: "What, in your opinion, are the necessary preconditions [to reestablish fixed parities within the European Community] regarding the price of gold?"

Giscard's reply was eminently cautious.

The French Government's position is not the gold standard and we are not heading for a system based on monometallism, but towards a rational system in which gold will retain a role for as long as it takes to achieve complete rationality, for as long as each country continues to feel it necessary to retain a certain holding as a precaution and, finally, for as long as the uncertainties of monetary behavior and devaluations continue to necessitate periodic references to gold. The gold standard is not the French Government's position. President Pompidou and we ourselves have been saying this for years. On the other hand, we find that gold still has a monetary role. I maintain that those who say the contrary do not carry their arguments through to their logical conclusions. The proof of this is that the countries which state their opposition to the monetary role of gold are never prepared to relinquish their gold assets. Logically, those in favor of the elimination of gold from the international system would say: We are not interested in gold, ours is for sale. No one has adopted this stance. The United States has not released its gold. West Germany is holding rather more than us and not rather less. Italy did not wish to release its gold under the European regulations. It is a fact that gold is used for monetary purposes.

Though gold had ceased to serve as a medium of international settlements in August 1971, it remained a monetary standard at the now fictitious official price of $42.22 per ounce.

Giscard continued:

A second fact is that gold is a raw material and must be treated as such. It is a raw material used for monetary purposes. At present, it is the only raw material which has an official price. An official price which, currently, is being flouted in the market place. It is not our objective to see gold with a new official price which could be the future basis of the monetary system. Our idea is that it should be possible for gold, as a monetary raw material, to play its role. It must be possible for settlements to be made in gold between European or non-European central banks exchanging gold as a monetary raw material. . . . The 1974 deficits will not be intra-European deficits. They will be deficits with countries outside Europe. The debtor countries will be much less worried about releasing part of their foreign exchange when they have gold reserves carrying a higher valuation behind them.

With that warning to the Arabs, Giscard withdrew from the public controversy on gold. He had already agreed with Helmut Schmidt that, faced by quadrupled, then quintupled oil prices, the members of the European Community should refrain from competitive devaluations, restrictions on trade or protectionist overbidding of any kind. That had been a repudiation of the flagrantly independent, futile maneuverings of Michel Jobert.

Among the finance ministers of the European Community, there were no longer any dogmatic arguments about gold. The questions were how to retain their gold stocks if they could, and how best to use them if they should be needed to pay for OPEC oil. The West Germans and the British were reluctant to see gold reenthroned by increasing its official price to the free-market price. But even the West Germans had begun to agree with Giscard that some kind of private arrangement among the Community's central banks was needed, to enable them to settle their internal debts with gold if necessary. Quietly they confided the technical problem of devising a plan to the Monetary Committee of the European Community, with instructions that it be ready for approval by April, when European finance ministers held their next meeting at Zeist in the Netherlands.

Meanwhile the deputies of the Committee of Twenty met in Washington on March 28 in an effort to draft new monetary rules before the June deadline. Their first sessions were devoted to discussion of possible rules for floating. Six had been proposed. First a country with a floating exchange rate would be allowed to intervene in the foreign-exchange markets, to maintain orderly conditions and to prevent sharp or erratic fluctuations, but not to affect the market trend. Second, intervention by a country with a floating rate should normally moderate rather than accelerate the market movement in its exchange rate. Normally a country with a floating rate should not accumulate reserves when the market trend of its currency was depreciation, or reduce them when the market trend was appreciation. Third a country with a floating rate should cooperate with the International Monetary Fund to determine in which direction its exchange rate should or should not move and, whenever possible, to determine an approximate range of fluctuation for its exchange rate. That country might then intervene in the foreign-exchange markets in accordance with (but not contrary to) any such determination. Fourth a country whose reserves were recognized to be disproportionately high or low might be encouraged to intervene while that disproportion should last, to restore its reserves to a more normal level, subject to the second rule. Fifth a country whose currency was floating, and had an effective choice of intervention currencies, should normally buy the weakest of those currencies or sell the strongest. If it should desire to intervene with any other currency, the agreement of the issuing country would be required. Sixth, intervention by other countries in a floating currency should not take place without the agreement of the floating country, except possibly for smoothing operations to maintain orderly market conditions and other small transactions.

The most interesting of those proposed rules was the stipulation that governments floating their currencies should agree with the Fund on a "normal zone" for their exchange rates, and that a central bank managing a float would be committed to intervene "aggressively" once it had moved outside that zone, to bring it back into line. There was also a brief discussion on the question of the official price of gold, in which familiar positions were restated. Paul Volcker emphasized that the United States remained hostile to any increase in the official price, and the European deputies preferred to withhold comment until their ministers had met at Zeist. On March 29, at the conclusion of that Washington meeting, Jeremy Morse announced full agreement that the Special Drawing Right should be redefined in terms of a weighted basket of standard currencies, coupled to a rate of interest. Then he cast doubt on the possibility of resolving the disagreements on the future role of gold before dissolution of the Committee of Twenty in June.

Prime Minister Heath's defeat at the hands of British coal miners had returned to power a Labour Government headed by Harold Wilson, with Denis Healey as his Chancellor of the Exchequer. In West Germany, Helmut Schmidt would soon succeed the worn Willy Brandt as Chancellor, in a surprising but well-arranged transfer of authority. The oil crisis had so vividly exposed the European Community's dependence on the United States that both Wilson and Schmidt hastened to make amends for the follies of their predecessors. When Denis Healey first met the other finance ministers of the Community on April 22 at the 17th century baroque castle of Zeist near Utrecht, he and Karl-Otto Pöhl were therefore confronted with a highly sensitive task. Quite conveniently, Valéry Giscard and the Belgian Finance Minister had failed to appear, the former pleading the French presidential election campaign and the latter a cabinet crisis in Brussels. But the Monetary Committee of the European Community had prepared for approval by the ministers a plan that would have officially freed their central bankers to buy and sell gold among themselves at the free-market price, then $170 per ounce. In the free markets of Western Europe, speculators were already celebrating their expectation that the Community's finance ministers would approve that plan. *"Nécessité fait loi,"* cried the Editor of *Le Monde.*

The Italian government had particularly pressing needs, and at Zeist the Bank of Italy's Guido Carli fervently expressed his belief that only a new official price of approximately $170 per ounce would solve Italy's difficulties. Somewhat mischievously, Denis Healey asked why Italy and others who needed cash did not sell their gold on the free markets. No reply was expected, and none was received. The answer was only too obvious. The price would have fallen sharply, and in France many of Valéry Giscard's most ardent supporters would have discarded him. Whenever the British and the West Germans have had so serious an argument with the French, they have had an unpleasant habit of withdrawing to the sidelines, construing resolution of the dispute as a "Franco–American confrontation." Faithful to that tradition of using the United States as their scapegoat, the finance ministers assembled at Zeist decided to accept the plan for a floating official gold price related to the free-market price, that would enable their central banks to buy and sell, but not to implement it until they could obtain the concurrence of the United States. They deputed Willem Duisenberg, the apprehensive Dutch Finance Minister, to obtain from Washington the American reaction they already knew he would receive: "No!"

Italy's balance-of-payments deficit for the first 5 months of 1974 had been 3.35 billion lire. That difficulty, and internal disputes over the measures needed to end it, caused collapse of the Italian government early in June. An alarmed Henry Kissinger had therefore been urging George Shultz and Arthur Burns to find a way to provide financial support for Guido Carli. The exhausted Shultz was being succeeded by a protégé, William Simon, a private bond dealer from New York who had been serving as Deputy Secretary of the Treasury and head of the Federal Energy Administration. The bemused Simon was faced with the dispute over an increase in the official price of gold during his first days as Secretary. But when European finance ministers arrived in Washington on Tuesday, June 11, they found him ready. Newspapers informed them that he would urge President Nixon to remove the 40-year ban on the private ownership of gold by American citizens. Simon described that ban as "repugnant to me", and he recommended raising it "before the end of the year unless there are damaging developments."

That evening, at a dinner given by Guido Carli for the finance ministers of the old Group of Ten, gold was the only topic for discussion. They agreed informally that Italy should be allowed to pledge its gold stocks as collateral for loans, at any price on which borrower and lender might agree. That dinnertable compromise, when West Germany reluctantly accepted its new responsibilities as Europe's rich though notoriously stingy uncle, provided a way for Europeans to use their gold reserves without relinquishing them and without any official revaluation. The French delegation, who feared they might be next in line for loans from Bonn, remained remarkably silent. Their new finance minister, Jean-Pierre Fourcade, had remained in Paris to introduce a tardy, deflationary budget. Domestic elections past, President Giscard had swiftly moved to curb inflation. His deputies in Washington were primarily concerned to determine whether the articles of the International Monetary Fund would be amended to legalize the new rules for floating. They insisted that floating should not be formally authorized and that the world should wait for a complete new "package" of reforms that would incorporate their ideas on gold. The dollar, the pound and many other currencies therefore continued to float without any formal blessing from the Fund.

Nevertheless, at that final meeting of the Committee of Twenty, ministers did agree on one section of the lengthy *Outline of Reform* prepared by their deputies. They approved the new definition for the Special Drawing Right, to become effective July 1, that would enable the "standard basket" to in-

clude both fixed and floating currencies. Sixteen had been chosen, each of
which had accounted for 1 percent or more of world trade during the 5-year
period 1968–1972. The Fund would collect their exchange rates daily, to
calculate and announce the daily rate of the SDR in terms of each of the
sixteen currencies. They had been weighted according to their shares of world
trade, except for the dollar, which would be a larger 33 percent because of its
additional financial role. Weightings were rounded to the nearest ½ percent,
as follows:

U.S. dollar	33	Belgian franc	3½
West German mark	12½	Swedish crown	2½
Pound sterling	9	Australian dollar	1½
French franc	7½	Danish crown	1½
Japanese yen	7½	Norwegian crown	1½
Canadian dollar	6	Spanish peseta	1½
Italian lira	6	Austrian schilling	1
Dutch guilder	4½	South African rand	1
			100

The rate of interest on Special Drawing Rights was increased from 1½ percent to 5, which was the basic rate of return on super gold tranche positions.
Adjustments would be made every 6 months, whenever necessary and on a
sliding scale, 5 percent to apply whenever commercial interest rates (the
weighted average of interest on 3-month bonds in the United States, Britain,
France, West Germany and Japan) were in the 9 to 11 percent band. For
each percentage point movement of commercial rates up or down from that
band, the SDR interest rate would be moved 0.6 percentage point up or
down. If commercial rates should drop to 7 percent, the rate on the SDR
would become 3.8 percent, and so on. That formula had reconciled the West
German insistence on a "hard" SDR and the American anxiety that SDRs
should not be so attractive that there might be a flight from the dollar into
them.

At last the official world of finance ministers and central bankers had a
new international monetary standard, entirely severed from gold. It remained to be seen whether the real world of private bankers and foreign-
exchange dealers would accept the change.

THE JAMAICA AGREEMENT

The rest was prologue.

Gold would have its fling. In 1974, speculators accounted for 65 percent of
the private demand for that metal. The South African Government was bas-

ing its economic development planning on the assumption that the minimum free-market price would continue to be at least $150 per ounce. Private French holdings were estimated at 192 million ounces. Their value at the official price of $42.22 per ounce was a mere $8.106 billion. However, if the Zeist agreement had been implemented, French owners of gold would have been awarded $32.64 billion by a new official price of $170 per ounce. If their 192 million ounces had been equally divided among the 16.6 million households of France, each would then have held a handsome nest egg of $1966. As a prisoner of the Gaullists in the French National Assembly, President Giscard had adopted a position of studied ambiguity. By June 27 the free-market price in London had fallen to $144.50 per ounce. Rising interest rates everywhere had begun to make speculation costly, and many speculators were liquidating their positions. Optimistic prospects were needed to encourage them, and the vast, virginal American market appeared to offer the possibility of an eternally rising price. South African and West European gold interests began an ambitious advertising campaign to persuade the supposedly gullible American people that gold would be a safer investment than paper securities denominated in their inflating dollar, even though gold could not yield the income they had learned to expect from their investments.

On June 18 the Money and Banking Committee of the United States House of Representatives had voted to allow American citizens to own gold by December 31. That provision had been attached as a rider to a bill that authorized $1.5 billion in new funds for the International Development Association, with the hope that it would ease passage of that bill regardless of growing Congressional opposition to foreign aid of all kinds. In July the gold stocks of the United States totaled 276 million ounces and were valued at $11.6 billion, at the official price of $42.22 per ounce. To counter President Giscard's jibe that the United States was not seriously intent on demonetization, Secretary Simon announced that he would feel free to begin selling from those stocks to satisfy any new domestic demand that might appear. Another element of uncertainty was added to the trend in the free-market price. The House passed the bill that restored the private right to own gold, and on July 2 it was sent to a conference committee to resolve differences with the Senate. In London and in Zürich, the free-market price fell to $136 per ounce the next day.

By July 29 the House Judiciary Committee had decided to recommend the impeachment of President Nixon, primarily for obstruction of justice. On July 30 the free-market price of gold soared to $158 per ounce in London. Most of the world was watching Washington with a certain horrified fascination. On July 31 the House voted final approval of the bill granting Americans the right to buy and sell gold by the end of that year, and forwarded it to the White House for presidential approval. There it would lie on President

Nixon's desk, an unsigned, symbolic reminder of his many failures as steward of the American economy. On August 4 Congressman Henry Reuss exploded: "The current economic management is inept. Its ideas are bankrupt. . . . We live on the brink of disaster." Though Reuss somewhat exaggerated the dangers, he voiced the apprehension of many millions. During the second quarter of 1974, the annual rate of inflation in the United States had risen to 11.1 percent, and the rate of unemployment to 5.4 percent. No one believed the Administration's forecasts of improved economic conditions during the last half of the year. Nothing could hide the failure of Nixon and Kissinger to achieve a peaceful settlement in the Middle East and a reduction in the price of OPEC oil. Scenting blood, other nations had begun to make demands on the United States that had become wildly exorbitant.

Though tardy, Richard Nixon's resignation on August 8 permitted his country to begin slowly to retreat from the perils that had awaited it. On August 14 President Gerald Ford signed into law the bill that authorized American citizens to own gold, beginning December 31. Despite lively trading in gold mining shares, the Dow Jones industrial average fell to a 4-year low of 750.54. It declined 99 points during Ford's first 3 weeks in office. Somehow that seemed an appropriate accompaniment to the fall from grace of Wall Street's chosen champion, Richard Nixon. Having allowed the dollar to appreciate, by the second quarter of 1974 the trade and payments accounts of the United States had once again fallen into serious trouble. The quarterly trade deficit had been $1.537 billion, and on the official settlements account, the quarterly payments deficit had been a staggering $4.192 billion. For August alone the trade deficit was $1.131 billion, the largest in the history of the United States. The cost of oil imports, a mere $3.9 billion in 1972, had been soaring to $24 billion in 1974. That recurring deterioration in the competitive position of the United States had been contributing substantially to the deepening recession. On October 14 Secretary of Commerce Frederick Dent bitterly protested:

> There is a danger that the exchange rate of the dollar will become unrealistic because of dirty floating by other countries and that this could produce increased calls for isolationist policies and trade protectionism.

In the third quarter, inflation had jumped to an annual rate of 11.5 percent. It reached a peak of 13.6 percent in October, and the Dow Jones average continued to fall, dropping to a 12-year low of 577.60 in December.

Throughout the world, stock exchanges had panicked. But inflation rather than recession had continued to be the problem that had disturbed most Americans. In the 12 months since October 1973, American wholesale prices had soared 22 percent. President Ford was also told that a Federal budget deficit of at least $35 billion was forecast for Fiscal Year 1975. With unemployment also rising sharply, to 5.8 percent during the third quarter of 1974, the choice was between evils. By October, Arthur Burns and the Federal Reserve Board had decided that recession was becoming the more immediate hazard. Abruptly they reversed course. Restraints on growth of the domestic money supply were eased, interest rates began to fall, and the long struggle to depreciate the dollar was resumed regardless of frantic European protests. Their unvarying insistence on the "protection" of an overvalued dollar, to give them export advantages in a new era of floating exchange rates, had become not merely archaic but pernicious to the welfare of the United States and its workers.

The change in Administration had not dampened the French monetary attacks on the United States that had dominated Franco–American relations since the First World War. President Ford had opened the 29th annual meeting of the International Monetary Fund with a brief speech on September 30 in which he had called for:

> solutions which serve broad interests rather than narrow, self-serving ones. We want cooperation, not more isolation. We want growth, not stagnation. . . . We believe that the same spirit of international cooperation which brought forth the Bretton Woods Agreements a generation ago can resolve the difficulties we face today.

Both Ford and Kissinger had been hopeful that a new President could resolve the interminable monetary disputes with France, and that French cooperation could be obtained for American efforts to find an Arab–Israeli peace agreement in the Middle East.

Yet on October 1 Secretary Simon had his first public clash with Jean-Pierre Fourcade, the French Finance Minister. Speaking for President Giscard, Fourcade proposed sweeping monetary reforms that would end floating exchange rates, would "banalize" gold by permitting central banks freely to buy and sell, and would make Special Drawing Rights the center of the new world monetary system. French official thinking had begun to change, but Fourcade concluded:

> The special status of gold should be eliminated and it should be treated like any other monetary asset. The concept of an official price, which no longer has any meaning, should be discarded and gold should be carried on the books at its true value.

To protect the value of French private holdings, he vehemently opposed Simon's suggestion that the gold stocks of the International Monetary Fund should be sold on the free markets, to finance development aid for poor nations. The next day, in Paris, after deploring Giscard's cunning choice of the word *banaliser* for an object so sacred as gold, the Editor of *Le Monde* huffed:

> The President of the United States has exalted international co-operation. . . .
> Was this the place, was this indeed the moment, to recall Bretton Woods? Espe-
> cially was it appropriate for the highest authority of American policy to evoke
> that memory when one knows that the United States respected those famous
> Bretton Woods Agreements only as long as they served American interests and
> did not hesitate deliberately to violate them three years ago in order to free the
> dollar from all restraint?

It is doubtful that the subjective French habit of rewriting monetary history
can ever be corrected.

A curious anomaly appeared. France alone could not have reestablished
and defended a new, high official price for gold. It had continued to adhere
to the rule among the Group of Ten that had prohibited their central banks
from buying gold in the free markets. Moreover, even if France had decided
to violate that rule, it lacked sufficient gold reserves to defend in the markets
the permanently fixed price that would have been the only way to reinstate
gold as an effective monetary standard. But that had not deterred French
officials from devising a scheme to provide some psychological support for a
high free-market price. Though Valéry Giscard had refused an official invitation to visit Washington, he had proposed a meeting with President Ford on
the French island of Martinique, beginning December 14. It was a cautiously
cordial occasion, an opportunity for Giscard to deploy his affability. Arguing
the supposed need of France and Italy to revalue their gold reserves at the
free-market price, to use them as collateral for loans, he persuaded Gerald
Ford and Henry Kissinger to agree. Perforce both had become familiar with
French thinking on gold. They chose politely to ignore the embarrassing fact
that only Congress could authorize a change in the American official price,
though fully aware that Congressional leaders were adamantly opposed to it.
On December 16 an official communiqué from Martinique announced:

> As one specific measure to strengthen the existing financial framework the presi-
> dents agreed that it would be appropriate for any government which wished to
> do so to adopt current market prices as the basis of valuation for its gold hold-
> ings.

West European investors and speculators in gold chose to construe that
Martinique agreement as another step on their road toward remonetization.
By December 30, anticipating the beginning of private gold sales in the United States, which European traders had forecast at 10 million ounces in the
initial boom alone, the London price had soared to $197.50 per ounce. Asked
by excited journalists whether he too might buy, Gerald Ford mildly replied:
"I am not a speculator." Yet in Paris, grateful for the support promised by
Papa Giscard, French buyers briefly pushed the price to a startling $201.40
per ounce, an historic record. They were quickly disappointed. When the

United States Treasury tried to auction 2 million ounces, on January 6, 1975, serious buyers appeared for only 754 thousand ounces at $153 or more. The widely heralded "Great American Gold Rush" had been a figment of its promoters. American buyers considered the free-market price excessive, and only Swiss, West German and British buyers prevented that auction from failing.

Though the speculative fever rapidly dissipated, it had thoroughly angered the Shah of Iran. On December 19 he had loudly, vigorously denounced the Martinique agreement and had claimed that the central bankers of the West had been "trying to set up a gold cartel, to match ingot for barrel OPEC's oil cartel." He had warned that:

> A rise in value of official gold holdings would pose a very grave problem. It could end the nine-month freeze on oil prices. Rising oil prices would surely follow, and bring about the collapse of the whole monetary system.

On December 26 Iraq had become the second oil-exporting country fiercely to demand international discussions on gold. Then the suspicious Algerians had protested, announcing that they might refuse to accept oil payments in devalued paper currencies. Nevertheless, on January 9, Jean-Pierre Fourcade announced that France alone would revalue its official gold reserves at $170.40 per ounce, the average price of January 7 on the London market. Thereafter the 3140 tons held by the Bank of France would be carried on its books at a value of 75.6 billion francs, rather than 19.6 billion at the official price of $42.22 per ounce. Fourcade added that the French valuation would be revised every 6 months, to conform to the free-market price.

Amid that public tumult, quiet official efforts had begun to answer the long-deferred questions on the role of gold in the reformed monetary system. The International Monetary Fund's do-nothing Committee of Twenty had been succeeded by a similarly constituted Interim Committee, and the Group of Ten had been resurrected. When its finance ministers met in Washington, on January 12, for a full week of conferences, they carried one step farther the gradual process of demonetizing gold by agreeing to eliminate the obligation of members to pay one-quarter (the "Gold Tranche") of their quotas in gold. But no agreement could be reached on the proposal to authorize the Fund to sell some of its gold. The French heatedly objected, arguing that the Fund's gold stocks should be returned to the nations that had subscribed them. Nor was there any agreement on the French insistence that central banks should again be allowed freely to buy gold in the markets. The Executive Directors of the Fund were instructed to continue their studies on those questions and on the abolition of any official price for gold.

Reporting to the Bundestag in Bonn, on January 23, West German Finance Minister Hans Apel felt compelled to protest against the efforts of the

French and the oil-exporting countries to turn the Fund into "a political forum." With some asperity he commented:

> There was the usual debate about the future of gold. Interests in this field differ considerably. There are central banks and member states who have large gold deposits—like West Germany and the Netherlands. We do not consider—and will not do so in the future—revaluing upward our gold reserves. We shall keep them at the present level. If the gold-holding countries should try to revalue their gold reserves upward, a renewed, massive injustice would arise by the creation of purchasing power. . . . We must make certain that the IMF is not turned into a political institution, sticks to its task as an instrument of the world monetary system, and does not become an instrument of inflation.

When the Interim Committee met again in Paris on June 10, they made additional progress toward the demonetization of gold. Ministers agreed that the official price should be abolished, that gold should be eliminated from the articles of the Fund, and that increases in the total gold stocks held by the Fund and by central banks should not be permitted. There was further agreement "in principle" that a portion of the Fund's gold should be sold on the free markets to finance development aid for poor countries, and that another portion should be sold to members at the official price of SDR 35 per ounce. The Executive Directors were told to study the possibility of setting up a "gold substitution account" through which members could exchange part or all of their gold for SDRs.

Unhappily, however, there was a theatrical display of Franco–American animosity, to please French Gaullists. The United States and most other countries favored a rule that central banks be allowed to buy gold from each other only in times of dire need, whereas France demanded restoration of complete freedom to buy and sell at will. When William Simon and Arthur Burns also called for "legalization" of floating, Jean-Pierre Fourcade became vitriolic. He denounced floating as "the cause of economic chaos and inflation," and demanded that the United States return to "fixed but adjustable rates." Regardless of serious doubts about the stability of the franc, President Giscard had decided "for political reasons" that France should rejoin the European joint float. West Germany had stipulated that France do so at the former parity between the mark and the franc, and Giscard had agreed. However, careful arrangements had been made to ensure that France would never be obliged to defend that parity with its gold reserves.

From a meeting of his own ministers on June 17 Giscard then stiffly warned other industrial countries: "It will be impossible to end the crisis affecting their economic relations until they have taken a clear stand on a return to a system of fixed parities." It was an arrogant, unequivocal attempt publicly to coerce the American officials who had disagreed with him for so many years, and to wring further concessions from them. He had misjudged them, and the change in circumstances. Both in private and in public, he was immediately informed that the dollar would continue permanently to float. There were no longer any compelling reasons, foreign or domestic, for Americans to tolerate the fallacies and hostilities of the French.

Unnoted by the public but carefully watched by bankers, the Special Drawing Right redefined as a "standard basket" had begun to gain a modicum of acceptance. To reduce the costs of imports, the Iranian Central Bank had announced on February 12 that thereafter the parity of the Iranian rial would be expressed in terms of the SDR, rather than the depreciating dollar. On March 14 Saudi Arabia had become the second major oil-exporting country formally to cut the link between its ryal and the dollar by declaring a new parity in SDRs. Then on May 8, members of the International Air Transport Association had agreed in principle to adopt the SDR as the basis for calculating worldwide air fares. The fluctuating rates of exchange for the floating dollar and the pound had been frequently disturbing airline charges, which were expressed in more than 60 currencies. On May 25 the Suez Canal Authority had announced in Cairo that new tolls for shipping through the Suez Canal would be expressed in SDRs. Four days later, on May 29, the Swiss aluminum company Alusuisse had become the first to float a private bond issue denominated in SDRs. It had offered a 5-year issue of SDR 30 million, approximately $37.5 million that day, and had found buyers for SDR 150 million.

In a new era of floating currencies many private investors had been anxiously seeking some kind of protection against unpredictable fluctuations in exchange rates. To the issuer, the advantage was a lower interest cost. Early in June, a 7-year issue of SDR 40 million by the Swedish Investment Bank was also oversubscribed. Heeding that example, the Nordic Council that coordinated the interests of Denmark, Finland, Iceland, Norway and Sweden was completing its preparations to found a Nordic Investment Bank, initially to be capitalized at SDR 400 million. And on June 23 the French State utility Electricité de France announced that President Giscard had approved French private financing denominated in SDRs, by authorizing it to issue SDR 50 million in 8-year notes. Though interest and principal would be paid in dollars, at last events had compelled France to recognize the desirability of an international monetary standard specifically designed for the new era ahead, in which many major currencies would continue permanently to float.

Adversity has many uses. In 1975 world trade had contracted 6 percent from its high level the year before. That recession, the most severe since the 1930s, had become a sobering experience for everyone. Early in July, President Giscard therefore proposed a summit meeting of the five leading industrial powers, the United States, Britain, France, West Germany and Japan, to discuss international monetary problems. West Europeans were also urging President Ford and Secretary Simon to inflate the American economy, to increase American demand for European exports. But the Federal budget deficit for Fiscal Year 1976 was forecast at more than $70 billion, the national debt of the United States had already soared beyond $600 billion and eventual repudiation of that debt was no longer unthinkable. "Moderation" was becoming the new key-note of economic planners, even in Britain, where a debilitating annual inflation rate of 29 percent had at last exposed the fallibility of its "neo-Keynesian" economists. The British Treasury announced that the value of the pound, in terms of its 1914 purchasing power, had fallen to 8 pence.

Behind the scenes, Chancellor Brandt was attempting to persuade President Giscard that France should also adapt to the new realities and should cooperate fully in the efforts of the Group of Ten to mitigate the worst effects of that recession. By Sunday, August 30, when the Interim Committee reassembled in Washington, a compromise on gold had been reached. All references to the monetary status of that metal would be written out of the articles of the Fund. Its gold stocks of 150 million ounces would be divided into three unequal parts. 100 million ounces would be retained by the Fund, 25 million ounces would be returned to members in proportion to their original subscriptions and the remaining 25 million ounces would gradually be sold on the free markets to finance aid for the poorest members. Outside its jurisdiction, among the Group of Ten, there was also an informal agreement that for the next 2 years central banks would be free to buy and sell among themselves and on the free markets at market-related prices, subject to an overriding prohibition against any new acquisition of gold by those countries as a whole. The American insistence on formal demonetization of gold was satisfied, and the French were allowed to hope that someday gold might recover its role as an international monetary standard. The next day in London, gold dropped $4 per ounce, to $155.50. Within the next 3 weeks, the free-market price would fall to $136.50 per ounce. By September 21 South Africa would be compelled to devalue its rand 17.9 percent.

Formal acceptance of the compromise on gold awaited precise drafting of new articles for the International Monetary Fund, and agreement on several related questions. The planned increase of 32.5 percent in quotas had given OPEC an opportunity to demand more power. The voting strength of those oil-exporting countries was therefore increased from 5 percent to 10, while the share of the poorest countries remained unchanged, and the Group of Ten accepted a 5 percent cut. The quota and voting power of the United States were reduced from 22.95 percent to 21.55, and those of Britain from 9.56 percent to 7.5. But there had not been any agreement between the United States and France on revision of the Fund's articles to authorize floating. William Simon was defiantly proclaiming his belief that only free, absolutely clean floating would conform to the American philosophy of letting the markets determine exchange rates. With equal determination, Jean-Pierre Fourcade informed everyone that France would remain "intransigent" in its insistence that "fixed but adjustable parities" be restored. Others had begun to suspect that those dramatic antagonists might yield to persuasion. As Managing Director, Johannes Witteveen had therefore appealed on September 1 for changes in the articles of the Fund that would "allow the exchange-rate system to develop in the manner best suited to evolving circumstances." Countries that wished to float should be permitted to do so, while others established fixed rates, and clearer rules should be drafted to create "a system which responds to the needs of individual countries, while continuing to assert the primacy of the general interest in a matter which concerns the welfare of all."

Worried by the resurgence of public disharmony among the Western democracies, President Ford quietly recalled a deft, experienced negotiator, George Shultz. Private discussions began in New York, on Sunday, October 5, to reconcile differences and to plan the economic summit conference of the United States, Britain, France, West Germany, Italy and Japan. Forewarned by Shultz that President Ford would not attend unless France dropped its opposition to the legalization of floating, President Giscard modified his position. He conceded that it was no longer realistic to consider a return to fixed exchange rates in the near future. However, he insisted that frequent intervention by central banks could "stabilize" the international monetary system, to permit "viscous but not fluid" changes in exchange rates. His primary purpose was to prevent the United States from retaining the export advantage of an undervalued dollar that had at last been earning the United States an adequate trade surplus of $9.146 billion for 1975. By November 15, the rainy Saturday morning when six chiefs of state and heads of government assembled at the Château de Rambouillet, another compromise had been formed.

Rambouillet, southwest of Paris and used as a hunting lodge by Louis XIV, had become a summer home for the Presidents of France. Its British visitors could not forget that, a dozen years before, Charles de Gaulle had entertained Harold Macmillan there before deciding that Britain was too pro-American to be allowed to enter the European Community. But times change, and sometimes people change. At the close of that six-nation summit conference, on November 17, a joint declaration was issued that stated:

> With regard to monetary problems, we affirm our intention to work for greater stability. This involves efforts to restore greater stability in underlying economic and financial conditions in the world economy. At the same time, our monetary authorities will act to counter disorderly market conditions, or erratic fluctuations, in exchange rates. We welcome the rapprochement reached at the request of many other countries, between the views of the United States and France on

the need for stability that the reform of the international monetary system must promote. This rapprochement will facilitate agreement through the IMF at the next session of the Interim Committee in Jamaica on the outstanding issues of international monetary reform.

They also endorsed a supplementary agreement, signed by William Simon and Jean-Pierre Fourcade, that specified the conditions in which the New York Federal Reserve Bank and the Bank of France would intervene to prevent "erratic fluctuations" in the exchange rate between the American dollar and the currencies of the European joint float. Interpretation of those provisions later became an onerous task for the New York Federal Reserve Bank, which was required to consult daily with the Bank of France. But the second part of that agreement defined the new draft of Article Four in the revised statutes of the International Monetary Fund, to authorize floating. At last the thousands of officials who had awaited some kind of settlement between the United States and France could proceed to draft new international rules.

The meeting of the Fund's Interim Committee in Kingston, Jamaica, began January 7, 1976. Though the finance ministers and central bankers of the Group of Ten were now agreed on the reforms they had been discussing so many years, they had not yet persuaded the poor countries that held the remaining ten seats. The latter had calculated that sale of 25 million ounces of the Fund's gold stocks over the next 4 years would at most provide them $1.6 billion. They demanded more, far more, before they would accept the package of reforms proposed. To be precise, they wanted a 50 percent increase in their rights to borrow from the Fund. After hours of noisy bargaining, the Group of Ten capitulated, by agreeing to a temporary increase of 45 percent that would last until the proposed increase of quotas to SDR 39 billion could take effect in 1977. Then the changes that would eliminate gold and would legalize floating in the articles of the Fund were accepted without demur. All were weary. Their negotiations had been hectic, their meeting had lacked the dignity of an historic occasion, and their Jamaica Agreement would not become legally binding until it had been ratified by most of the 128 governments represented in Kingston. But a beaming Jean-Pierre Fourcade proudly announced: "It marks the start of a new economic and monetary era."

Scant months later, in Paris, the morning of Monday, March 15, would dawn cold and drear. To defend the parity of the weakening franc, the Bank of France had spent 6 billion francs worth of its reserves in January and February, another 4 billion during the first 2 weeks in March, and a further 4 billion the preceding Friday, March 12. Before the foreign-exchange markets could reopen that Monday morning, President Giscard would decide once again to float the franc. *Nécessité fait loi.*

APPENDIX

Table 1 Gold Reserves , 1913 and 1921

(in millions of dollars, at $20 per fine ounce)	1913	1921	Increase + Decrease −
Belligerent States on the Continent			
France	678.9	688.3	
Italy	288.1	236.5	
Belgium	59.1	51.4	
Germany	278.7	260.0	
Austria-Hungary	251.4	0.0	
Russia	787.0	Unknown	
Total	2343.2	1236.2	− 1107.0
Great Britain	175.2	763.3	+ 583.1
Neutral States (including Japan)			
Sweden	27.4	75.5	
Norway	12.8	39.5	
Denmark	19.7	61.0	
Netherlands	60.9	245.6	
Spain	92.5	479.2	
Switzerland	32.8	104.9	
Argentina	225.0	450.1	
Japan	65.0	558.8	
Total	536.1	2014.6	+1478.5
United States	691.5	2529.6	+1838.1
Sum total	3741.0	6543.7	+3589.7

Source: Cassel, *Money and Foreign Exchange after 1914,* p. 67.

Table 2 Gold Reserves of Central Banks and Governments, 1938 and 1945

Reporting Countries	End of 1938 (In millions of dollars, at $35 per ounce)	End of 1945	Loss (−) or Gain (+)
Argentina	431	1,351	+920
Switzerland	701	1,342	+641
South Africa	220	914	+694
Cuba	—	191	+191
Venezuela	52	202	+150
Mexico	29	294	+265
Uruguay	69	195	+126
Colombia	24	127	+123
Brazil	32	354	+322
Turkey	29	241	+212
Sweden	321	482	+161
Spain	525	110	−415
Iran	26	131	+105
Chile	30	82	+52
Romania	133	485	+352
Canada	192	7	−185
British India	274	274	0
Czechoslovakia	83	61	−22
Egypt	55	52	−3
New Zealand	23	23	0
Portugal	69	60	−9
United Kingdom	2,690	1	−2689
Peru	20	28 ·	+8
Denmark	53	38	−15
Belgium	581	716	+135
Holland	998	270	−728
United States	14,512	20,065	+5553
France	2,430	1,090	−1340
Reserves			
Reported	25,700	30,100	+4400
Unreported	?	7,600	—
Total	?	37,700	—

Source: Bank for International Settlements, *Seventeenth Annual Report,* dated June, 1947.

Table 3 Gold Reserves of Central Banks and Governments, 1938-1958

Countries or Institutions	End of 1938	1945	1950 (In millions of dollars, at $35 per ounce)	1956	1957	1958	Change During 1958
European Countries							
Britain	2877	1980	2900	1800	1600	2850	+1250
Italy	193	24	256	338	452	1086	+634
Belgium	780	733	587	928	913	1270	+357
Netherlands	998	270	311	844	744	1050	+306
Switzerland	701	1342	1470	1676	1718	1925	+207
Germany	29	0	0	1494	2542	2639	+97
Austria	88	0	50	71	103	194	+91
Portugal	86	433	192	448	461	493	+32
France	2757	1550	523	861	575	589	+14
Denmark	53	38	31	31	31	31	0
Finland	26	3	12	35	35	35	0
Greece	27	28	2	10	13	13	0
Iceland	1	1	1	1	1	1	0
Ireland	10	17	17	18	18	18	0
Turkey	29	241	150	144	144	144	0
Norway	84	80	50	50	45	43	−2
Sweden	321	482	90	266	219	204	−15
Spain	525	110	110	116	89	60	−29
Others							
Australia	6	53	288	107	126	162	+36
Japan	230	125	128	128	128	159	+31
Colombia	24	127	74	57	62	72	+10
Iran	26	131	140	138	138	141	+3
Belgian Congo	6	16	23	122	81	83	+2
Brazil	32	354	317	324	324	325	+1
Chile	30	82	40	41	40	40	
Ecuador	3	21	19	22	22	22	
Guatemala	7	29	27	27	27	27	
India	274	274	247	247	247	247	
Lebanon	—	2	20	77	91	91	
New Zealand	23	23	29	33	33	33	
Pakistan	—	—	27	49	49	49	
El Salvador	7	13	23	28	31	31	
Thailand	—	86	118	112	112	112	
Uruguay	73	195	236	186	180	180	
Venezuela	54	202	373	603	719	719	

Indonesia	80	201	209	45	39	37	−2
Union of South Africa	220	914	197	224	217	211	−6
Peru	20	28	31	35	28	19	−9
Egypt	55	53	97	188	188	174	−14
Mexico	29	294	208	167	180	143	−37
Canada	192	361	590	1,113	1,115	1,078	−37
Cuba	1	191	271	136	136	80	−56
Argentina	431	1,197	216	224	126	53	−73
United States	14,592	20,083	22,820	22,058	22,857	20,582	−2275
International Institutions							
B.I.S.	14	39	167	179	165	339	+174
I.M.F.	—	—	1,494	1,692	1,180	1,332	+152
E.P.U.	—	—	—	268	254	126	−128
Total	26,014	32,426	34,981	37,766	38,598	39,312	+714
Others (exclusive of USSR and Eastern Europe)	406	1,344	829	479	372	553	+181
Estimated total (exclusive of USSR and Eastern Europe)	25,420	33,770	35,810	38,245	38,970	39,865	+895

Source: Bank for International Settlements, *Twenty-Ninth Annual Report,* dated June, 1959.

Table 4 World Gold Reserves, 1969-1971

Countries or Areas	Changes in 1969	1970	1971	Holdings at end of 1971
	(In millions of dollars, at $35 per ounce)			
United States	+970	−785	−865	10,205
Britain	−5	−125	−575	775
Others in West Europe	−745	−435	+510	19,755
Belgium	−5	−50	+75	1545
France	−330	−15	−10	3525
Germany	−460	−100	+100	4075
Italy	+30	−70	−5	2885
Netherlands	+25	+70	+120	1910
Sweden	—	−25	—	200
Switzerland	+20	+90	+175	2910
Others	−25	−335	+55	2705
Canada	+10	−80	+5	795
Japan	+60	+120	+145	680
Latin America	+55	−5	−55	1,030
Middle East	−35	−80	+35	1,010
Other Asia	−20	−30	−30	675
Africa	−90	−470	−255	810
South Africa	−130	−450	−255	410
Australia	+5	−25	+20	260
Other countries	−15	−30	+5	130
Total for all countries	+190	−1,945	1060	36,125
International Institutions				
BIS	−130	+200	+590	310
European Fund	+20	−5	+10	55
IMF	+20	+2,030	+390	4730
Grand total (at $35 per ounce)	+100	+280	−70	41,220
Total Revaluation			+3535	3,535
Effect on Holdings of				
Countries	—	—	+3095	3095
International Institutions			+440	440
Grand Total, including revaluation effect	—	—	+3465	44,755

Source: Bank for International Settlements, *Forty-Second Annual Report,* dated June 1972.

BIBLIOGRAPHY

The bibliography that follows includes only those titles I have found useful, or interesting in one way or another. It is not comprehensive, and anyone who attempts a more thorough study than mine should consider it merely a starting point.

Two libraries have served most of my needs. Among the many collections in Zürich, I found the private library of the Swiss National Bank the most helpful. Its holdings of Central European materials are extensive, but it is deficient in Anglo–American publications prior to 1944. By contrast, the collections of the Bodleian Library in Oxford have been selected by scholars whose primary interests have been the monetary affairs of Great Britain and its former empire. Too few of the studies prepared by Continental scholars and experts are available there, partly because they have seldom appeared in English translations. In the field of money, a narrowly national approach still prevails and international studies are rare. Thus the resources of the Swiss National Bank and the Bodleian Library tend to complement one another, and I shall remain grateful to their attentive staffs. To the librarians of the Bodleian, I shall add a complaint. Perhaps the time has come to cease housing all of their materials on the United States within the imperial precincts of Rhodes House. It is doubtful that the prodigal will ever return, and it has been tiresome simultaneously to consult books stored in four separate buildings.

While preparing the last third of this book, I became increasingly dependent on periodicals and the press. Readers who critically compare their often contradictory reports will find that few monetary "secrets" remain hidden for long. Among the weeklies, I have found London's *Economist* the most useful. The dailies from which I have gleaned bits of information have been *Le Monde* and *The International Herald Tribune,* the London *Times* and *Financial Times,* and the *Neue Zürcher Zeitung.* The Princeton "Studies in International Finance" provide brief articles on monetary controversies since 1943. Statistical materials can be found in the *Annual Reports* and other publications of the Bank for International Settlements, the International Monetary Fund, the Organization for Economic Cooperation and Development, and the Federal Reserve Board. Reliable information on the hopes and fears of the gold markets appears in the *Annual Bullion Reviews* of Samuel Montagu and Company Limited.

Abetz, Otto, *Pétain et les allemands,* Paris, 1948.

Alexandre, Philippe, *Le Duel: De Gaulle et Pompidou,* Paris, 1971.

Aliber, R. Z., *The International Money Game,* London, 1973.

Allen, G. C., *Japan's Economic Expansion,* London, 1965.

Alphand, Hervé, *The Financial and Economic Situation of France,* London, 1942.

Amery, L. S., *The Washington Loan Agreements,* London, 1946.

Andréadès, A., *History of the Bank of England, 1640 to 1903,* London, 1966.

Angell, J. W., *The Recovery of Germany,* New Haven, 1929.

Angell, R. N., *The Story of Money,* London, 1930.

Arndt, H. W., *The Economic Lessons of the Nineteen-Thirties,* London, 1944.

Aron, Raymond, *France Steadfast and Changing,* London, 1960.

———, *The Imperial Republic,* London, 1975.

Artz, F. B., *France Under the Bourbon Restoration, 1814–1830,* Cambridge, Massachusetts, 1931.

Ashton, T. S. and Sayers, R. S., *Papers in English Monetary History,* Oxford, 1953.

Aubrey, H. G., *The Dollar in World Affairs,* New York, 1964.

Aufricht, Hans, *The International Monetary Fund: Legal Bases, Structure, Functions,* London, 1964.

Bagehot, Walter, *Lombard Street,* London, 1931.

Barbour, Sir D. M., *The Influence of the Gold Supply on Prices and Profits,* London, 1913.

Bartlett, Randall, *Economic Foundations of Political Power,* London, 1974.

Baster, A. S. J., *The International Banks,* London, 1935.

Baynes, N. H. and Moss, H., editors, *Byzantium,* Oxford, 1948.

Beach, W. E., *British International Gold Movements and Banking Policy, 1881–1913,* Cambridge, Massachusetts, 1935.

Bemis, S. F., editor, *The American Secretaries of State and Their Diplomacy,* New York, 1927– , 17 vols.

Bendix, Ludwig, *Krieg und Geldmarkt,* Berlin, 1915.

Bergsten, C. F., *The Dilemmas of the Dollar,* New York, 1976.

Bernstein, E. M., *International Effects of U.S. Economic Policy,* Washington, 1960.

Beyen, J. W., *Money in a Maelstrom,* London, 1951.

Bisschop, W. R., *The Rise of the London Money Market, 1640–1826,* London, 1968.

Blankart, Charles, *Die Devisenpolitik während des Weltkrieges,* Zürich, 1919.

Blum, J. M., *From the Morgenthau Diaries,* Boston, 1959–1967, 3 vols.

———, *Roosevelt and Morgenthau,* Boston, 1970.

Böttger, Hugo, *Das Geld im Kriege,* Stuttgart, 1915.

Bouthillier, Yves, *Le Drame de Vichy,* Paris, 1950, 2 vols.

Brandon, Henry, *The Retreat of American Power,* London, 1973.

Bresciani-Turroni, Costantino, *The Economics of Inflation,* London, 1937.

Brittan, Samuel, *Steering the Economy,* London, 1971.

Brown, W. A. Jr., *The Groping Giant,* New Haven, 1920.

———, *England and the New Gold Standard, 1919–1926,* London, 1929.

———, *The International Gold Standard Re-interpreted,* New York, 1940, 2 vols.

———, *The United States and the Restoration of World Trade,* Washington, 1950.

————, and Opie, Redvers, *American Foreign Assistance,* Washington, 1953.

Buchan, Alistair, *The End of the Post-War World,* London, 1974.

Burgess, W. R., *The Reserve Banks and the Money Market,* New York, 1936.

Burns, A. F., *Prosperity Without Inflation,* New York, 1957.

Cannan, Edwin, *The Paper Pound of 1797–1821, A Reprint of the Bullion Report,* London, 1919.

Carson, Deane, *Banking and Monetary Studies,* Homewood, Illinois, 1963.

Cassel, C. G., *Deutschlandswirtschaftliche Widerstandskraft,* Berlin, 1916.

————, *Money and Foreign Exchange After 1914,* London, 1922.

————, *Post-War Monetary Stabilization,* New York, 1928.

————, *The Crisis in the World's Monetary System,* Oxford, 1932.

————, *The Downfall of the Gold Standard,* Oxford, 1936.

Cassell, Francis, *Gold or Credit?,* London, 1965.

Cecco, Marcello de, *Money and Empire,* London, 1975.

Chalon, J. V., *La hausse des prix et la production de l'or entre 1914 et 1924,* Paris, 1924.

Chandler, L. V., *Benjamin Strong, Central Banker,* Washington, 1958.

Chang Kia-ngau, *The Inflationary Spiral,* London, 1958.

Chou Shun-hsin, *The Chinese Inflation 1937–1949,* New York, 1963.

Churchill, Randolph, *The Rise and Fall of Sir Anthony Eden,* London, 1959.

Clapham, Sir John, *An Economic History of Modern Britain,* Cambridge, England, 1930, 3 vols.

————, *The Bank of England,* Cambridge, England, 1944, 2 vols.

Clarke, S. V. O., *Central Bank Co-operation, 1924–1931,* New York, 1967.

Clendenning, E. W., *The Euro-Dollar Market,* Oxford, 1970.

Coffey, Peter and Presley, J. R., *European Monetary Integration,* London, 1971.

Cohen, J. B., *Japan's Postwar Economy,* Bloomington, Indiana, 1958.

Cohen, S. D., *International Monetary Reform, 1964–1969,* New York, 1970.

Cole, C. W., *Colbert and a Century of French Mercantilism,* New York, 1939, 2 vols.

Cole, G. D. H., *Gold, Credit and Employment,* London, 1930.

————, *Money, Its Present and Future,* London, 1944.

Cooke, Colin, *The Life of Richard Stafford Cripps,* London, 1957.

Coombs, C. A., *The Arena of International Finance,* New York, 1976.

Coppieters, Emmanuel, *English Bank Note Circulation, 1694–1954,* The Hague, 1955.

Couve de Murville, Maurice, *Une politique étrangère 1958–1969,* Paris, 1971.

Craig, Sir John, *The Mint,* Cambridge, England, 1953.

Croome, D. R. and Johnson, H. G., editors, *Money in Britain 1959–1969,* Oxford, 1970.

Crowther, Sir Geoffrey, *An Outline of Money,* London, 1948.

Crozier, Bryan, *De Gaulle,* London, 1970–1973, 2 vols.

Crump, Norman, *The ABC of the Foreign Exchanges,* London, 1963.

Dalberg, Rudolf, *Die Entthronung des Goldes,* Stuttgart, 1916.

Dalton, Hugh, *Memoirs,* London, 1962.

Davidson, Ian and Weil, Gordon, *The Gold War,* London, 1970.

Dawes, C. G., *A Journal of Reparations,* London, 1939.

Dawson, W. H., *The Evolution of Modern Germany,* London, 1919.

De Kock, M. H., *Central Banking*, London, 1954.

Del Mar, A., *History of the Precious Metals*, New York, 1902.

Diebold, William Jr., *The Schuman Plan*, New York, 1959.

Diehl, Karl, *Über Fragen des Geldwesens und der Valuta*, Jena, 1918.

Dieterlin, Pierre and Rist, Charles, *The Monetary Problems of France*, New York, 1948.

Dodwell, D. W., *Treasuries and Central Banks*, London, 1934.

Dulles, E. L., *The French Franc*, New York, 1929.

———, *The Bank for International Settlements at Work*, New York, 1932.

Duroselle, J. B., *De Wilson à Roosevelt*, Paris, 1960.

———, *Les relations franco-allemandes de 1914 à 1939*, Paris, 1969.

Duveen, Sir Geoffrey and Stride, H. G., *The History of the Gold Sovereign*, London, 1962.

Edwards, D. S., *Gold Reserves and the Monetary Standard*, London, 1933.

Einzig, Paul, *International Gold Movements*, London, 1931.

———, *The Bank for International Settlements*, London, 1932.

———, *Behind the Scenes of International Finance*, London, 1932.

———, *The Fight for Financial Supremacy*, London, 1932.

———, *The Sterling–Dollar–Franc Tangle*, London, 1933.

———, *The Future of Gold*, London, 1934.

———, *Germany's Default: The Economics of Hitlerism*, London, 1934.

———, *World Finance Since 1914*, London, 1935.

———, *Monetary Reform in Theory and Practice*, London, 1936.

———, *Primitive Money*, London, 1966.

———, *Foreign Exchange Crises*, London, 1970.

———, *The History of Foreign Exchange*, London, 1970.

———, *The Destiny of the Dollar*, London, 1972.

Erhard, Ludwig, *The Economics of Success*, London, 1963.

Eshag, Eprime, *From Marshall to Keynes*, Oxford, 1963.

Eyck, Erich, *A History of the Weimar Republic*, Cambridge, Massachusetts, 1963–1964, 2 vols.

Faulkner, H. U., *American Economic History*, New York, 1963.

Feaveryear, Sir Albert, *The Pound Sterling*, Oxford, 1963.

Feis, Herbert, *Europe: The World's Banker, 1870–1914*, New Haven, 1930.

———, *The Sinews of Peace*, New York, 1944.

———, *Petroleum and American Foreign Policy*, Stanford, 1944.

———, *The Diplomacy of the Dollar*, Baltimore, 1950.

———, *The Road to Pearl Harbor*, Princeton, 1950.

———, *Foreign Aid and Foreign Policy*, New York, 1964.

———, *1933: Characters in Crisis*, Boston, 1966.

Felix, David, *Walther Rathenau and the Weimar Republic*, Baltimore, 1971.

Fellner, William, Machlup, Fritz, Triffin, Robert et al., *Maintaining and Restoring Balance in International Payments*, Princeton, 1966.

Fergusson, Adam, *When Money Dies*, London, 1975.

Fetter, F. W., *Development of British Monetary Orthodoxy, 1797–1875*, Cambridge, England, 1965.

Fisk, H. E., *French Public Finance,* New York, 1922.

———, *The Inter-Ally Debts, 1914–1923,* New York, 1924.

Flandin, P.-E., *Politique française 1919–1940,* Paris, 1947.

Flux, A. W., *The Foreign Exchanges,* London, 1924.

Forbin, Victor, *L'or dans le monde,* Paris, 1941.

Ford, A. G., *The Gold Standard, 1880–1914: Britain and Argentina,* Oxford, 1962.

Frazer, W. J. Jr. and Yohe, W. P., *The Analytics and Institutions of Money and Banking,* Princeton, 1966.

Frenkel, J. A. and Johnson, H. G., *The Monetary Approach to the Balance of Payments,* London, 1975.

Friedberg, Robert, *Gold Coins of the World, Complete from 600 A.D. to 1958,* New York, 1958.

Friedman, E. M., *International Finance and Its Reorganization,* New York, 1922.

Friedman, Irving, *Inflation,* London, 1973.

Friedman, Milton and Schwartz, A. J., *A Monetary History of the United States, 1867–1960,* Princeton, 1963.

Friedman, Milton, *The Optimum Quantity of Money,* London, 1969.

Galbraith, J. K., *The Great Crash,* London, 1955.

———, *Money: Whence It Came, Where It Went,* Boston, 1975.

Gardner, R. N., *Sterling-Dollar Diplomacy,* New York, 1969.

Gayer, A. D., *Monetary Policy and Economic Stabilisation,* London, 1937.

———, Rostow, W. W. and Schwartz, A. J., *The Growth and Fluctuation of the British Economy,* Hassocks, 1975, 2 vols.

Gide, Charles and Rist, Charles, *A History of Economic Doctrines,* London, 1967.

Giffen, Robert, *The Case Against Bimetallism,* London, 1892.

Giscard d'Estaing, E. J. L., *Misères et splendeurs des finances allemandes,* Paris, 1924.

———, *Capitalisme,* Paris, 1930.

———, *La maladie du monde,* Paris, 1933.

———, *La France et l'unification économique de l'Europe,* Paris, 1953.

Goldenweiser, E. A., *American Monetary Policy,* New York, 1951.

Goschen, George Viscount, *The Theory of the Foreign Exchanges,* London, 1843.

Grady, H. F., *British War Finance, 1914–1919,* New York, 1927.

Gregory, Sir T. E., *The First Year of the Gold Standard,* London, 1926.

———, *Gold, Unemployment and Capitalism,* London, 1933.

———, *The Gold Standard and Its Future,* London, 1934.

———, *Ernest Oppenheimer and the Economic Development of South Africa,* Cape Town, 1962.

Greidanus, Tjardus, *The Value of Money,* London, 1950.

Grigg, Sir P. J., *Prejudice and Judgement,* London, 1948.

Grosser, Alfred, *Western Germany, From Defeat to Rearmament,* London, 1955.

Group of Ten, *Report of the Study Group on the Creation of Reserve Assets,* Rome, 1965.

Grubel, H. G. editor, *World Monetary Reform,* Stanford, 1964.

Guillebaud, C. W., *The Economic Recovery of Germany,* London, 1939.

Gutt, Camille, *La Belgique au carrefour 1940–1944,* Paris, 1971.

Hahlweg, Werner, *Lenins Rückkehr nach Russland 1917,* Leiden, 1957.

Haig, R. M. et al., *The Public Finances of Post-War France,* New York, 1929.

Halm, G. N., *International Monetary Cooperation,* Chapel Hill, 1945.

Hancock, W. K., *Problems of Economic Policy 1918–1939,* Oxford, 1940.

Hancock, W. K. and Gowing, M. M., *British War Economy,* London, 1949.

Hankel, Wilhelm, *Währungspolitik,* Stuttgart, 1971.

Haring, C. H., *Trade and Navigation Between Spain and the Indies,* Cambridge, Massachusetts, 1918.

Harris, S. E., *The Assignats,* Cambridge, Massachusetts, 1929.

————, *Monetary Problems of the British Empire,* New York, 1931.

————, *The European Recovery Program,* Cambridge, Massachusetts, 1948.

————, *Foreign Economic Policy for the United States,* Cambridge, Massachusetts, 1948.

————, *The Dollar in Crisis,* New York, 1961.

————, *Economics of the Kennedy Years,* New York, 1964.

Harrod, Sir Roy, *The Life of John Maynard Keynes,* London, 1951.

————, *The Dollar,* London, 1953.

————, *Reforming the World's Money,* London, 1965.

————, *Money,* London, 1969.

Hawtrey, Sir R. G., *Monetary Reconstruction,* London, 1926.

————, *Trade Depression and the Way Out,* London, 1933.

————, *Economic Destiny,* London, 1944.

————, *Bretton Woods: For Better or Worse,* London, 1946.

————, *The Gold Standard in Theory and Practice,* London, 1947.

————, *Currency and Credit,* London, 1950.

————, *Towards the Rescue of Sterling,* London, 1954.

————, *The Art of Central Banking,* London, 1962.

Hayek, F. A. von, *Monetary Nationalism and International Stability,* London, 1937.

Heckscher, E. F., *The Continental System,* Oxford, 1922.

Hegeland, Hugo, *The Quantity Theory of Money,* Güteborg, 1951.

Heichelheim, F. M., *An Ancient Economic History,* Leiden, 1958, 3 vols.

Helfferich, Karl, *Der Weltkrieg,* Karlsruhe, 1925.

Henderson, H. D., *The Inter-War Years,* Oxford, 1955.

Henderson, W. O., *The Zollverein,* Cambridge, England, 1939.

Hertz, Frederick, *The Economic Problems of the Danubian States,* London, 1947.

Hirsch, Fred, *The Pound Sterling: A Polemic,* London, 1965.

————, *Money International,* London, 1967.

Hinshaw, Randall, editor, *Monetary Reform and the Price of Gold,* Baltimore, 1967.

His Majesty's Stationery Office, *Proposals for an International Clearing Union,* London, 1943.

Hobson, J. A., *Imperialism,* London, 1905.

————, *The Economics of Reparation,* London, 1921.

————, *Gold, Prices and Wages,* London, 1924.

Hodson, H. V., *Slump and Recovery, 1929–1937,* London, 1938.

Hoover, Herbert, *Memoirs,* London, 1952–1953, 3 vols.

Horie, Shigeo, *The International Monetary Fund,* London, 1964.

Horsefield, J. K., *British Monetary Experiments, 1650–1710*, London, 1960.

Huizinga, J. H., *Gold Points a Moral*, The Hague, 1935.

Iklé, Max, *Die Schweiz als internationaler Bank- und Finanzplatz*, Zürich, 1970.

Inouye, Junnosuke, *Problems of the Japanese Exchange, 1914–1926*, London, 1931.

International Monetary Fund, *International Reserves and Liquidity*, Washington, 1958.

Iversen, Carl, *International Capital Movements*, London, 1936.

Jack, D. T., *The Economics of the Gold Standard*, London, 1925.

———, *The Restoration of European Currencies*, London, 1927.

———, *The Crises of 1931*, London, 1931.

———, *Studies in Economic Warfare*, London, 1940.

Jacobsson, Per, *Some Monetary Problems, International and National*, London, 1958.

———, *Towards a Modern Monetary Standard*, London, 1959.

———, *International Monetary Problems 1957–1963*, Washington, 1964.

Jèze, Gaston and Truchy, Henri, *The War Finance of France*, London, 1925.

Johnson, L. B., *The Vantage Point*, London, 1971.

Johnson, P. B., *Land Fit For Heroes*, Chicago, 1968.

Katzenellenbaum, S. S., *Russian Currency and Banking, 1914–1924*, London, 1925.

Kawai, Kazuo, *Japan's American Interlude*, Chicago, 1960.

Kemmerer, E. W., *Gold and the Gold Standard*, New York, 1944.

Kemp, W., *Precious Metals as Money*, London, 1923.

Kerner, R. J., *The Urge to the Sea, The Course of Russian History*, Berkeley, 1942.

Keynes, J. M. Baron, *Indian Currency and Finance*, London, 1913.

———, *The Economic Consequences of the Peace*, London, 1920.

———, *A Revision of the Treaty*, London, 1922.

———, *A Tract on Monetary Reform*, London, 1923.

———, *The Economic Consequences of Mr. Churchill*, London, 1925.

———, *A Treatise on Money*, London, 1930.

———, *A General Theory of Money, Interest and Employment*, London, 1936.

Kindleberger, C. P., *The Dollar Shortage*, Cambridge, Massachusetts, 1950.

———, *Power and Money*, London, 1970.

Kirkaldy, A. W., *British Finance, 1914–1921*, London, 1921.

Klopstock, F. H., *The International Status of the Dollar*, Princeton, 1957.

Knorr, Klaus, *Power and Wealth*, London, 1973.

Kriz, Miroslav, *Postwar International Lending*, Princeton, 1947.

———, *The Price of Gold*, Princeton, 1952.

———, *Gold in Monetary Affairs Today*, Princeton, 1959.

Langer, W. L. and Gleason, S. E., *The Challenge to Isolation, 1937–1940*, London, 1952–1953, 2 vols.

Laqueur, Walter, *The Struggle for the Middle East*, London, 1972.

Latouche, Robert, *The Birth of Western Economy*, London, 1967.

Lawson, W. R., *British War Finance*, London, 1915.

League of Nations, *Currencies After the War*, London, 1920.

———, *Production mondiale et les prix, 1936–1937*, Geneva, 1938.

Lehfeldt, R. A., *Gold Prices and the Witwatersrand,* London, 1919.

——, *Restoration of the World's Money,* London, 1923.

Lenormant, François, *La monnaie dans l'Antiquité,* Paris, 1878.

Lester, R. A., *International Aspects of Wartime Monetary Experience,* Princeton, 1946.

Lewis, W. A., *Economic Survey 1919–1939,* London, 1957.

Liefmann, Robert, *Geld und Gold,* Stuttgart, 1916.

Link, A. S., *Wilson,* Princeton, 1947–1965, 5 vols.

Luther, Hans, *Politiker Ohne Partei,* Stuttgart, 1960.

McCloy, J. J., *The Atlantic Alliance: Its Origin and Its Future,* New York, 1968.

McDonald, I. S., *Anglo–American Relations Since the Second World War,* London, 1974.

McGuire, C. E., *Italy's International Economic Situation,* London, 1926.

Machlup, Fritz, *International Monetary Economics,* London, 1966.

——, *Remaking the International Monetary System,* Baltimore, 1968.

Manderson-Jones, R. B., *The Special Relationship,* London, 1972.

Mansergh, Nicholas, *Problems of Wartime Co-operation and Post-War Change 1939–1952,* London, 1958.

Mantoux, Étienne, *The Carthaginian Peace,* London, 1946.

Mattingly, Harold, *Roman Coins,* London, 1960.

Maynard, Geoffrey and Ryckeghem, W., *A World of Inflation,* London, 1975.

Mertens, J. E., *La naissance et le développement de l'étalon-or, 1696–1922,* Paris, 1944.

Mikesell, R. F., *Foreign Exchange in the Postwar World,* New York, 1954.

Milne, J. G., *Greek Coinage,* London, 1931.

Mogg, William Rees-, *Sir Anthony Eden,* London, 1956.

Moggridge, D. E., *British Monetary Policy 1924–1931,* London, 1972.

——, *Keynes,* London, 1976.

Monroe, A. E., *Monetary Theory Before Adam Smith,* Cambridge, Massachusetts, 1923.

Monroe, W. F., *International Monetary Reconstruction,* London, 1974.

Morgan, E. V., *Studies in British Financial Policy, 1914–1925,* London, 1952.

——, *The Theory and Practice of Central Banking 1797–1913,* London, 1965.

——, *A History of Money,* London, 1969.

Morrell, W. P., *The Gold Rushes,* London, 1968.

Mossé, Robert, *Les problèmes monétaires internationaux,* Paris, 1967.

Moulton, H. G. and McGuire, C. E., *Germany's Capacity to Pay,* New York, 1923.

Myers, M. G., *The New York Money Market,* New York, 1931–1932, 4 vols.

Myers, W. S. and Newton, W. H., *The Hoover Administration,* New York, 1936.

National Industrial Conference Board, *Gold and World Monetary Problems,* New York, 1966.

Netzband, K.-B. and Widmaier, H. P., *Währungs- und Finanzpolitik der Ära Luther 1923–1925,* Basle, 1964.

Nevin, Edward, *The Mechanism of Cheap Money,* Cardiff, 1955.

Nogaro, Bertrand, *A Short Treatise on Money and Monetary Systems,* London, 1949.

Notzke, Johann, *Deutschlands Finanz- und Handelsgesetze im Kriege,* Berlin, 1917.

Oman, Sir Charles, *The Coinage of England,* London, 1931.

Ostrogorski, George, *History of the Byzantine State,* Oxford, 1968.

Paris, J. D., *Monetary Policies of the United States 1932–1938,* New York, 1938.

Perrenound, Jean, *L'Étalon-or. Son avenir après l'accord monétaire de Bretton Woods,* Paris, 1947.

Pigou, A. C., *The Veil of Money,* London, 1949.

Pohl, Helga, *Gold: Macht und Magie in der Geschichte,* Stuttgart, 1958.

Pollard, Sidney, *The Gold Standard and Employment Policies Between the Wars,* London, 1970.

Pompidou, Georges, *The Gordian Knot,* London, 1974.

Rees, David, *Harry Dexter White,* London, 1974.

Reuss, H. S., *The Critical Decade,* New York, 1963.

Rist, Charles, *La déflation en pratique,* Paris, 1924.

——, *History of Money and Credit Theory,* London, 1940.

——, *Défense de l'or,* Paris, 1953.

——, *The Triumph of Gold,* London, 1962.

Ritter, Gerhard, *The Sword and the Sceptre,* London, 1972–1973, 4 vols.

Robbins, Lionel, *The Great Depression,* London, 1934.

——, *The Economic Causes of War,* London, 1940.

Robertson, D. H., *Money,* London, 1922.

Robey, Ralph ed., *The Monetary Problem, Gold and Silver: Final Report of the Royal Commission of 1888,* New York, 1936.

Röpke, Wilhelm, *The Solution of the German Problem,* New York, 1947.

Rolfe, S. E. and Burtle, J. L., *The Great Wheel,* London, 1974.

Roosa, R. V., *Monetary Reform for the World Economy,* New York, 1965.

——, *The Dollar and World Liquidity,* New York, 1967.

Ross, Sir F. W. Leith-, *Money Talks,* London, 1968.

Rostovtzeff, M., *Social and Economic History of the Hellenistic World,* London, 1941.

——, *Social and Economic History of the Roman Empire,* London, 1957.

Royal Institute of International Affairs, *The International Gold Problem,* Oxford, 1931.

——, *The Future of Monetary Policy,* Oxford, 1935.

Rueff, Jacques, *Théorie des phénomènes monétaires,* Paris, 1927.

——, *Le péché monétaire de l'Occident,* Paris, 1971.

——, *Combats pour l'ordre financier,* Paris, 1972.

Rufener, L. A., *The Economic Position of Switzerland During the War,* Washington, 1919.

Runciman, Sir Steven, *Byzantine Civilisation,* London, 1936.

Salter, Sir Arthur et al., *The World's Economic Crisis,* London, 1932.

——, *Recovery,* London, 1933.

Sauvy, Alfred, *Histoire économique de la France entre les deux guerres, 1918–1939,* Paris, 1965–1967, 2 vols.

Sayers, R. S., *Bank of England Operations 1890–1914,* London, 1936.

Scammell, W. B., *International Monetary Policy,* London, 1961.

Schacht, H. G. H., *The Stabilization of the Mark,* London, 1927.

——, *The End of Reparations,* London, 1931.

——, *Germany and World Trade,* Munich, 1939.

————, *Account Settled,* London, 1949.

————, *Gold for Europe,* London, 1950.

————, *My First Seventy-Six Years,* London, 1955.

————, *The Magic of Money,* London, 1967.

Schloss, H. H., *The Bank for International Settlements,* Amsterdam, 1958.

Schwartz, Harry, *Russia's Soviet Economy,* London, 1951.

Sebald, W. J. and Brines, Russell, *With MacArthur in Japan,* London, 1967.

Sédillot, René, *Le drame des monnaies,* Paris, 1937.

————, *Le franc enchaîné,* Paris, 1945.

————, *Le Franc,* Paris, 1953.

————, *Du franc Bonaparte au franc de Gaulle,* Paris, 1959.

Select Committee, *Report, Together with Minutes of Evidence and Accounts, from the Select Committee Appointed to Inquire into the Cause of the High Price of Gold Bullion,* London, 1810.

Shaw, W. A., *The History of Currency, 1252 to 1894,* London, 1895.

————, editor, *Select Tracts and Documents Illustrative of English Monetary History, 1626–1730,* London, 1935.

Shirer, W. L., *The Collapse of the Third Republic,* London, 1970.

Shonfield, Andrew, editor, *International Economic Relations of the Western World, 1959–1971,* London, 1976, 2 vols.

Shrigley, I., *The Price of Gold,* London, 1925.

Soustelle, Jacques, *Envers et contre tout,* Paris, 1947.

————, *L'espérance trahie,* Paris, 1962.

Spalding, W. F., *The London Money Market,* London, 1938.

Spanier, David, *Europe, Our Europe,* London, 1972.

Speer, Albert, *Inside the Third Reich,* London, 1970.

Stamp, Sir Josiah, *Papers on Gold and the Price Level,* London, 1931.

Stevenson, Hugh, *The Coming Clash,* London, 1972.

Strakosch, Sir H., *Monetary Stability and the Gold Standard,* London, 1928.

Sutherland, C. H. V., *Coinage in Roman Imperial Policy, 31 B.C.–A.D. 68,* London, 1961.

Tew, Bryan, *International Monetary Co-operation 1945–1960,* London, 1962.

Thomas, Brinley, *Monetary Policy and Crises,* London, 1936.

Thomas, Georg, *Geschichte der Deutschen Wehr- und Rüstungswirtschaft (1918–1943/45),* Boppard am Rhein, 1966.

Thompson, J. W., *Economic and Social History of Europe in the Later Middle Ages,* New York, 1966.

Tobin, James, *The New Economics One Decade Older,* Princeton, 1974.

Toutain, Charles, *The Economic Life of the Ancient World,* London, 1930.

Triffin, Robert, *Europe and the Money Muddle,* New Haven, 1957.

————, *Gold and the Dollar Crisis,* New Haven, 1961.

————, *The World Money Maze,* New Haven, 1966.

United Nations Monetary and Financial Conference, Bretton Woods, New Hampshire, U.S.A., July 1 to July 22, 1944, *Final Act,* London, 1944.

United Nations Monetary and Financial Conference, *Proceedings and Documents of,* Washington, 1948, 2 vols.

United States Congress, Joint Economic Committee, *An Economic Profile of Mainland China*, New York, 1958.

Vandenberg, A. H. Jr., *Private Papers*, New York, 1954.

Vissering, Gerard, *The Netherlands Bank and the War*, The Hague, 1915–1916.

———, *Das Goldproblem*, The Hague, 1918.

Walker, F. A., *International Bimetallism*, London, 1896.

Wallich, H. C., *Mainsprings of the German Revival*, New Haven, 1955.

Warren, G. F. and Pearson, F. A., *Gold and Prices*, New York, 1935.

Webb, Sir C. M., *The Rise and Fall of the Gold Standard*, London, 1934.

Weymar, Paul, *Konrad Adenauer*, London, 1957.

Whicher, G. F., editor, *William Jennings Bryan and the Campaign of 1896*, Lexington, Massachusetts, 1953.

Whittlesey, C. R. and Wilson, J. S. G., editors, *Essays in Money and Banking in Honour of R. S. Sayers*, Oxford, 1968.

Williams, J. H., *Post-War Monetary Plans*, Oxford, 1949.

Willis, H. P. and Beckhart, B. H., *Foreign Banking Systems*, London, 1929.

Withers, Hartley, *War and Lombard Street*, London, 1915.

Wolfe, Martin, *The French Franc Between the Wars*, New York, 1951.

Wu Yuan-li, *An Economic Survey of Communist China*, New York, 1956.

Yeager, L. B., *International Monetary Relations*, New York, 1966.

Yoshida, Shigeru, *Memoirs*, London, 1961.

Yurovsky, L. N., *Currency Problems and Policy of the Soviet Union*, London, 1925.

Index